DATE DUE

CAREER OPPORTUNITIES in

SCIENCE

SECOND EDITION

CAREER
OPPORTUNITIES
in
SCIENCE

SECOND EDITION

SUSAN ECHAORE-McDAVID

Checkmark Books®
An imprint of Infobase Publishing

Dedicated to Frank Percy Yoon
Chemist, Environmentalist, Humanitarian 1920–1995

Career Opportunities in Science, Second Edition

Copyright © 2008, 2003 by Susan Echaore-McDavid

Checkmark Books
An imprint of Infobase Publishing
132 West 31st Street
New York NY 10001

Library of Congress Cataloging-in-Publication Data

Echaore-McDavid, Susan.
   Career opportunities in science / Susan Echaore-McDavid.—2nd ed.
     p. cm.
   Includes bibliographical references and index.
   ISBN-13: 978-0-8160-7132-6 (hardcover: alk. paper)
   ISBN-10: 0-8160-7132-2 (hardcover : alk. paper)
   ISBN-13: 978-0-8160-7133-3 (pbk. : alk. paper)
   ISBN-10: 0-8160-7133-0 (pbk. : alk. paper) 1. Science—Vocational guidance. I. Title.
   Q147.E33 2008
   502.3—dc22   2007040659

Checkmark Books are available at special discounts when purchased in bulk quantities for businesses, associations, institutions, or sales promotions. Please call our Special Sales Department in New York at (212) 967-8800 or (800) 322-8755.

You can find Facts On File on the World Wide Web at http://www.factsonfile.com

Cover design by Takeshi Takahashi

Printed in the United States of America

Bang Hermitage 10 9 8 7 6 5 4 3 2 1

This book is printed on acid-free paper.

CONTENTS

INTRODUCTION

Have you ever dreamed about one day having a job in which you can seek cures for cancer or other diseases, or create robots to handle boring chores, or design the fastest, yet most fuel-efficient, car around? Have you ever wondered if you could have a job that allows you to investigate such questions as: Besides the Colorado River, what other natural phenomenon could have contributed to carving the Grand Canyon? What is the rate of oxygen depletion in our atmosphere over the last 100 years? What causes the different types of cells in our body to distinguish themselves from each other? What really came first, the chicken or the egg?

If so, a career in science may be right for you.

Science is an awesome and amazing endeavor. It is about research, experimentation, and discovery. You could be involved in studying topics that interest you—such as atoms, bacteria, plants, animal behavior, human systems, artificial intelligence, fossils, volcanoes, radiation, or outer space.

Science is also about applying scientific knowledge to solve problems, invent new technologies, and develop new products. Look around you, and you can see the endless results of science: the food we eat; the clothes we wear; the vehicles we ride in; the computers, telephones, and electronic gadgets that we use for work and play; the medicines we take to treat our illnesses; and much more.

Many career opportunities are available in science and technology. The more familiar occupations are those of scientists, engineers, and technicians. They work in academia and government agencies as well as in various industries, including the pharmaceutical, biomedicine, health, biotechnology, agriculture, food processing, energy, aviation, chemical manufacturing, and telecommunications industries, among others.

There are also other career options that you may not have considered to be part of science because they are found in such fields as business, finance, law, education, and communications. However, these professions also require scientific training and skills. For example, you might choose to become a patent agent, science writer, science curator, actuary, regulatory affairs specialist, technology policy analyst, math teacher, or management consultant.

In *Career Opportunities in Science* you can read 93 profiles about different scientific and technical careers. These profiles are designed to introduce you to basic career information and to encourage you to continue investigating the professions that you might choose to pursue.

What's New in the Second Edition?

Twenty-three new profiles have been added to this revised edition of *Career Opportunities in Science*. In addition, all the original profiles have been updated with information about salaries, employment prospects, job requirements, and job duties. Furthermore, contact information and Web site addresses throughout the book have been made current at the time this book was being revised.

Many of the new occupations that have been added to the book are technician and technologist positions, which may require an associate, bachelor's, or master's degree for entry. The profiles about engineers and all but one of the profiles about forensic scientists have been left out of this edition. Those professions are covered more thoroughly in two other *Career Opportunities* books—*Career*

Opportunities in Engineering and *Career Opportunities in Forensic Science.*

A Note to High School Students

Now is the time to start preparing for your future career, whether it is in science or another area that interests you. While you are in high school, take courses that can help you succeed in college. For any college program, you need a foundation in English, mathematics, science, history, and social science. If you are planning to major in a science discipline, it would be a good idea to take as many science and math classes as you can to help you handle a college curriculum.

Other courses that can help you meet the challenges of college include computer, public speaking, and foreign language classes. Also be sure to develop your writing, critical-thinking, and problem-solving skills, which will be essential to performing well in college as well as in your future jobs.

You can start getting an idea of what lies ahead in college by checking out various college catalogs. (School and public libraries usually carry catalogs of different colleges and universities.) These catalogs describe the school enrollment process, the different academic departments and majors, and campus life.

Also be sure to talk with your high school counselor or teachers. Let them know about your interest in going to college and perhaps pursuing a career in science. They can help you choose appropriate courses, as well as advise you on the different college and career options that are available.

Start Exploring Your Options

Career Opportunities in Science provides you with basic information about 93 professions. When you come across occupations that look intriguing, take the time to learn more about them. The references mentioned throughout the book and in the appendixes can help you further research careers that interest you. In addition, here are a few other things you might do to explore a profession or field in more depth:

- read books about the profession or field
- check out professional and trade magazines, journals, newspapers, and other periodicals
- look at Web sites of professional societies, trade associations, businesses, and other organizations related to your desired occupation
- talk with professionals who work in those jobs that interest you
- visit different work settings, if possible
- enroll in courses related to the profession
- browse through career resources that are available at libraries and career centers
- obtain part-time, seasonal, volunteer, or internship positions at science laboratories, science centers, or other organizations

As you explore various occupations, you will discover the kind of careers you might like—and not like. You will also be gaining valuable knowledge and experience. Furthermore, you will be building a network of contacts that may be able to help with your next steps—obtaining further education and training, as well as future jobs.

Go for it! You can make your career goals and dreams come true.

—Susan Echaore-McDavid

ACKNOWLEDGMENTS

To all the people and organizations who have provided me with information about the various professions described in this book, thank you! I couldn't have written it without you all.

In particular, I would like to express my gratitude to Alan A. Andolsen, CMC, CRM, President, Naremco Services Inc.; American Geophysical Union; Dr. Russ Altman, President, International Society for Computational Biology; Dr. Daniel Baker, Director, Laboratory for Atmospheric and Space Physics, University of Colorado; Dr. Francis Belloni, Chair of the American Physiological Society Career Opportunities in Physiology Committee.

Jeanine L. Bussiere, Ph.D., DABT, Director, Pharmacology/Toxicology, Immunex Corp., Seattle; John A. Boyle, Professor and Head of the Department of Biochemistry and Molecular Biology, Mississippi State University; Dr. James L. Carew, Department of Geology, College of Charleston, South Carolina; Kelly L. Classic, Media Relations Liaison, Health Physics Society; Nick Claudy, Manager, Human Resources, American Geological Institute.

David M. Danko, GIS Standards, Environmental Systems Research Institute; Mike Dion, National Weather Service; Betty J. Eidemiller, Ph.D., Director of Education, Society of Toxicology; Richard A. Engberg, RPH, Technical Specialist, American Water Resources Association; Ken Goddard, Lab Director, National Fish and Wildlife Forensics Laboratory; Kelly A. Gull, Manager, Meetings and Educational Programs, American Society for Biochemistry and Molecular Biology; Shai Halevi, Ph.D; Health Physics Society.

Dr. Jill Karsten, Manager, Education and Career Services, American Geophysical Union; Nancy Kirner, CHP, President-Elect, American Academy of Health Physics; Paul R. Koch, Ph.D., P.E.; Penelope Jones, Director of Education and Customer Services, American Board of Clinical Chemistry; Dr. Gene Likens, International Association of Theoretical and Applied Limnologists; Melinda E. Lowy, Higher Education Programs Coordinator, American Physiological Society.

Ed Maher, Sc.D, CHP, President, American Academy of Health Physics; Timothy B. Mihuc, Chair of the North American Benthological Society Publicity and Public Information Committee; Dr. Elizabeth Murray, College of Mt. Saint Joseph, Cincinnati, Ohio; Sharlotte Neely, Ph.D., Professor of Anthropology, Northern Kentucky University; North American Benthological Society; Alan Rowen, Technical Director, Society of Naval Architects and Marine Engineers.

Dr. Wendy Ryan, Department of Biology, Kutztown University, Pennsylvania; Kathy San Roman; Suzanne Scarlata, Department of Physiology & Biophysics, S.U.N.Y. Stony Brook; Bruce Schneier, CTO of BT Counterpane; Joshua M. Scott, P.E.; Frank Shephard, Executive Secretary of the Society of General Physiologists; Professor Marjorie Skubic, Computer Engineering and Computer Science Department, University of Missouri at Columbia, Missouri; Rosalyn Snyder, Homepage Editor, IEEE Robotics and Automation Society.

Society for Integrative and Comparative Biology (SICB) Education Council; Society of Toxicology; Marvin Specter, Executive Director, National Academy of Forensic Engineers; Lisa Spurlock, Entomological Society of America; Dr. Paula Stephan, Andrew Young School of Policy Studies, Georgia State University; Lance Strawn, P.E.

Hilary Troester, Research Assistant, Research and Publications, Association of Science-Technology Centers; Dr. C. Susan Weiler, Whitman College, Walla Walla, Washington; John Winchester, P.E., Water Resources Engineer; and Alan C. York, Professor, Department of Entomology, Purdue University.

And thank you, James Chambers, Sarah Fogarty, and Dick McDavid.

HOW TO USE THIS BOOK

In *Career Opportunities in Science,* you will learn about 93 professions that you can enter in the scientific and technical fields. You will learn about various scientists, specialists, and technicians. In addition, you will learn about some career options that are available to individuals with scientific training and a background in such areas as business, education, and communications.

Career Opportunities in Science provides basic information about the different professions described in this book. You will read about what the occupations are like, what job requirements are needed, and get a general idea of the salaries, job markets, and advancement prospects for each occupation.

Sources of Information

The information presented in *Career Opportunities in Science* comes from a variety of sources—scientists, engineers, educators, professional societies, trade associations, government agencies, and so on. In addition, books and periodicals related to the different occupations were consulted as well as brochures and other written materials from professional associations, federal agencies, businesses, and other organizations. Job descriptions, work guidelines, and other work-related materials for the different professions were also studied.

The World Wide Web was also a valuable source. A wide range of Web sites were visited to learn about each of the professions that are described in this book. These Web sites included professional societies, trade associations, medical schools, universities, government agencies, companies, and on-line professional periodicals.

How This Book Is Organized

Career Opportunities in Science is designed to be easy to use and read. Altogether there are 93 profiles in 13 sections. A section may have as few as three profiles or as many as 14 profiles. The profiles are usually two or three pages long. The profiles all follow the same format so that you may read the job profiles or sections in whatever order you prefer.

Sections one through four describe opportunities in the biological sciences, physical sciences, and earth sciences. Sections five and six cover occupations in the fields of mathematics and computer science. Sections seven through nine discuss professions in applied sciences while sections ten through thirteen describe other options that are available for individuals with scientific backgrounds and training.

The Job Profiles

The job profiles give you basic information about 93 career opportunities. Each profile starts with the *Career Profile,* a summary of a job's major duties, salary, job outlook, and opportunities for promotion. It also sums up general requirements and special skills needed for a job, as well as personality traits that successful professionals may share. The *Career Ladder* section is a visual presentation of a typical career path.

The rest of the occupational profile is divided into the following parts:

- The "Position Description" details major responsibilities and duties of an occupation.
- "Salaries" presents a general idea of the wages that professionals may earn.
- "Employment Prospects" provides a general idea of the job market for an occupation.
- "Advancement Prospects" discusses possible ways that professionals may advance in their careers.
- "Education and Training" describes the type of education and training that may be required to enter a profession.
- "Special Requirements" lists any professional license, certification, or registration that may be required.
- "Experience, Skills, and Personality Traits" generally covers the job requirements needed for entry-level positions. It also describes some employability skills that employers expect job candidates to have. In addition, this section describes some personality traits that successful professionals have in common.
- "Unions and Associations" provides the names of some professional associations and other organizations that professionals are eligible to join.
- "Tips for Entry" offers general advice for gaining work experience, improving employability, and finding jobs. It also provides suggestions for finding more career information on the World Wide Web.

The Appendixes

At the end of the book are four appendixes that provide additional resources for the professions described in *Career Opportunities in Science.* You can learn about resources for educational training for some professions. You can also find contact information for professional associations and other organizations that can provide you with additional career information. Further, you can find a list of books, periodicals, and Web sites that may give you further information about and insight into the occupations that interest you.

Also at the back of the book is a glossary that defines some of the scientific and nonscientific terms used in this book. In addition, you will find a bibliography that offers you more resources to check out for further exploration on your own.

The World Wide Web

Throughout *Career Opportunities in Science,* Web site addresses for various professional organizations and other resources are provided so that you can learn more on your own. All the Web sites were accessible as the book was being written. Keep in mind that the Web site owners may change addresses, remove the web pages to which you have been referred, or shut down their Web sites completely. Should you come across a URL that does not work, you may still be able to find the Web site by entering its title or the name of the organization or individual in a search engine.

This Books Is Yours

Career Opportunities in Science is your reference book. Use it to read about jobs you have often wondered about. Use it to learn about professions in the science world that you never knew existed. Use it to start your search for the career of your dreams.

Good luck!

BIOLOGICAL SCIENCES

BIOLOGIST

Duties: Study living organisms; design and conduct research projects; perform duties as required

Alternate Title(s): Life Scientist, Biological Scientist, Medical Scientist, Research Scientist; Botanist, Microbiologist, Entomologist, or other title that reflects a specialty

Salary Range: $45,000 to $146,000

Employment Prospects: Good

Advancement Prospects: Good

Prerequisites:

Education or Training—An advanced degree required for research scientist positions

Experience—Work and research experience related to position usually required

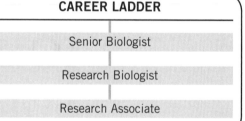

Special Skills and Personality Traits—Math, computer, communication, writing, interpersonal, teamwork, and self-management skills; be analytical, creative, clever, flexible, and persistent

Position Description

Biology is a life science. It is the study of how all living organisms function. They may be one-celled organisms (such as bacteria and algae), plants, animals, or humans.

Biologists are concerned with understanding the structure and life processes of all living organisms. They are also involved with the classification of plant and animal species, as well as with examining the distribution of the different species. In addition, Biologists investigate the relationships that living organisms have with each other and with their environments. Further, Biologists seek to understand plant, animal, and human diseases and search for ways to prevent and cure diseases.

Biology covers many disciplines and subdisciplines, and together these various fields are referred to as the biological sciences. From time to time, new biological fields emerge to meet challenges of new health and environmental problems, or new subdisciplines develop as a result of scientific discoveries and technological advancements. The following are some of the fields in which Biologists specialize:

- taxonomy, the study of how organisms are classified into certain categories
- anatomy, the study of an organism's structure, such as the human skeleton

- microbiology, the study of bacteria, viruses, fungi, and other organisms that can only be seen through microscopes
- botany, the study of the plant world
- zoology, the study of the animal kingdom
- physiology, the study of the life processes (such as the respiratory system or circulatory system) that keep organisms alive
- cell biology, the study of the smallest units of life that make up all organisms
- genetics, the study of how characteristics (or traits) are passed on through generations
- molecular biology, the study of how genetic information is read and controlled
- biochemistry, the study of how chemicals combine and react within the cells
- ecology, the study of how ecosystems are organized and how plants and animals interact with each other in their surroundings

Biological scientists also specialize in various applied biology fields, such as biotechnology, medical science, agriculture, food science, environmental science, and conservation.

Many Biologists engage in research and development, working mostly in academic, government, and industrial laboratories. Oftentimes, they work on research projects that involve the collaboration of various biological scientists or with scientists from other disciplines, such as chemists, physicists, or geologists.

Biologists conduct basic research to seek further knowledge and understanding about living organisms. For example, they study questions such as: How does the human brain work? How are trees affected by pollution? How do apes communicate with each other?

Biologists are also concerned with applied research. They use the findings of basic research to create technologies and processes that can solve general problems in different fields. For example, the various biotechnologies used to manipulate living organisms are results of applied research.

In addition, biological scientists are involved in the development of new or improved consumer products. They usually work in private industry. These scientists generally research ways to refine technologies and processes to create useful products. For instance, various biological scientists have used biotechnologies to develop new drugs, medical diagnostic tests, and disease-resistant crops.

Biologists conduct research on a wide range of subjects. Academic researchers normally explore topics that interest them, while researchers in government and industrial laboratories carry out studies that fit the particular purposes and goals of their employers.

Biologists work in offices and laboratories. Depending on their specialty, their research might involve any of the following: manipulating cells, examining tissues and organs, devising experiments that involve greenhouse plants or lab animals, or conducting tests on human subjects.

Many Biologists also conduct research in the field to make observations and to gather samples to study when they return to their laboratories. Sometimes they travel to remote locations, such as wildernesses, islands, rain forests, or oceans, and spend several days or months working and living there.

Biologists' duties vary, depending on their position and experience. In general, research scientists are responsible for designing and conducting research projects. Senior researchers and principal investigators may perform supervisory and management duties. Some of the general tasks that research scientists perform include: conducting experiments, gathering data, analyzing and interpreting data, writing reports, and performing administrative tasks. Biologists who conduct independent research are usually responsible for seeking research grants from the federal government and other sources to fund their research projects. This involves writing grant proposals that describe goals, methodologies, budgets, and other aspects about their proposed projects.

Biologists typically share the results of their research work with colleagues. They might write scientific papers which they submit to scientific journals or make presentations at scientific conferences.

Many academic researchers are employed as professors at colleges where they teach courses in their areas of expertise. Their duties also include advising students, supervising student research projects, writing scholarly works, performing administrative duties, and participating in community service.

Biologists can also find employment in various other professions that utilize their biological training. Some occupations include biological technician, research assistant, forensic biologist, high school biology teacher, environmental educator, biological sales representative, patent examiner, park ranger, museum curator, technical writer, safety and health inspector, medical laboratory technologist, and science policy analyst, among others.

With additional education and training, Biologists can pursue careers in medical and health professions. For example, they can become medical doctors, dentists, veterinarians, physical therapists, and psychologists.

Salaries

Salaries for Biologists vary, depending on such factors as their education, experience, position, employer, and geographical location. According to a 2006 salary survey by the American Association for the Advancement of Science, the median salary for life scientists in academic settings ranged from $45,000 to $146,000, and for those in industrial settings, from $47,000 to $145,500.

Employment Prospects

Research scientists are hired by government agencies, academic institutions, research institutes, and non-governmental organizations. Additionally, they are employed throughout the various private industries. The competition for research opportunities is strong in all work settings.

According to the U.S. Bureau of Labor Statistics, job growth for biological scientists is predicted to increase by 9 percent through 2016. Many opportunities will also arise as a result of Biologists retiring, being promoted, or transferring to other jobs.

Job prospects vary in the different biological fields. For example, opportunities for marine biologists are limited in comparison to those for molecular biologists. Many experts in the field report that job opportunities for biological scientists should be strongest in the biotechnology and pharmaceutical industries.

Advancement Prospects

Biologists with administrative or management ambitions can advance to such positions within their specialty. Research scientists can become project leaders, program managers, laboratory directors, and executive officers. Technicians and research assistants can advance to managerial positions as laboratory managers and nonlaboratory administrative positions. Some Biologists become consultants. Professors receive promotional rankings as assistant professors, associate professors, or full professors.

Many Biologists achieve advancement by earning higher pay, by conducting independent research projects, and through receiving professional recognition.

Education and Training

Research scientists must hold either a master's or a doctoral degree in their specialties. A Ph.D. degree is required in order to teach in universities and four-year colleges, to conduct independent research, or to obtain top management positions. Some Ph.D. scientists also earn medical degrees (M.D.) to obtain additional training for careers in medical research.

Individuals with a bachelor's degree in a biological science discipline may qualify for research assistant or biological technician positions.

Experience, Skills, and Personality Traits

Requirements vary for the various positions as well as among the different employers. For entry-level positions, employers generally choose candidates who have related work and research experience, which may have been gained through research projects, internships, fellowships or employment. Many employers expect Ph.D. candidates for research scientist positions to have several years of postdoctoral experience.

Biologists need strong math and computer skills for their work. They also need excellent communication and writing skills as they must be able to report their results and conclusions clearly to fellow scientists and to nontechnical personnel. Additionally, Biologists need effective interpersonal and teamwork skills as well as self-management skills such as being able to meet deadlines, prioritize multiple tasks, work independently, and make sound judgments.

Some personality traits that successful Biologists share are being analytical, creative, clever, flexible, and persistent.

Unions and Associations

Many Biologists join professional societies to take advantage of professional services and resources such as professional certification, education programs, and current research information. Membership also provides them with opportunities to network with their colleagues. Biologists are eligible to join societies that serve scientists from all disciplines, such as the American Association for the Advancement of Science, or societies that serve Biologists in general such as the American Institute of Biological Sciences.

In addition, many Biologists join associations that serve their particular fields. For example, animal biologists might join the Society for Integrative and Comparative Biology while microbiologists might join the American Society of Microbiology.

See Appendix III for contact information for the above organizations.

Tips for Entry

1. As an undergraduate student, take a wide variety of biological courses to get an idea of the various career paths that are available.
2. To gain experience, become a research assistant with a professor in whose work you are interested.
3. Establish positive working relationships with colleagues, professors, supervisors, and principal investigators, as they may be able to help you with your future job searches.
4. Contact employers directly about job vacancies. Also inquire about their job selection process. Many companies, government agencies, and other organizations post job announcements at their Web sites.
5. You can learn more about various biology careers on the Internet. One source is the "Careers in Biology" Web page by Emporia State University (Kansas) at http://www.emporia.edu/biosci/carebiol.htm. For more links, see Appendix IV.

MICROBIOLOGIST

Duties: Study the characteristics and growth of micro-organisms; design and conduct research projects; may provide clinical laboratory services; perform duties as required

Alternate Title(s): Virologist, Medical Microbiologist, or other title that reflects a specialty

Salary Range: $35,000 to $108,000

Employment Prospects: Good

Advancement Prospects: Good

Prerequisites:

Education or Training—Bachelor's or advanced degree in biology, microbiology, or a related field

Experience—Postdoctoral experience may be required for research scientists

Special Skills and Personality Traits—Math, computer, writing, communication, interpersonal, and

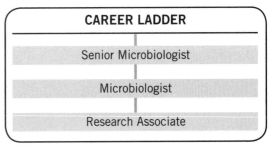

CAREER LADDER

Senior Microbiologist

Microbiologist

Research Associate

teamwork skills; be precise, creative, flexible, and self-motivated

Special Requirements—Licensure or certification may be required for Clinical Microbiologists; board certification required to run clinical laboratories

Position Description

Microbiology is the study of microbes (or microorganisms) such as bacteria, viruses, molds, yeast, algae, and protozoa. These are very tiny living organisms that can be only seen with the help of microscopes.

Microbiologists seek to understand how microbes exist by studying their characteristics as well as how they grow, develop, reproduce and function. Additionally, these scientists examine how the different microbes interact with other living organisms. Microbiologists are also concerned in understanding how some microbes act as infectious agents and affect the health of plants, animals, and humans.

Many Microbiologists are research scientists who conduct basic research to gain further knowledge about microorganisms and infectious agents. These scientists also develop new methodologies and techniques by which to study the various microbes.

Some Microbiologists devote themselves to a specialty. Some specialize in the type of microbes that they study. For example, bacteriologists examine bacteria, parasitologists study tiny parasites, and virologists investigate viruses that are active inside living cells. Other Microbiologists concentrate in a particular specialty of biology. For example, they might study only the physiology, cytology, biochemistry, immunology, or genetics of microorganisms.

Microbiologists sometimes collaborate on projects with other scientists. Their duties vary, depending on their position and experience. In general, Microbiologists are responsible for designing and conducting research projects. Some of their tasks include conducting experiments, gathering data, analyzing and interpreting data, writing reports, and performing administrative tasks. Most senior researchers and principal investigators also perform supervisory and management duties. Some Microbiologists are responsible for obtaining research grants to fund their projects.

Microbiologists typically exchange information about their research results with colleagues. They might submit articles, or scientific papers, to scientific journals or give presentations at scientific conferences that are sponsored by professional associations.

Some Microbiologists provide technical and administrative support to scientists. They are usually called research assistants or technicians. Some of their duties include conducting experiments, collecting specimens, analyzing data, writing reports, maintaining laboratories, and performing routine administrative tasks.

A large number of Microbiologists are involved in medicine, industry, agriculture, and other areas of applied microbiology. They use the findings of basic microbiological research to solve problems in their respective fields.

The duties of applied microbiologists vary, depending on their specialty. Medical and veterinary microbiologists work closely with physicians, dentists, and medical scientists. These Microbiologists identify and examine microbes that cause diseases in humans and animals. In addition, they investigate ways to prevent, treat, and eliminate those diseases.

Clinical microbiologists provide laboratory services to physicians. They perform tests to identify pathogenic microbes in specimens from patients; assist physicians with the interpretation and evaluation of tests; and suggest further test procedures.

Public health microbiologists provide laboratory services to local public health agencies. They perform testing and other services to detect, diagnose, treat, and control infectious diseases and other health hazards in the community.

Industrial microbiologists are involved in the research and development of new products and production methods in pharmaceutical, biotechnology, food, dairy, cosmetics, and other industries. These products include medicines, antibiotics, foods, beverages, and health care products.

Agricultural microbiologists are concerned with ways to improve the production of crops and livestock. Some agricultural microbiologists may work on projects that use microbes to increase crops or to control insect pests. Environmental microbiologists are involved in the protection of ecosystems. Their jobs may involve inspecting manufacturing plants, testing bodies of water for pollutants, or controlling disease that is spread by wildlife, insects, or rodents infected with pathogenic microbes.

Microbiologists mostly work in sterile laboratories and offices. They use computers, electron microscopes, and other sophisticated laboratory equipment. Many of them use biotechnology techniques to manipulate microbes to understand how they work or to produce new or improved products, processes, or systems. They wear protective clothing and follow strict safety rules and regulations to minimize the risks that are involved in handling microbes, chemicals, and other potentially dangerous elements.

Microbiologists usually work 40 hours a week. They often put in additional hours to monitor experiments and complete various tasks.

Salaries

Salaries for Microbiologists vary and depend on their education, experience, type of employer, duties, geographical location, and other factors. The U.S. Bureau of Labor Statistics reports in its May 2006 *Occupational Employment Statistics* survey that the estimated annual salary for most Microbiologists ranged between $35,460 and $108,270. According to a 2006 salary survey by the American Association for the Advancement of Science, the median annual salary for academic researchers in microbiology was $62,000, and for industrial researchers, $89,000.

Employment Prospects

Microbiologists are employed by government agencies, academic institutions, and nonprofit organizations, as well as throughout private industry.

Job prospects for experienced Microbiologists are reported as being favorable by many in the field, particularly in the biotechnology and pharmaceutical industries. However, competition for jobs is keen. Most opportunities will become available as Microbiologists retire, transfer to other positions, or leave their fields.

Advancement Prospects

Microbiologists can pursue management and administrative positions in any work setting. Experienced Microbiologists can become consultants to businesses, government agencies, and policy makers. An advanced degree is usually required for advancement to higher positions.

Education and Training

A bachelor's degree in biology or microbiology may qualify candidates for positions as research assistants, quality assurance technologists, medical technologists, food microbiologists, industrial microbiologists, environmental microbiologists, clinical microbiologists, and veterinary microbiologists. Some employers, however, prefer to hire applicants with a master's degree.

To qualify for research associate, research manager, or laboratory manager positions, individuals must possess at least a master's degree.

Microbiologists normally need a doctoral degree (Ph.D.), medical doctor degree (M.D.), or a joint Ph.D. and M.D. degree to conduct independent research, teach in four-year colleges and universities, and obtain top management posts.

Special Requirements

Clinical and public health microbiologists may be required to be certified or licensed in the state where they practice. For requirements for a specific location, contact the appropriate licensing agency that governs that jurisdiction.

Experience, Skills, and Personality Traits

In general, employers choose candidates who have related work and research experience to the positions they are applying for. Recent college graduates may have gained experience through student research projects, internships, fellowships, or employment. Many employers prefer that Ph.D. candidates have several years of postdoctoral experience.

Microbiologists need strong math, computer, writing, and communication skills. In addition, they need effective interpersonal and teamwork skills. Being precise, creative, flexible, and self-motivated are a few of the personality traits that successful Microbiologists share.

Unions and Associations

Many Microbiologists join societies to take advantage of professional services such as education programs, professional certification programs, and networking opportunities. Some professional associations are the American Society for Microbiology, the Society for Industrial Microbiology, and the American Society for Virology. See Appendix III for contact information.

Tips for Entry

1. Take advantage of your school's career center when searching for internships, cooperative education programs, fellowships, part-time work, and permanent positions.
2. A background in business can help you succeed in private industry.
3. Many employers allow applicants to complete an application at their Web sites.
4. Use the Internet to learn more about microbiology. One Web site you might visit is Microbe World, http://www.microbeworld.org. For more links, see Appendix IV.

BIOTECHNOLOGIST

Duties: Study the use of living cells and biomolecular materials to solve problems and create useful products for society; design and conduct research projects; perform duties as required

Alternate Title(s): Research Scientist, Research Associate, Research Assistant, Technician; a title that reflects a specialty such as Microbiologist or Biochemist

Salary Range: $30,000 to $130,000

Employment Prospects: Good

Advancement Prospects: Good

Prerequisites:

   Education or Training—Bachelor's or advanced degree in a scientific discipline

   Experience—Previous biotechnology research experience preferred

CAREER LADDER

Senior Biotechnologist

Biotechnologist

Biotechnologist (Entry-level)

Special Skills and Personality Traits—Communication, interpersonal, teamwork, analytical, problem-solving, troubleshooting, and self-management skills; flexible, hard working, patient, creative, innovative, detail-oriented, determined, and self-motivated

Position Description

All microbes, plants, animals, and humans each have their own set of genes that are contained within the DNA molecules inside their cells. By using various technologies, scientists can manipulate the genetic and biochemical characteristics in living organisms to produce specific traits. For example, scientists might transfer DNA from a plant with desired traits (such as being a certain color or being resistant to specific insects) into another plant to enhance its features. The targeted plant may or may not be of the same species.

The science and practice of using living cells and biomolecular materials to solve problems and create useful products is called biotechnology. The scientists who work in this field are generally known as Biotechnologists. They enter this field with different scientific backgrounds, including microbiology, biochemistry, chemistry, biophysics, genetics, mathematics, biomedical engineering, botany, animal science, food science, and environmental engineering, among others.

Biotechnology is an applied biological science. Some people think that biotechnology is a new science, but it has actually been around for many centuries. For example, farmers have long collected seeds with the best attributes for the next year's planting and bred livestock with the most desirable traits; and people have used bacteria, yeasts, molds, and other microorganisms to produce bread, cheese, beer, wine, and other foods and drinks. Several breakthroughs that occurred during the last 30 years—such as the testing of genetically engineered plants and the mapping and sequencing of the human genome—have caused biotechnology to become one of the most active research and development fields in the United States, as well as in the world. For example, Biotechnologists have helped to develop new drugs, vaccines, and medical diagnostic tests; to improve the resistance of plants and animals to disease; to preserve food products; to design industrial processes that use less energy and water; to clean up hazardous waste more effectively; to develop methods for detecting land mines; and to enhance criminal investigations with such tools as DNA fingerprinting.

Biotechnologists conduct research in academic, government, and industrial settings. They typically specialize in a particular area, such as agriculture, food technology, pharmaceuticals, clinical diagnostics, medical therapies, genetics, industrial microbiology, waste management, wastewater treatment, alternative fuels, or forensics.

These scientists engage in different types of research and development. Some of them conduct basic research to gain further understanding and knowledge about cellular and biomolecular processes in various life-forms.

Their discoveries are the basis upon which technologies, processes, products, and services are created.

Many Biotechnologists are involved in applied research. They utilize the findings of basic research to solve practical problems in their areas of concern. For example, applied researchers might be concerned with seeking methods to eliminate cancerous cells, designing drugs without toxic side effects, or developing tests that can uncover microbial contaminants in food. In private industry, many Biotechnologists participate in product development. They are part of research teams that utilize both basic and applied research to invent new or improved commercial products and services.

Industrial and government researchers typically work on projects that fulfill the mission and goals of their employers, while academic researchers perform research on whatever subject matter interests them. Depending on their projects, Biotechnologists may work alone or collaborate with fellow scientists and engineers. They perform a wide variety of tasks, which vary according to their position, experience, and skills levels. Some general tasks that most of these scientists perform include:

- planning and developing research projects
- designing and conducting experiments or tests
- keeping accurate and detailed records and logs of their experiments or tests
- searching for and reading research literature
- analyzing and interpreting data
- writing technical summaries and reports
- meeting with colleagues to discuss projects
- planning and organizing work schedules
- keeping up-to-date with the latest research developments
- supervising junior scientists, research assistants and associates, science technicians, and administrative support staff members

Senior scientists may also be responsible for leading project teams and managing research units or departments.

Researchers typically share and exchange information with other scientists, including those in other disciplines. Many write papers about their findings and conclusions for scientific journals, as well as give presentations at scientific conferences.

Most academic researchers hold professorships at colleges and universities where they teach undergraduate and graduate students in biotechnology or other subjects. These researchers are responsible for teaching courses, advising students, supervising students'

research projects, producing scholarly work, fulfilling community service, and performing administrative duties. In addition, they are responsible for seeking grants to fund their research projects.

Biotechnologists work in laboratories and offices. They generally work a 40-hour week, but it is not uncommon for them to put in additional hours on evenings and weekends to monitor experiments, attend conferences, and complete various tasks.

Salaries

Salaries for Biotechnologists vary, depending on such factors as their field, education, experience, employer, and geographic location. Formal salary information about this occupation is unavailable. In general, they earn salaries similar to other scientists within their discipline. The U.S. Bureau of Labor Statistics reported the following estimated annual salaries for most of these scientists in its May 2006 *Occupational Employment Statistics* survey:

- animal scientists, $31,540 to $81,430
- food scientists and technologists, $29,620 to $97,350
- biochemists and biophysicists, $40,820 to $129,510
- chemists, $35,480 to $106,310
- microbiologists, $35,460 to $108,270
- environmental scientists, $34,590 to $94,670
- plant scientists, $33,650 to $93,460

Employment Prospects

Although biotechology is a young field (having emerged during the 1970s), the job market for Biotechnologists is strong and is expected to continue to grow in the coming years. These scientists are employed by government agencies, academic institutions, research institutes, and private companies. They also work for biotechnology firms, many of which are located in San Francisco, San Diego, Seattle, Denver/Boulder area, Boston, Chicago, and Research Triangle Park, North Carolina. In addition, increasingly more companies in different industries are hiring Biotechnologists to improve their products and manufacturing processes. Some of these industries include the pharmaceutical, medical manufacturing, agriculture, food processing, energy, and chemical manufacturing industries.

According to the *2005–2006 Guide to Biotechnology* by BIO (Biotechnology Industry Organization), 1,473 biotechnology companies existed in the United States in 2003, and 198,300 people overall were employed in the biotechnology industry. The report further states that in 2003, the U.S. biotechnology industry spent $17.9 billion on research and development.

Advancement Prospects

Biotechnologists can advance in any number of ways, depending on their interests and ambitions. They can become technical specialists or pursue supervisory and managerial positions. They may choose to seek research jobs in other settings. In industry, they may move into production, quality control, marketing, sales, or another area within their company. Entrepreneurial individuals may choose to become independent consultants or start their own companies.

Many Biotechnologists measure their success through making important discoveries, through job satisfaction, and by earning professional recognition among their peers.

Education and Training

Educational requirements vary with the different positions. Employers typically seek scientists who hold bachelor's or advanced degrees in different scientific disciplines, including biology, microbiology, biotechnology (or applied biology), chemistry, biochemistry, biophysics, genetics, animal science, plant science, and environmental science, among others.

Depending on the employer, candidates for lab technician and research assistant positions may need an associate or bachelor's degree in an appropriate field or a professional certificate in biotechnology. Applicants for research associate positions must usually hold a bachelor's or master's degree, while those seeking research scientist positions are normally required to possess a master's or doctoral degree. Scientists must hold doctorates if they plan to conduct independent research, teach in four-year colleges and universities, or advance to top management positions.

Entry-level Biotechnologists are usually provided on-the-job training. Throughout their careers, Biotechnologists enroll in workshops, seminars, and courses to update their skills and knowledge.

Experience, Special Skills, and Personality Traits

Employers generally seek candidates who have experience working in biotechnology research. Entry-level applicants may have gained their experience through internships, work-study programs, student research projects, or employment. Many employers prefer to hire Ph.D. applicants who have a few years of postdoctoral experience.

Because they must work well with others in their research teams, Biotechnologists need excellent communication, interpersonal, and teamwork skills. Their work also requires that they have effective analytical, problem-solving, and troubleshooting skills. In addition, they must have strong self-management skills, including the abilities to work independently, understand and follow directions, prioritize multiple tasks, and handle stressful situations. Being flexible, hardworking, patient, creative, innovative, detail-oriented, determined, and self-motivated are some personality traits that successful Biotechnologists have in common.

Unions and Associations

Biotechnologists can join professional associations to take advantage of networking opportunities, training programs, job listings, and other professional services and resources. A few national societies that serve their diverse interests include the Society for Industrial Microbiology, the American Chemical Society, the American Dairy Science Association, the Institute of Food Technologists, and the American Association for the Advancement of Science. For contact information, see Appendix III.

Tips for Entry

1. You will need a fundamental understanding of various scientific disciplines to work in biotechnology. While in high school and college, take courses in biology, molecular biology, genetics, chemistry, and bioinformatics.

2. Many companies sponsor summer employment or internship programs for college students. Some also have summer programs for high school students. Contact local companies early in the spring to find out what jobs they may have available and how you can apply for a summer position.

3. Biotechnologists need to have an understanding of how business works. Hence, take some fundamental courses in business, finance, and management. Ask your college adviser for suggestions of classes that would be most helpful to you.

4. Some people sign up with a scientific staffing agency, such as Kelly Scientific Resources, to work on a temporary or contractual basis with different companies. Along with building up their work experience, individuals can get an idea of the types of work environments in which they would like to work on a permanent basis.

5. Use the Internet to learn more about the biotechnology field. You might start by visiting BIO (Biotechnology Industry Organization) at http://bio.org. For more links, see Appendix IV.

BOTANIST

Duties: Study plants and their environments; design and conduct research projects; perform duties as required

Alternate Title(s): Plant Biologist, Plant Scientist; Plant Pathologist or another title that reflects a specialty

Salary Range: $34,000 to $95,000

Employment Prospects: Fair

Advancement Prospects: Good

Prerequisites:

    Education or Training—A bachelor's or advanced degree in botany or related field

    Experience—Postdoctoral experience may be required for research scientists

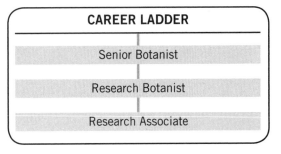

CAREER LADDER

Senior Botanist

Research Botanist

Research Associate

Special Skills and Personality Traits—Math, computer, communication, writing, interpersonal, teamwork, and self-management skills; be patient, ambitious, creative, and flexible

Position Description

Botany is the biological study of plants—lichens, mosses, ferns, flowers, shrubs, grasses, vines, trees, and so on. Botanists, or plant biologists, are concerned with the identification and classification of the thousands of plant species. They seek to understand the structure and life processes of plants, as well as how plants relate to each other and to other living organisms. Botanists also study how plants have developed and changed through time and how plants adapt to their surroundings. In addition, they investigate the practical uses of plants and study the causes and cures of plant diseases.

Many Botanists devote themselves to studying the biology of particular plant species. For example, mycologists study fungi, and marine biologists study different plant species that live in the oceans. Botanists also specialize in studying one (or more) biology fields, such as:

- anatomy, the structure of plants
- physiology, the internal processes that take place in order for plants to grow and reproduce
- biophysics, the application of physics principles to study how plants function
- plant genetics, the heredity of plants
- molecular biology, the study of how genes affect the form and function of plants
- plant ecology, the relationships between plants as well as with their surroundings
- paleobotany, the biology and evolution of fossil plants

Many Botanists focus their work in an applied plant science field such as biotechnology, horticulture, medical botany, or natural resources management. For example, plant breeders develop better types of plants; plant pathologists study how to manage, prevent, or control plant diseases; horticulturists investigate ways to improve the production of fruits and vegetables; and conservationists study and manage natural resources such as rangelands and forests.

Most Botanists engage in research and development in academic, government, and industrial settings. They work in three general research areas. Basic researchers seek further knowledge about the biology of plants. Applied researchers use the findings of basic botanical research to produce technologies and processes that can solve problems in different fields. Researchers in product development take results of both basic and applied research to create new or improved consumer products.

Academic Botanists usually choose their own research topics while those who work in nonacademic settings typically perform research that is determined by their employers. Those who conduct independent research are responsible for seeking grants to fund their projects.

In general, research scientists are responsible for designing and conducting research projects. They study plants in controlled conditions in greenhouses as well as in their natural habitats. They also examine plant cells and tissues under microscopes. Some of their tasks include conducting experiments; collecting, analyzing, and interpreting data; preparing reports; and performing administrative tasks. Sometimes Botanists conduct field expeditions to remote areas, such as rain forests, islands, and wildernesses. They may spend several weeks or months working and living there.

Most academic Botanists are employed as professors. In addition to conducting research, they are responsible for planning and teaching undergraduate and graduate courses. They also advise students, supervise student research projects, perform administrative duties, and participate in community service.

Botanists can also seek other occupations in which they may use their training. Some of these occupations are: science teacher, botanical garden director, naturalist, landscape designer, farmer, seed company sales representative, botanical illustrator, and environmental scientist.

Salaries
Salaries for Botanists vary, depending on such factors as their education, experience, position, employer, and geographical location. Formal salary information is unavailable for this occupation. The U.S. Bureau of Labor Statistics (BLS) reports in its May 2006 *Occupational Employment Statistics* survey that the estimated annual salary for most biological scientists, who were not listed separately in its survey, ranged between $34,300 and $95,130.

Employment Prospects
Research scientists work for academic institutions, government agencies, and nongovernmental organizations. They also find employment in seed companies, nurseries, food processing plants, pharmaceutical companies, biotechnology firms, and other establishments in private industry.

According to the BLS, employment for biological scientists, including Botanists, is expected to increase by 7 to 13 percent through 2016. In addition to job growth, opportunities for Botanists will become available as individuals retire, transfer to other jobs, or advance to higher positions.

In general, competition for research positions is strong.

Advancement Prospects
Botanists with administrative or management ambitions can advance to such positions within their specialty. They can become project leaders, program managers, laboratory directors, executive officers, and so on. Some Botanists become consultants. Professors receive promotional rankings as assistant professors, associate professors, or full professors.

Education and Training
In general, a bachelor's or master's degree in botany or a related field is required for research assistant, technician, and technologist positions. Doctorate degrees are required to conduct independent research, teach in universities and four-years colleges, or to obtain top management positions.

Experience, Skills, and Personality Traits
Employers typically choose candidates for entry-level positions who have related work and research experience, which may have been gained through student research projects, internships, fellowships, or employment. Ph.D. candidates for research scientist positions are usually expected to have a few years of postdoctoral experience.

Botanists need basic math and computer skills for their work. They also need excellent communication and writing skills to report their results clearly to fellow scientists and others. In addition, they need strong interpersonal, teamwork, and self-management skills.

Some personality traits that successful Botanists share are being patient, ambitious, creative, and flexible.

Unions and Associations
Many Botanists join professional associations to take advantage of education programs, networking opportunities, and other professional services and resources. Some societies that serve the diverse interests of Botanists are the American Society of Plant Biologists, the Botanical Society of America, the American Society for Horticulture Science, the American Society of Agronomy, and the American Institute of Biological Sciences. See Appendix III for contact information.

Tips for Entry
1. Gain research experience as an undergraduate by doing independent research projects or working as a research assistant for a professor whose work interests you.
2. Start searching for internships in summer employment early, as many positions are filled by late spring.
3. Use the Internet to learn more about Botanists. One Web site you might visit is the Botanical Society of America, http://www.botany.org. For more links, see Appendix IV.

ECOLOGIST

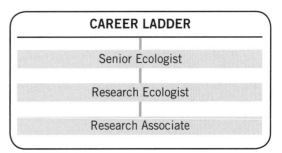

Position Description

Ecologists are concerned with the diversity of life within ecosystems, which include backyards, ponds, suburban hillsides, cities, beaches, wetlands, oceans, forests, and canyons, among other geographical areas. An ecosystem refers to a location and all the living organisms and nonliving things that reside there.

Ecologists study the different plant and animal species that live within an ecosystem, how many there are of each species, and how they are distributed within the ecosystem. These scientists also seek to understand how different organisms interact with each other and with their physical surroundings. In addition, Ecologists examine how ecosystems provide humans, animals, and plants with food, shelter, and other natural resources. Further, they investigate how environmental problems and issues affect ecosystems and what can be done to restore, protect, and preserve them.

Most Ecologists are research scientists. Many of them conduct basic research to expand our knowledge about various ecosystems. Some Ecologists carry out studies in the applied field of environmental science where they seek solutions to environmental problems and issues, such as air pollution, water pollution, land use, and hazardous waste management. In addition to conducting research, these Ecologists perform other tasks. For example, they might monitor natural resources within an ecosystem, design plans to restore ecosystems, write environmental impact statements, or advise lawmakers on the best practices for healthy ecosystems within their local communities.

In general, research scientists are responsible for designing and conducting research projects. They may handle one or more research projects at a time. They often collaborate on projects with other scientists.

Ecologists perform a wide range of tasks. They conduct experiments and tests; gather, analyze, and interpret data, and perform administrative tasks. They also write scientific papers and give presentations about the results of their research projects. Those who conduct independent research are responsible for obtaining grants to fund their projects.

Ecologists work in offices and laboratories, as well as conduct research in the field. Field expeditions may sometimes require working and living for several weeks or months in remote locations such as islands, deserts, rain forests, and wildernesses.

Many Ecologists are employed as professors at colleges and universities. They teach ecology courses, and sometimes teach biology or other courses, to undergraduate or graduate students. As professors, their duties include advising students, supervising student research projects, writing scholarly works, performing administrative duties, and participating in community service.

Ecologists can also find employment in various other professions that utilize their training and background.

For example, they can become biological technicians, high school teachers, naturalists, environmental educators, museum curators, planners, environmental analysts, conservationists, lobbyists, and science journalists.

Salaries

Salaries for Ecologists vary, depending on such factors as their experience, education, employer, and geographical location. According to a 2006 salary by the American Association for the Advancement of Science, the median annual salary for academic researchers in ecology was $61,474, and for industrial researchers, $75,000. The U.S. Bureau of Labor Statistics reports in its May 2006 *Occupational Employment Statistics* survey that the estimated annual salary for most biological scientists, who were not listed separately in its survey, ranged between $34,300 and $95,130.

Employment Prospects

Ecologists work in academic, governmental, industrial, nongovernmental, and nonprofit settings. Some employers include academic institutions, government agencies, research institutes, zoos, environmental organizations, agribusiness companies, and environmental consulting firms, among others.

With the growing awareness of the environment and the need to manage it more carefully, opportunities are expected to be good for Ecologists. However, keep in mind that job opportunities go up and down, depending on the changes in the economy, political administrations, and other factors. The best opportunities are predicted to be in the private sector and with nongovernmental organizations.

Advancement Prospects

Advancement opportunities vary. Research Ecologists can advance to management and administrative positions, such as project leaders, program managers, and executive directors. Professors can advance in rank (assistant, associate, and full professor) as well as obtain job tenure.

Education and Training

Minimally, Ecologists must hold a bachelor's degree in ecology, biology, or another related field. A mas-

ter's or doctoral degree is generally required of candidates to qualify for research scientist positions. To become professors, conduct independent research, or obtain top management positions, Ecologists must hold a Ph.D.

Experience, Skills, and Personality Traits

For entry-level positions, employers generally choose candidates who have related work and research experience, which may have been gained through research projects, internships, fellowships, or employment. Many employers expect Ph.D. applicants to have worked in one or more postdoctoral positions.

Ecologists need strong math, statistics, and computer skills as well as excellent writing, communication, organizational, teamwork, and interpersonal skills. Being flexible, determined, creative, analytical, and resourceful are some personality traits that successful Ecologists share.

Unions and Associations

Many Ecologists belong to professional societies to take advantage of resources and services such as education programs, professional certification and networking opportunities. Some associations that serve the various interests of Ecologists are the American Association for the Advancement of Science, the American Institute of Biological Sciences, the Ecological Society of America, the Society of Wetland Scientists, and the Society for Conservation Biology. See Appendix III for contact information.

Tips for Entry

1. You can start getting involved in ecology while in high school. You might join ecological or environmental organizations, as well as participate in activities that support the environment.
2. You can learn about internships and jobs from various sources, such as professors, college career centers, professional societies, and conservation groups.
3. Use the Internet to learn more about Ecologists. One Web site you might visit is Ecological Society of America, http://www.esa.org. For more links, see Appendix IV.

ZOOLOGIST

CAREER PROFILE

Duties: Study animals in their natural habitats; design and conduct research projects; perform duties as required

Alternate Title(s): Animal Biologist; Entomologist, Wildlife Biologist, or other title that reflects a specialty

Salary Range: $33,000 to $85,000

Employment Prospects: Good

Advancement Prospects: Good

Prerequisites:

  Education or Training—A bachelor's or advanced degree in zoology or a related field

  Experience—Postdoctoral experience may be required for research scientists

CAREER LADDER

Senior Zoologist

Research Zoologist

Research Associate

Special Skills and Personality Traits—Math, computer, data management, problem-solving, communication, and technical writing skills; be curious, creative, analytical, committed, and flexible

Position Description

Zoology is the biological study of the animal kingdom. It deals with the origin, characteristics, life processes, and behavior of animals. Additionally, it is concerned with the identification, classification, and distribution of the many thousands of different animal species.

The animal biologists who study this science are Zoologists. People often confuse them with zookeepers. Although zookeepers usually have a background in zoology, their primary job is to take care of the animals in aquariums and zoological parks. Zoologists, on the other hand, are research scientists. Some conduct basic research to add further knowledge about the biology of animals, while others apply the findings of basic research to develop useful products or find solutions to problems in such applied fields as agriculture, medical science, biotechnology, conservation, and environmental science.

Many Zoologists focus their studies in one or more biology specialties, such as:

- taxonomy, the naming and classification of animals
- comparative anatomy, examining how body structures are different or the same
- physiology, the study of animal life processes such as the nervous and muscular systems
- endocrinology, the study of the tissues and glands that produce and secrete hormones
- genetics, the study of how characteristics are passed from one generation to the next
- animal behavior, the way animals behave

- animal ecology, the relationship of animals to their environment
- phylogeny, the evolution of animals

Some Zoologists study the overall biology of particular types of animals. For example: protozoologists examine protozoa; invertebrate Zoologists study animals without a backbone; herpetologists examine amphibians and reptiles; ornithologists investigate the world of birds; and primatologists study apes and other primates. Other Zoologists specialize in studying animals within a particular environment. For example, wildlife biologists study animals in the wilderness while limnologists examine animals that live in freshwater bodies.

Many Zoologists work in the applied sciences, such as conservation or animal husbandry (the management of animal welfare and breeding). For example, they may be employed as animal breeders, fisheries biologists, dairy scientists, food technologists, and wildlife forensic scientists. Conducting basic or applied research may be their primary duty or one of many duties.

Zoologists often conduct more than one research project at a time. They sometimes collaborate on projects with other zoologists, biological scientists, and scientists from other disciplines.

Zoological research involves designing and conducting research projects. Their duties include conducting experiments; collecting, interpreting, and analyzing data; preparing reports; and performing administrative tasks. Those who conduct independent research are usually responsible for seeking grants from the federal government and other sources to fund their projects. Senior researchers and principal investigators may perform supervisory and management duties.

Zoologists often exchange research information with their colleagues. They might write articles, or scientific papers, which are published in scientific journals. Some might make presentations at scientific meetings that are sponsored by professional associations.

Zoologists observe animals in their natural habitats as well as in zoos, laboratories, and other controlled environments. Some conduct field expeditions to remote locations, such as wildernesses, rain forests, or islands, where they spend several days or months working and living.

Many Zoologists are employed as university and college professors to teach zoology courses to undergraduate and graduate students. Zoologists juggle various tasks each day. Along with conducting research, they advise students, supervise student research projects, write scholarly works, perform administrative duties, and participate in community service.

Some Zoologists work as technicians and research assistants. In these positions they provide research scientists with technical support.

Zoologists also find employment in other occupations in which they may use their training. Some of these occupations are science teacher, environmental educator, zookeeper, animal trainer, museum curator, environmental scientist, park naturalist, and pharmaceutical sales representative. With additional education and training, Zoologists can pursue careers as veterinarians, medical doctors, dentists, or other medical or healthcare professionals.

Salaries

Salaries for Zoologists vary, depending on their education, experience, geographical location, and other factors. The U.S. Bureau of Labor Statistics (BLS) reports in its May 2006 *Occupational Employment Statistics* (OES) survey that the estimated annual salary for most Zoologists ranged between $32,800 and $84,580. According to a 2006 salary by the American Association for the Advancement of Science, the median annual salary for industrial researchers in zoology was $47,000, and for academic researchers, $59,300.

Employment Prospects

Zoologists are employed by various organizations, including academic institutions, government agencies, research laboratories, medical laboratories, animal hospitals, fisheries, wildlife preserves, zoological gardens,

conservation groups, and agricultural product manufacturers, among others.

According to the BLS May 2006 OES survey, about 18,000 Zoologists (and wildlife biologists) are employed in the United States. This agency further projects that this occupation will grow 9 percent during the 2006–16 period. In addition to job growth, opportunities will become available as individuals retire, transfer to other positions, or leave the profession for any number of reasons. Job candidates can expect keen competition, particularly for research and teaching positions. Zoologists with advanced degrees increase their chances of employment.

Advancement Prospects

Zoologists can advance in various ways, depending on their interests and ambitions. For example, those with managerial and administrative ambitions can pursue management opportunities in their work settings. Many Zoologists measure success through job satisfaction, by earning higher wages, and by gaining professional recognition.

Academicians can advance in rank from instructor to assistant, associate, and full professor, as well as gain tenure at their institution.

Education and Training

A bachelor's degree in zoology, biology, psychology, anthropology, or another related field can qualify Zoologists for research assistant or technician positions. Having a master's degree typically offers candidates a wider range of opportunities. A Ph.D. is required to teach in universities and four-year colleges, to conduct independent research, or to obtain top management positions.

Experience, Skills, and Personality Traits

Requirements vary for the different positions as well as among the various employers. For entry-level positions, employers generally choose candidates who have related work and research experience. This may have been gained through research projects, internships, fellowships, or employment. Ph.D. candidates for research scientist positions may be required to have a few years of postdoctoral experience.

Zoologists need strong math, computer, data management, and problem-solving skills for their work. In addition, excellent communication and technical writing skills are needed in order to write and present comprehensible reports to others.

Being curious, creative, analytical, committed, and flexible are a few of the personality traits that successful zoologists share.

Unions and Associations

Professional societies offer Zoologists many professional resources and services such as current research information and networking opportunities. Zoologists can join general scientific societies such as the American Association for the Advancement of Science or the Society for Integrative and Comparative Biology. They can also join professional societies that serve their particular interests such as the Animal Behavior Society, the Society for Marine Mammalogy, the American Society of Animal Science, or the American Physiological Society. See Appendix III for contact information.

Tips for Entry

1. You can begin acquiring practical experience in high school. Do volunteer work at zoos, nature centers, aquariums, or animal shelters.
2. Contact professional societies for leads to internships, fellowships, postdoctoral positions, and permanent positions.
3. Use the Internet to learn more about zoology. To start, you might visit the Society for Integrative and Comparative Biology Web site at http://www.sicb.org. For more links, see Appendix IV.

AQUATIC BIOLOGIST

Duties: Study plants and animals in marine and freshwater settings; design and conduct research projects; perform duties as required

Alternate Title(s): Marine Biologist, Limnologist, Fisheries Biologist, or other title that reflects a specialty

Salary Range: $34,000 to $95,000

Employment Prospects: Good

Advancement Prospects: Good

Prerequisites:

> **Education or Training**—A bachelor's or advanced degree in biology, aquatic biology, or related field
>
> **Experience**—Research experience required

CAREER LADDER

Senior Aquatic Biologist

Research Aquatic Biologist

Research Associate

Special Skills and Personality Traits—Laboratory, statistics, computer, data management, communication, technical writing, organizational, interpersonal, and teamwork skills; be independent, flexible, persistent, creative, enthusiastic, and self-motivated

Position Description

Aquatic Biologists study the structure and life processes of the various plants and animals that live in the oceans, estuaries, lakes, rivers, and other bodies of water. They are also interested in learning about the origins and evolution of aquatic species, as well as in their classification and distribution.

Many of these scientists examine how aquatic organisms behave and relate to each other as well as with their surroundings. In addition, they study problems such as the effects of pollution, the invasion of exotic species into an ecosystem, diseases of aquatic plants, and how to increase production in fish farms.

Aquatic Biologists typically focus their research in areas that most interest them. The following are a few specialties:

- marine mammal science, the study of dolphins, seals, polar bears, and other aquatic mammals
- marine biology, the study of bacteria, plankton, worms, fish larvae, and other small creatures that live in oceans and other saltwater bodies
- biological oceanography, the interaction of organisms with each other and with their saltwater surroundings
- limnology, the study of organisms that live in inland water systems such as lakes, ponds, rivers, and wetlands
- benthology, the study of organisms that live on, in, or near the bottom of seas, lakes, and other bodies of water

- aquatic botany, the study of algae and other aquatic plants
- fisheries biology, the management of fish programs
- aquaculture, the study of farming fish, shellfish, and aquatic plants for food, aquarium fish tanks, ornamental purposes, sportfishing, and other purposes

Most Aquatic Biologists work as research scientists in universities, government, industry, research institutes, zoological parks, and other work settings. They may handle one or several research projects at a time, and sometimes collaborate with other scientists on a project. They conduct their research in laboratories as well as in the field on small boats or large research ships. The amount of fieldwork varies with different projects. For example, field expeditions may be conducted on a weekly basis or last for several weeks or months.

Specific duties vary, but in general, Aquatic Biologists are responsible for designing and conducting their research projects. Some of their tasks include conducting experiments, collecting samples, analyzing and interpreting data, writing reports, and performing administrative tasks.

Many independent research projects are funded through grants from the federal government and other sources. Thus scientists must seek out appropriate research grants and write grant proposals.

Academic researchers are usually appointed to professorships. They are responsible for teaching courses to undergraduate and graduate students. They also advise students, supervise student research projects, fulfill community service duties, and perform administrative tasks.

Some Aquatic Biologists are employed as research assistants or biological technicians. They provide technical support to research scientists in the laboratory as well as in the field. Other professionals pursue other careers where they apply their training and background. For example, they may become fish farmers, fish and game wardens, animal health technicians, aquarium educators, science writers, wildlife conservation officers, or high school biology teachers.

Salaries

Salaries for Aquatic Biologists vary, depending on such factors as their education, experience, employer, and geographical location. Formal salary information is unavailable for this occupation. The U.S. Bureau of Labor Statistics (BLS) reports in its May 2006 *Occupational Employment Statistics* survey that the estimated annual salary for most biological scientists, who were not listed separately in its survey, ranged between $34,300 and $95,130.

Employment Prospects

Overall, opportunities become available as Aquatic Biologists retire, transfer to other positions, or resign. Some Aquatic Biologists expect opportunities to increase in the next decade due to the large number of colleagues reaching retirement age.

Competition for jobs is strong, especially in the field of marine biology. According to the Career Prospects in Virginia Web site, the general job outlook for aquatic scientists, including Aquatic Biologists, is good.

Advancement Prospects

Aquatic Biologists are generally required to pursue management positions in order to earn higher salaries. A typical career path would be 10 to 15 years of field experience followed by 10 years of management experience.

Education and Training

Aquatic Biologists who wish to conduct independent research or advance to management positions must obtain a master's or doctoral degree in aquatic biology, limnology, oceanography, or another related field. A Ph.D. is required to teach in universities and four-year colleges.

For research assistant and technician positions, candidates need a bachelor's degree in biology, chemistry, or another discipline with relevant course work in aquatic biology. Having a master's degree in the appropriate field is usually preferred by most employers.

Experience, Skills, and Personality Traits

Entry-level candidates need practical research experience in the laboratory and the field. This could be in the form of internships, summer jobs, student research projects, and postdoctoral training.

Aquatic Biologists need strong laboratory, statistics, and computer, and data management skills. In addition, they must have proficient communication and technical writing skills. Excellent organizational, interpersonal, and teamwork skills are also important. Successful Aquatic Biologists share personality traits such as being flexible, creative, persistent, enthusiastic, and self-motivated.

Unions and Associations

Most Aquatic Biologists join professional associations to take advantage of professional services and resources such as continuing education programs, professional publications, and networking opportunities. Some national societies that serve their interests are the American Society of Limnology and Oceanography, the North American Benthological Society, the Society for Integrative and Comparative Biology, the Society of Wetland Scientists, and the American Fisheries Society. See Appendix III for contact information.

Tips for Entry

1. The more experience you can get in the field, the greater chances you have of being hired.
2. Having skills in any of the following may strengthen your employability: computer programming, global information systems (GIS), photography, boat handling, engine maintenance, and scuba diving.
3. Learn more about aquatic biology on the Internet. One Web site you might visit is Aquatic Network at http://www.aquanet.com. For more links, see Appendix IV.

ENTOMOLOGIST

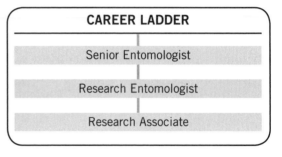

Position Description

Entomology is the biological study of insects, which are tiny, six-legged animals such as ants, flies, beetles, crickets, and butterflies. It also includes the study of related arthropods such as spiders, ticks, and centipedes.

Entomologists are concerned with the taxonomy, distribution, and evolution of the many thousands of species of insects. They examine the morphology and physiology of insects, as well as study their life cycle, behavior, and ecology. Entomologists also study the genetics of insects along with their cellular and molecular composition. In addition, they investigate the relationships that insects have with each other and with their physical surroundings. Furthermore, they study how insects are beneficial or harmful to humans and the environment, as well as how insect pests can be controlled.

Many Entomologists engage in research and development. Basic researchers seek further knowledge about the various species of insects. Many devote themselves to examining specific insects; for example, lepidopterists study moths and butterflies while coleopterists study beetles.

Many Entomologists are involved in applied research in which they utilize results of basic research to find solutions to problems in agriculture, conservation, and other fields. For example, they might work on technologies that can help increase crop production or protect the environment. Entomologists also conduct research on product development in private industry. Their objective is to use research findings to help create new or improved consumer products for their employers.

Entomologists usually focus their work in a particular subfield. Forensic Entomologists apply the principles and techniques of their discipline to help solve crime. Medical entomologists study disease-carrying insects and how they may affect the health of humans. Agricultural entomologists are involved in pest management. They also investigate how insects can benefit agriculture. Conservation entomologists are concerned with the restoration of habitats or ecosystems. A few other subfields include forest entomology, insect ecology, veterinary entomology, molecular entomology, and integrated pest management, among others.

Entomologists work in offices and labs where they design and conduct research projects. Their tasks include conducting experiments, examining specimens, analyzing and interpreting data, writing reports, reading scientific literature, and performing administrative tasks. Those who conduct independent research are usually responsible for seeking grants to fund their projects.

Their research involves the use of computers, electron microscopes, and other sophisticated scientific equipment. Many Entomologists go out in the field to collect samples and observe insects in their natural habitats. Field trips may involve living and working in forests and other remote locations for several days, weeks, or months at a time.

Many Entomologists are employed as professors at colleges and universities where they teach entomology courses to undergraduates and graduates. Professorial duties include preparing for and teaching courses, advising students, supervising student research projects, writing scholarly works, performing administrative duties, and participating in community service.

Some Entomologists are research assistants and technicians who provide scientists with technical support in the laboratory and the field. Other professionals apply their training and background in other related occupations. For example, many have become science teachers, cooperative extension agents, beekeepers, pest control specialists, vector control specialists, public health inspectors, and technical writers.

Salaries

Salaries for Entomologists vary, depending on their education, experience, geographical location, and other factors. Formal salary information is unavailable for this occupation. The U.S. Bureau of Labor Statistics (BLS) reports in its May 2006 *Occupational Employment Statistics* survey that the estimated annual salary for most biological scientists, who were not listed separately in its survey, ranged between $34,300 and $95,130.

Employment Prospects

Entomologists are employed by universities, colleges, government agencies, military services, research institutes, environmental organizations, agricultural companies, biotechnology firms, pest control companies, pest management consulting firms, and so on.

The job outlook is favorable for Entomologists, particularly in areas of applied entomology. Many opportunities will be created to replace individuals who retire, advance to other positions, or resign from the field.

Advancement Prospects

As in any field, Entomologists can advance to become project leaders, program managers, department administrators, and executive officers. The highest ambition for some Entomologists is to become consultants.

Education and Training

A master's or doctoral degree in entomology, biology, zoology, or related field is required for most research and teaching positions. Most graduate programs require that applicants have earned a bachelor's degree in entomology, biology, or zoology.

Experience, Skills, and Personality Traits

Employers typically look for candidates who have previous experience in the area in which they would be working. This may be in the form of internships, summer jobs, undergraduate or graduate research projects, postdoctoral research positions, and so on.

Entomologists need strong communication and writing skills as well as effective teamwork, and interpersonal skills to be able to work well with others. Entomologists should also have a good grasp of math and statistics and have adequate computer skills. Being creative, dependable, flexible, self-motivated, and persistent are some personality traits that successful Entomologists share.

Unions and Associations

Entomologists can join professional associations to take advantage of networking opportunities, education programs, professional certification, and other professional services and resources. Some societies are the Entomological Society of America, the American Institute of Biological Sciences, and the Society for Integrative and Comparative Biology.

Many Entomologists join societies that serve their particular interests—such as the Association of Applied IPM Ecologists, the Coleopterists Society, and the American Arachnological Society. See Appendix III for contact information.

Tips for Entry

1. You can begin training for a career in entomology while still in high school. Learn about the insect world through books, videos, and museums. Start your own insect collections. Join youth groups that have entomological activities such as the Young Entomologists' Society.
2. Professional societies are good sources of information on internships, postdoctoral positions, and permanent positions.
3. Use the Internet to learn more about entomology. One Web site you might visit is the Iowa State Entomology Index of Internet Resources, http://www.ent.iastate.edu/list. For more links, see Appendix IV.

PHYSIOLOGIST

Special Skills and Personality Traits—Communication, writing, interpersonal, teamwork, and self-management skills, be innovative, creative, flexible, analytical, and persistent

Position Description

Physiology is the study of how living organisms (microbes, plants, animals, and humans) function. All organisms are made up of cells, tissues, and organs that form different life systems such as the respiratory, circulatory, digestive, excretory, and reproductive systems. These life systems all work together to keep organisms healthy, fit, and alive.

Physiologists are research scientists who mostly work in academic, government, medical, and industrial laboratories. They are concerned with understanding how the different life systems work individually and with each other. They also seek to understand how tissues or organs can become dysfunctional and cause abnormal conditions or disease in living organisms. In addition, many are involved in the practical applications of physiology in such fields as medicine, agriculture, or environmental science.

Physiologists apply the knowledge and methodologies of biology, chemistry, and physics to their studies. They focus their research in any number of ways. Many Physiologists concentrate on studying only plants, animals, or humans. Some focus further by specializing in particular plant or animal species. Some Physiologists concentrate on studying how life functions at the molecular, cell, tissue, or organ level. Others investigate a particular life process, such as plant photosynthesis, the animal endocrine system, or the human cardiovascular system.

Some Physiologists confine their investigations to certain applications. For example, medical physiolo-gists are concerned with the physiology of diseases such as diabetes, hypertension, and atherosclerosis; exercise physiologists examine how the body responds to various forms of physical activities; and space physiologists study how the different life processes handle the stresses of space travel.

Physiologists use a wide variety of tools in their research, including computers, polygraphs, electron microscopes, and nuclear magnetic resonance machines. Depending on the nature of their research, Physiologists may manipulate cells by extracting molecules from the cell nucleus, or devise experiments that involve greenhouse plants or laboratory animals. Some Physiologists examine the life processes in a different species to gain a better understanding of how the processes work in the particular species that they are studying. For example, a Physiologist might study the cardiovascular system of a mouse to understand how that system would function in the human body.

Physiologists are responsible for designing and conducting research projects. Some of their general duties include designing and conducting experiments, analyzing and interpreting data, and performing routine administrative tasks. In addition, Physiologists write scientific papers or give presentations at scientific meetings about their research results. Senior research scientists and principal investigators usually have additional supervisory and project management duties.

Physiologists sometimes handle more than one research project at a time, and often collaborate with other Physiologists and bioscientists on projects. Academic Physiologists are able to choose the topics in which they wish to research, while most nonacademic Physiologists conduct research that is determined by their employers. Physiologists who conduct independent research are usually responsible for obtaining grants to fund their research projects.

Many Physiologists are full-time professors or adjunct instructors in colleges, universities, and medical schools. Depending on their expertise, professors teach courses in animal, human, or plant physiology, as well as related courses, such as biology, molecular biology, botany, biochemistry, anatomy, and zoology.

As full-time professors, Physiologists must juggle research and teaching duties with other responsibilities. Professors are also involved in advising students, supervising student research projects, and fulfilling community service duties.

Salaries

Salaries for Physiologists vary, depending on such factors as their experience and geographical location. According to a 2006 salary survey by the American Association of Medical Colleges, the mean annual salary for survey respondents ranged from $48,700 for physiology instructors to $213,000 for physiology department chairpersons.

Employment Prospects

Physiologists are employed by universities, colleges, medical schools, medical centers, hospitals, pharmaceutical firms, biotechnology companies, agricultural companies, and government laboratories. Many also work for the U.S. Air Force and with the U.S. Food and Drug Administration, the U.S. Environmental Protection Agency, and other government agencies that are concerned with health, medicine, epidemiology, pollution, or toxicity.

Most positions become available as individuals retire, resign, or transfer to other positions.

Advancement Prospects

Positions as laboratory directors, research managers, and executive-level administrators are available to Physiologists who wish to pursue management and administration careers. Academic professors can advance in rank (assistant, associate, and full professor) as well as by obtaining job tenure.

Education and Training

Physiologists must have doctoral degrees in physiology or a related field in order to conduct independent research, teach in four-year colleges, universities, and medical schools, or to pursue top management posts.

Physiologists who wish to work with patients, must complete an M.D. program. Some universities offer programs that grant a joint M.D. degree and Ph.D. in physiology.

Experience, Skills, and Personality Traits

Requirements vary with the various employers. In general, Physiologists should have appropriate work and research experience related to the positions for which they are applying. Many employers generally require or prefer to hire Ph.D.'s who have worked in one or more postdoctoral positions.

Physiologists need excellent communication and writing skills as they must be able to report their results and conclusions clearly to fellow scientists and nontechnical personnel. Additionally, they need strong interpersonal, teamwork, and self-management skills. Some personality traits that successful Physiologists share are being innovative, creative, flexible, analytical, and persistent.

Unions and Associations

Many Physiologists join professional associations to take advantage of professional services and resources, such as networking opportunities. Some national societies that serve their diverse interests are American Physiological Society, Society of General Physiologists, American Society of Plant Biologists, Society for Integrative and Comparative Biology, and American Association for the Advancement of Science. See Appendix III for contact information.

Tips for Entry

1. List research projects on your résumé that are relevant to the position for which you apply.
2. Get experience writing grant proposals while you are an undergraduate or postdoctoral fellow.
3. If you plan to work with patients, you will need to obtain a medical license.
4. Use the Internet to learn more about physiology. One Web site to visit is the American Physiological Society, http://www.the-aps.org. For more links, see Appendix IV.

GENETICIST

CAREER PROFILE

Duties: Study heredity and genetic mutations; design and conduct research projects; may provide diagnosis, treatment, education, or counseling services to patients; perform duties as required

Alternate Title(s): Plant Geneticist, Medical Geneticist, or other title that reflects a specialty

Salary Range: $34,000 to $146,000

Employment Prospects: Good

Advancement Prospects: Good

Prerequisites:

    Education or Training—A master's degree, Ph.D., or M.D., depending on occupation

    Experience—Postdoctoral experience for research scientists may be required

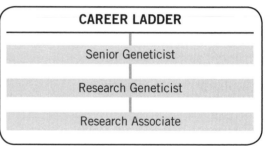

CAREER LADDER

Senior Geneticist

Research Geneticist

Research Associate

Special Skills and Personality Traits—Communication, writing, computer, statistics, analytical, interpersonal, and teamwork skills; be curious, creative, persistent, precise, detail-oriented, and dedicated

Special Requirements—A medical (M.D.) license may be required for clinical geneticists

Position Description

Over the last several decades, genetics has become an essential component for developing technologies that solve problems in agriculture, medicine, health care, biotechnology, law enforcement, scientific research, and other fields. For example, genetics has been the foundation for counseling families who are at risk of producing children with genetic disorders, developing treatments for diseases, breeding new crops, and designing forensic tests to identify individuals.

Genetics is the study of heredity. That is how an organism's traits are passed from one generation to the next through its genes. Genes are found in the nucleus of every cell of an organism, and contain the DNA (deoxyribonucleic acid) code which defines the organism's traits. For example, the genes of an orange tree determine its size, the shape of its leaves, and the type of fruit it bears.

Geneticists examine the biochemical and physiological aspects of heredity. They are interested in learning about the structure and function of genes. They investigate how genes duplicate within the cell and form organisms, as well as study how genes evolve through generations. They are also concerned with understanding gene mutations, the changes that occur within the genetic code, how mutations cause diseases, and how organisms inherit genetic disorders.

Most Geneticists are involved in research and development, working in academic, government, and industrial laboratories. They generally devote their studies in plant, animal, or human genetics. Some of them further specialize by examining genetics at the molecular level.

Research scientists engage in three types of studies. They conduct basic research to gain further knowledge about genes and the genetic process. They perform applied research. That is, they use findings of basic research to develop new or improved technologies or processes that may resolve problems in agriculture, medicine, and other fields. For example, Geneticists might work on a process to alter certain traits in plants.

Research Geneticists also are involved in product development. These research scientists generally work in private industry where they apply the results of both basic and applied research to create new or improved consumer products. For example, Geneticists in a biomedical company may be part of research teams concerned with developing diagnostic tests that identify genetic disorders in patients.

Research scientists are in charge of designing and conducting research projects. Their duties vary, depending on their position and experience. Some of their tasks include conducting experiments or tests, gathering data, analyzing and interpreting data, writing reports, and performing administrative tasks. Geneticists who conduct independent research are usually responsible for seeking research grants from the federal government and other sources to fund their projects. Most senior researchers and principal investigators also perform supervisory and management duties.

Geneticists sometimes handle several research projects at a time. They often collaborate on research projects with colleagues, other biological scientists, and scientists (such as chemists and physicists) from other disciplines.

Research scientists typically exchange information about their research with each other. Many publish scientific papers and give presentations at scientific meetings.

Geneticists also perform roles besides research scientists. Some Geneticists are health professionals who provide various services to patients. Clinical geneticists diagnose, test, manage, and treat patients who have inherited genetic conditions. Some patients are pregnant women whose unborn babies are at risk of birth defects. These geneticists work directly with patients, providing medical care along with genetic counseling services. Other clinical geneticists work in the laboratory performing and interpreting biochemical, molecular, or cytogenetic analyses. In addition, they act as consultants regarding genetic disorders.

Medical geneticists provide assessment and education services to patients. These specialists work closely with patients, conducting risk assessments and informing them about their disorders and their medical options. Medical geneticists also provide patients with supportive counseling, as well as refer patients to appropriate health-care resources.

Many Geneticists are employed as adjunct instructors or full-time professors at colleges, universities, and medical schools. Full-time professors have a number of responsibilities, which include conducting independent research; preparing for and teaching courses; advising students; supervising student research projects; writing scholarly works; performing administrative duties; and participating in community service.

Geneticists typically work more than 40 hours a week. Researchers, for example, often work evenings and weekends to conduct and monitor experiments.

Salaries

Salaries for Geneticists vary, depending on their experience, position, geographical location, and other factors. According to a 2006 salary survey by the American Association for the Advancement of Science, the median annual salary for academic researchers in genetics was $73,458, and for industrial researchers, $83,750.

The U.S. Bureau of Labor Statistics (BLS) reports in its May 2006 *Occupational Employment Statistics* survey that the estimated annual salary for most biological scientists, who were not listed separately in its survey, ranged between $34,300 and $95,130. Most postsec-

ondary biological science instructors earned an estimated annual salary between $37,620 and $145,600.

Employment Prospects

Geneticists find employment in both the public and private sectors. Employers include universities, medical schools, hospitals, clinical laboratories, research institutions, government agencies, biotechnology firms, agribusiness companies, and pharmaceutical companies. Some Geneticists are self-employed.

Typically, job openings become available as scientists transfer to other positions, retire, or resign. Employers may create additional positions to meet their growing needs, if funds are available. Opportunities in the private sector are particularly good in the agricultural, biotechnology, pharmaceutical, and biomedical industries.

New opportunities, as well as new fields (such as pharmacogenetics), are expected to increase in the coming years as more details of the human genome develop.

Advancement Prospects

Geneticists with administrative or management ambitions can advance to such positions within their specialty. Entrepreneurial individuals may start up their own genetic research, consulting, or counseling services. Professors receive promotional rankings as assistant professors, associate professors, or full professors.

Many Geneticists achieve advancement by earning higher pay, by conducting independent research projects, and through receiving professional recognition.

Education and Training

Educational requirements vary for the various Geneticist positions, as well as with different employers. Research scientists and medical geneticists must possess a doctoral degree in genetics or another related field. Geneticists who perform clinical laboratory analyses must possess a bachelor's or master's degree in a biological science.

Being licensed physicians, clinical geneticists possess a medical doctor's degree. After earning their degree, they complete a two- to four-year residency program in medical genetics. Alternatively, they may fulfill a three- to five-year residency program in another medical specialty (such as internal medicine or pediatrics) followed by a fellowship in clinical genetics, which may be two to three years long.

Special Requirements

Clinical geneticists must be licensed to practice medicine. Many employers prefer to hire candidates who are board-certified in medical genetics by the American Board of Medical Genetics.

Experience, Skills, and Personality Traits

Requirements vary with the different positions as well as among various employers. In general, Geneticists should have appropriate work and research experience related to the positions for which they are applying. Most employers prefer or require that candidates have several years of post-doctoral experience.

Geneticists need excellent communication, writing, and computer skills. They should be knowledgeable about statistics and have the ability to analyze data. They also need excellent interpersonal and teamwork skills, as they must be able to work well with scientists and others.

Successful Geneticists share personality traits such as being curious, creative, persistent, precise, detail-oriented, and dedicated.

Unions and Associations

Many professional societies are available to Geneticists. By joining local, state, or national associations, they can take advantage of various professional services and resources, such as networking opportunities and professional certification. Some national societies are the American Society of Human Genetics, the Genetics Society of America, the Botanical Society of America, and the American Association for the Advancement of Science. See Appendix III for contact information.

Tips for Entry

1. Talk with Geneticists to learn more about the work they do, the types of courses they took in college, and what their career path has been like so far.

2. Go to job or careers fairs to meet with prospective employers. Find out beforehand who will be at a fair so that you can identify employers for whom you would most like to work.

3. Learn more about Geneticists on the Internet. One Web site you might visit is the Genetic Education Center (hosted by the Kansas Medical Center) at http://www.kumc.edu/gec/geneinfo.html. For more links, see Appendix IV.

MOLECULAR BIOLOGIST

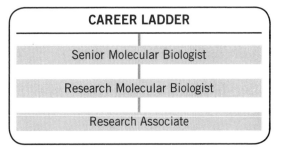

Position Description

Molecular biology deals with the study of basic molecules that reside in the nucleus of all living cells. One of these basic molecules is deoxyribonucleic acid (DNA), which is the genetic code of a living organism. It conveys the characteristics that an organism has inherited from its parents. Ribonucleic acid (RNA), another molecule, transmits the DNA code to other parts of the cell where it is translated and forms appropriate protein molecules. Proteins are also basic molecules, and they form tissues, enzymes, hormones, and other parts of a living organism.

Molecular Biologists are concerned with understanding how basic molecules combine and interact so that living organisms grow, develop, reproduce, and stay alive. They seek answers to such questions as: How do cells know when to divide and when to stop dividing? How do cells recognize one another? How can mutant genes be suppressed so that disease does not occur? How can DNA or proteins be altered to produce better or stronger organisms? Molecular Biologists typically conduct in vitro experiments in which they extract molecules from cells to study.

Most Molecular Biologists are involved in research and development, working in academic, government, and industrial laboratories. Because molecular biology is a fundamental science, Molecular Biologists work in diverse fields (such as botany, zoology, genetics, and immunology), as well as in a wide range of industries (such as biotechnology, pharmaceutical, and agriculture).

These research scientists engage in different types of studies. They may conduct basic research to further knowledge and understanding of molecular biology. They may be involved in applied research, in which they use results of basic research to develop new technologies and processes to solve problems in their different fields.

Molecular Biologists also work in product development for private industry. They apply findings of both basic and applied research to create new or improved consumer products, such as foods, drugs, or medical diagnostic tests.

Duties for Molecular Biologists vary, depending on their positions and experience. In general, these research scientists are responsible for designing and conducting research projects. Their tasks include conducting experiments or tests, gathering data, analyzing and interpreting data, writing reports, and performing administrative tasks. Usually, scientists who conduct independent research are responsible for obtaining grants to fund their projects. Many Molecular Biologists present their research results to their colleagues as papers in scientific journals or presentations at scientific meetings.

Many research scientists are employed as professors at colleges and universities. Along with their research duties, they are responsible for teaching molecular biology and other biology courses to undergraduate and graduate students. They also advise students, supervise student research projects, perform administrative duties, and participate in community service.

Research assistants and technicians who work in this field are also considered Molecular Biologists. They provide research scientists with technical support. Their tasks include conducting experiments, analyzing data, writing reports, and maintaining laboratories.

All Molecular Biologists keep up with developments in their fields as well as update their skills. For example, they read professional literature, network with colleagues, and enroll in training programs.

Salaries

Salaries for Molecular Biologists vary, depending on such factors as their education, experience, employer, and geographical location. According to the May 2006 *Occupational Employment Statistics* survey by the U.S. Bureau of Labor Statistics, the estimated annual salary for most biological scientists, who were not listed separately in its survey, ranged between $34,300 and $95,130. Most postsecondary biological science instructors earned an estimated annual salary between $37,620 and $145,600.

Employment Prospects

Experts in the field report that opportunities for experienced Molecular Biologists are favorable in academic, government, and industrial settings. The demand for these scientists is particularly strong in the biotechnology and pharmaceutical industries.

According to the U.S. Bureau of Labor Statistics, job growth for Molecular Biologists is expected to increase by 11 percent through 2016. Many opportunities will also arise as scientists retire, advance to higher positions, or transfer to other jobs.

Advancement Prospects

Positions such as project leader, program manager, laboratory director, and executive officer are available for those who wish to pursue supervisory or administrative careers. Professors can advance in rank (assistant, associate, and full professor) as well as obtaining job tenure.

Education and Training

Research assistants and technicians must have a bachelor's degree in biochemistry, molecular biology, biology, or another related field. Research scientists must hold either a master's degree or a Ph.D. in molecular biol-ogy, biochemistry, or another related field. A Ph.D. is required in order to teach in universities and four-year colleges, to conduct independent research, or to pursue top management posts.

Experience, Skills, and Personality Traits

Employers generally choose candidates who have related work and research experience, which may have been gained through research projects, internships, fellowships, or employment. Ph.D. candidates for research scientist positions may be required to have a few years of postdoctoral experience.

Molecular Biologists need excellent writing and communication skills to report their results clearly to fellow scientists and others. In addition, they need strong interpersonal, teamwork, and self-management skills. Being creative, analytical, persistent, and flexible are some personality traits that successful Molecular Biologists share.

Unions and Associations

Molecular Biologists join professional societies to take advantage of professional services and resources such as networking opportunities. Some associations that serve their interests are the American Society for Biochemistry and Molecular Biology, the American Institute of Biological Sciences, and the American Association for the Advancement of Science. See Appendix III for contact information.

Tips for Entry

1. Choose a doctoral program that fits your needs. Also make sure that it offers specialties that interest you, as well as has faculty with whom you would like to work.
2. Take courses in bioinformatics to enhance your employability.
3. Many universities and colleges offer certificate programs in laboratory techniques. These programs may enhance employability for those who want to enter the job market after completing their bachelor's degrees.
4. Use the Internet to learn more about molecular biology. One Web site you might visit is Cell and Molecular Biology Online, http://www.cellbio.com. For more links, see Appendix IV.

BIOINFORMATICS SCIENTIST

CAREER PROFILE

Duties: Develop and manage biological information systems; perform analyses on biological data; design and conduct research projects; perform duties as required

Alternate Title(s): Bioinformatician, Bioinformatics Research Analyst, Bioinformatics Associate

Salary Range: $34,000 to $95,000+

Employment Prospects: Excellent

Advancement Prospects: Good

Prerequisites:

    Education or Training—A bachelor's or advanced degree in bioinformatics or a related field

    Experience—Previous work experience in bioinformatics required

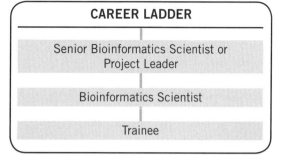

CAREER LADDER

Senior Bioinformatics Scientist or Project Leader

Bioinformatics Scientist

Trainee

Special Skills and Personality Traits—Programming, database management, math, statistics, interpersonal, teamwork, problem-solving, and communication skills; be creative, flexible, curious, and self-motivated

Position Description

Bioinformatics, a young field, plays an important role in biological and medical science research. It is the science and technology of managing, processing, and analyzing enormous amounts of biological information that is generated by research and kept in computer databases and networks. For example, researchers who are developing various new drugs might use computers to store and catalog data collected from experiments, tests, and clinical trials.

The research scientists, data analysts, programmers, and other specialists who work in this field are known as Bioinformatics Scientists. They work in academic, government, and industrial laboratories where their primary concern is with the management and analysis of the biological data in public and proprietary databases. They also engage in the development and application of effective information technology and computational tools to store, catalog, retrieve, and analyze biological data more efficiently.

Bioinformatics is an interdisciplinary field that requires professionals to be knowledgeable about the principles and techniques of biology, molecular biology, chemistry, computer science, mathematics, and statistics.

Bioinformatics Scientists work as part of multidisciplinary research teams in the various biological and medical fields. They may be involved in basic research, applied research, or product development. For example, these scientists might work on research projects that are concerned with identifying the genetic code in various plant or animal species, seeking the cause of certain cancers, developing new drug treatments for skin conditions, or designing improved bioinformatics technologies to address specific problems.

Bioinformatics Scientists collaborate with bench scientists to generate and analyze biological information for research projects. Their job is to help bench scientists obtain reliable and useful information. Bioinformaticians perform a wide range of duties. Depending on their position, experience, and skill level, they may be responsible for some or all of the following duties:

- set up and maintain databases
- assess the needs of other scientists in regard to data submissions and retrievals
- set up and run experiments—searching (or mining) databases for the appropriate data
- analyze and interpret data
- identify new areas for bioinformatics investigations
- develop new bioinformatics approaches for analyzing data in proprietary and public databases
- develop and apply computer programs and software to store, organize, manage, retrieve, and analyze data

Bioinformatics Scientists are usually involved with several projects at a time. Senior scientists may have the additional duties of leading and managing projects, as well as training and supervising new and junior scientists.

All Bioinformatics Scientists are responsible for keeping up with new technologies and developments in their fields. They participate in training programs, enroll in continuing education programs, attend professional conferences and meetings, network with colleagues, and so forth.

Some academic researchers are appointed as professors in colleges and universities. In addition to their research projects, they are responsible for teaching courses in bioinformatics as well as in biology or computer science to undergraduate and graduate students. Their professorial duties also include advising students, supervising student research projects, writing scholarly works, fulfilling community service obligations, and performing administrative duties.

Bioinformatics Scientists typically work more than 40 hours a week to perform their various tasks.

Salaries

Salaries for Bioinformatics Scientists vary, depending on their education, experience, employer, geographical location, and other factors. According to a 2006 salary survey by the American Association for the Advancement of Science, the median annual salary for academic researchers in bioinformatics was $65,000, and for industrial researchers, $103,000.

The U.S. Bureau of Labor Statistics reports in its May 2006 *Occupational Employment Statistics* survey that the estimated annual salary for most biological scientists, who were not listed separately in its survey, ranged between $34,300 and $95,130.

Salaries are generally higher for these scientists than other bioscientists because the demand is greater than the number of available bioinformaticians. As more trained scientists enter this field, salaries will likely decrease.

Employment Prospects

Bioinformatics emerged in the 1990s from the need for biologists with programming skills to store and catalog vast amounts of data about human DNA for the Human Genome Project. This field had been rapidly growing, and the demand for bioinformaticians continues to be strong for highly skilled and experienced individuals in the United States, as well as worldwide. Opportunities are especially favorable in the pharmaceutical and biotechnology industries.

Advancement Prospects

Bioinformatics Scientists can advance in any number of ways, depending on their ambitions and interests.

Those interested in management and administrative work can pursue such positions as project leader, program manager, and executive officer. Professors can advance in rank (assistant, associate, and full professor) as well as by obtaining job tenure.

Education and Training

Educational requirements for entry-level positions vary among employers. Minimally, candidates for data analysis and programming positions need a bachelor's degree in molecular biology, bioinformatics, computer science, or another biological science field. Entry-level candidates for research positions generally need a master's or doctoral degree in bioinformatics, computational biology, molecular biology, biochemistry, or another related field.

Biology majors should have training in programming while computer science majors should have completed course work in biology.

Each year, increasingly more schools are offering certificate and degree programs in bioinformatics. Some schools now offer a professional science masters (P.S.M.) degree in bioinformatics, which is a two-year program designed to train students in specific skills desired by industrial employers.

Experience, Skills, and Personality Traits

Employers look for candidates who have previous experience in bioinformatics. Candidates for entry-level positions may have obtained experience through research projects, internships employment, or postdoctoral training.

Bioinformatics Scientists must have basic knowledge and skills in biology, particularly in molecular biology. In addition, they need math (especially algebra and logic), statistics, programming, and database management skills. Because they must be able to work well with others, these scientists need excellent communication, interpersonal, and teamwork skills. Furthermore, they need effective problem-solving, organizational, time management, and self-management skills. Being creative, flexible, curious, and self-motivated are a few personality traits that Bioinformatics Scientists share.

Unions and Associations

Many Bioinformatics Scientists join professional associations to take advantage of professional resources and services such as education programs and networking opportunities. Some societies that serve their interests are: International Society for Computational Biology, American Society for Biochemistry and Molecular Biologists, American Institute of Biological Sciences,

Association for Computing Machinery, and American Association for the Advancement of Science. See Appendix III for contact information.

Tips for Entry

1. Because bioinformatics is a new discipline, job opportunities and requirements will continually change to reflect the evolving needs of employers.
2. Talk with your college adviser to develop an education program that reflects your interests and ambitions in bioinformatics.
3. Smaller companies may be more willing to hire bioinformatics applicants with little work experience.
4. Some experts say that the best candidates possess degrees in biological science and computer science, as well as have information technology experience.
5. Use the Internet to learn more about bioinformatics. One Web site you might visit is BioPlanet—The Bioinformatics Homepage, http://www.bioplanet.com. For more links, see Appendix IV.

BIOLOGICAL TECHNICIAN

Duties: Provide technical support and assistance to scientists and engineers; may work in research, production, operations, or program administration; perform duties as required

Alternate Title(s): Laboratory Technician, Research Assistant; a title that reflects a particular occupation such as Wildlife Technician or Agricultural Science Research Technician

Salary Range: $24,000 to $58,000

Employment Prospects: Good

Advancement Prospects: Good

Prerequisites:

    Education or Training—Associate or bachelor's degree required

    Experience—One or more years of work experience preferred

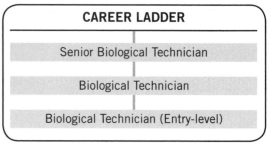

CAREER LADDER

Senior Biological Technician

Biological Technician

Biological Technician (Entry-level)

Special Skills and Personality Traits—Analytical, problem-solving, organizational, writing, computer, communication, interpersonal, and teamwork skills; be curious, enthusiastic, self-motivated, detail-oriented, flexible, methodical, patient, and reliable

Position Description

Biological Technicians are valuable members of scientific teams that engage in various life sciences projects. Their job is to provide technical support and assistance to scientists and engineers as they solve problems in research, production, operations, or program administration.

These technicians apply the principles and techniques of science and mathematics in such fields as microbiology, molecular biology, plant science, animal science, resource management, environmental science, and medical science. They work under the direction of a laboratory supervisor, scientist, or engineer, but generally work independently as they conduct experiments, perform analyses, and prepare reports.

Due to the breadth of biological sciences, Biological Technicians engage in a wide range of activities. For example, they may be involved in:

- studying living microscopic organisms or infectious agents such as bacteria and viruses
- performing chemical and DNA analysis of blood and other body fluids
- conducting medical research to find a cure for cancer
- developing or manufacturing medicinal preparations
- using organisms, such as bacteria or DNA to improve plants, animals, or other products

- improving management practices for producing poultry, beef, or other meat products more economically
- studying soil and water to improve cropping practices used in agricultural work
- developing new techniques and products to control insects
- managing fish hatcheries, greenhouse production, or other operational programs
- identifying, surveying, and detecting threatened or endangered plant species
- developing methods to assess and monitor conditions and trends of endangered animals species

Biological Technicians work in various settings. Many of them work primarily in research laboratories where they monitor experiments as well as conduct biological, microbiological, chemical, and biochemical tests on organic substances such as human tissue, plants, drugs, or food. Some technicians work in industrial plants where they are involved in checking manufacturing processes as well as ensuring the quality of finished products.

Many Biological Technicians perform some of their duties outdoors, such as conducting surveys, gathering specimens, or monitoring plants or animals. Some work in greenhouses, vegetable fields, fruit orchards, and livestock pens. Others work in forests, on rangelands, by rivers and ponds, along coastlines, on oceans, and in other remote locations.

Biological Technicians perform a variety of routine tasks, which vary according to their experience, skill level, and position. For example, they may be responsible for:

- collecting samples, such as human tissue, water, or soil for testing
- isolating, identifying, and preparing specimens for examination
- growing cultures under controlled conditions
- preparing compounds and solutions for experiments or tests
- conducting field or laboratory tests
- monitoring experiments and recording observations
- analyzing and interpreting experimental data or test results
- making sure work is in compliance with established standards and protocols
- using computers, robotics, or high-tech industrial applications to perform tasks
- setting up, adjusting, calibrating, troubleshooting, cleaning, and maintaining equipment and instruments
- setting up and maintaining laboratory areas
- keeping detailed logs and records of work activities
- preparing technical reports
- supervising subordinate staff members

Technicians who work with livestock or laboratory animals may be responsible for feeding, watering, and caring for them, as well as maintaining the enclosures and cages where the animals live. Biological Technicians who are engaged in studying plant life may be assigned to care for plants growing in fields or in greenhouses.

Biological Technicians wear protective equipment as well as follow strict safety procedures when they perform tasks that may expose them to toxic chemicals, radiation, or harmful bacteria, viruses, and other biological agents.

These science technicians generally work a 40-hour week. Some of them work irregular hours, including evenings and weekends, or are assigned to rotating shifts in order to monitor experiments. Production technicians may be assigned to day, evening, or night shifts. Those who perform fieldwork might conduct their tasks in all types of weather. They may be required to live and work several days, weeks, or months in remote locations.

Salaries
Salaries for Biological Technicians vary, depending on such factors as their education, experience, job duties, employer, industry, and geographical location. Accord-

ing to the May 2006 *Occupational Employment Statistics* (OES) survey, by the U.S. Bureau of Labor Statistics (BLS), the estimated annual salary for most Biological Technicians ranged between $23,670 and $57,890.

Employment Prospects
Biological Technicians are employed throughout private industry, including the biotechnology, pharmaceutical and medicine manufacturing, agriculture, food processing, chemical manufacturing, environmental protection, and scientific research and development services industries, among others. They also find employment with government agencies, such as the U.S. Department of Agriculture and state fish and wildlife departments. In addition, these technicians are employed by colleges and universities as well as by nonprofit organizations such as conservation research groups.

The BLS reports in its May 2006 OES survey that an estimated 71,590 Biological Technicians were employed in the United States. This federal agency further reports that employment of Biological Technicians is expected to increase by 14 to 20 percent through 2016. Opportunities are reported to be strongest in the biotechnology, the pharmaceutical and medicine manufacturing, and the scientific research and development services industries.

In addition to job growth, opportunities will become available as technicians advance to higher positions, transfer to other jobs, or leave the workforce for various reasons.

Advancement Prospects
Biological Technicians may advance in various ways, depending on their interests and ambitions. Many technicians measure their success through job satisfaction, by assuming greater responsibilities, and by earning higher wages. Senior technicians may specialize by working in a particular field, such as microbiology, plant science, or environmental science.

Those with supervisory and managerial ambitions can pursue such opportunities. With additional training, laboratory technicians may advance to research assistant and research associate positions. (A bachelor's degree may be required.) Those working in private industry may pursue opportunities in other areas such as sales, technical service, technical writing, or marketing.

Some technicians choose to continue their education to become research scientists, engineers, or educators, or to work in other professions that interest them.

Education and Training

Educational requirements for entry-level positions vary with the different employers, as well as with the different positions. Some employers require that candidates possess at least a bachelor's degree in biology, chemistry, or another life science discipline, while others require only an associate's degree in applied science or science-related technology.

Entry-level Biological Technicians receive on-the-job training. They work under the guidance and supervision of experienced technicians, scientists, and engineers.

Throughout their careers, Biological Technicians enroll in workshops, seminars, and courses to update their skills and keep up with advancements in their fields.

Experience, Special Skills, and Personality Traits

Employers generally prefer to hire entry-level candidates who have one or more years of work experience relevant to the position for which they apply. Recent college graduates may have gained experience through internships, work-study programs, research assistantships, or employment.

Analytical, problem-solving, organizational, writing, and computer skills are some essential skills that Biological Technicians need for their work. These technicians also need excellent communication, interpersonal, and teamwork skills, as they must be able to work well with colleagues, scientists, engineers, managers, and various others. Being curious, enthusiastic, self-motivated, detail-oriented, flexible, methodical, patient, and reliable are some personality traits that successful Biological Technicians share.

Unions and Associations

Some Biological Technicians are members of a labor union that represents them in contract negotiations for better wages and working conditions. The union also handles any grievances that union members have against their employers.

Biological Technicians can join professional associations at the local, state, or national level that serve their particular interests. By joining a society they may take advantage of networking opportunities, continuing education programs, current research findings, and other professional services and resources.

Tips for Entry

1. Part-time, temporary, or internship positions can sometimes turn into full-time, permanent positions.
2. If you do not have much practical experience to list on your application, then be sure to mention the various laboratory-based courses that you have completed.
3. Temporary and permanent positions can be found with different federal government agencies. To learn about job openings throughout the federal government, visit its official job site (called USAJOBS) at http://usajobs.opm.gov.
4. Use the Internet to learn more about the different biological sciences. You might start by visiting The WWW Virtual Library Biosciences Web site at http://vlib.org/Biosciences. For more links, see Appendix IV.

VETERINARY TECHNICIAN

Duties: Provide medical and surgical support to veterinarians; perform duties as required

Alternate Title(s): Veterinary Technologist, Animal Care Technician, Animal Lab Technician

Salary Range: $18,000 to $39,000

Employment Prospects: Excellent

Advancement Prospects: Good

Prerequisites:

Education or Training—Associate or bachelor's degree in veterinary technology preferred

Experience—One or more years of work experience

Special Skills and Personality Traits—Interpersonal, communication, teamwork, organizational, problem-solving, time management, and self-management skills; be tactful, calm, positive, honest, dependable, detail-oriented, flexible, and self-motivated

Special Requirements—State license, certification, or registration may be required

CAREER LADDER

Senior Veterinary Technician

Veterinary Technician

Veterinary Technician (Entry-level) or Assistant Veterinary Technician

Position Description

Pets, livestock, zoo animals, wildlife, and laboratory animals need medical attention from time to time. Among those trained to provide animal health care are Veterinary Technicians who work under the direction of veterinarians. Some of these paraprofessionals are called veterinary technologists.

Most people think of veterinarians and Veterinary Technicians as working only in private practices, veterinary clinics, and animal hospitals. However, these animal care practitioners also work in animal shelters, animal control facilities, stables, kennels, zoos, animal parks, and wildlife facilities.

Some Veterinary Technicians are employed in research laboratories, where they are often referred to as animal lab technicians. These technicians may work in an academic, a government, or an industrial laboratory where animals are utilized in agricultural or biomedical research or in the research and development of drugs, medical devices, and other consumer products.

Veterinary Technicians perform several roles as they assist veterinarians in the medical and surgical treatment of animals. They help veterinarians perform physical examinations by obtaining medical histories of patients; take and record their temperatures, pulse, and respiration rate; restrain patients as veterinarians examine them; and collect blood samples and specimens for laboratory tests. Some Veterinary Technicians are also trained to take and develop X rays, which are used to help diagnose and treat animal health problems.

Under the supervision of veterinarians, Veterinary Technicians perform such procedures as dispensing medications to patients, cleaning and extracting teeth, applying splints to injured limbs, dressing and suturing wounds, and administering immunizations. They also carry out life saving procedures, such as emergency resuscitation, when directed by veterinarians. Some Veterinary Technicians assist with euthanizing animals that are too sickly, severely injured, or unwanted.

Veterinary Technicians are responsible for preparing animal patients, as well as surgical instruments and equipment, for surgery. Additionally, they assist veterinarians during surgery by providing them with the proper instruments and equipment as they are needed. Technicians, with the proper training, administer anesthesia to animals and monitor their responses throughout surgery. During their recovery from surgery, animal patients are observed closely and attended to by Veterinary Technicians.

Veterinary Technicians also assist with client education, by teaching pet owners and animal caretakers how to care for injured and ill animals properly.

Technicians who work in research laboratories are also responsible for making general observations of animals that are being studied. They monitor as well as maintain a record of the animals' behavior and condition. For example, Veterinary Technicians note any signs of pain or distress an animal may be showing, what it is eating, and what medications it has taken. If they notice any irregular conditions in an animal, they notify the proper authority, which may be a veterinarian, scientist, or another lab technician.

Veterinary Technicians perform a wide range of tasks, which vary depending on their experience, skills, and position. For example, they may be assigned such tasks as:

- preparing vaccines and serums
- filling prescriptions for patients
- preparing and labeling samples for laboratory testing, culture, or microscopic examination
- cleaning and sterilizing instruments, equipment, and materials
- maintaining facilities in an orderly and hygienic condition
- keeping an inventory of pharmaceuticals, equipment, and supplies
- maintaining accurate records regarding patients or lab animals
- completing required forms, reports, and other paperwork
- feeding and watering animals

Entry-level Veterinary Technicians perform basic routine tasks under the supervision and direction of experienced staff members. As they gain experience and skills, they are assigned more complex responsibilities. Senior technicians may be assigned a supervisory role, in which they provide guidance and direction to veterinary assistants and volunteer staff.

Senior Veterinary Technicians can specialize in various ways. They may work with certain types of animals, such as birds, horses, wildlife, or lab animals. They may choose to work in certain environments, such as zoos, emergency clinics, humane facilities, or research laboratories. They may specialize in particular technical areas such as animal dental care, anesthesiology, or emergency and critical care.

Depending on their work setting, Veterinary Technicians may work mostly indoors or outdoors. Their job can be stressful at times. On occasion, they lift and carry animals and objects that weigh 50 pounds or more. They are also at risk of being injured by frightened, hostile, or dangerous animals. They may need to cope with personal anxiety when they handle seriously neglected and injured animals or when they must euthanize animals. Veterinary Technicians who work in private practice sometimes must handle angry, demanding, or distressed pet owners.

Veterinary Technicians work full time or part time. They may be required to work weekends and holidays. Full-time staff work 40 hours a week, and put in additional hours as needed. In some research facilities, animal hospitals, and animal shelters, Veterinary Technicians are assigned to work day, evening, or night shifts.

Salaries

Salaries for Veterinary Technicians vary, depending on such factors as their education, experience, employer, and geographical location. According to the May 2006 *Occupational Employment Statistics* (OES) survey by the U.S. Bureau of Labor Statistics (BLS), the estimated annual salary for most Veterinary Technicians ranged between $18,280 and $38,850.

Employment Prospects

The BLS reports in its May 2006 OES survey that an estimated 69,700 veterinary technicians and technologists were employed in the United States. Over the 2006–16 period, the BLS predicts that employment of Veterinary Technicians should increase by 41 percent. The demand for Veterinary Technicians is particularly strong in private practice, mostly due to the rising number of pet owners who are willing to seek advanced medical care for their pets.

In addition to job growth, opportunities will become available as individuals advance to higher positions, transfer to other jobs, or leave the occupation for other careers.

With their experience and skills, Veterinary Technicians may be able to find employment as animal inspectors as well as sales representatives for companies that sell pet food or animal products.

Advancement Prospects

Veterinary Technicians may advance in various ways, depending on their interests and ambitions. Many technicians seek success through job satisfaction and by earning higher wages. Some pursue opportunities as supervisors, administrators, or managers. In research laboratories, Veterinary Technicians may be promoted to research assistant positions.

Individuals can also continue their education to become veterinarians, zookeepers, research scientists, or other professionals. Those with entrepreneurial aspirations may start animal care businesses, such as kennels, stables, animal training services, dog grooming services, or pet care services.

Education and Training

In general, employers prefer to hire candidates who have earned an associate or bachelor's degree in veterinary technology. Veterinary Technicians usually possess the former degree, while veterinary technologists hold the latter degree.

Veterinary technology programs are offered by two-year colleges, four-year colleges, and universities. Students complete course work in such areas as animal husbandry and diseases, comparative anatomy, physiology, anesthesiology, radiography, surgical principles, or animal medical techniques. Students also receive practical experience in handling animals while giving them injections and medications, taking X rays, preparing them for surgery, and other skills.

Entry-level Veterinary Technicians receive on-the-job training. They work under the supervision and direction of senior technicians, veterinarians, and scientists.

Throughout their careers, Veterinary Technicians enroll in seminars, workshops, and courses to continue to update their skills and keep up with advancements in their fields.

Special Requirements

In many states, Veterinary Technicians must obtain the proper credential to practice. States may require that qualified individuals become licensed veterinary technicians (LVT), certified veterinary technicians (CRT), or registered veterinary technicians (RVT). To become licensed, certified, or registered, applicants must pass an examination that is administered by the appropriate state agency. For specific information about the credentialing requirements in a state, contact the state board of veterinary examiners.

Experience, Special Skills, and Personality Traits

Employers prefer to hire candidates for entry-level positions who have one or more years of practical experience caring for animals. They may have gained their experience through internships, volunteer work, or employment as veterinary assistants or animal lab assistants.

Veterinary Technicians need to be able to work well with various people from diverse backgrounds; hence they must have effective interpersonal and communication skills. Their job also requires that they have strong teamwork, organizational, problem-solving, and time management skills. In addition, these technicians need excellent self-management skills, including the ability to understand and follow instructions, prioritize multiple tasks, work independently, and handle stressful situations.

Some personality traits that successful Veterinary Technicians have in common include being tactful, calm, positive, honest, dependable, detail-oriented, flexible, and self-motivated.

Unions and Associations

Veterinary Technicians can join professional associations to take advantage of professional resources and services such as certification programs, training programs, and networking opportunities. These organizations are available at the local, state, and national levels. Some national societies that serve the interests of this profession include:

- National Association of Veterinary Technicians in America
- Society of Veterinary Behavior Technicians
- American Association of Equine Veterinary Technicians
- American Veterinary Dental Society
- Association of Zoo Veterinary Technicians
- American Association for Laboratory Animal Science

For contact information, see Appendix III.

Tips for Entry

1. You can get an idea if working with animals is right for you by volunteering at an animal shelter or a humane society, or working at a kennel, pet store, dog grooming service, or other animal-related services.
2. Apply directly to employers for whom you would like to work. Some employers allow candidates to apply online at their Web site.
3. Veterinary Technicians may enhance their employability by obtaining professional certification from organizations that are recognized by employers. For example, the American Association for Laboratory Science and Academy of Veterinary Dental Technicians offer certification programs to qualified candidates.
4. Learn more about Veterinary Technicians on the Internet. You might start by visiting the Web site of the National Association of Veterinary Technicians in America at http://www.navta.net. For more links, see Appendix IV.

CHEMISTRY
AND MATERIALS
SCIENCE

CHEMIST

CAREER PROFILE

Duties: Study the chemical make-up of substances and how they behave and interact with each other; design and conduct projects; perform duties as required

Alternate Title(s): Organic Chemist, Analytical Chemist, Biochemist, Forensic Chemist, or other title that reflects a specialty

Salary Range: $35,000 to $117,000

Employment Prospects: Good

Advancement Prospects: Good

Prerequisites:

    Education or Training—An advanced degree required for research scientist positions

    Experience—Postdoctoral experience for research scientists may be required

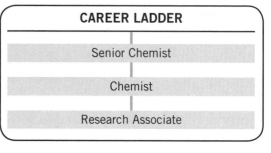

Special Skills and Personality Traits—Self-management, mathematical, computer, analytical, problem-solving, communication, writing, interpersonal and teamwork skills; be curious, creative, self-motivated, persistent, and flexible

Special Requirements—State licensure or professional certification may be required

Position Description

Chemistry is a physical science that deals with the substances (or chemicals) which make up matter. All matter, whether it forms living organisms or nonliving things, is composed of chemical compounds. A compound is made up of elements, which are chemicals that cannot be broken down any further. For example, when the elements hydrogen and oxygen combine in a certain way, the compound known as water is formed. So far, 110 natural and manmade elements have been discovered.

The scientists who study elements and compounds are called Chemists. They seek to understand the chemical composition, structure, and properties (or characteristics) of living organisms and nonliving things. Chemists are also concerned with understanding how substances behave under certain conditions and how different chemicals interact with each other. In addition, Chemists investigate what occurs during chemical changes. For example, food goes through several chemical changes in the body in order for the body to absorb nutrients from the food.

Most Chemists are involved in research and development in academic, government, and industrial settings. Some of them perform basic research to further scientific knowledge about chemical elements, compounds, interactions, chemical processes, and so forth. Other Chemists conduct applied research. They use findings of basic research to solve problems in fields such as medicine, the environment, agriculture, food processing, biotechnology, energy, and nanotechnology.

Other Chemists engage in the research and development of consumer products for a wide range of private companies. For example, they may be involved in the creation of new or improved food products, cosmetics, drugs, medical diagnostic tests, soaps, textiles, plastics, industrial chemicals, paints, and electronic products, among many others.

Chemistry is divided into several major fields of study, and Chemists may work in more than one field throughout their careers. Some of these major fields are:

- organic chemistry, the study of carbon compounds (carbon is an element that is found in all living organisms)
- inorganic chemistry, the study of substances (such as minerals and metals) that are made up of elements other than carbons
- physical chemistry, the application of physical laws and mathematical formulas to study the physical and chemical characteristics of matter
- analytical chemistry, the precise investigation into the composition, structure, and properties of matter
- biochemistry, the study of the chemistry of living organisms

Many Chemists concentrate on devoting their studies to a particular type of matter or a chemical process. Geochemists, for example, examine substances in rocks and minerals; surface chemists study the surface properties of chemical compounds; and synthetic chemists investigate the possibility of creating new chemical compounds. Some Chemists specialize in the method they use to approach their studies. For example, computational chemists use computer technologies to solve problems in chemistry.

Chemists also specialize in one of the various applied fields of chemistry. The following are just a few examples: forensic chemists analyze physical evidence (such as blood stains, human hair, glass fragments, paint chips, or soil) found at crime scenes. Clinical chemists apply their expertise to the health field by evaluating blood and tissue samples. Medicinal chemists work in the area of pharmaceuticals, studying the structural properties of compounds to develop new drugs and medicines. Agricultural chemists, on the other hand, focus their training in developing new products (feed, fertilizers, and pesticides) that improve the production, protection, and use of crops and livestock. Environmental chemists are involved in the protection of the environment, where they conduct or develop pollution monitoring or remediation programs.

Chemists work in laboratories and offices. Their duties vary, depending on Chemists' positions. Technicians and research assistants typically work under the supervision of research scientists. They provide research and administrative support in chemical labs. Their duties include conducting experiments or tests, analyzing data, writing reports, maintaining laboratory equipment, and performing routine administrative tasks.

Research Chemists are responsible for designing and conducting research projects. Some of their tasks include conducting experiments or tests, gathering data, analyzing and interpreting data, writing reports, and performing administrative tasks. Senior researchers or principal investigators typically perform supervisory and management tasks. In addition, Chemists who conduct independent research are usually responsible for obtaining grants to fund their research projects. Their tasks involve seeking out available grants from the federal government and other sources and writing grant proposals that describe the goals, objectives, methodologies, and other aspects of their projects.

Chemists often collaborate on research projects with other chemists as well as with scientists from other disciplines—such as biologists, physicists, and geologists. Many Chemists share the results of their research with colleagues by writing articles (or scientific papers) for scientific journals or giving presentations at scientific meetings that are sponsored by professional associations.

Many Chemists are adjunct instructors and full-time professors at colleges and universities. They teach basic chemistry courses as well as advanced courses in their areas of expertise. Full-time professors must juggle various tasks each day. Their responsibilities include conducting independent research, preparing courses, teaching classes, advising students, supervising student research projects, and performing administrative duties. In addition, professors are required to publish scholarly work and to participate in community service.

All Chemists use a variety of specialized computers and instruments to help them identify, measure, and evaluate chemicals. Further, they must follow specific safety measures while handling chemicals to keep health and safety hazards down to a minimum.

Salaries

Salaries for Chemists vary, depending on their education, experience, geographical location, and other factors. According to the May 2006 *Occupational Employment Statistics* (OES) survey by the U.S. Bureau of Labor Statistics (BLS), the estimated annual salary for most Chemists ranged between $35,480 and $106,310, and for most chemistry professors, between $36,160 and $116,910.

Employment Prospects

The BLS reports in its May 2006 OES survey that an estimated 80,500 Chemists were employed in the United States. Nearly 19 percent of them worked in the pharmaceutical and medicine manufacturing industry, the largest employer of Chemists. The next largest employers were the scientific research and development services industry (about 17 percent) and the architectural, engineering, and related services industry (about 13 percent).

Chemists are also employed by academic institutions, as well as by local, state, and federal government agencies in such areas as consumer protection, public health, safety and inspection, environmental protection, and forensics.

Job competition is strong for all Chemist positions. Most job openings will be created to replace Chemists who retire, advance to higher positions, or transfer to other jobs. The BLS predicts that employment growth for Chemists should increase by 9 percent through 2016.

Experts in the field report that job opportunities for Chemists should be strongest in the pharmaceutical, biotechnology, nanotechnology, advanced manufacturing, and homeland security industries.

With a chemistry background, individuals can follow other career paths by becoming high school chemistry teachers, environmental lawyers, patent agents, quality control personnel, technical sales representatives, technical writers, software developers, museum curators, safety and health inspectors, physicians, and pharmacists.

Advancement Prospects

Chemists with management or administrative ambitions can advance to such positions in any work setting. Professors receive promotional rankings as assistant professors, associate professors, or full professors.

Many Chemists measure their success by being able to conduct independent research, by making discoveries or inventions, by making higher earnings, and through gaining professional recognition.

Education and Training

Bachelor's and advanced degrees may be earned in chemistry or another discipline—such as biochemistry, toxicology, or materials science—that is related to the area in which Chemists wish to work.

For technician and research assistant jobs, candidates need a bachelor's degree. Many employers prefer or require that candidates have a master's degree. For research scientist positions, a master's degree or a Ph.D. is typically required. To teach at the university level, conduct independent research, or advance to top management posts, a Ph.D. is a mandatory requirement.

Special Requirements

Some Chemists such as marine chemists and directors of clinical laboratories, are required to obtain appropriate state licensure or professional certification. For information about a specific occupation, contact professionals in the field, professional societies, or chemistry professors.

Experience, Skills, and Personality Traits

Employers generally choose candidates who have work and research experience related to the position for which they are applying. For example, a job applicant for a position in a pharmaceutical company should have previous work experience in the industry. Experience may have been gained through student research projects, internships, fellowships or employment. Ph.D. candidates for research scientist positions may be required to have several years of postdoctoral experience.

Chemists need good self-management skills, including the ability to work independently, organize and prioritize tasks, and make appropriate decisions. In addition, they must possess strong mathematical and computer skills, excellent analytical and problem-solving skills, and effective communication and writing skills. Furthermore, Chemists must have good interpersonal and teamwork skills in order to work well with others.

Some personality traits that successful Chemists share are being curious, creative, self-motivated, persistent, and flexible.

Unions and Associations

Many Chemists belong to professional associations so that they can take advantage of education programs, professional certification, networking opportunities, and other professional resources and services. The American Chemical Society, the American Institute of Chemists, and the American Association for the Advancement of Science are three of the general scientific societies that many Chemists join. Many professional associations serve specific interests in chemistry, including the American Association for Clinical Chemistry, the Society of Cosmetic Chemists, the Geochemical Society, and the AACC International.

Chemistry professors are eligible to join professional societies such as the American Association of University Professors or the National Association of Scholars.

See Appendix III for contact information for all of the above organizations.

Tips for Entry

1. You can find out about scholarships, internships, fellowships, postdoctoral positions, and permanent jobs from college career centers and professional associations.

2. As an undergraduate, vary the settings in which you intern or work part time. This way, you can get an idea of the types of work that interest you as well as the settings in which you would like to work.

3. Having a willingness to relocate may increase your chances to obtain the type of job you want.

4. Contact employers for whom you would like to work, and ask about current openings.

5. Learn more about Chemists on the Internet. One Web site you might visit is for the American Chemical Society. Its URL is http://www.chemistry.org. For more links, see Appendix IV.

BIOCHEMIST

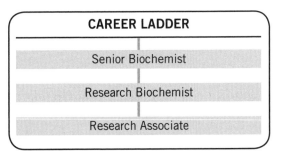
Position Description

Biochemistry is the chemical study of microbes, plants, animals, and humans. Biochemists seek to understand the chemical composition and structure of living organisms. In addition, they are interested in learning about the chemical reactions that are involved in reproduction, heredity, metabolism, and growth.

Biochemists conduct research in various fields, including agriculture, food science, pharmacology, physiology, toxicology, genetics, medicine, biotechnology, nanotechnology, and environmental science, among others. They might engage in basic research to further our knowledge about the chemistry of living organisms, studying such questions as: How do chemical changes take place during muscle contraction? What is DNA's role in heredity? How do toxins break down in an organism?

These scientists also conduct applied research in which they use the results of basic research to design technologies and processes that can help solve problems within their particular field. For example, Biochemists in the agriculture field might apply basic findings to the development of improved techniques for crop cultivation.

In addition, Biochemists are involved in product development for pharmaceutical, agribusiness, food, biotechnology, and many other companies. These researchers contribute to the creation of new and improved drugs, foods, and other consumer products.

Research scientists are responsible for designing and conducting research projects. Some of their tasks include conducting experiments, gathering data, analyzing and interpreting data, writing reports, and performing administrative tasks. Senior researchers and principal investigators usually perform supervisory and management duties. Biochemists who conduct independent research are usually responsible for seeking grants from the federal government and other sources to fund their projects. This involves preparing grant proposals that include the goals, methodologies, budgets, and other aspects for their projects.

Biochemists sometimes collaborate on research projects with other scientists, engineers, and specialists. Most Biochemists share results of their research with colleagues by writing papers for scientific publications or making presentations at scientific conferences.

Many Biochemists hold faculty positions at universities, colleges, and medical schools. They teach biochemistry courses in chemistry and biochemistry departments as well as in such departments as medicine, veterinary science, pharmacy, and agriculture. They are responsible for planning and teaching courses in addition to conducting research projects. Their duties also include advising students, supervising student research projects, writing scholarly work, performing administrative duties, and participating in community service.

Biochemists are responsible for keeping up with new technologies and developments in their fields. They participate in training programs, enroll in continuing education programs, attend professional conferences and meetings, and network with colleagues.

Biochemists generally work 40 hours a week, but it is not uncommon for them to put in additional hours to monitor experiments and complete various tasks.

Salaries

Salaries for Biochemists vary, depending on their experience, education, geographical location, and other factors. According to the May 2006 *Occupational Employment Statistics* survey by the U.S. Bureau of Labor Statistics, the estimated annual salary for most Biochemists ranged between $40,820 and $129,510.

Employment Prospects

Biochemists are employed by academic institutions, government agencies, research institutes, and hospitals. They also work throughout private industry.

According to the U.S. Bureau of Labor Statistics, job growth for biological scientists, including Biochemists, is expected to increase by 7 to 13 percent through 2016. Some experts report that opportunities are expected to be favorable for Biochemists in the biotechnology, pharmaceutical, and nanotechnology industries in the next several years. Many opportunities will also arise as a result of Biochemists advancing to higher positions, transferring to other jobs, and retiring.

Advancement Prospects

Most Biochemists measure their success by being able to conduct independent research, through earning professional recognition, and by earning higher incomes. Some Biochemists pursue management or administrative positions.

Education and Training

Entry-level candidates for research scientist positions generally need a doctoral degree in biochemistry, biology, chemistry, or another related field. (Doctorates are required for candidates who seek professorships.) Some employers require only a master's degree for applied research positions. Individuals with a bachelor's degree may be able to obtain technician or other nonresearch positions.

Some experts suggest that undergraduates earn a bachelor's degree in biochemistry. Alternatively, they might earn a bachelor's in chemistry with coursework in cell biology, genetics, molecular biology, biochemistry, and biophysics; or they might obtain a bachelor's in biology with coursework in chemistry, biochemistry, physics, and mathematics.

Experience, Skills, and Personality Traits

Employers generally choose candidates who have related work and research experience, which may have been gained through research projects, internships, fellowships, or employment. Many employers prefer that Ph.D. applicants have relevant postdoctoral experience.

Biochemists need effective writing and communication skills, as they must be able to present their findings clearly to others. Strong interpersonal and teamwork skills are also important for their work. Some personality traits that successful Biochemists share are being cooperative, creative, imaginative, hardworking, persistent, and flexible.

Unions and Associations

Many Biochemists join professional associations to take advantage of professional services and resources, such as education programs and networking opportunities. One national association that serves Biochemists is the American Society for Biochemistry and Molecular Biology. Biochemists are also eligible to join general biology or chemistry societies such as the American Institute of Biological Sciences, the American Institute of Chemists, or the American Chemical Society. See Appendix III for contact information.

Tips for Entry

1. Many universities and colleges offer cooperative education programs in which undergraduate students integrate their academic study with supervised work experience in government or industry settings. Often, employers hire students after they have completed their bachelor's degree. Speak with your chemistry adviser or a career placement counselor for more information.
2. You can find job listings for biochemistry positions on the Internet. Some sources are professional societies, college departments, and job banks such as Monster.com, http://www.monster.com. In addition, many employers post job openings on their Web sites.
3. Learn more about Biochemists on the Internet. To get a list of relevant Web sites to read, enter the keyword *biochemistry* or *biochemists* in any search engine. For some links, See Appendix IV.

TOXICOLOGIST

Position Description

Toxicology is the study of poisons, which may be solid, liquid, or gaseous substances. All chemicals are potentially toxic and any substance absorbed in excess can be extremely harmful.

Toxicologists engage in various types of research that help ensure the safety of human health, as well as the health of animals and the environment. These scientists identify the toxicity of substances and determine their levels of safe and dangerous use. They investigate how specific chemicals, processes, or situations can affect ecosystems. In addition, they are concerned with the safety of drugs, cleaning supplies, pesticides, paints, fuel, cosmetics, and dyes, and other products as well as natural and industrial chemicals to which living organisms and the environment are constantly exposed.

Toxicologists work in academic, government, and industrial laboratories, where they perform research in such areas as medicine, public health, animal science, environmental science, food science, and forensic science. These scientists apply principles of chemistry and biology to their studies, and utilize molecular, genetic, and analytical techniques to examine how cellular, biochemical, and molecular processes react to toxic chemicals. Their studies may involve the use of laboratory animals.

Toxicologists are involved in basic research, applied research, and product development. With basic research, Toxicologists engage in projects to further scientific knowledge about different poisons, the risks of using various chemicals, how substances cause injury or disease, what are safe conditions for using various chemicals and so forth.

Toxicologists who conduct applied research utilize the findings of basic research to solve particular problems in their fields. For example, Toxicologists might perform studies to identify chemicals that may be responsible for a specific disease in a population of workers.

Toxicologists also work on product development teams in chemical, pharmaceutical, biotechnology, and other industries. These Toxicologists are responsible for researching harmful effects of potential products. They identify any risks (such as birth defects, cancer, or illnesses) that may occur if a product is used under certain conditions. For example, a Toxicologist might determine that a new drug for allergies may cause such side effects as nausea or headaches. With approved products, Toxicologists design and conduct various tests to ensure that they are safe for consumers to use and that they meet industrial standards.

Toxicologists work in various applied areas. Their duties may include conducting research and performing analysis services. The following are a few other types of Toxicologists:

- Forensic toxicologists are involved in criminal and postmortem investigations. They perform chemical analyses on human and animal corpses to determine the type and amount of poisons that caused their deaths.
- Medical and clinical toxicologists are concerned with how poisons and pollutants affect human health. Many are directly involved with the diagnosis and treatment of human diseases. Some are medical doctors who work with patients; others work in hospital labs where they analyze the levels of medication or other substances in blood and tissue samples.
- Veterinary toxicologists study the effects of poisons and pollutants on animals, both domestic and wild; many are involved with the diagnosis and treatment of diseases.
- Environmental toxicologists study the effects that chemical pollutants have on humans, animals, plants, and the environment.
- Food safety toxicologists are concerned with understanding how poisons or pathogens (such as bacteria or viruses) in food affect human health.
- Regulatory toxicologists work for local, state, and federal government agencies. They assist in the enforcement as well as development of laws and regulations that protect human health and the environment.

Some Toxicologists are consultants, being independent contractors or employees of consulting firms. They offer research, analytical, and other services to private industries and public agencies on a contractual basis.

Many academic researchers are appointed to professor positions. They have the additional duty of teaching toxicology courses to graduate and medical students. On smaller campuses, Toxicologists might also teach basic chemistry or biology courses to undergraduate students. As faculty members, their duties include advising students, supervising student research projects, writing scholarly work, performing administrative duties, and participating in community service. Further, they are responsible for obtaining grants for their research projects.

Toxicologists work in laboratories and offices. Some Toxicologists take field trips to conduct research and testing services. Their field work may involve traveling to isolated areas, such as forests and wilderness areas.

Salaries

Salaries for Toxicologists vary, depending on such factors as their education, experience, position, employer, and geographical location. According to a 2006 salary survey by the American Association for the Advancement of Science, the median annual salary for academic researchers in toxicology was $78,000, and for industrial researchers, $105,000. The U.S. Bureau of Labor Statistics reports in its May 2006 *Occupational Employment Statistics* survey that the estimated annual salary for most chemists, including Toxicologists, ranged between $35,480 and $106,310.

Employment Prospects

Toxicologists are employed by colleges, universities, and medical schools. They also work for a wide range of local, state, and federal government agencies (for example: public health, regulatory, law enforcement, and defense agencies). Many Toxicologists work in pharmaceutical, chemical, biotechnology, manufacturing, and other industries. In addition, many are independent consultants or employed in consulting firms, providing services to local public agencies, industries, and attorneys. Some Toxicologists work for nonprofit research foundations.

Job opportunities are favorable for experienced Toxicologists in all settings. Most job openings are created to replace individuals who retire, transfer to other positions, or resign.

Advancement Prospects

In any setting, Toxicologists can advance to supervisory and administrative positions, such as project leader, program manager, lab director, and executive officer. As professors, Toxicologists can move up through the ranks as assistant professor, associate professor, or full professor.

Education and Training

Employers generally require that entry-level candidates possess a master's or doctoral degree in toxicology or another related discipline. Doctoral degrees are required for Toxicologists to teach in universities and four-year colleges, to conduct independent research, and to pursue top management positions.

To enter a graduate program in toxicology, students are usually required to possess a bachelor's degree in chemistry, biology, or another relevant field. Many programs require that undergraduates have completed at least one year of general biology, as well as courses in general physics, statistics, calculus, and computer science. In addition, they should have completed advanced coursework in chemistry, including organic chemistry, and have gained laboratory experience.

Special Requirements

Clinical Toxicologists may be required to obtain state licensure or appropriate professional certification from the National Registry in Clinical Chemistry or other organization. Toxicologists who plan to become clinical laboratory directors or consultants must obtain proper board certification from the American Board of Toxicology or the American Board of Clinical Chemistry.

Toxicologists can obtain professional certification on a voluntary basis from organizations that offer credentials for their field. For example, forensic toxicologists may seek board certification from the American Board of Forensic Toxicology while veterinary toxicologists may apply for board certification from the American Board of Veterinary Toxicology.

Experience, Skills, and Personality Traits

Employers generally choose candidates who have related work and research experience, which may have been gained through research projects, internships, fellowships, or employment. Many employers prefer that Ph.D. applicants have a few years of postdoctoral experience.

Along with being able to work independently, Toxicologists need to work collaboratively with others in team projects. Thus, having effective interpersonal and teamwork skills is important. Toxicologists also need strong communication and writing skills and should have good math and computer skills.

Being flexible, creative, organized, and analytical are a few of the personality traits that successful Toxicologists share.

Unions and Associations

Many Toxicologists join professional associations to take advantage of education programs, professional publications, networking opportunities, and other professional resources and services. Some of the various societies that serve the diverse interests of Toxicologists are the Society of Toxicology, the American College of Toxicology, the Society of Forensic Toxicologists, the Association of Government Toxicologists, and the Society of Environmental Toxicology and Chemistry. See Appendix III for contact information.

Tips for Entry

1. Contact government and private sector employers directly for information about available internships, postdoctoral opportunities, and permanent positions.

2. Admission requirements for graduate programs in toxicology vary from school to school. Get an early start learning about the programs that interest you so that you can be sure to take appropriate courses during your undergraduate years.

3. Use the Internet to learn more about toxicology. One Web site you might visit is for the Society of Toxicology at http://www.toxicology.org. For more links, See Appendix IV.

MATERIALS SCIENTIST

CAREER PROFILE

Duties: Study the structures and properties of natural and man-made materials; design and conduct research projects; perform duties as required

Alternate Title(s): Glass Scientist, Metallurgist, or other title that reflects a specialty

Salary Range: $42,000 to $119,000

Employment Prospects: Good

Advancement Prospects: Good

Prerequisites:

    Education or Training—Master's or doctoral degree in materials science or another related field

    Experience—Previous work experience required

CAREER LADDER

Senior Materials Scientist

Research Materials Scientist

Research Associate

Special Skills and Personality Traits—Leadership, problem-solving, teamwork, interpersonal, communication, writing, and computer skills; be curious, determined, focused, resourceful, and creative

Position Description

Do you ever wonder how materials are chosen to make items as diverse as food packaging, clothing, household items, cell phones, hip implants, bicycles, high-rise buildings, and spacecraft? All materials—natural and man-made—are composed of unique properties, or characteristics, that make them well suited for specific uses.

The men and women who engage in the scientific study of materials are known as Materials Scientists. They are interested in understanding the molecular makeup of a material; the relationships between its structure and properties; how it reacts under pressure, in water, at different temperatures, and in other conditions; how a material changes during processing; and how well it performs when used in a particular application. These scientists also study how to maintain the desired properties in a material as they attempt to use it to produce practical things.

Materials Scientists examine various metals, alloys, ceramics, glass, fiberglass, polymers, rubber, semiconductors, biomaterials, and other materials. They are constantly seeking ways to improve the use of the many different materials, as well as finding ways to create entirely new materials with new or specific properties.

Over the years, the research work that Materials Scientists have performed has led to many technical advances in diverse fields, including electronics, computing, medicine, biotechnology, aerospace, transportation, environmental remediation, energy, construction, manufacturing, and national security, among others.

Furthermore, their research has contributed to the development and design of thousands upon thousands of new and improved consumer products.

Materials Scientists work in industrial, academic, and government settings where they are involved in research and development. Some conduct basic research to gain further understanding and knowledge about different materials. Many of them perform applied research in which they utilize the findings of basic research to develop new materials or improve existing materials for use in various products.

Materials Scientists in industrial settings are usually involved in product development. For example, a Materials Scientist in the medical device industry may be involved in developing materials that are compatible with human tissues for artificial hearts. Some industrial scientists are involved in the full cycle of the development and production of a product, which includes working with other scientists and engineers to design manufacturing processes. Industrial scientists sometimes provide technical assistance for customers on products on which they have worked.

Materials science is made up of many subfields. Materials Scientists specialize in one or more areas throughout their careers. For example, they may be involved in:

- biomaterials, the study of materials that are used in medical devices such as teeth implants, contact lenses, heart valves, and hip joints
- crystallography, the study of crystals

- electronic and magnetic materials, the study of semiconductors and other materials that are used to create integrated circuits, sensors, and other devices
- glass science, the study of solid substances that are formed by melting and cooling without crystallizing
- metallurgy, the study of metals and their alloys, as well as their extraction and processing
- nanotechnology, the study and development of materials, devices, and systems at the atomic, molecular, or macromolecular level
- tribology, the study of the wear, friction, lubrication, corrosion, and erosion of materials

Materials Scientists are responsible for designing and conducting research projects. They may work alone or collaborate with other scientists on a project. Industrial and government researchers typically work on topics that fulfill the mission and goals of their employers, while academic researchers perform research on subject matter that interests them. Researchers, regardless of their setting, perform such tasks as reading literature, planning and conducting experiments and tests, collecting and analyzing data, preparing technical reports, and completing administrative tasks. Senior researchers and principal investigators usually perform supervisory and administrative duties.

Researchers typically share and exchange information with other scientists, including those in other disciplines. Many write papers about their findings and conclusions for scientific journals, as well as give presentations at scientific conferences.

Most academic researchers hold professorships at colleges and universities where they teach undergraduate and graduate students in materials sciences, chemistry, physics, or other subjects. These researchers are responsible for teaching courses, advising students, supervising students' research projects, producing scholarly work, fulfilling community service, and performing administrative duties. In addition, they are responsible for seeking grants to fund their research projects.

Materials Scientists work in offices and laboratories. Industrial scientists may also spend some time working in manufacturing plants. Typically, Materials Scientists put in long hours to complete their various tasks.

Salaries

Salaries for Materials Scientists vary, depending on such factors as their education, experience, position, employer, and geographical location. According to the May 2006 *Occupational Employment Statistics* survey by the U.S. Bureau of Labor Statistics, the estimated annual salary for most Materials Scientists ranged between $41,810 and $118,670.

Employment Prospects

Most Materials Scientists are employed in the private sector, working in a wide range of materials-producing industries (such as metals and plastics) and manufacturing industries. They work for start-up firms as well as established companies throughout the United States. Materials Scientists also find employment with government and academic laboratories.

In general, job openings become available as Materials Scientists retire, advance to higher positions, or transfer to other jobs. Employers will create additional positions to meet growing needs, as long as funding is available.

Some experts in the field say that the job outlook for experienced Materials Scientists will continually be favorable due to the essential role materials play in developing new and improved consumer products. In recent years, companies in the United States have hired Materials Scientists from other countries due to the low number of students graduating from materials science programs.

Advancement Prospects

Many Materials Scientists measure their success through making important discoveries, through job satisfaction, and by earning professional recognition among their peers. Those with management and administrative ambitions can pursue such positions in government, industrial, and academic laboratories. Entrepreneurial individuals might choose to become independent consultants or start up their own companies.

Academicians can advance in rank from instructor to assistant, associate, and full professor, as well as gain job tenure at their institution.

Education and Training

Because materials science is an interdisciplinary field, Materials Scientists need a strong background in such fields as chemistry, physics, engineering, biological science, and mathematics. Individuals typically need a master's or doctoral degree in materials science, materials engineering, chemistry, physics, or another related field to qualify for research scientist positions. A doctorate is generally required for individuals to perform independent research, teach in colleges and universities, and to advance to top management positions.

Individuals with bachelor's degrees may qualify for research assistant and technician positions, in which they work under the supervision and direction of research scientists.

Throughout their careers, Materials Scientists enroll in continuing education programs to update their skills and keep up with advancements in their fields.

Experience, Special Skills, and Personality Traits

Employers generally seek candidates who have work experience as well as have completed research work relevant to the positions for which they apply. Entry-level applicants may have gained their experience through internships, work-study programs, student research projects, or employment. Many employers prefer to hire Ph.D. applicants who have a few years of postdoctoral experience. Employers in private industry usually favor candidates who have a fundamental understanding of business, marketing, and economics.

To be effective at their job, Materials Scientist need strong leadership, problem-solving, teamwork, interpersonal, communication, writing, and computer skills. Being curious, determined, focused, resourceful, and creative are some personality traits that successful Materials Scientists share.

Unions and Associations

Many Materials Scientists join professional associations to take advantage of networking opportunities, training programs, job listings, and other professional services and resources. Some national societies that serve their diverse interests include:

- American Ceramic Society
- American Chemical Society
- ASM International
- Materials Research Society
- Minerals, Metals & Materials Society
- Society for Biomaterials

For contact information, see Appendix III.

Tips for Entry

1. As a college student, ask your adviser or a college career counselor for help in finding an internship or work-study position in a private company.
2. Many professional associations offer student memberships. Consider joining a society that serves your particular interests, and participate in its activities.
3. If you plan to work in the private sector, carefully research the industries in which you would like to work. For example, you might talk with professionals, contact trade and professional associations, or visit company Web sites.
4. When doing a job hunt, contact current and former instructors, supervisors, and classmates as well as friends and college alumni for job leads.
5. Use the Internet to learn more about the field of materials science. You might start by visiting the Materials Research Society Web site, http://www.mrs.org. For more links, see Appendix IV.

CHEMICAL TECHNICIAN

Duties: Provide laboratory and technical support to scientists and engineers; may work in research, process control, quality control, or another area; perform duties as required

Alternate Title(s): Laboratory Technician, Research Assistant, Process Control Technician; a title that reflects a particular specialty such as Environmental Technician

Salary Range: $25,000 to $60,000

Employment Prospects: Good

Advancement Prospects: Good

Prerequisites:

    Education or Training—An associate in applied science degree, minimally required

    Experience—One or more years of work experience preferred

CAREER LADDER

Senior Chemical Technician

Chemical Technician

Chemical Technician (Entry-level)

Special Skills and Personality Traits—Analytical, problem-solving, organizational, self-management, math, computer, writing, public speaking, communication, interpersonal, and teamwork skills; be curious, detail-oriented, dependable, flexible, self-motivated, enthusiastic, patient, and dedicated

Position Description

Chemical Technicians play a valuable role in scientific teams, providing scientists and engineers with technical support and assistance on various projects. These science technicians are very knowledgeable about the application of chemistry principles and techniques, and they are highly skilled in operating standard laboratory equipment. Over the last few decades, their jobs have evolved from conducting simple laboratory tests into ones in which they perform many complex duties that were once the responsibilities of chemists.

Chemical Technicians are involved from basic research to the research and development of products and chemical processes to the manufacturing of products. These technicians generally work in one of two areas—the experimental laboratory or the manufacturing plant.

Those working in experimental laboratories are sometimes called laboratory technicians or research and development technicians. They might participate in basic research in which they help scientists increase further knowledge of a particular topic. They might assist scientists in performing applied research, which involve using the results of basic research to solve problems in a specific field such as health care, pollution control, or energy production. They might be part of research teams that engage in the development of new or improved consumer products. Chemical Technicians work under the direction of a laboratory supervisor, scientist, or engineer, but generally conduct experiments and tests, perform analyses, and write reports on their own.

Technicians who work in manufacturing or other industrial plants perform a variety of roles to ensure that chemical processes are being executed safely, in a cost-effective manner, and according to the highest professional standards. For example, different technicians assist in developing and improving the manufacturing processes; performing chemical tests to check for quality of raw materials and final products; monitoring pollution levels in the air, soil, and water; auditing manufacturing processes to ensure they meet the federal Good Manufacturing Practice (GMP) regulations; and defining shipping procedures for hazardous material.

As Chemical Technicians gain experience, many of them choose to specialize in terms of where they work and what type of role they perform. Many of them focus their work in a particular field, such as industrial chemicals, polymers, pharmaceuticals, environmental protection, or food processing. Some also choose to engage in a particular activity, such as quality control, data management, or research and development.

Chemical Technicians work on projects that range from simple, routine jobs to complex assignments. Their responsibilities vary, depending on their experience, skills, and position. Experienced technicians, for instance, may assist in developing and conducting quality programs to ensure that high standards of raw materials, chemical intermediates, and products are being met in manufacturing plants.

Chemical Technicians perform various tasks each day, such as:

- conducting chemical and physical laboratory tests
- preparing chemical solutions by following standard formulas or experimental procedures
- setting up, adjusting, operating, and maintaining laboratory instruments and equipment
- using appropriate techniques (such as microscopy, chromatography, or physical and chemical separation techniques) to conduct tests, experiments, and analyses
- compiling, analyzing, and interpreting results of tests or experiments
- making sure that their work is in compliance with standards, laws, and regulations
- keeping precise and detailed records of their work
- preparing technical reports, graphs, and charts to document experimental results
- maintaining an inventory of materials and supplies
- keeping up with emerging technologies

Chemical Technicians operate various equipment and instrumentation, such as test tubes, gas burners, microscopes, laboratory balances, vacuum pumps, chromatographs, centrifuges, and spectrophotometers. They operate calculators as well as computers and use a variety of software, including scientific, analytical, database, word processing, and spreadsheet applications.

These scientific technicians mostly work indoors in laboratories and manufacturing plants. Some of them work in the field, sometimes in remote locations, to collect samples or conduct tests. Because they are exposed to dangerous chemicals, fumes, equipment, and other hazards, Chemical Technicians follow safety procedures and wear protective equipment.

Most Chemical Technicians work 40 hours a week. They put in additional hours as needed to complete tasks and meet deadlines. Some technicians work irregular hours to monitor experiments. Chemical Technicians in manufacturing plants may be assigned to night or weekend work shifts.

Salaries

Salaries for Chemical Technicians vary, depending on such factors as their education, experience, position, employer, and geographical location. The U.S. Bureau of Labor Statistics (BLS) reports in its May *2006 Occupational Employment Statistics* (OES) survey that the estimated annual salary for most Chemical Technicians ranged between $24,560 and $60,120.

Employment Prospects

Most Chemical Technicians are employed in the private sector, working in various industries including the chemical, rubber, steel, paints, pharmaceutical, cosmetics, food, agriculture, biotechnology, electronics, and petroleum and oil industries, among others. Chemical Technicians also find employment in academic institutions as well as in local, state, and federal government agencies.

The BLS reports in its May 2006 OES survey that an estimated 59,900 Chemical Technicians were employed in the United States. This federal agency projects that job growth for Chemical Technicians should be increasing by 6 percent during the 2006–16 period. Most job openings will become available as individuals advance to higher positions, transfer to other jobs, or leave the workforce for various reasons. Some experts in the field state that jobs for Chemical Technicians could become plentiful in the next several years due to the large number of baby boomers who are reaching retirement age.

Opportunities are reported to be most prevalent in the pharmaceutical, medical, biotechnology, and environmental management and testing industries.

Advancement Prospects

Chemical Technicians may advance in various ways, depending on their interests and ambitions. Many technicians measure their success through job satisfaction and by earning higher wages. As they gain experience, some pursue opportunities as supervisors, administrators, or managers. Others seek industrial opportunities in sales, technical service, marketing, technical writing, or another area. Advancement opportunities are generally best for individuals who obtain a bachelor's degree.

Some technicians choose to continue their education to become chemists, biochemists, chemical engineers, or high school science teachers, or to pursue other professions that interest them.

Education and Training

In general, most employers prefer to hire entry-level candidates who possess at least an associate degree in applied science (A.A.S.) degree in chemical technology or another science discipline. Without an A.A.S. degree, most employers prefer that applicants have two years of specialized training. Some employers seek applicants with a bachelor's degree in chemistry, chemical technology, or another degree.

Chemical technology programs are two-year programs offered by community colleges, technical colleges, and technical institutes, which are designed to meet the workforce needs of employers within the surrounding communities. These programs teach fundamental academic courses as well as provide students with practical laboratory experience. Some schools focus their programs in a particular area such as biotechnology, pharmaceutical manufacturing, or environmental technology.

Entry-level Chemical Technicians receive on-the-job training. They work under the guidance and supervision of experienced technicians, as well as chemists, chemical engineers, and others.

Throughout their careers, Chemical Technicians enroll in workshops, seminars, and courses to update their skills and keep up with advancements in their fields.

Experience, Special Skills, and Personality Traits

Employers prefer to hire candidates for entry-level positions who have one or more years of practical experience. They may have gained their experience through internships, work-study programs, volunteer work, or employment.

To perform well at their job, Chemical Technicians need excellent analytical, problem-solving, organizational, and self-management skills. They must also have strong math and computer skills. In addition, they need proficient writing and public speaking skills, as they must be able to write comprehensible technical reports and make clear presentations. Because they must work well with scientists, engineers, and others, Chemical Technicians must have effective communication, interpersonal, and teamwork skills.

Some personality traits that successful Chemical Technicians have in common include being curious, detail-oriented, dependable, flexible, self-motivated, enthusiastic, patient, and dedicated.

Unions and Associations

Some Chemical Technicians are members of a labor union that represents them in contract negotiations with their employers. The union also handles any grievances that union members have against their employers.

Many Chemical Technicians join professional associations to take advantage of networking opportunities, continuing education programs, and other professional services and resources. One national society that serves their particular interests is the Division of Chemical Technicians, which is part of the American Chemical Society. For contact information, see Appendix III.

Tips for Entry

1. Sometimes employers hire high school graduates for trainee or assistant technician positions, if they have a strong background in science and mathematics. These employees then receive formal and on-the-job training that allows them to eventually advance to technician positions.

2. Take advantage of your career counseling office or school placement office for help in finding a job.

3. Check newspaper classifieds for job openings.

4. Individuals who are willing to relocate may be able to find more opportunities in the fields in which they wish to work.

5. Use the Internet to learn more about the field of chemical technology. You might start by visiting the Web site for the American Chemical Society Division of Chemical Technicians at http://membership.acs.org/t/tech. For more links, see Appendix IV.

PHYSICS AND ASTRONOMY

PHYSICIST

Duties: Study the structure and behavior of matter and energy, as well as their relationships and the effects they have on each other; design and conduct research projects; perform duties as required

Alternate Title(s): Experimental Physicist, Theoretical Physicist; Optics Physicist, Nuclear Physicist, Biophysicist, or other title that reflects a specialty

Salary Range: $40,000 to $144,000

Employment Prospects: Good

Advancement Prospects: Good

Prerequisites:

Education or Training—An advanced degree required for research scientist positions

Experience—Postdoctoral experience may be required for research scientists

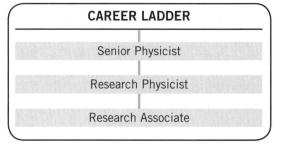

CAREER LADDER

Senior Physicist

Research Physicist

Research Associate

Special Skills and Personality Traits—Math, writing, computer, problem-solving, analytical, self-management, interpersonal, communication, and teamwork skills; be imaginative, persistent, inquisitive, and self-motivated

Position Description

Physicists seek to understand how everything works: atoms and molecules; living cells and tissues; electrical circuits and supercomputers; liquid, solid, and gaseous matter; the Earth and other celestial bodies; and so on. These physical scientists are committed to the study of matter and energy. They investigate the structure and behavior of matter as well as the various forms of energy. Additionally they are interested in learning about the relationships between matter and energy, including how they affect each other over time and through space.

Physics is a fundamental science, and the laws of physics form the basis for all other natural science and engineering disciplines. Most of the technologies that we have today (such as cell phones, microwave ovens, medical imaging, vehicles, lasers, radar, the Internet, atomic power, and global positioning system tools) are founded on physics research. In addition, the principles and techniques of physics have helped solve diverse problems in such fields as medicine, biotechnology, chemistry, nanotechnology, engineering, communications, energy, and environmental science.

Physicists are involved in research and development in academic, government, and industrial settings. Some of them conduct basic research to increase scientific knowledge in their areas of interest. Through observation and analysis, Physicists continue to discover physical laws and theories that explain gravity, electromagnetism, chemical reactions, the transfer of energy, nuclear reactions, and various other processes and interactions that occur in the world.

Many Physicists are involved in applied research or product development. Applied researchers utilize findings of basic research to develop technologies and processes to solve general problems in their fields of interest. Physicists working on product development teams use physics principles and applied research results to create new or improved consumer products for private companies.

Physicists usually specialize in performing experimental or theoretical research. Experimental Physicists design and run experiments and make careful observations and measurements to explain what happened in the experiments. Theoretical Physicists, on the other hand, analyze the results of experiments (usually done by other Physicists) and determine whether the experiments obey particular theories. Theoretical Physicists create computer models to help them with their investigations.

Physicists also specialize in one of the many subfields of physics. Some Physicists switch from one specialty to another throughout their careers. Some subfields are:

- astrophysics, the study of the physical and chemical composition and processes of stars, star systems, and interstellar materials

- acoustics, the study of sound and sound waves
- optics, the study of light (including ultraviolet and infrared radiation) and the phenomena related to its generation, transmission, and detection
- electromagnetism, the study of electricity and magnetic fields
- atomic physics, the study of atoms and their properties, as well as their interactions with atomic particles and fields
- particle physics (or high-energy physics), the study of electrons, neutrons, protons, and other elementary particles that are the building blocks of all matter in the universe
- solid-state physics (or condensed-matter physics), the study of solid matter and its properties
- plasma physics, the study of highly ionized (electrically charged) gases, which are found in space as well as in thermonuclear reactors (Plasma is sometimes called the fourth state of matter. Solids, liquids, and gases are the three known states of matter.)
- cryogenics, the study of matter at extremely low temperatures (near absolute zero)
- vacuum physics, the study of matter in an environment that contains very few atoms or molecules
- nuclear physics, the study of atomic nuclei and their interactions, as well as of nuclear energy

Some Physicists work in a field that combines physics with another scientific discipline. For example, biophysicists apply physics to biological problems, geophysicists study the physics of the earth, and astrophysicists incorporate the principles and theories of physics to the study of astronomy.

Most Physicists collaborate on research projects with other Physicists as well as with other scientists, engineers, and specialists. Physicists usually share the results of their research work with colleagues. Many write scientific papers which they submit to scientific journals. Some also make presentations at scientific meetings that are sponsored by professional associations.

Physicists' duties vary, depending on their position. Technicians and research assistants typically work under the supervision of research Physicists. Their duties may include: performing experiments, analyzing data, writing reports, maintaining laboratory equipment, and performing routine administrative tasks.

Research physicists are responsible for designing and conducting research projects. They work in laboratories to conduct their research, but also work in offices to analyze data, write reports, and perform other research and administrative tasks. Physicists sometimes are involved in designing complex equipment (such as lasers, telescopes, radiation detectors, and particle accelerators) for their particular type of research. They might also create computer software programs necessary for data analysis, modeling, and other purposes.

Many Physicists are responsible for obtaining research grants to fund their projects. This involves learning about available grants from the federal government and other sources, as well as writing grant proposals that describe the objectives, methodologies, budgets, and other aspects of their projects.

Many research physicists are also faculty members at colleges and universities. In addition to conducting independent research, they are responsible for teaching physics courses to undergraduate and graduate students. They also perform other duties that include advising students, supervising student research projects, writing scholarly works, fulfilling administrative duties, and participating in community services.

Physicists sometimes travel to laboratory facilities in other cities or countries to use special equipment for their research projects. They may be exposed to radiation, toxic materials, and high-voltage electrical equipment in the laboratory. Thus, they follow specific safety measures to keep health and safety hazards to a minimum.

Salaries

Salaries for Physicists vary, depending on their education, experience, employer, geographical location, and other factors. According to the May 2006 *Occupational Employment Statistics* survey by the U.S. Bureau of Labor Statistics (BLS), the estimated annual salary for most Physicists ranged between $52,070 and $143,570, and for most physics professors, between $39,580 and $120,210.

Employment Prospects

Physicists are employed by academic institutions, where they work in the physics, engineering, mathematics, materials science, or other department. Physicists also find employment in private industry, as well as with government agencies, government laboratories, and federally funded research and development centers.

Most job opportunities become available as Physicists retire, advance to higher positions, or transfer to other jobs. Employers may create additional positions to meet growing needs, as long as funding is available.

With a background in physics, individuals can pursue career paths in various areas, such as engineering, computer science, energy, education, medicine, law, finance, and journalism.

Advancement Prospects

Physicists with management and administrative interests can pursue such positions in any work setting. For example, research scientists in industry or government settings may advance by becoming a project leader, program director, or executive officer. Professors receive promotional rankings as assistant professors, associate professors, or full professors.

Education and Training

For research scientist positions, Physicists must possess either a master's degree or a Ph.D. in physics, a subfield of physics (such as biophysics), or another related field (such as engineering). A Ph.D. is necessary for those wishing to teach in universities and four-year colleges, to conduct independent research, or to pursue top management positions.

A bachelor's degree in physics is usually the minimum requirement for research assistant and lab technician positions.

Experience, Skills, and Personality Traits

Employers generally choose candidates who have previous work and research experience related to the positions being sought. Entry-level applicants may have gained experience through research projects, internships, fellowships, or employment. Many employers generally prefer that Ph.D. applicants for research scientist positions have a few years of postdoctoral experience. Candidates for industry positions should have some related industry experience or some background in business or economics.

Physicists should have strong math, writing, and computer skills, as well as effective problem-solving, analytical, and self-management skills. They also need excellent interpersonal, communication, and teamwork skills, as they must be able to work well with others.

Some personality traits that successful Physicists have in common are being imaginative, persistent, inquisitive, and self-motivated.

Unions and Associations

Most Physicists join professional organizations to take advantage of professional services and resources such as education programs and networking opportunities. Some general societies are the American Institute of Physics, the American Physical Society, and the American Association for the Advancement of Science. Physicists might also join professional societies that serve their specialties, such as the American Geophysical Union, the Biophysical Society, the Acoustical Society of America, or the American Association of Physicists in Medicine. Academic faculty might join professional societies such as the National Association of Scholars. See Appendix III for contact information.

Tips for Entry

1. Talk with Physicists of various specializations and in various settings to learn about the types of opportunities that are available.
2. Many sources can provide you with information about job openings. For example, you might talk with physics professors, visit college and university placement centers, contact professional societies, or check out the Internet for job listings. You might also contact human resource departments of those employers for whom you would like to work.
3. To learn about job openings with the federal government, contact the nearest U.S. Office of Personnel Management. Check out the white pages in your telephone directory. Or visit its Web site at http://usajobs.opm.gov.
4. The Internet can provide you with more information about physics. One Web site you might visit is for the Society Physics Students at http://www.spsnational.org. For more links, see Appendix IV.

BIOPHYSICIST

Position Description

Biophysicists apply the principles and techniques of physics to understand how life processes (such as the muscular, nervous, and cardiovascular systems) function in humans, plants, and animals. These scientists study the physical properties and structures of life processes, as well as examine the interrelationships among the life systems. They investigate such questions as: What is the structure of the cell membrane? How do nucleic acids get their shapes? How do animals respond to light? How do plants make food? How does the brain send messages to the body? What causes disease at the molecular level?

Most Biophysicists conduct basic or applied research in various areas, including medical science, pharmaceuticals, nutrition, biotechnology, agriculture, clinical chemistry, food science, toxicology, and environmental science. Their research projects often involve collaboration with biologists, chemists, geneticists, and other scientists and engineers.

Biophysicists focus their studies in several ways. Some choose to conduct only molecular or cellular investigations. Others specialize in the type of organ (such as brain or heart) or type of organism (such as a plant or microbe) that they study. Some Biophysicists are involved in the development of instruments and methodologies that other Biophysicists can use in their research work.

Many Biophysicists choose to specialize in one of two approaches that is used to explore the mechanisms of life. Experimental biophysicists design and run experiments and make careful observations and measurements to explain what happened in the experiments. Theoretical biophysicists, on the other hand, analyze the results of experiments to see whether or not they obey particular theories, and to explain what happened in the experiments in mathematical equations.

Biophysicists use a variety of techniques and technologies in their research. For example, they use electron microscopes, magnetic resonance spectroscopy, X-ray crystallography, and particle accelerators. It is common for Biophysicists to design and build instruments and equipment for their research, as well as to create software for data analysis, data transference, modeling, or other purposes.

Duties for Biophysicists vary, depending on their position. As research scientists, they are responsible for designing and conducting research projects. Some of their tasks include conducting experiments, gathering data, analyzing and interpreting data, writing reports, and performing administrative tasks. Those who conduct independent research are usually responsible for seeking research grants from the federal government and other sources. Most senior researchers and principal investigators also perform supervisory and management duties.

Some Biophysicists are research assistants and technicians, who provide technical support to scientists. Their duties include conducting experiments, analyzing data, writing reports, maintaining equipment and facilities, and performing routine administrative tasks.

Many research biophysicists are faculty members at colleges, universities, medical schools, and dental schools. In addition to their research duties, they are responsible for teaching undergraduate and graduate courses, such as biophysics, physics, chemistry, biology, and engineering. They also advise students, supervise student research projects, write scholarly works, perform administrative duties, and participate in community service.

Salaries

Salaries for Biophysicists vary, depending on their experience, job duties, geographical location, and other factors. The U.S. Bureau of Labor Statistics reports in its May 2006 *Occupational Employment Statistics* survey that the estimated annual salary for most Biophysicists ranged between $40,820 and $129,510.

Employment Prospects

Some employers of Biophysicists are universities, medical centers, drug companies, biotechnology firms, agricultural companies, government agencies, and research institutions.

According to the BLS, employment for Biophysicists is predicted to increase by 16 percent through 2016. Some experts say Biophysicists are in particular demand in the biotechnology, homeland security, and nanotechnology industries.

With a background in biophysics, individuals can pursue careers in various other fields.

Advancement Prospects

Management and administrative positions are available to research scientists who have managerial ambitions. Academic faculty members receive promotional rankings as assistant professors, associate professors, or full professors.

Education and Training

The minimum requirement for research assistant or technician positions is a bachelor's degree. Because few undergraduate programs in biophysics are available, many Biophysicists earn degrees in such disciplines as physics, chemistry, biology, and mathematics.

Requirements for entry-level candidates for research scientist positions vary. Some employers require only a master's degree in biophysics, physics, or another related field, while others require either a doctorate or a combined medical and doctoral (M.D./Ph.D.) degree.

In a joint M.D./Ph.D. degree program, students earn a doctorate in biophysics, physics, physiology, or another related field. This program is usually seven years long. Students complete medical courses during their first two years, followed by two to three years fulfilling their doctoral program requirements. The last two years are comprised of clinical training.

Experience, Skills, and Personality Traits

Entry-level candidates should have relevant work and research experience. This may have been gained through research projects, internships, or employment. Ph.D. candidates for research scientist positions should have postdoctoral experience.

Biophysicists need strong math, computer, critical thinking, problem-solving, communication, and writing skills. They must also have strong interpersonal and teamwork skills, as they must be able to work well with others from diverse backgrounds. Being inquisitive, determined, creative, and self-motivated are a few personality traits that successful Biophysicists have in common.

Unions and Associations

Biophysicists can join professional associations to take advantage of networking opportunities, education programs, and other professional services and resources. Some societies that specifically serve the interests of Biophysicists are the Biophysical Society, the Division of Biological Physics (American Physical Society), and the International Union for Pure and Applied Biophysics. See Appendix III for contact information.

Tips for Entry

1. If you think you would like to pursue a Ph.D., talk with your college adviser to learn what courses would best prepare you for a graduate program.
2. Are you having difficulty finding a graduate program in biophysics at a particular school? Try checking with the school's chemistry, physics, or physiology department.
3. Use the Internet to learn more about biophysics. To get a list of relevant Web sites to read, enter the keyword *biophysics* or *biological physics* in any search engine. For some links, see Appendix IV.

NUCLEAR PHYSICIST

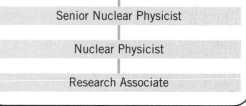

Position Description

Nuclear physics is the study of the atomic nucleus, the most basic level of matter. All matter (living organisms and nonliving things) are made up of billions of tiny atoms. At the core of each atom is the nucleus which contains most of an atom's mass. The nucleus consists of neutrons, protons, and other elementary particles which are the building blocks of all matter. Nuclear Physicists seek to understand the structure and properties of atomic nuclei as well as to learn about their reactions and interactions.

Most Nuclear Physicists engage in research and development in academic, government, and industrial settings. Those who conduct basic research extend knowledge about nuclear science. For example, they may examine the interactions of elementary particles at the subatomic level or investigate questions about the formation of stars.

Nuclear Physicists also are involved in applied research and product development, contributing to such fields as medicine, electronics, communications, energy, national security, the environment, and archaeology. They usually work as part of research teams, which are composed of various scientists, engineers, and specialists. These teams work on various projects concerned with the design and development of new or improved technologies, processes, or products, such as:

- nuclear medicine procedures that help physicians diagnose and treat patients
- research tools that help environmental scientists to monitor air quality, learn more about global warning, or search for alternative water supplies
- processes used to enhance the safety and security of nuclear power plants
- processes that are used for quality control and quality assurance testing in various industries
- nuclear techniques that help scientists determine when artifacts and artwork were made

Nuclear Physicists, like other physicists, generally specialize in one of two types of research methods. Some are experimental physicists. They design and run experiments and make careful observations and measurements to explain what happens in the experiments. Others are theoretical physicists. They use computer models to analyze the results of completed experiments to determine whether certain physical laws are being followed.

The most common tools that Nuclear Physicists use in their research are computers, radiation detectors, nuclear reactors, and particle accelerators. Nuclear Physicists sometimes build instrumentation and write computer software programs that are needed for their research.

All researchers have virtually the same duties. These include designing research projects, gathering data, conducting experiments, analyzing and interpreting research data, and preparing reports. Senior researchers and principal investigators might also perform supervisory and administrative tasks. Many Nuclear Physicists are involved in writing research proposals and seeking grants to fund their projects. In addition, Nuclear Physicists write scientific papers or make presentations at scientific conferences to share the results of their research work with colleagues.

Many Nuclear Physicists are employed as faculty members at universities and colleges. In addition to conducting research, they teach physics courses to undergraduate and graduate students. They are responsible for writing scholarly works, advising students, supervising student research projects, performing administrative tasks, and fulfilling community service obligations.

Nuclear Physicists often work long hours to complete their duties. They sometimes travel to laboratories in other localities to use special equipment for their projects.

Salaries

Salaries for Nuclear Physicists vary, depending on such factors as their education, experience, employer, and geographical location. According to the May 2006 *Occupational Employment Statistics* survey by the U.S. Bureau of Labor Statistics, the estimated annual salary for most physicists, including Nuclear Physicists, ranged between $52,070 and $143,570, and for most physics professors, between $39,580 and $120,210.

Employment Prospects

Nuclear Physicists are generally employed by academic institutions and national laboratory facilities, as well as in private industry.

Most positions become available as individuals retire or transfer to other positions. Although the competition for permanent positions is high, the need for qualified Nuclear Physicists should continue for the coming years. Some experts report a particular demand for physicists in the homeland security industry.

Some experts are concerned about a potential shortage of qualified Nuclear Physicists in the future due to the lower number of Nuclear Physicists graduating from U.S. schools over the last several years.

Advancement Prospects

Positions such as program director, laboratory director, and executive officer are available for those with management and administrative ambitions. Faculty members may advance through the academic ranks as assistant professors, associate professors, or full professors.

Education and Training

Nuclear Physicists must hold either a master's degree or Ph.D. in nuclear physics, physics, or another related field. A Ph.D. is required in order to teach in universities and four-year colleges, conduct independent research, or pursue top management positions.

Experience, Skills, and Personality Traits

Employers generally choose candidates who have previous work and research experience related to the position being sought. Entry-level applicants may have gained experience through research projects, internships, or employment. Many employers prefer to hire Ph.D. applicants who have a few years of postdoctoral experience.

Nuclear Physicists must have excellent communication, interpersonal, and teamwork skills, as they must be able to work well with others. In addition, they need strong problem-solving, analytical, and writing skills. Being creative, determined, self-motivated, and curious are a few personality traits that successful Physicists share.

Unions and Associations

Many Nuclear Physicists join societies to take advantage of networking opportunities, education programs, and other professional resources and services. The American Nuclear Society and the Division of Nuclear Physics (part of the American Physical Society) are some of these professional associations. Faculty members are eligible to join professional societies that serve their interests such as the National Association of Scholars and the American Association of University Professors. See Appendix III for contact information.

Tips for Entry

1. To prepare yourself for graduate school, obtain a summer internship with a university or government lab or get a lab assistant position with a physics professor.

2. Join a professional association, and participate in its activities to begin building a network of contacts.

3. Use the Internet to learn more about nuclear physics. Here are some Web sites that you might visit: Office of Nuclear Physics (U.S. Department of Energy), http://www.er.doe.gov/np; and Division of Nuclear Physics (The American Physical Society), http://dnp.nscl.msu.edu. For more links, see Appendix IV.

HEALTH PHYSICIST

CAREER PROFILE

Duties: Study radiation, its risks, and its problems; develop, implement, and manage radiation protection problems; conduct research; perform duties as required

Alternate Title(s): Specialist in Radiation Safety, Specialist in Radiation Protection, Radiation Safety Officer

Salary Range: $34,000 to $175,000

Employment Prospects: Good

Advancement Prospects: Good

Prerequisites:

Education or Training—A bachelor's or advanced degree required

Experience—Practical experience in health physics preferred

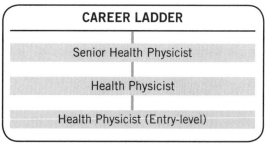

CAREER LADDER

Senior Health Physicist

Health Physicist

Health Physicist (Entry-level)

Special Skills and Personality Traits—Organizational, analytical, problem-solving, communication, and writing skills; be detail-oriented, flexible, cooperative, self-motivated, honest, trustworthy, and dependable

Position Description

Radiation is found naturally in the ground and air, as well as from space. It is also made artificially for a wide range of useful medical, commercial, industrial, and scientific applications. For example, radiation is used for X-ray and MRI imaging, producing electricity, extending the shelf life of food products, testing new drugs, detecting flaws in industrial equipment, sterilizing manufactured products, determining the age of biological specimens, locating mineral deposits, and powering spacecraft. Radiation is also used in many household and work products such as smoke detectors, lightbulbs, nonstick pans, computer disks, televisions, and photocopiers. Too much exposure to radiation, in particular ionizing radiation, can cause cancer, genetic defects, and other adverse health effects in people. Radiation can also damage the environment.

Health physics is the science—and practice—dedicated to the study of radiation and the risks and problems created by this carcinogenic substance. The field emerged during the 1940s as scientists addressed health and safety concerns during the development of the atomic bomb. Today, Health Physicists play an important role in protecting workers, the general public, and the environment from harmful exposure to radioactive materials, ionizing radiation, and nonionizing radiation sources such as lasers, magnetic fields, and ultraviolet light.

These professionals perform various functions in research laboratories, universities, medical centers, nuclear facilities, manufacturing plants, military establishments, and other organizations. Many are involved in the development, implementation, and management of radiation safety programs in the workplace. Some Health Physicists create employee-safety training programs about the principles of radiological protection, radiation detection, and radiation emergency response. Other professionals design educational programs aimed at the general public.

Health Physicists are also responsible for surveying and monitoring levels of radiation in the environment, investigating radiological health hazards and contamination incidents, and developing new methods of radioactive waste disposal. Additionally, they provide technical advice to managers, engineers, and scientists regarding the design of facilities and radiation-control programs. As part of regulatory agencies, Health Physicists enforce laws and regulations as well as establish guidelines for adequate radiation control.

Medical health physicists work in hospitals, clinics, and medical centers to make sure that employees are safely using X-ray machines and other radioactive materials. These Health Physicists are not to be confused with medical physicists who are concerned with the safe use of radiation dosages for patients.

Many Health Physicists are involved in research. Some conduct basic research to gain further understanding and knowledge about radiation and their effects on people and the environment. Many of them conduct applied or operational research in which they apply findings of basic research to solve problems in nuclear energy, medicine, occupational safety, public health, defense, the environment, and other areas. These scientists may be involved in the research and development of new or improved processes, practices, equipment, or instrumentation.

Some Health Physicists work as instructors in colleges and universities, where they teach courses in health physics and other subjects. Full-time professors are responsible for conducting scholarly research in their areas of interest and for having their research findings published as books or in professional journals.

The nature of their work requires that Health Physicists have a broad understanding of various disciplines, including physics, chemistry, biology, biophysics, human physiology, genetics, engineering, toxicology, ecology, environmental science, mathematics, and industrial hygiene. These professionals are also knowledgeable about instrumentation, as well as have familiarity with laws and regulations regarding the procurement, storage, usage, handling, disposal, and monitoring of radiation sources.

Health Physicists perform various duties, which vary according to their position. For example, they may be assigned to:

- develop safe working methods and inspection standards
- select and maintain radiation protection, laboratory, and detection equipment
- develop and implement emergency response plans and procedures
- respond to accidents or incidents involving radiation or radioactive materials
- monitor radiation exposure of workers, patients, or others in a facility
- evaluate potential radiation hazards
- establish new rules and regulations regarding the use, manufacture, and disposal of radioactive material
- develop, modify, test, or evaluate new or improved instrumentation and equipment
- make sure that federal and state radiation safety regulations are observed
- meet with officials
- supervise and direct the work of subordinate staff
- prepare reports for information and evaluation purposes
- keep accurate records of radiation hazards

Health Physicists work in offices and laboratories. Some of them occasionally travel and work in the field to perform their duties. They wear the necessary protective clothing and equipment to protect themselves from hazardous materials.

Salaries

Salaries for Health Physicists vary, depending upon their education, experience, job duties, employer, geographical location, and other factors. According to salary surveys conducted in 2006 by the Health Physics Society, the annual salaries for survey respondents ranged from $48,750 to $175,008 for certified Health Physicists, and from $33,750 to $173,750 for noncertified professionals.

Employment Prospects

Health Physicists are employed in a wide range of private industries, including agriculture, food, pharmaceuticals, medical device, aerospace, petroleum, and manufacturing industries, among others. They also work for academic institutions, research institutes, health care facilities, government agencies, and the military.

The demand for experienced Health Physicists is strong, particularly in the nuclear energy industry. According to some experts, there is currently an insufficient number of qualified Health Physicists, and that trend is expected to continue for the next several years.

Advancement Prospects

Many Health Physicists realize advancement by receiving more complex assignments, through job satisfaction, and by earning higher wages. Those with supervisory, administrative, and managerial ambitions can pursue such positions. Individuals usually need an advanced degree to obtain top management jobs. Entrepreneurial individuals can become independent consultants or business owners. Academicians are promoted in rank from instructor to assistant, associate, and full professor.

Education and Training

Minimally, individuals need a bachelor's degree to enter the health physics field. Their degree may be in health physics, physical science, engineering, health science or another related field. For many positions, employers prefer to hire candidates with a master's or doctoral degree in health physics.

Throughout their careers, Health Physicists enroll in continuing education programs to update their skills and to keep up with advancements in their fields.

Experience, Special Skills, and Personality Traits

Employers prefer to hire candidates for entry-level positions who have one or more years of practical experience in health physics. They may have gained their work experience through internships, work-study programs, employment, research assistantships, or postdoctoral training. Additionally, employers seek candidates who have experience working in their particular field.

To perform their job effectively, Health Physicists need strong organizational, analytical, problem-solving, communication, and writing skills. Being detail-oriented, flexible, cooperative, self-motivated, honest, trustworthy, and dependable are some personality traits that successful Health Physicists share.

Unions and Associations

Health Physicists can join professional associations to take advantage of networking opportunities, certification programs, training programs, and other professional services and resources. Some national societies that serve their interests include the Health Physics Society, the American Academy of Health Physics, and the American Nuclear Society. For contact information, see Appendix III.

Tips for Entry

1. You might consider getting a job as a Health Physicist technician to see if health physics is the right field for you. Some two-year colleges offer associate programs in health physics.

2. One expert in the field suggests that students take some business, management, and leadership courses to prepare for future administrative, managerial, and teaching responsibilities as a Health Physicist.

3. To enhance your employability, you might consider obtaining the professional certification granted by the American Board of Health Physics. For more information, visit its Web site at http://www.hps1.org/aahp/abhp/abhp.htm.

4. Learn more about Health Physicists on the Internet. You might start by visiting the Health Physics Society Web site at http://www.hps.org. For more links, see Appendix IV.

ASTRONOMER

CAREER PROFILE

Duties: Study the universe; design and conduct research projects; perform duties as required

Alternate Title(s): Astrophysicist

Salary Range: $45,000 to $146,000

Employment Prospects: Fair

Advancement Prospects: Good

Prerequisites:

Education or Training—A doctoral degree in astronomy or a related field

Experience—Postdoctoral experience in specialty

Special Skills and Personality Traits—Computer, programming, math, statistics, analytical, problem-

CAREER LADDER

Senior Astronomer

Astronomer

Research Associate

solving, observation, writing, communication, and interpersonal skills; be patient, precise, determined, curious, self-motivated, and imaginative

Position Description

Astronomy is the scientific study of the solar system and the universe. It is an ancient science, but over the years this discipline has evolved from solely an observation science to a discipline that uses the principles and techniques of physics and mathematics to understand the phenomena of the universe. Today, astronomy is considered to be a subdiscipline of physics, and the terms astronomy and astrophysics are used interchangeably.

Astronomers (or astrophysicists) seek to understand the physical nature, origin, and development of stars, planets, and other celestial bodies as well as of galaxies and the universe. Their studies involve such questions as: How are stars born? What happens when stars die? Where do comets come from? What is the surface like on other planets in the solar system? Does life exist elsewhere in the universe?

Professional Astronomers work in offices, laboratories, and observatories, mostly in academic and government settings. Academic Astronomers normally research topics within their own interests, while most nonacademic Astronomers conduct research in areas that fulfill their employers' specific goals and missions.

Astronomers gather data about their subject matter by making direct observations of the skies or from information gathered by colleagues, amateur astronomers, and other scientists. They also use supercomputers and high-powered telescopes, X-ray spectrometers, radar, magnetometers, and other instrumentation to gather data about celestial bodies and phenomena. Furthermore, Astronomers obtain data from observa-

tions made by satellites and other spacecraft traveling through the solar system.

Astronomers are often characterized by their method of study, either theoretical or observational. Theoretical Astronomers conduct much of their research on computers, developing theories that they base on observations made mostly by other Astronomers. Theoretical scientists usually create computer models which they use to analyze data and interpret observations. Observational Astronomers, or observers, analyze data based on the observations that they gather from telescopes as well as from observations gathered by spacecraft. Observers usually spend several days or weeks at a time making observations. This sometimes involves traveling to research facilities in remote areas, and living and working there for the duration of their observing run.

Most Astronomers have teaching, administrative, or other responsibilities in addition to their research work. Many Astronomers are employed as professors in colleges and universities. Their duties include teaching astronomy courses to undergraduate and graduate students. (Some professors also teach physics courses.) They also advise students, supervise student research projects, write scholarly works, perform administrative tasks, and fulfill community service duties.

Some Astronomers are employed by astronomy observatories and laboratories. They may assist in or be in charge of managing and running research facilities. Their responsibilities may include any of the following: maintaining facilities, designing instrumentation, and developing education programs. Some Astronomers also give presentations to schools, community organizations, and the general public.

All Astronomers are responsible for keeping up with the technology and developments in their specialties as well as in astronomy in general. Most Astronomers participate in scientific conferences to network with colleagues and to share research information. In addition, Astronomers write scientific papers about their research work and submit the papers to scientific journals for publication.

Salaries

Salaries for Astronomers vary, depending on such factors as their experience, employer, and geographical location. According to the May 2006 *Occupational Employment Statistics* by the U.S. Bureau of Labor Statistics, the estimated annual salary for most Astronomers ranged between $44,590 and $145,600.

Employment Prospects

About 7,000 professional Astronomers are employed in North America, according to the American Astronomical Society. Astronomers work for academic institutions, national observatories, federally funded research centers, museums, and planetariums. They are also employed by the aerospace, satellite communications, and other private industries. Job turnover is low, and competition for available positions is high.

Opportunities are more favorable for postdoctoral positions than for permanent ones. In general, new doctoral graduates work several years in postdoctoral positions before obtaining a full-time job.

With a degree in astronomy, individuals can follow any number of career paths. For example, they can become telescope operators, observing assistants, optical engineers, high school science teachers, science journalists, or computer scientists.

Advancement Prospects

Astronomers can pursue management and administrative positions by becoming a project leader, program manager, lab director, or observatory director. As faculty members, Astronomers receive promotional rankings as assistant professors, associate professors, or full professors.

Education and Training

A doctorate in astronomy, astrophysics, or physics is the minimum educational requirement to become an Astronomer. Individuals must first earn a bachelor's degree in physics, astronomy, or another field. They then complete a master's program followed by a doctoral program. As part of their doctoral program, students conduct original research projects.

Experience, Skills, and Personality Traits

Employers generally choose candidates who have related work and research experience. Entry-level applicants may have gained relevant experience through research projects, internships, postdoctoral training, or employment. It is common for Astronomers to hold several postdoctoral positions before obtaining a permanent position.

Astronomers must be highly skilled in computers, programming, math, and statistics. They also need excellent analytical, problem-solving, observation, writing, communication, and interpersonal skills. Being patient, precise, determined, curious, self-motivated, and imaginative are a few personality traits that successful Astronomers have in common.

Unions and Associations

Many Astronomers join professional associations to take advantage of networking opportunities, education programs, and other professional resources and services. Some national societies that serve their interests include the American Astronomical Society, the American Geographical Union, and the American Institute of Physics. See Appendix III for contact information.

Tips for Entry

1. Join an amateur astronomy group, such as the American Association of Variable Star Observers, to learn more about stars and the universe.
2. Be sure you have a strong foundation in physics, mathematics, and computer science before enrolling in a graduate program.
3. While an undergraduate, get as much experience as you can. You might work as a research assistant for an astronomy professor, or you might volunteer, intern, or work at an astronomy observatory or astronomy laboratory.
4. Use the Internet to learn more about Astronomers. One Web site you might visit is for the American Astronomical Society at http://www.aas.org. For more links, see Appendix IV.

SPACE PHYSICIST

CAREER PROFILE

Duties: Study the physical properties of phenomena in space; design and conduct research projects; perform duties as required

Alternate Title(s): Astrophysicist; Space Plasma Physicist, or other title that reflects a specialty

Salary Range: $37,000 to $122,000

Employment Prospects: Fair

Advancement Prospects: Good

Prerequisites:

    Education or Training—A doctoral degree in space physics or related field

    Experience—Work and research experience related to the position one is applying for

CAREER LADDER

Senior Space Physicist

Space Physicist

Research Associate

Special Skills and Personality Traits—Writing, communication, analytical, problem-solving, interpersonal, and teamwork skills; enthusiastic; honest; curious; persistent; imaginative; creative

Position Description

Space Physicists engage in the study of the physical properties and phenomena—such as plasma, magnetic fields, and solar wind—that occur naturally in space, beyond the Earth's atmosphere. They are also concerned with examining the relationship between the Sun and the Earth, as well as the Sun's connection with the other planets and celestial bodies in the solar system. The results of their studies have been used in such practical applications as satellites that help in weather forecasting, navigation, and transmission of communications around the world.

Space physics is a broad, and evolving, discipline with a wide range of subfields. Space Physicists typically specialize in one or more of these throughout their career. Some of these specialties are:

- solar physics—the study of the Sun's composition and properties, its activities (such as sun spots and sun flares), and its outer atmosphere (also known as the corona)
- the planetary magnetospheres, which are the magnetic fields that surround magnetic planets (such as the Earth) and protects them from solar activities
- the physics of solar wind, which is composed of streams of particles coming from the Sun and rushing through interplanetary space at very supersonic speeds
- the effect of solar wind, sun spots, solar flares, and other activities upon the celestial bodies in the solar system; for example, the phenomena known as the

aurora borealis (northern lights) on the Earth is the interaction of the solar wind with particles in the Earth's atmosphere

Many Space Physicists are involved in basic research. They seek to expand knowledge about the phenomena and processes that occur in space. Many other Space Physicists are involved in applied research. They apply the findings of basic research to the search for solutions to technological problems caused by solar phenomena. For example, solar activities have caused the destruction of satellites and have interfered with the transmission of communication signals.

Space Physicists obtain data through a variety of tools and instruments that are able to monitor and measure details of the Sun, interplanetary matter, planetary magnetospheres, and so on. Along with supercomputers, they use various specialized telescopes, radar, magnetometers, special cameras, and other instrumentation based in observatories throughout the world. Data is also gathered by instrumentation on board satellites and other spacecraft.

To help them analyze and interpret data, Space Physicists create computer models, which are scientific models based on sets of mathematical equations. Scientists use these models to help them develop theories about what is happening in space. For example, Space Physicists have developed computer models that simulate the theoretical flow of plasma around Mars. In addition, many Space Physicists develop instrumentation and spacecraft that are needed for their research.

Space Physicists are responsible for designing and conducting research projects. Independent researchers choose topics that reflect their interests, while others conduct studies that fulfill their employers' goals and missions. Space Physicists might work on more than one research project at a time, and sometimes collaborate with others on research projects.

Most space physics projects are funded by federal grants or other sources. Thus, many Space Physicists are involved in writing grant proposals and seeking research grants from the federal government and other sources.

Space Physicists typically share information about their research by writing articles (or scientific papers) which they submit to scientific journals for publication. Some of them also make presentations at scientific conferences that are sponsored by professional associations.

Some Space Physicists are employed as professors at colleges and universities. They teach courses in solar physics, as well as in astronomy or physics. Their duties include conducting independent research, preparing courses, teaching classes, advising students, supervising student research projects, writing scholarly works, performing administrative duties, and participating in community service.

Salaries

Salaries for Space Physicists vary, depending on such factors as their experience, employer, and geographical location. According to the May 2006 *Occupational Employment Statistics* survey by the U.S. Bureau of Labor Statistics, the estimated annual salary for most space sciences professors ranged between \$37,330 and \$121,500.

Employment Prospects

Universities, national laboratories, and aerospace companies are major employers of Space Physicists.

Some experts in the field describe the job market for permanent research positions as being tight, but opportunities are reasonably good for postdoctoral positions. Most job opportunities are created to replace Space Physicists who retire or transfer to other positions.

Advancement Prospects

Space Physicists can advance to supervisory, administrative, and executive-level management positions. Professors can rise through the ranks as assistant professors, associate professors, and full professors.

Education and Training

To conduct independent research, teach in universities and colleges, and hold top management positions, a doctorate is required.

Few institutions currently offer a Ph.D. program in space physics. Many Space Physicists have earned their degrees in astrophysics, astronomy, or physics, with an emphasis in space physics.

Experience, Skills, and Personality Traits

Employers generally choose candidates who have work and research experience related to the position they are applying for. Experience may have been gained through research projects, internships, fellowships, employment, or postdoctoral training.

Space Physicists should have writing, communication, analytical, problem-solving, interpersonal, and teamwork skills. Being enthusiastic, honest, curious, persistent, imaginative, and creative are some personal personality traits that successful Space Physicists share.

Unions and Associations

The American Astronomical Society, the Physics and Aeronomy Section of AGU (American Geophysical Union), and the International Association of Geomagnetism and Aeronomy are some societies that serve the interests of Space Physicists. Academicians are eligible to join academic societies such as the National Association of Scholars. By joining a society, individuals can take advantage of networking opportunities, job listings, and other professional services and resources. (For contact information for the above groups, see Appendix III.)

Tips for Entry

1. The U.S. National Aeronautics Space Administration (NASA) offers programs that allow students to participate in space research. For information, visit NASA's student opportunities Web page at http://www.nasajobs.nasa.gov/studentopps/employment.

2. Many physics and astronomy departments provide employment information at their Web sites.

3. Learn more about space physics on the Internet. For pertinent Web sites to read, enter the keyword *space physics* or *space physicists* into a search engine. For some links, see Appendix IV.

EARTH SCIENCES
(OR GEOSCIENCES)

GEOLOGIST

Duties: Study the structure, composition, processes, and history of the Earth; design and conduct research projects; perform duties as required

Alternate Title(s): Geoscientist; Hydrologist, Engineering Geologist, Environmental Geologist, or other title that reflects a specialty

Salary Range: $37,000 to $136,000

Employment Prospects: Good

Advancement Prospects: Good

Prerequisites:

Education or Training—An advanced degree usually required for research scientist positions

Experience—Work and research experience related to the position for which one is applying

Special Skills and Personality Traits—Computer, observation, analytical, problem-solving, com-

munication, writing, presentation, teamwork, and interpersonal skills; be flexible, patient, inquisitive, self-motivated, honest, and cooperative

Special Requirements—State licensure as registered geologist (R.G.) may be required

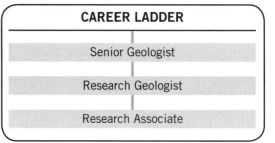

CAREER LADDER

Senior Geologist

Research Geologist

Research Associate

Position Description

Geology is an earth science (or geoscience). It deals with the study of the structure, composition, processes, and history of the Earth.

Geologists estimate that the Earth was formed several billion years ago. They seek to understand how it came into being and how it took shape as well as how it has changed and continues to change today. Geologists examine the materials—rocks, minerals, and soils—that make up the Earth as well as the landforms, such as mountains, volcanoes, valleys, plains, and rivers, on the Earth's surface. Geologists also explore the layers of rock in the Earth's crust and the fossils found there to get an idea on how the Earth has developed over thousands, millions, and billions of years. Further, Geologists study the various processes (such as weather, erosion, earthquakes, and tectonics) that shape the Earth and investigate how human activities (such as dredging, mining, and development) affect and change the Earth.

Geologists are also involved in various activities that benefit society. For example, Geologists search for new sources of water, energy, and minerals; they help develop community emergency plans for natural hazards (such as earthquakes, floods, and landslides); and they investigate proposed sites for waste treatment plants, dams, freeways, bridges, harbors, and other

structures to make sure they are geologically safe and sound. In addition, Geologists apply their expertise to helping solve problems and issues about the environment, including air quality, water pollution, energy conservation, global warming, endangered species, brownfields, and land use.

Geologists are involved in research and development in academic, government, industrial, and nongovernmental settings. Some conduct basic research to further knowledge and understanding about the different areas of geology. Some engage in applied research in which they use the findings of basic research to design technologies and processes to solve problems in their particular fields. Other Geologists participate in product development for industrial employers. These geoscientists are part of research teams that develop new or improved consumer products and services.

Geologists typically focus their studies in one of the many subdisciplines that make up geology. Some of these specialties are:

- planetary geology (or astrogeology), the study of the surface of the planets, moons, asteroids, and other celestial bodies
- petrology, the study of igneous (volcanic), metamorphic, and sedimentary rocks

- geomorphology, the study of the Earth's surface, the origins of its landforms, and the processes that shape and change landforms
- hydrology, the study of the movement and distribution of water on the Earth's surface as well as beneath it
- oceanography, the investigation of the oceans
- glacial geology, the study of the characteristics and movements of glaciers and how they change the Earth's surface
- geochemistry, the study of the chemical composition of the Earth
- geophysics—the study of the Earth's crust and interior, using the principles of mathematics and physics
- seismology, the study of earthquakes
- structural geology, the study of how mountains and other features inside the Earth's crusts are formed
- volcanology, the study of volcanoes
- sedimentology, the study of sedimentary rocks and how they are formed and deposited
- stratigraphy, the study of the origin, composition, sequence, and relationship of the layers of rock in the Earth's crust
- geochronology, the study of geological time
- paleontology, the study of animal and plant fossils to understand the evolution of species as well as the geological history of the Earth
- quaternary geology, the study of geological processes that have occurred over the last two million years

Many Geologists specialize in a particular area in which they apply their geological expertise. Petroleum geologists are involved in the exploration for oil and natural gas. Economic geologists study the development of minerals, coal, and other geological materials for profitable uses. Environmental geologists are concerned with solving human-made problems (such as pollution, waste management, and urban development) and natural hazards (such as flooding, landslides, and coastal erosions). Engineering geologists provide geological expertise on the design, construction, operation, and maintenance of such structures as dams, bridges, freeways, and skyscrapers.

Geologists are responsible for designing and conducting research projects. In academic settings, Geologists choose research topics that reflect their personal interests while those working in other settings usually conduct research that is determined by their employers' missions. Many Geologists collaborate on projects with geologists from other specialties.

Geologists spend much of their time working in offices and laboratories. They complete such tasks as designing experiments, conducting library research, developing theoretical models, analyzing and interpreting data, writing reports, and performing administrative tasks. Geologists also prepare scientific papers or presentations about their research findings to share with their colleagues. Some Geologists are responsible for obtaining grants to fund their research projects, which involves preparing proposals and budgets that meet the specifications of different funding sources.

Many Geologists spend some time conducting research in the field, where they perform such tasks as taking measurements, examining rocks, collecting samples, conducting geological surveys, making field maps, or searching for sites that may potentially hold water, fossils, oil, or mineral deposits. Field research is often conducted in remote areas that can only be reached by walking long distances or by using four-wheel drive vehicles or helicopters. Some conduct research on vessels that sail along coastlines or out at sea. It is not uncommon for Geologists to live and work at field sites for several weeks or months.

Along with their research duties, most Geologists have other major responsibilities. Many teach undergraduate or graduate courses in colleges and universities, while others develop educational programs and materials for the general public. Some Geologists provide consultation services to government agencies, policy makers, industry, and the general public. Others are responsible for the management and administration of laboratories, academic departments, research institutes, and companies.

Some Geologists provide technical support to the research scientists. These Geologists are the research assistants and technicians. Their duties vary, depending on their experience. Some general tasks include collecting data, maintaining computer databases, running experiments, assisting with fieldwork, writing reports, and maintaining equipment and facilities.

Salaries

Salaries for Geologists vary, depending on such factors as their education, experience, employer, position, and geographical location. According to the May 2006 *Occupational Employment Statistics* survey by the U.S. Bureau of Labor Statistics (BLS), the estimated annual salary for most geoscientists ranged between $39,740 and $135,950, and for most earth science professors, between $37,330 and $121,500.

Employment Prospects

Major employers of Geologists are the oil and mining industries; geological and environmental consulting firms; colleges and universities; and local, state, and federal government agencies. Some federal agencies that hire Geologists include the U.S. Geological Survey, the U.S. Department of Agriculture Forest Service, the National Oceanic and Atmospheric Administration, the National Aeronautics and Space Administration, the U.S. Army Corps of Engineers, and the U.S. Department of Energy.

The BLS reports that job growth for geoscientists is predicted to increase by 22 percent through 2016. Some experts say that Geoscientists should find favorable opportunities within the management, scientific, and technical consulting services industries. There is a continued demand for qualified Geologists to provide technical and management assistance to companies and other organizations in such areas as complying with environmental laws and regulations, addressing environmental issues, and assessing construction sites for potential geological hazards.

In general, the rise or fall of job opportunities is dependent on such factors as the health of the economy, changes in government policies about the environment or energy, and the availability of federal grants for science research.

With a background in geology, individuals can pursue other career paths. They might become high school science teachers, community college geoscience instructors, science journalists, science librarians, environmental lawyers, land surveyors, cartographers, urban planners, civil engineers, park rangers, conservation scientists, or environmental engineers.

Advancement Prospects

In nonacademic settings, Geologists may be promoted to administrative and management positions such as project leader, program manager, and executive-level administrator. Professors advance in rank (assistant, associate, and full professor). They may also be promoted to department chairs, academic deans, or school administration positions.

Many Geologists measure their success by earning higher salaries, by being able to conduct independent research projects, and through receiving professional recognition.

Education and Training

The minimum educational requirement for most entry-level research positions is a master's degree in geology or another geoscience. A doctorate is required for Geologists to teach in academic institutions, conduct independent research, or obtain high-level research opportunities, and to advance to top management positions.

Many employers provide entry-level employees with training programs, which may include both on-the-job training and formal classroom instruction.

Special Requirements

Geologists who provide services that involve public health, safety, and welfare may be required to be licensed as registered geologists (R.G.) in the states where they practice.

Licensure requirements vary from state to state. For information, contact the board of geology in the state where you wish to practice. You can also obtain general licensure information from the National Association of State Boards of Geology Web site, http://www.asbog.org.

Experience, Skills, and Personality Traits

Employers typically choose candidates who have work and research experience related to the position for which they are applying. Entry-level scientists may have obtained experience through employment, internships, research projects, or postdoctoral training. Many employers prefer that candidates have field experience. In addition, job candidates should have a basic understanding of the industry, business, or mission in which prospective employers are involved.

Geologists need strong computer skills, and should have some experience with computer modeling, data analysis and integration, geographic information systems (GIS), global positioning system (GPS), digital mapping, and remote sensing. In addition, Geologists need excellent observation, analytical, and problem-solving skills as well as communication, writing, and presentation skills. They must also have effective teamwork and interpersonal skills, as they must be able to work with people of diverse backgrounds and technical abilities.

Some personality traits that successful Geologists have in common are being flexible, patient, inquisitive, self-motivated, honest, and cooperative.

Unions and Associations

Most Geologists join professional associations to take advantage of education programs, networking opportunities, and other professional resources and services. The American Geological Institute, the Geological Society of America, the Association for Women Geoscientists, the American Institute of Professional Geologists, and the National Association of Black Geologists and Geophysicists are a few examples of these organizations. Many Geologists also join societies that serve specific interests, such as the American Association of Petroleum Geologists, the Seismological Society of America, the Association of Engineering Geologists, or the Society of Vertebrate Paleontology. See Appendix III for contact information.

Tips for Entry

1. While you are a high school student, seek opportunities to go on geological field trips to learn how professionals make observations and describe geological features and processes. Talk to your parents, science teachers, or school librarians for suggestions. Another option is to contact science museums or geology instructors at nearby colleges.

2. The U.S. Geological Survey offers student employment programs for college students in geology, hydrology, administration, and other fields. For more information visit its Web page at http://www.usgs.gov/ohr/student.

3. Some sources for job listings include professors, college career centers, professional associations, professional journals, and state employment offices. Also check for job announcements at Web sites of employers for whom you are interested in working.

4. Some Geologists obtain the registered geology license on a voluntary basis to enhance their employability.

5. You can learn more about geology on the Internet. Two Web sites you might visit are American Geological Institute, http://www.agiweb.org; and U.S. Geological Survey, http://www.usgs.org. For more links, see Appendix IV.

OCEANOGRAPHER

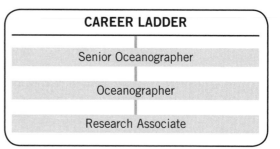

Position Description

Oceanography is the scientific study of the oceans, which cover about 70 percent of the Earth's surface. This discipline integrates the knowledge and applications of geology, geophysics, geography, physics, chemistry, biology, mathematics, and engineering.

Oceanographers seek to understand everything about the ocean and coastal environments. They study the properties of the ocean waters (such as tides, currents, and salt content), the structure and form of the oceans, the composition of sediments on the ocean floors, the various species of sea plants and animals, and the geological history of the oceans. In addition, they seek solutions to such diverse problems as coastal pollution, global warming, the decline of the world's fisheries, the search for oil deposits under the ocean floor, and the effects of human development along coastlines.

Oceanographers usually specialize in one of the discipline's major subfields—biological oceanography, chemical oceanography, physical oceanography, geological oceanography, or ocean engineering. Oceanographers from these diverse disciplines often collaborate on research projects to gain an integrated understanding of the topics or problems they are investigating.

Biological oceanographers are involved in learning about the species of sea plants and animals. They study the various aspects of biology in regards to sea life, including their anatomy, physiology, genetics, evolu-

tion, taxonomy, and distribution. These Oceanographers are also known as marine biologists or fisheries scientists.

Chemical oceanographers study the chemical composition and properties of the ocean waters. They investigate the various chemical reactions that occur in the ocean and on the sea floor, including interactions with solar energy, atmospheric compounds, sea life, and natural substances (such as minerals and petroleum). These Oceanographers are also known as marine chemists or marine geochemists.

Physical oceanographers seek to understand how the oceans work. They study the physical properties of ocean water and the relationship of the ocean to the atmosphere which influences weather and climates. They also examine the interaction that the ocean has with coastlines and underwater formations as well as with solar, sound, wind, and other forms of energy.

Geological oceanographers, or marine geologists, are involved in understanding the Earth's history. Their focus is studying the physical and chemical properties of rock and sediments found at the coastlines and on the ocean floors. Ocean engineers design, build, and maintain the instruments and equipment that scientists need to conduct their field research in, on, and under the ocean waters.

Oceanographers conduct basic and applied research while working in academic, government, industry, nonprofit, and nongovernmental settings. Most Oceanographers conduct field trips along coastlines, in estuaries, or at sea to make observations and collect samples. Their research expeditions sometimes require living and working on ships for several weeks or months. Back at their offices and laboratories, they analyze and interpret data, conduct experiments, develop theoretical models, do library research, write reports, and perform other tasks.

Oceanographers' duties vary, depending on their specialty and position. In general, research assistants and laboratory technicians provide scientists with technical support. Their tasks may include setting up experiments in the laboratories, collecting samples in the field, analyzing data, repairing instruments, maintaining labs, and completing routine administrative tasks.

Research scientists are responsible for designing and managing research projects. Many of them have other major responsibilities, such as overseeing the daily operations of programs and laboratories, providing consulting services to policy makers, or developing educational materials for the public.

Many Oceanographers hold permanent teaching positions at universities and colleges. In addition to conducting independent research projects, they prepare course syllabuses and lessons, deliver class lectures, advise students about their course work, and supervise student research projects. Furthermore, they are required to publish scholarly works, perform administrative duties, and participate in community services.

Many Oceanographers are responsible for seeking out grants from the federal government and other sources to fund their research projects. This involves writing comprehensive proposals that describe the goals, objectives, methodologies, budget, and other aspects of their projects.

All Oceanographers keep up with developments in their fields by networking with colleagues, attending professional meetings, and reading professional journals. Most research scientists share information about their research work by writing scientific papers for publication in scientific journals or making presentations at scientific meetings that are sponsored by professional associations.

Salaries

Salaries for Oceanographers vary, depending on factors such as their education, experience, employer, and job duties. According to the May 2006 *Occupational Employment Statistics* survey by the U.S. Bureau of Labor Statistics, the estimated annual salary for most geoscientists (including Oceanographers) ranged between $39,740 and $135,950.

Employment Prospects

Oceanography is a young discipline with new subfields continually emerging. For example, the fields of marine biotechnology and marine molecular biology have emerged in recent years. Some Oceanographers predict the job market to grow in areas that are related to aquaculture, environmental protection, and deep sea geology and exploration.

With a background in oceanography, individuals can pursue careers in other areas such as environmental science, communications, museum science, archeology, recreation and tourism, marine electronics, engineering, and water quality management.

Advancement Prospects

Research scientists can advance to administrative or management positions by becoming project leaders, program managers, laboratory directors, or executive officers. Technicians and research assistants can advance to managerial positions such as laboratory manager or to other nonlaboratory administrative positions. As professors, Oceanographers can advance through the ranks as assistant professors, associate professors, and full professors.

Education and Training

The minimum requirement for research assistant and technician positions is a bachelor's degree in oceanography, earth science, biology, mathematics, or other related field. Some employers prefer that candidates hold a master's degree.

Research scientists must have either a master's degree or a Ph.D. A Ph.D. is required in order to teach in universities and four-year colleges, to conduct independent research, or to pursue top management positions.

Experience, Skills, and Personality Traits

Employers generally choose candidates who have related work and research experience, which may have been gained through research projects, internships, fellowships, or employment. Ph.D. applicants for research scientist positions are usually expected to have several years of related postdoctoral experience.

Oceanographers need strong math and computer skills as well as excellent writing and communication skills. In order to work well with others, they must possess effective interpersonal and teamwork skills.

Being curious, creative, innovative, patient, enthusiastic, and flexible are a few personality traits that successful Oceanographers have in common. They are also physically fit and have the stamina and strength to work long periods of time on research cruises.

Unions and Associations

Most Oceanographers join professional associations to take advantage of networking opportunities, current research information, education programs, and other professional services and resources. Many join societies such as the Oceanography Society, the American Geophysical Union, and the Association for Women Geoscientists. Oceanographers also join societies that serve their particular interests, such as the American Society of Limnology and Oceanography, the Marine Technology Society, or the Oceanic Engineering Society. For contact information see Appendix III.

Tips for Entry

1. While you are an undergraduate student (or a high school student), take the opportunity to get practical experience. You might work as a research assistant, intern, or volunteer for a professor, science museum, government lab, research institute, or private company.

2. Join a campus or local branch of a professional society and participate in its activities. If possible, attend conferences to learn more about the field as well as to network with scientists and others.

3. Some experts say that graduates with experience in more than one field of science have better chances of employability, as do those with backgrounds in computer programming or mathematical modeling.

4. Other desirable skills that employers look for are sailing, mechanical (the ability to fix equipment), and scuba-diving skills.

5. Learn more about oceanography on the Internet. To get a list of relevant Web sites, enter the keyword *oceanography* or *oceanographers* into a search engine. For some links, See Appendix IV.

HYDROLOGIST

CAREER PROFILE

Duties: Study the water cycle and water-related issues; design and conduct research projects; may be involved in locating and managing water resources; perform duties as required

Alternate Title(s): Hydrogeologist, Civil Engineer, or other title that reflect a specific specialty or occupation

Salary Range: $42,000 to $98,000

Employment Prospects: Good

Advancement Prospects: Good

Prerequisites:

Education or Training—A bachelor's or advanced degree in hydrology or related field

Experience—Fieldwork experience and familiarity with employer's business or industry are desirable

Special Skills and Personality Traits—Computer, writing, communication, interpersonal, and team-

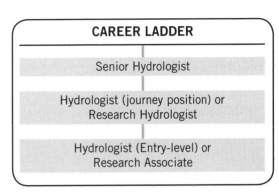

CAREER LADDER

Senior Hydrologist

Hydrologist (journey position) or Research Hydrologist

Hydrologist (Entry-level) or Research Associate

work skills; be self-motivated, imaginative, dedicated, inquisitive, logical, and open-minded

Special Requirements—Licensure as Hydrologist required in Wisconsin; geologists and engineers with hydrologist duties may be required to have appropriate state licensure

Position Description

Hydrologists study the water cycle, or hydrologic cycle, which is nature's system of circulating water from the atmosphere to the surface of the Earth and back. The hydrologic cycle consists of several stages and has no beginning or end. The cycle includes the storage and movement of water in its gaseous state in the atmosphere; its change from a gas to precipitation (rain, snow, or ice) which falls to the Earth; the storage of water on the surface as well as beneath it; the various stages in which water moves upon land as it travels toward the seas; and the processes in which water changes into a gas and evaporates into the atmosphere.

Hydrologists are interested in understanding the water cycle on a regional and global basis. They examine the physical and chemical properties of water; and seek measurable information and knowledge about the occurrence and distribution of water at each phase of the water cycle.

Hydrologists also assist in the search and management of fresh water supplies for public, industrial, agricultural, and other uses. In addition, they address a wide range of such water-related issues and problems as the availability of fresh water sources; water allocation; water quality; water pollution; groundwater contamina-

tion; flood control; water conservation; and environmental protection.

Many Hydrologists specialize in a particular area of the hydrologic cycle, and usually hold other job titles. For example, hydrogeologists specialize in the study of groundwater; glaciologists examine glaciers; limnologists study lakes; geochemists investigate the quality of groundwater; and hydrometeorologists investigate water in the atmosphere.

Hydrologists work in academic, government, industry, nonprofit, and nongovernmental settings. Many of them design and conduct basic research projects to further knowledge about the hydrologic cycle. Others are involved in applying findings of basic research to develop useful products or to solve water-related problems. For example, some research scientists are involved in developing tools and systems for making predictions about water availability, flooding, effects of water pollution, or other phenomena. Hydrologists often collaborate on research projects with scientists from other disciplines (such as meteorology, agriculture, and forestry).

Many other Hydrologists work in applied areas, performing roles as researchers, educators, consultants, technicians, engineers, and administrators. They usually work directly with the public, engineers, other scientists, public officials, policy makers, and others. Their duties might include

- designing and conducting technical investigations about specific hydrologic problems
- performing assessments or appraisals on proposed development or construction of bridges, dams, waste treatment centers, or other structures
- providing hydrologic information and technical support to engineers, other scientists, policy makers, and the general public
- monitoring surface and underground water supplies to ensure that they are in compliance with health standards and environmental laws and regulations
- advising government officials and policy makers about hydrologic issues
- educating the public about water conservation and preservation of water resources
- creating and producing maps, graphs, interpretive reports, computer models, and other products that explain hydrologic information
- managing hydrologic projects or water resource programs

Some Hydrologists are professional engineers (P.E.), registered geologists (R.G.), or engineering hydrologists. They are involved in the planning, designing, control, use, and management of water resources.

Many Hydrologists are adjunct instructors or full-time professors at colleges and universities. They teach hydrology courses to undergraduate and graduate students. Some also teach courses in geology, engineering, geography, or other disciplines. Along with conducting research and teaching courses, professors advise students, supervise student research projects, perform administrative tasks, write scholarly works, and participate in community service.

Most Hydrologists spend some time in the field, hence they need to be physically fit and have stamina. Their fieldwork might involve such tasks as collecting water samples, measuring rainfall, evaluating groundwater resources, and assessing environmental factors that affect the hydrologic cycle in specific locations. Back in their offices and labs, Hydrologists design and conduct experiments or develop computer models to test their theories. They also conduct library research, analyze and interpret data, write technical reports, complete administrative tasks, and so on. Those who conduct independent research are responsible for writing grant proposals and applying for scientific research grants to fund new or ongoing projects.

Salaries

Salaries for Hydrologists vary, depending on such factors as their education, experience, position, employer, and geographical location. According to the May 2006 *Occupational Employment Statistics* survey by the U.S. Bureau of Labor Statistics (BLS), the estimated annual salary for most Hydrologists ranged between $42,080 and $98,320.

Employment Prospects

Hydrologists are employed by federal government agencies, such as the U.S. Geological Survey and the U.S. Bureau of Land Management, as well as by state departments of natural resources and other state government agencies. They are also hired by nonprofit groups, nongovernmental organizations, academic institutions, and research institutes. In addition, many Hydrologists find employment with engineering services and technical consulting services, such as environmental consulting firms. Some Hydrologists are self-employed consultants.

Employment of Hydrologists is predicted to increase by 24 percent through 2016, according to the BLS. In addition, opportunities will become available as Hydrologists retire, are promoted, or transfer to other jobs.

Some experts say that the demand for Hydrologists should be strongest with consulting firms that help organizations to comply with environmental laws and regulations. In addition, Hydrologists will be needed to address such hydrologic issues as flood control, water pollution, water conservation, waste disposal, and groundwater contamination.

Advancement Prospects

Hydrologists advance in their careers in various ways, depending on their career path, ambitions, and interests. Those interested in management and administrative work can find opportunities in any work setting. Hydrologists with entrepreneurial ambitions can become independent consultants or owners of consulting firms.

Hydrologists with a bachelor's degree in engineering or geology might also pursue advancement by becoming licensed as a professional engineer (P.E.) or registered geologist (R.G.). With licensure, a hydrologist has better chances of commanding higher salaries and receiving more complex assignments.

Education and Training

To enter this field, Hydrologists need at least a bachelor's degree in hydrology, geology, engineering, water resource management, or another related discipline. Many employers prefer to hire candidates with a master's degree. A Ph.D. is normally required to conduct independent research, teach in four-year colleges and universities, and to hold top management positions.

Special Requirements

As of June 2007, Wisconsin is the only state known to require Hydrologists to be licensed if they provide services that involve public health, safety, and welfare.

Geologists and engineers who perform hydrology duties may be required to be licensed as a registered geologist (R.G.) or professional engineer (P.E.) in the states where they practice. Individuals take the examination for licensure after they have met the required number of years of work experience as set by their state.

Experience, Skills, and Personality Traits

Employers generally choose candidates for entry-level positions who have related work and research experience, which may have been gained through research projects, internships, employment, or postdoctoral training. Many employers look for applicants who have fieldwork experience. Employers typically prefer candidates who are familiar with the business or industry in which they are employed.

Hydrologists need strong computer, writing, and communication skills for their jobs. In addition, they should have excellent interpersonal and teamwork skills as they usually work with others on team projects. Those planning to be involved in fieldwork must be in good health and have physical stamina. Some personality traits that successful Hydrologists share are being self-motivated, imaginative, dedicated, inquisitive, logical, and open-minded.

Unions and Associations

Many Hydrologists join professional associations to take advantage of professional resources and services, such as networking opportunities and education programs. The American Institute of Hydrology, the American Water Resources Association, the National Groundwater Association, the American Institute of Professional Geologists, and the American Society of Civil Engineers are some organizations that Hydrologists are eligible to join. See Appendix III for contact information.

Tips for Entry

1. To learn more about the variety of career paths available in this field, talk to various Hydrologists in different settings.
2. Obtaining skills in any of the following areas can enhance your employability: computer programming, computer modeling, remote, sensing, and geographic information systems (GIS).
3. Many Hydrologists voluntarily obtain professional certification from the American Institute of Hydrology to establish their professional credibility, as well as to enhance their employability.
4. Use the Internet to learn more about hydrology. Some Web sites you might visit are the Hydrology Web, http://hydrologyweb.pnl.gov; and Water Resources of the United States (U.S. Geological Survey), http://water.usgs.gov. For more links, see Appendix IV.

METEOROLOGIST

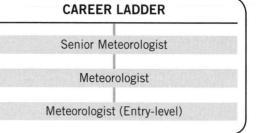
Position Description

Meteorology is the study of the Earth's atmosphere as well as the atmospheric conditions (such as wind, temperature, sunlight, and precipitation) that are continually changing to produce weather on the Earth. Meteorology also deals with weather forecasting—making predictions about the weather—by applying physical and mathematical principles to atmospheric conditions.

Meteorologists are also known as atmospheric scientists. They typically specialize in one of the different subfields of meteorology. For example:

- Physical meteorologists investigate electrical and chemical properties of the atmosphere.
- Synoptic meteorologists study weather forecasting.
- Dynamic meteorologists examine the movements of weather systems and what controls them.
- Climatologists study long-term weather patterns.
- Instrumentation specialists are concerned with designing instruments and weather information systems for measuring and recording weather variables.
- Aviation meteorologists prepare weather reports and forecasts that serve the needs of pilots, airports, and others in the aviation community.
- Air quality meteorologists study air quality issues (such as acid rain and air pollution) and provide scientific and technical advice on such problems.
- Forensic meteorologists apply their expertise to criminal investigations and other legal matters.

Many Meteorologists are engaged in research while working in academic, government, military, industry, and other settings. Those who conduct basic research seek further scientific knowledge about the atmosphere, clouds, weather, and climate; causes of hurricanes, flash floods and other events; the effects of long-term droughts; and so on. Other Meteorologists are involved in applied research, addressing meteorological problems and issues in such areas as agriculture, aviation, sea transportation, satellite communication, national defense, and environmental science.

Research meteorologists often collaborate on projects and sometimes work closely with chemists, physicists, geologists, oceanographers, and other scientists. They also work with mathematicians and computer scientists who help them design computer models of atmospheric processes.

The largest group of Meteorologists work in the area of weather forecasting, which is an applied field of meteorology. They are called operational meteorologists. Broadcast meteorologists are probably the most familiar type of weather forecaster. They are employed by television networks, newspapers, radio stations, and Internet weather service providers to forecast the weather and provide weather reports. They may give air quality reports as well. (Note: Not all weather reporters are Meteorologists.) Some operational meteorologists work as private forecasters. They generally provide specialized forecasts to clients in such industries as aviation, shipping, defense, agriculture, fishing, utilities, sports, or securities and commodities.

The majority of operational meteorologists work in weather stations around the world, collecting and recording atmospheric data several times each day. Their information is transmitted to other operational meteorologists who produce analyses of global weather forecasts. In the United States, these analyses are sent to regional and local National Weather Service centers where Meteorologists interpret the data and make predictions for their particular regions or local areas. Many operational meteorologists assist local authorities and the general public to develop emergency plans when hurricanes, blizzards, and other severe and dangerous weather conditions are being predicted.

To make their weather predictions, Meteorologists use a variety of instruments to take measurements of the different atmospheric conditions and to track weather conditions, such as severe storms or tornadoes. Some of these instruments are thermometers, barometers, radar, acoustic sounders (that use sound waves to measure winds), ocean buoys, and weather balloons. Meteorologists also obtain observations from aircraft which are specially equipped with measuring and sampling instruments. In addition, they get observations from weather satellites which use remote-sensing techniques to measure conditions at many levels of the atmosphere.

Computers are also an essential tool in their work. Meteorologists can make long-term predictions with the aid of computer models, which are sets of mathematical equations that represent atmospheric conditions. By changing the variables in the equations, the computer models simulate how weather systems may behave over several days, weeks, and even years.

Some Meteorologists are employed as consultants. They provide a wide range of meteorological services to clients in the public and private sectors on a fee basis. For example, a Meteorologist might provide farmers with consultation about climate-related problems; another might help planners find the best location for an airport; and still another might provide expert witness testimony at a court trial about specific weather conditions.

Duties for Meteorologists vary, depending on their specialty, area of work, position, and other factors. For example, some Meteorologists are employed as professors in colleges and universities. They divide their time among these duties: conducting research projects, teaching meteorology or other courses, advising students, supervising student research projects, writing scholarly works for publications, performing administrative tasks, and participating in community services.

Research meteorologists work in offices and laboratories, as well as in the field. Operational meteorologists mostly work in large field offices located at airports or in urban areas; some work in isolated and remote areas and may work alone. Those working in weather stations may be required to work nights and weekend shifts on a rotating basis.

Salaries

Salaries for Meteorologists vary, depending on such factors as their job duties, employer, education, experience, and geographical location. According to the May 2006 *Occupational Employment Statistics* survey by the U.S. Bureau of Labor Statistics (BLS), the estimated annual salary for most atmospheric scientists ranged between $39,090 and $119,700, and for atmospheric professors, $37,330 and $121,500.

Employment Prospects

In the United States, the federal government is the largest employer of Meteorologists. Most of them work for the National Oceanic and Atmospheric Administration. Meteorologists also find employment with state governments, private meteorological consulting firms, air carriers, and radio and television broadcasting stations. In addition, some work for research institutes, and some are hired as faculty members at colleges and universities.

The BLS reports that employment of atmospheric scientists, which include Meteorologists, is expected to increase by 11 percent through 2016. In addition to job growth, Meteorologists will be needed to replace those who retire, are promoted, or transfer to other jobs.

Because this is a small but popular occupation, job competition is high. Experts say that the private industry offers more job prospects than the federal government. For example, opportunities should increase in consulting firms that provide weather services to industries (such as agriculture, utilities, aviation, construction, and transportation) that are dependent on the weather.

Advancement Prospects

Meteorologists with management or administrative ambitions can advance to such positions within their specialty. Many Meteorologists pursue advancement by earning higher pay, by being able to conduct independent research projects, and through receiving professional recognition.

Education and Training

Minimally, applicants need a bachelor's degree in meteorology, atmospheric science, or another related field (with coursework in meteorology) for most entry-level positions. Candidates for applied research positions are generally required to possess a master's degrees, while a doctorate is typically required for basic research and university teaching positions.

Employers provide entry-level Meteorologists with on-the-job training while working under the supervision and guidance of experienced staff members. They may also attend formal training courses.

Experience, Skills, and Personality Traits

Employers prefer to hire entry-level candidates who have one or more years of work experience related to the position for which they apply. Their experience may have been gained through internships, research projects, employment, or postdoctoral training.

Meteorologists need to have strong math and computer skills. In addition, they need to be able to communicate effectively as well as have excellent writing skills. Further, they should have strong teamwork and interpersonal skills, as they must be able to work well with various people of diverse backgrounds and with different technical levels. Some personality traits that successful Meteorologists share are being creative, flexible, versatile, analytical, and enthusiastic.

Unions and Associations

Many Meteorologists join societies to take advantage of professional services and resources, such as networking opportunities, training programs, and professional certification. Some professional associations are the American Meteorological Society, the National Weather Association (for operational meteorologists), the National Council of Industrial Meteorologists, and the Air Weather Association (for military meteorologists), See Appendix III for contact information.

Tips for Entry

1. Gain experience by obtaining internships with public or private meteorological employers. Talk with your college adviser or the college placement center for assistance in finding out about relevant internship programs in your area.

2. If you are interested in becoming a broadcast meteorologist, take courses in speech, journalism, and other related fields to develop communication skills.

3. Applicants who are knowledgeable about business, economics, and statistics have a greater chance of obtaining a job with a weather consulting firm.

4. To obtain information about Meteorologist jobs with the federal government, contact the United States Office of Personnel Management. Look in your telephone book under U.S. Government for a local phone number. Or visit its Web site at http://usajobs.opm.gov.

5. Use the Internet to learn more about Meteorologists. Two Web sites you might visit are: American Meteorological Society, http://www.ametsoc.org/; and the National Weather Service, http://www.nws.noaa.gov. For more links, see Appendix IV.

CLIMATOLOGIST

Position Description

Climatology is the scientific study of climate, the pattern of weather that occurs in a place over a period of time. Every location on the Earth has its own unique climate. If a location, for example, is said to have a tropical wet climate, then the weather is generally hot and humid with high temperatures and heavy and frequent rainfall throughout the year. Climates, however, are not constant. They can change over time because of variations that take place in the conditions—such as temperature, precipitation, and air pressure—that shape weather.

Climatologists are concerned with understanding the climates of specific locations (such as towns, cities, states, or countries) as well as the climate on a global basis. They examine how climates in different locations change over time. Additionally, they investigate how changes in the climate affect the vegetation, soils, and other physical features of a location as well as how such changes affect the way people live and work. Further, Climatologists are involved in predicting long-term changes in climates.

Urban climatologists specialize in studying climates that occur in and around cities. They address problems such as air pollution, the effects of urban climate on people's health, and how to improve urban climates. Other specialists are paleoclimatologists who study global and regional climates that occurred over thousands or millions of years ago.

Most Climatologists conduct basic and applied research, while working in academic, government, private sector, and other settings. They often collaborate on projects with colleagues as well as with scientists from other disciplines.

Their research work involves searching for weather data about the location they are investigating. They collect past records of temperature, rainfall, wind speed, and other weather conditions. Many Climatologists also gather information about plant and animal species, as their responses to the weather are clues that climates may be changing. Paleoclimatologists study fossils and rocks to learn about weather conditions that occurred in the past.

To help them analyze and interpret data, Climatologists create computer models, which are mathematical equations that represent the various weather conditions. The models help Climatologists learn how climates have changed in the past as well as predict how climates may change in the future. For example, Climatologists might develop a computer model to help them understand what could happen to the climate if the rate of carbon dioxide in the atmosphere continues to increase at a certain percentage each year.

In general, Climatologists are responsible for designing and conducting research projects. When they complete their projects, they prepare scientific papers and presentations about their findings to share with colleagues. Independent researchers are also responsible for seeking research grants to fund their projects.

Some Climatologists are responsible for providing climate data services to individuals, farmers, businesses, companies, government agencies, and others who use the information to help them make decisions about their personal and economic activities. These Climatologists generally work in climate data centers for government agencies and private firms. Their duties include acquiring, analyzing, and interpreting data for their clients. They also write reports and summaries of climatology information. In addition, Climatologists are responsible for maintaining and distributing the climatological data of their assigned locations.

Many Climatologists are professors or adjunct instructors in universities and colleges. They teach climatology courses and may teach other courses in geography, atmospheric science (or meteorology), or geoscience. Full-time professors conduct independent research in addition to teaching their courses. Further, they advise students, supervise student research projects, write scholarly works, participate in community service, and perform administrative duties.

All Climatologists are responsible for keeping up with developments in their field as well as with updating their skills. They enroll in training programs, read professional journals, attend professional conferences, and network with colleagues.

Salaries

Salaries for Climatologists vary, depending on such factors as their education, experience, and geographical location. The U.S. Bureau of Labor Statistics reports in its May 2006 *Occupational Employment Statistics* survey that the estimated annual salary for most atmospheric scientists (including Climatologists) ranged between $39,090 and $119,700.

Employment Prospects

Climatologists are employed by state and federal government agencies, universities, colleges, research institutes, and meteorology consulting firms.

Climatology is a young field. Opportunities in general will become available as Climatologists retire or transfer to other positions. Employers will create additional positions to meet growing needs, as long as funding is available.

Advancement Prospects

Climatologists can advance to management and administrative positions in any work setting. Academic professors typically advance in terms of rank (assistant, associate, and full professor).

Many Climatologists measure their success by earning higher wages, by conducting independent research, and through gaining professional recognition among their colleagues.

Education and Training

A bachelor's degree in atmospheric science, geography, agronomy, or other related field is the minimum education requirement to enter this field. For most research positions, a master's or doctoral degree in climatology (or another major with an emphasis in this field) is needed. To teach in universities and four-year colleges or to advance to top management positions, a doctoral degree is required.

Experience, Skills, and Personality Traits

Employers generally require that job candidates have related work and research experience. Entry-level applicants may have gained experience through internships, research projects, part-time employment, or volunteer work. Ph.D. candidates for research scientist positions are usually expected to have a few years of postdoctoral experience.

Climatologists must have strong math and computer skills. In addition, they need to be able to communicate effectively as well as have excellent writing skills. Further, they should have strong teamwork and interpersonal skills, as they must be able to work well with various people of diverse backgrounds and with different technical levels. Some personality traits that successful Climatologists share are being enthusiastic, creative, flexible, and analytical.

Unions and Associations

Many Climatologists are members of professional associations which provide networking opportunities and other professional resources and services. Some of the various societies that Climatologists might join are the American Meteorological Society, the Climate Specialty Group (part of the Association of American Geographers), and the American Geological Institute. See Appendix III for contact information.

Tips for Entry

1. Obtain a research assistantship or volunteer to work with a professor who is doing research in areas that interest you.
2. Before sending a résumé to a company, phone the company to learn to whom you should send it. Get the person's exact job title as well as the correct spelling of his or her name.
3. You can learn more about Climatologists on the Internet. One Web site you might visit is for the National Climatic Data Center at http://www.ncdc.noaa.gov/oa/ncdc.html. For more links, see Appendix IV.

PALEONTOLOGIST

CAREER PROFILE

Duties: Study fossilized remains of ancient organisms; design and conduct research projects; perform duties as required

Alternate Title(s): Palynologist, Invertebrate Paleontologist, or other title that reflects a specialty

Salary Range: $40,000 to $136,000

Employment Prospects: Poor

Advancement Prospects: Good

Prerequisites:

    Education or Training—Ph.D. or master's degree required for research scientist positions

    Experience—Lab and field experience required

    Special Skills and Personality Traits—Computer, writing, communication, interpersonal, and self-management skills; be flexible, patient, persevering, creative, and analytical

    Special Requirements—Licensure as a registered geologist (R.G.) may be required

CAREER LADDER

Senior Paleontologist

Research Paleontologist

Research Associate

Position Description

Paleontology is the scientific study of the remains (or fossils) of ancient organisms—microbes, plants, and animals—that lived on the Earth over thousands or millions of years ago. Fossils may be bones, shells, leaf impressions, animal footprints, or other things that had been preserved in the sedimentary layers of rock. Paleontologists examine fossils to learn about the structure, evolution, distribution, and environment of ancient life on the Earth. They are trained in geology, biology, chemistry, and physics.

Many people confuse archaeologists with Paleontologists. However, archaeologists do not study fossils; their expertise is in the investigation of artifacts, such as tools and clothing, made by ancient humans.

Much of paleontological research is applied in other fields such as archaeology, geology, geography, botany, zoology, forensic science, and environmental science. The study of fossils can provide clues about various facets of the geological past, including prehistoric climates, migration paths of plant and animal life, rates of evolution, the past positions of continents and oceans, and so on. For example, knowledge about the natural changes in prehistoric climates can help environmental scientists who are investigating global warming.

Paleontologists conduct basic or applied research, while specializing in a subfield of paleontology. Some of these specialties are:

- vertebrate paleontology, the study of fossils of animals with backbones (examples: fish, amphibians, mammals, and dinosaurs)
- invertebrate paleontology, the study of remains of animals without backbones (examples: corals and mollusks)
- micropaleontology, the study of fossils of very small organisms (such as conodonts) that are found in large numbers in rock
- paleobotany, the study of plant fossils
- palynology, the study of remains of pollen, spores, algae, and other microscopic plant bodies
- biostratigraphy, the study of the distribution of fossils in rock strata (or layers of rock)
- paleoecology, the study of ancient ecosystems and their development

Part of Paleontologists' research involves conducting fieldwork, which may require traveling to remote areas—such as mountains, deserts, or islands—anywhere in the world. They live and work at field sites for extended periods of time. They carefully remove fossils with such tools as brushes, picks, chisels, shovels, and drills.

Back in their laboratories and offices, Paleontologists examine fossils with the aid of such tools as electron microscopes and computers. They compare their discoveries with other paleontological findings as well as with modern life forms to help them understand the fossils. Paleontologists classify their findings according to their age as well as to their botanical or zoological family. In some instances, Paleontologists discover fossils of previously unknown species of animals or plants.

Paleontologists work in a variety of settings. Many Paleontologists are employed as professors in colleges and universities, teaching courses in paleontology, geology, anatomy, biology, and other disciplines. Professors typically divide their time among the following duties: conducting independent research, planning courses, teaching, writing scholarly works, advising students, supervising student research projects, performing administrative tasks, and fulfilling community service obligations.

Many Paleontologists conduct applied research in industry settings (such as oil, coal, and mining companies). They may be employed as staff members or consultants. In general, these Paleontologists study fossils to determine the potential presence of oil, coal, or other materials in particular areas.

Some Paleontologists are hired as museum curators. Some of their duties include conducting basic research, leading field trips, preparing exhibits, developing educational programs, teaching workshops to the general public, writing scientific papers, and managing daily operations of museums or paleontology departments.

Some Paleontologists work for geological surveys, which are federal and state government agencies that conduct geological studies and research. Paleontologists in these work settings might conduct basic or applied research. Some other duties might include providing consulting services to individuals, industry, or legislatures; writing technical reports; developing educational materials; making public presentations; and so on.

Paleontologists typically share information about their research work with colleagues. They might write scientific papers and submit them to scientific journals for publication or make presentations at scientific conferences sponsored by professional associations.

All Paleontologists are responsible for keeping up with technologies and developments in their specialties. They may attend professional conferences, network with colleagues, read professional journals, and so on. Many Paleontologists are responsible for obtaining research grants to fund their projects.

Salaries

Salaries for Paleontologists vary, depending on factors such as their education, experience, position, employer, and geographical location. The U.S. Bureau of Labor Statistics reports in its May 2006 *Occupational Employment Statistics* survey that the estimated annual salary for most geoscientists (including Paleontologists) ranged between $39,740 and $135,950.

Employment Prospects

Paleontologists are mostly employed by colleges, universities, museums, research institutions, and state and federal geological surveys. Many work in the petroleum and other industries.

In general, opportunities for Paleontologists are limited. The turnover rate is quite low, with positions becoming available as Paleontologists retire or transfer to other positions. In addition, the last two decades have seen a slow decrease in the number of permanent jobs, thus the competition for available positions is high.

Advancement Prospects

Most Paleontologists measure their success by being able to conduct independent research, by making discoveries, and through earning professional recognition among their peers.

Management and administrative positions are available in any work setting. For example, depending on their particular circumstances, Paleontologists can become department chairs, administrative deans, museum directors, program directors, or executive officers.

Education and Training

Entry-level candidates need either a master's or doctoral degree to obtain research positions. To conduct independent research, teach in four-year colleges and universities, or to advance to top management positions, Paleontologists must possess a doctorate. A bachelor's degree is usually sufficient for entry-level candidates seeking research assistant or technician positions. Technicians provide technical support and assistance to Paleontologists.

Few schools in the United States offer paleontology degrees. Alternatively, students can obtain their degree in zoology, geology, biology, physical anthropology, or another related field with an emphasis in paleontology.

Special Requirements

Professional licensure is not required for Paleontologists. However, Paleontologists who provide geological services to the public may be required to be registered geologists (R.G.) in the states where they practice.

Experience, Skills, and Personality Traits

Employers prefer to hire entry-level candidates who have previous work and research experience related to the position for which they apply. They may have gained their experience through research projects, internships, employment, or volunteer fieldwork. Some employers prefer that Ph.D.'s have completed a few years of post-doctoral training.

Paleontologists need strong computer, writing, and communication skills for their work. In addition, they should have effective interpersonal skills and self-management skills, such as being able to work independently, organize tasks, and handle deadlines. Some personality traits that successful Paleontologists share are being flexible, patient, persevering, creative, and analytical. In addition, Paleontologists must be physically fit and enjoy hiking and being out-of-doors for long periods of time.

Unions and Associations

Many Paleontologists are members of professional societies to take advantage of networking opportunities, publications, and other professional resources and services. Some associations that serve this profession are the Paleontological Society, the American Association of Stratigraphic Palynologists, and the Society of Vertebrate Paleontology.

Paleontologists are also eligible to join geology societies, such as the American Geological Institute. In addition, they can join academic, museum, or other professional associations that serve the particular areas in which they work.

For contact information for the above organizations, see Appendix III.

Tips for Entry

1. As a high school or college student, learn as much as you can about fossils. For example, you might visit nearby museums with paleontology collections or you might join a local fossil or gem and mineral club.
2. Talk with Paleontologists for advice about the best graduate schools for the type of research or area of paleontology that you wish to enter.
3. Being fluent in a modern foreign language (particularly German, French, Russian, or Chinese) may enhance your employability.
4. Learn more about paleontology on the Internet. One Web site that you might visit is the PaleoNet Pages (by Norman MacLeod), http://www.nhm.ac.uk/hosted-sites/paleonet.

GEOPHYSICIST

CAREER PROFILE

Duties: Study the structure and behavior of matter and energy, as well as their relationships and the effects they have on each other; design and conduct research projects; perform duties as required

Alternate Title(s): Geoscientist, Geologist; Seismologist, Marine Geophysicist, Mining Geophysicist, or other title that reflects a specialty

Salary Range: $40,000 to $136,000

Employment Prospects: Good

Advancement Prospects: Good

Prerequisites:

Education or Training—An advanced degree required for research scientist positions

Experience—Work and research experience related to the position one is applying for

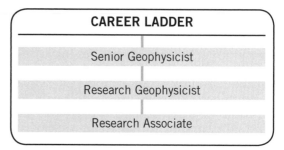

CAREER LADDER

Senior Geophysicist

Research Geophysicist

Research Associate

Special Skills and Personality Traits—Computer, writing, communication, observation, analytical, problem-solving, teamwork, and interpersonal skills; be flexible, patient, curious, and self-motivated

Special Requirements—State licensure as registered geologist or registered geophysicist may be required

Position Description

Geophysics is a branch of geology in which earth scientists study the Earth's interior by applying the principles and methods of physics. Without doing any drilling or excavating, Geophysicists are able to measure the depth of bedrock, locate earthquake faults, map ancient river channels buried beneath the surface, identify soil compositions, evaluate the integrity of man-made structures, search for mineral deposits, and engage in various other research and exploration activities. They use instrumentation that are able to probe far beneath the surface to detect and measure a variety of physical properties—such as magnetism, gravity, and electricity—that humans would not be able to sense.

Many Geophysicists engage in basic research to advance scientific knowledge. Their particular interests involve learning about the Earth's physical properties and its internal structure, as well as about its earthquake, volcanic, and other internal activities. They also investigate the physical properties of the Earth's atmosphere, oceans, and fresh water systems. Many study plate tectonics, the theory that describes the movements and evolution of the continents and ocean floors and explains the location of earthquakes, volcanoes, and mountain building. Other geologists investigate the physical properties of space and of the other celestial bodies in the solar system to gain an understanding of the Earth's structure and evolution.

Geophysicists are also involved in conducting applied research. They take the findings of basic research to develop technologies and processes that can solve problems in communications, defense, construction, engineering, agriculture, environmental protection, and many other fields.

Typically, researchers specialize in the various subfields of the discipline. For example, Geophysicists might conduct research in seismology (the study of earthquakes); geothermal energy; physical oceanography; hydrology (the study of fresh surface water and groundwater); the Earth's gravity field; geodesy (the size and form of the Earth); atmospheric electricity; climate change; or magnetic fields.

Many Geophysicists work in exploration geophysics, an applied branch of geophysics. While using geophysical methods, they search for natural resources such as groundwater, oil, or minerals.

Another applied branch is engineering geophysics. Geophysicists in this specialty investigate engineering and environmental problems which affect the safety, health, and welfare of people and other living things. For example, Geophysicists might be asked to identify potential geological hazards at proposed construction sites, or track contaminants in groundwater, or locate sites for underground nuclear waste disposal.

Exploration and engineering geophysicists often work as part of multidisciplinary teams that usually include geologists from other specialties, engineers, technicians, and scientists from other disciplines. Research geophysicists also collaborate on projects with other scientists from time to time.

All Geophysicists make sure that they collect accurate and precise data. They operate ground-based instruments and employ instrumentation installed in planes and satellites to identify various types of rock, obtain measurements, detect variations in gravity, and so on. To collect their data, Geophysicists use electromagnetic, seismic, and other geophysical methods that enable them to detect and measure the diverse properties of the Earth beneath its surface. For example, Geophysicists can measure the speed of sound waves traveling through the Earth's crust by using the seismic method. Seismologists also use this method to investigate earthquakes while petroleum geophysicists use it to locate new sources of oil.

Geophysicists perform a variety of tasks that generally include collecting field data, conducting experiments or tests, developing computer models, analyzing and interpreting data, and preparing technical reports. They also have other tasks that are unique to their specializations.

Geologists are responsible for designing and conducting their research projects, in addition to guiding and supervising research assistants and technicians. Many Geophysicists in nonindustry settings are responsible for obtaining research grants from the federal government and other sources to fund their research projects.

Many Geophysicists are faculty members at colleges and universities. Along with conducting research, they are responsible for planning courses, teaching classes, advising students, supervising student research projects, performing administrative tasks, writing scholarly works, and participating in community service.

Geophysicists work in offices and laboratories as well as in the field. Those involved in exploration and engineering projects often work and live in remote areas anywhere in the world, for several weeks or months at a time.

Salaries

Salaries for Geophysicists vary, depending on such factors as their education, experience, position, employer, and geographical location. The U.S. Bureau of Labor Statistics reports in its May 2006 *Occupational Employment Statistics* survey that the estimated annual salary for most geoscientists (including Geophysicists) ranged between $39,740 and $135,950.

Employment Prospects

Major employers of Geophysicists include the petroleum and mining industries, environmental and geotechnical consulting firms, colleges and universities, and government laboratories and agencies.

Although job competition among Geophysicists is high, opportunities should be favorable. Employment for geoscientists, including Geophysicists, is predicted to grow by 22 percent through 2016, according to the BLS. Most opportunities will become available as Geophysicists retire, transfer to other positions, or resign.

Advancement Prospects

Geophysicists can advance to management and administrative positions in the various work settings. Professors advance in rank (assistant, associate, and full professor) as well as by obtaining job tenure, which generally assures professors a job until they retire. Entrepreneurial individuals can pursue careers as independent consultants or owners of consulting firms.

Many Geophysicists measure their success by earning higher salaries, by being able to conduct independent research projects, and through professional recognition.

Education and Training

Educational requirements vary with the different positions, as well as among employers. Entry-level candidates for jobs in applied geophysics must possess at least a bachelor's degree in geophysics, geology, engineering, chemistry, or another related field. Many employers prefer to hire candidates with a master's degree, particularly in the area of exploratory geophysics.

Depending on the employer, a master's or doctoral degree is required for candidates to obtain entry-level positions as research scientists. To conduct independent research, teach in four-year colleges and universities, and to advance to top management positions, Geophysicists must hold a doctorate in their specialty.

Special Requirements

Geophysicists may be required to be licensed as a registered geologist or registered geophysicist in the states where they practice. Engineering geologists may be required to obtain separate licensure. Further, entry-level applicants may be required to register as a geologist-in-training, which leads to professional registrations.

Licensure requirements vary from state to state. For information, contact the board of geology in the state where you wish to practice. You can also obtain general licensure information from the National Association of State Boards of Geology Web site, http://www.asbog.org.

Experience, Skills, and Personality Traits

Employers seek entry-level candidates who have work and research experience related to the position for which they are applying. Many employers look for candidates who have field experience. Recent graduates may have obtained experience through employment, internships, or research projects. Many employers expect Ph.D. candidates to have completed postdoctoral training. In addition, job candidates should have a basic understanding of the industry, business, or mission in which prospective employers are involved.

Geophysicists need excellent computer, writing, and communication skills. They must also have strong observation, analytical, and problem-solving skills as well as effective teamwork and interpersonal skills. In addition, Geophysicists who are involved in extensive fieldwork must be physically fit and have physical stamina.

Some personality traits that successful Geophysicists have in common are being flexible, patient, curious, and self-motivated.

Unions and Associations

Geophysicists can join geological societies to take advantage of various professional services and resources such as education programs, job listings, and networking opportunities. Some associations that serve the various interests of Geophysicists are the American Geophysical Union, the Environmental and Engineering Geophysical Society, the Society of Exploration Geophysicists, and the Seismological Society of America. See Appendix III for contact information.

Tips for Entry

1. Gain experience by seeking internships or summer employment with consulting firms, petroleum companies, or government agencies. Another option is obtaining a research assistant position with a professor who is conducting research in an area in which you are interested.

2. Many positions in industry require travel to other countries; thus, knowledge of a foreign language can be a valuable asset.

3. Many Geophysicists obtain licensure on a voluntary basis to enhance their employability, as many employers prefer to hire licensed Geophysicists, even if states where they practice do not require licensure.

4. Use the Internet to learn more about Geophysicists. A Web site you might visit is American Geophysical Union, http://www.agu.org. For more links, see Appendix IV.

SEISMOLOGIST

Position Description

Seismology is the scientific study of earthquakes, the natural phenomena that occur on the fractures, or faults, in the Earth's crust. When the sides of a fault slip against each other and rupture, energy is released in the form of seismic waves that travel in all directions through the crust. Most earthquakes, which occur on a daily basis throughout the world, are mild and not felt at all by people.

The scientists who investigate the nature and behavior of earthquakes are known as Seismologists. They monitor earthquake activity with seismographs that measure and record seismic waves as earthquakes occur. By analyzing and interpreting the data from those instruments, Seismologists can determine on which faults that earthquakes took place, their magnitudes, where the epicenters (points of rupture) were, and other characteristics.

Seismologists conduct research while working in academic, government, industry, and other settings. They apply principles and techniques of geology, physics, and mathematics to understand how and why earthquakes occur. Many study seismic waves to understand the internal structure of the Earth. Some Seismologists examine the nature and behavior of specific earthquake faults, including those on the ocean floors. Some study strong earthquakes that occurred hundreds or thousands of years ago to determine whether a fault may

still be active. Other Seismologists are concerned with the potential of earthquake hazards and their effects on heavily populated areas such as the San Francisco Bay Area or the Pacific Northwest. (Note: Few Seismologists are involved in research related to earthquake predictions. Most Seismologists believe that predicting earthquakes is not possible.)

Their research may involve designing experiments to simulate processes associated with earthquakes, and comparing their results with the actual events. Some Seismologists develop computer models (sets of mathematical equations) to enable them to create simulations of seismic activities and effects. By changing the variables in the models, Seismologists can vary hypothetical conditions and get an idea of what might occur if such conditions were actually created.

As part of their research, many Seismologists conduct field trips to earthquake faults, which are often in remote locations. Their fieldwork might involve examining and measuring the earth's surface after an earthquake occurs, mapping fault lines, searching for hidden fault lines, seeking evidence of seismic activity that occurred hundreds or thousands of years ago, or other tasks.

Many Seismologists are involved in applied research, using seismic technology for specific purposes. For example, some Seismologists are involved in monitoring seismic activity in active volcanoes. A sudden series of earthquakes is one of several clues that helps scientists determine if there is a potential for a volcanic eruption. Other Seismologists, who work for petroleum and mining companies, apply seismic techniques when they study sound waves that are generated by small explosions or mechanical devices to find oil, natural gas, or minerals.

Many Seismologists hold academic positions in colleges and universities. Along with conducting independent research, they teach courses in seismology, geophysics, and other fields. They also advise students and supervise student research projects. Additionally, professors are required to publish scholarly works, perform administrative duties, and participate in community service.

Seismologists perform duties that vary, depending on their positions. Some of these duties may include designing research projects, supervising research assistants, performing administrative tasks, writing scientific papers (which may be published in professional journals), attending science conferences, and providing consulting services to public officials and authorities. Some Seismologists are involved in developing educational materials for the public, covering such topics as earthquake hazards and how to prepare for earthquakes and emergency situations.

Seismologists typically put in long hours to complete their various tasks and to meet deadlines. Their fieldwork may require that they travel to remote locations where they live and work for several days or weeks at a time.

Salaries

Salaries for Seismologists vary, depending on factors such as their employer, education, experience, and geographical location. According to the May 2006 *Occupational Employment Statistics* survey by the U.S. Bureau of Labor Statistics, the estimated annual salary for most geoscientists (including Seismologists) ranged between $39,740 and $135,950.

Employment Prospects

Seismologists are employed by colleges and universities, government agencies, private industries (especially petroleum and mining industries), and research institutes.

Most opportunities are created to replace individuals who retire, resign, or transfer to other positions. In general, opportunities vary each year as funding of most earthquake research depends on the availability of federal grants.

Advancement Prospects

Seismologists can advance to administrative or management positions, which may require moving to other employers. Academic professors can advance in rank (assistant, associate, and full professor) as well as by obtaining job tenure.

Education and Training

The minimum qualification for most Seismologist positions is a doctoral degree in seismology, geophysics, or another related field. Doctoral degrees are necessary for those wishing to teach in universities and four-year colleges, conduct independent research, or pursue top administrative positions.

Some industry positions require only a bachelor's degree, though many employers prefer candidates with a master's degree.

Experience, Skills, and Personality Traits

Seismologists generally need work and research experience that is related to the positions for which they are applying. Experience may have been gained through research projects, internships, fellowships, or employment. Many employers prefer that Seismologists have several years of postdoctoral experience.

To do well at their jobs, Seismologists must have excellent computer, writing, communication, and analytical skills. They also need strong interpersonal and teamwork skills, as they often work with other scientists, technicians, engineers, and others. Some personality traits that successful Seismologists have in common are being curious, creative, meticulous, detail-oriented, patient, and flexible.

Unions and Associations

Many Seismologists join professional associations to take advantage of professional services and resources such as education programs and networking opportunities. Some societies that serve the interests of Seismologists are the Seismological Society of America; the International Association of Seismology and Physics of the Earth's Interior; the American Geophysical Union; and the Geological Society of America. See Appendix III for contact information.

Tips for Entry

1. Volunteer or complete internships at geological surveys, seismic labs, or other settings that can provide you with valuable training and experience.

2. If you do not plan to enroll in a graduate program immediately after earning your bachelor's degree, you might gain experience by obtaining a research assistant or technician position at a seismological logical or geological research facility.

3. Use the Internet to learn more about seismology. One Web site that you might visit is for the National Earthquake Information Center (U.S. Geological Survey) at http://neic.usgs.gov. For more links, see Appendix IV.

VOLCANOLOGIST

CAREER PROFILE

Duties: Study the characteristics and processes of volcanoes; design and conduct research projects; perform duties as required
Alternate Title(s): Geoscientist, Geologist
Salary Range: $40,000 to $136,000
Employment Prospects: Poor
Advancement Prospects: Good
Prerequisites:
  Education or Training—A doctoral degree in geophysics or geology with an emphasis in volcanology
  Experience—Work experience required
  Special Skills and Personality Traits—Computer, writing, communication, interpersonal, and self-management skills; be creative, persistent, flexible, calm, and analytical

Position Description

Volcanology is the study of volcanoes that are openings in the Earth's surface through which built-up pressures from within the Earth's interior can escape. Volcanic eruptions may be gentle or violent explosions in which lava (superhot melted rock), steam, gasses, and rock spew out of the vents. At least 1,500 volcanoes are known to be active or potentially active throughout the world, including approximately 70 volcanoes in the United States. Most volcanoes are mountains or islands, which are actually the tops of volcanic mountains that formed on the ocean floors.

Volcanologists are the research scientists who seek to understand the nature and causes of volcanic eruptions. They study the actual processes as well as the deposits of volcanic eruptions. Volcano observatories have been built at the rims or slopes of several active volcanoes around the world. There, Volcanologists can monitor volcanic activities on a regular basis. They use seismometers, spectrometers, laser surveying instruments, and other equipment to measure changes in:

- seismic activity, as earthquakes normally occur before an eruption
- the shape of the volcano surface
- geophysical properties (such as the magnetic field strength and the force of gravity)
- the composition or emission rate of gasses

- the temperature, level, flow, and other characteristics of ground water

Volcanologists also make observations at field sites before, during, and after eruptions. They draw detailed geological maps of flow fields, which may require that they hike over young lava flows. They also collect samples of superhot lava to test and analyze later in the labs. In addition, many Volcanologists design experiments that simulate volcanic conditions and activities to test their theories about the phenomena they have directly observed. Some Volcanologists test their understanding of volcanic processes by applying mathematical formulas and developing computer models.

Many Volcanologists focus their work by specializing in a particular area. Some specialize in the study of a specific type of eruption (such as gentle eruptions that form shield mountains) or a particular type of volcanic product such as volcanic ash. Other Volcanologists focus on a specific volcanic activity; for example, Volcanologists might specifically study seismic activity, the geochemistry of volcanoes, or the changing shapes of the volcanic surface.

Many Volcanologists are involved with studying inactive volcanoes, by examining the remains of their past eruptions. Some volcanoes are considered to be extinct; that is, they have not been active since the beginning of recorded history. Others have been dormant for a long period of time, but Volcanologists believe they may come alive again. Some Volcanologists specialize in the study of volcanic activities that occur on the ocean floors. Still others study volcanic processes on the moon and other planets in the solar system, using data gathered by spacecraft.

Volcanologists are also concerned with the effects that volcanic eruptions have on life and the environment. Some Volcanologists are involved in educating communities near active volcanoes about the hazards of volcanic eruptions. They also provide warnings to local authorities and leaders about potential hazards and eruptions.

In addition to working in observatories and in the field, Volcanologists work in offices and labs. In general, their duties include designing and conducting research projects; supervising research assistants and technicians; conducting experiments; gathering, analyzing, and interpreting data; writing reports; and performing administrative tasks. Volcanologists also share information about their research work with colleagues by writing scientific papers for publication in scientific journals or making presentations at scientific meetings that are sponsored by professional associations.

Many Volcanologists are faculty members at colleges and universities. In addition to their research work, they are responsible for the following duties: teaching geology, geophysics, volcanology, and other courses; advising students; supervising student research work; performing administrative tasks; writing scholarly works; and fulfilling community service obligations. They are also responsible for obtaining grants from the federal government and other sources for their research projects. Professors typically conduct field research during the summer and other college breaks.

Salaries

Salaries for Volcanologists vary, depending on such factors as their education, experience, and job duties. The U.S. Bureau of Labor Statistics reports in its May 2006 *Occupational Employment Statistics* survey that the estimated annual salary for most geoscientists (including Volcanologists) ranged between $39,740 and $135,950.

Employment Prospects

Most Volcanologists work for colleges, universities, government volcanic observatories, or state or federal geological surveys (which are government agencies that conduct geological research).

Volcanology is a young and small discipline. Opportunities are limited, with only a few positions becoming available as Volcanologists retire, resign, or transfer to other positions.

Advancement Prospects

Most Volcanologists measure their success by being able to conduct independent research, by making higher salaries, and through earning professional recognition among their peers.

Education and Training

Becoming a Volcanologist generally requires earning a Ph.D. in geophysics or geology with a specialization in volcanology, or in another related field. Most Volcanologists also have a solid foundation in chemistry, physics, mathematics, and computer science.

Experience, Skills, and Personality Traits

In general, employers prefer to hire Volcanologists who have related work and research experience, which may have been gained through research projects, internships, fellowships, or employment. Volcanologists typically have several years of postdoctoral experience before obtaining a permanent job.

Volcanologists need strong computer, writing, and communication skills for their work. They should have effective interpersonal skills and self-management skills, including the ability to handle stressful situations. In addition, they must be physically fit and enjoy hiking and being outdoors. Being creative, persistent, flexible, calm, and analytical are some personality traits that successful Volcanologists share.

Unions and Associations

Many Volcanologists are members of professional societies in order to take advantage of networking opportunities and other professional resources and services. Some associations that serve the interests of Volcanologists are the American Geophysical Union and the International Association of Volcanology and Chemistry of the Earth's Interior. See Appendix III for contact information.

Tips for Entry

1. Check out various graduate programs to make sure they offer the courses and research areas that interest you.

2. While you are an undergraduate student, do volunteer work or internships at volcano observatories, geological surveys, or other settings that can provide you with valuable training and experience.

3. Many employers advertise job openings in scientific publications and professional journals, as

well as on job banks at Web sites for professional societies.

4. Use the Internet to learn more about volcanology. Here are two Web sites you might visit: Volcano World, http://volcano.und.nodak.edu, and Volcano Hazards Program (U.S. Geological Survey), http://volcanoes.usgs.gov. For more links, see Appendix IV.

GEOGRAPHER

Duties: Study the physical processes and human activities that occur within particular locations; design and conduct research projects; perform duties as required

Alternate Title(s): Economic Geographer, Climatologist, Cartographer, GIS Specialist, Urban Planner, or other title that reflects a specialty

Salary Range: $34,000 to $98,000

Employment Prospects: Good

Advancement Prospects: Good

Prerequisites:

Education or Training—A bachelor's or advanced degree in geography or related field

Experience—Work experience preferred

Special Skills and Personality Traits—Organization, research, writing, computer, communication, statistics, and math skills; analytical, open-minded, curious, creative

Special Requirements—Licensure is required for specific occupations such as high school teachers and surveyors

CAREER LADDER

Senior Geographer

Geographer

Geographer (Entry-level)

Position Description

Geography is the scientific study of the physical processes and human activities that occur on the surface of the Earth. It is an interdisciplinary science that may be classified as a physical (or natural) science or a social science.

Geographers are interested in learning everything there is to know about any particular place on the planet. They study the physical features—landforms, vegetation, soils, water, climates, and so forth—that are found at different locations. They investigate such questions as: How did features form and develop? What changes may be occurring? and Why are they important for being in a particular location?

Geographers also examine the cultural, social, economic, and political activities of people in various locations. Additionally, they investigate how people interact with and affect their environments. Further, Geographers seek to understand how locations differ from each other, as well as understand the relationship between locations. Geographers are also concerned with understanding the natural and human forces that influence the distribution and patterns of physical features and human activities.

Most Geographers are research scientists who work in academic and government settings. Some conduct basic research to further scientific knowledge about the many subfields of geography. Others engage in applied research in which they utilize the findings of basic research to solve problems in such diverse areas as agriculture, the environment, public health, finance, transportation, and technology.

Geography is a broad discipline that is divided into two general branches, with each branch having several specialties. Physical geographers make up one branch. They study the physical characteristics of the Earth and the processes that shape and change them. Many physical geographers deal with a particular feature. For example, climatologists study climate patterns, geomorphologists examine landforms, and soil scientists investigate the different types of soils.

Human geography is another major branch of geography subdivided into several areas. Social geographers study the relationships between groups of people, while cultural geographers examine how cultural traits (such as beliefs, customs, and values) pass between generations and spread among locations.

Economic geographers are concerned with the distribution of natural resources and how people use natural resources in various economic activities such as agriculture, forestry, mining, manufacturing, trade, and transportation. Political geographers study political systems, historical geographers investigate how places and patterns of human activity have changed over time, and demographers study the patterns of human populations.

Some Geographers specialize in the types of locations they study. Urban geographers examine how cities develop and grow and are involved in the planning of housing, transportation, industrial sites, and other urban developments. Regional geographers, on the other hand, focus on a particular area on Earth, such as an island, valley, state, country, continent, or regional area. They are interested in understanding the physical, social, economic, political, and other geographical characteristics of the area.

Geographers are responsible for designing and conducting their research projects. They perform a variety of tasks that generally involve:

- designing and performing experiments
- collecting, analyzing, and interpreting statistical data, maps, satellite imagery, and other geographic information
- developing computer models or constructing maps to understand patterns and processes
- conducting fieldwork that may involve direct observation, conducting interviews, taking measurements, or gathering samples
- writing reports
- preparing scientific papers or presentations of research findings

Some Geographers are also responsible for obtaining grants to fund their research projects, which involves preparing proposals and budgets that meet the specifications of different funding sources.

Many academic researchers are appointed as faculty members in geography departments. In addition to their research duties, they are responsible for teaching and advising students, writing scholarly works, fulfilling community service, and performing administrative tasks.

Geographers mostly work in offices and laboratories. Some conduct fieldwork that requires traveling to remote locations where they live and work for several days or weeks.

Many Geographers are employed in other occupations besides research. They apply their geographical knowledge and skills in such roles as technicians, engineers, planners, mapmakers, educators, resource specialists, analysts, administrators, and consultants, among others. Most hold positions with job titles that describe their particular responsibilities. Hence, Geographers can be geography teachers, urban planners, GIS specialists, cartographers, water resources analysts, forestry technicians, interpretive specialists, location experts, surveyors, housing specialists, and tourism planners, to name a few occupations.

Salaries

Salaries for Geographers vary, depending on their education, experience, position, geographical location, and other factors. The U.S. Bureau of Labor Statistics (BLS) reports in its May 2006 *Occupational Employment Statistics* survey that the estimated annual salary for most Geographers ranged between $37,530 and $93,930, and for most geography professors, between $34,300 and $98,200.

Employment Prospects

As an occupational category, Geographers are members of a small group. The BLS reports in its May 2006 OES survey that about 960 Geographers are employed in the United States. Job competition is high, and most opportunities will become available as Geographers retire or transfer to other positions.

Opportunities for Geographers in a wide range of occupations are available. They are employed by government agencies, schools, nonprofit groups, and nongovernmental organizations. Some employers in the private sector who employ individuals with geography backgrounds are real estate developers, architectural firms, construction companies, engineering companies, satellite companies, utilities, medical services, environmental consulting firms, finance companies, manufacturing firms, publishers, and tour companies.

Advancement Prospects

Geographers can advance in any number of ways, depending on their positions, ambitions, and interests. Those interested in management and administrative positions may find opportunities in any work setting. Some Geographers choose to become consultants in their areas of expertise. Academic professors can advance in rank (assistant, associate, and full professor) as well as by obtaining job tenure.

Many Geographers with bachelor's degrees return to school to earn their master's or doctoral degree in order to increase their opportunities for better paying positions.

Education and Training

Depending on the employer, the minimum requirement for entry-level candidates for research scientist positions is a master's or doctoral degree in geography or another related field. A doctorate is needed for Geographers to conduct independent research, teach in four-year colleges and universities, and to advance to top management positions.

Many technician and nonresearch positions can be entered with a bachelor's degree. However, some employers prefer hiring candidates with a master's degree.

Jobs in other fields generally require knowledge obtained not only in geography but in other disciplines as well—such as economics, political science, environmental science, urban planning, computer science, geology, and landscape architecture.

Special Requirements

Some occupations, such as surveyor and geography teacher, require state licensure. For information about a specific occupation, talk with your college adviser or contact a professional association that serves that profession.

Experience, Skills, and Personality Traits

Requirements vary for the different positions as well as among the various employers. For entry-level positions, employers generally choose candidates who have related work experience, which may have been gained through research projects, internships, fellowships, or employment. Ph.D. applicants for a research scientist position are usually expected to have a few years of postdoctoral experience.

Strong organizational, research, writing, computer, and communication skills are essential for Geographers to have in their work. In addition, they should be proficient in statistics and math. Some personality traits that successful Geographers share are being analytical, open-minded, curious, and creative.

Unions and Associations

Geographers join professional associations to take advantage of services and resources (such as education programs and professional publications) as well as opportunities for networking with colleagues. Many are members of the Association of American Geographers and the American Geographical Society. Many geography professors are members of the American Association of University Professors or other associations that serve the interests of academic faculty. See Appendix III for association contact information.

Tips for Entry

1. To learn about the various career options that are available, talk with several different types of Geographers.
2. Directly contact employers for whom you would like to work to find out if positions are available.
3. Finding a job can be a job itself. If you need help with your job search skills, visit your college career center. Most centers usually offer job skills workshops on writing résumés, job interviews, and job search strategies.
4. To enhance your employability, learn the skills needed to work with computer cartography and GIS technologies.
5. Learn more about the geography field on the Internet. One Web site you might visit is for the Association of American Geographers at http://www.aag.org. For more links, see Appendix IV.

CARTOGRAPHER

Duties: Design, create, and produce maps; design and conduct research projects; perform duties as required

Alternate Title(s): Research Scientist or other title that describes a particular position

Salary Range: $31,000 to $81,000

Employment Prospects: Good

Advancement Prospects: Good

Prerequisites:

    Education or Training—A bachelor's degree or advanced degree in cartography, geography, or a related field

    Experience—One or more years of work experience

CAREER LADDER

Senior Cartographer

Cartographer

Cartographer (Entry-level)

Special Skills and Personality Traits—Mathematics, computing, GIS, GPS, interpersonal, organizational analytical, and self-management skills; be imaginative, artistic, adaptable, detail-oriented, accurate, precise, and patient

Position Description

Cartography is the scientific discipline that deals with the making of maps. They may be static maps (paper maps or maps bound in atlases) or digital maps that are displayed on computer monitors. Individuals, government officials, businesses, corporations, and others use maps to help them solve problems and make important decisions.

Cartographers make different types of maps. Navigational maps (such as street maps) and topographical maps are probably the most familiar types that they create. They also produce statistical maps that are based on quantitative data. For example, a statistical map for a state might show the age breakdown of that state's population. In addition, Cartographers make maps that depict relationships among geographic facts. For example, a city map might show its voting precincts, the party affiliations of the voters, and the sex, age, and income level of the voters.

The map-making process involves several stages. The first phase starts with Cartographers drawing up general guidelines, which may include discussing requirements with those who came up with the original idea. The next stage is conducting research. Cartographers collect, analyze, and interpret geographic data that is to be presented on the maps. They rarely do fieldwork—that is, to go and view the places that they map. Instead, they gather data from geodetic surveys, aeronautical photographs, statistical reports, existing maps, and other records. They also obtain data by such automation techniques as global positioning system (GPS) satellites

which can pinpoint any position on Earth, or geographic information systems (GIS) data banks.

Next, Cartographers research the best way to present the geographic information so that map readers can easily understand how to use the map. Cartographers then develop the graphic design for a map. They make decisions on the scale and size of a map, what the layout should look like, what shapes the symbols should be, and so forth.

The production phase usually goes through several stages, starting with drawing or revising the base map, then adding the layers of geographic information. Today, most Cartographers create maps on computers with graphics and mapping software. Maps are edited throughout the production phase to ensure that no errors have been made. Cartographers check that maps are drawn accurately, names are typed correctly, and symbols are positioned in the right place.

Some Cartographers are involved in research and development. Basic researchers are concerned with advancing understanding about maps and mapmaking. For example, a researcher might study the processes that people use to read maps. Applied researchers engage in developing technologies or processes, or they create map designs to solve problems in various fields. Some applied researchers participate in developing new or improved consumable products for their employers.

Some Cartographers are adjunct instructors or full-time professors who teach courses in cartography, geography, and other subjects. Full-time faculty members divide their time by performing research and writing scholarly works, teaching and advising students, and fulfilling community service and completing administrative tasks.

Salaries

Salaries for Cartographers vary, depending on such factors as their education, experience, and geographical location. According to the May 2006 *Occupational Employment Statistics* survey by the U.S. Bureau of Labor Statistics (BLS), the estimated annual salary for most Cartographers ranged between $30,910 and $80,520.

Employment Prospects

Some federal government agencies that employ Cartographers are the U.S. Geological Survey, the National Oceanic and Atmospheric Administration, the National Imagery and Mapping Agency, and the Federal Emergency Management Agency. At the local and state government levels, Cartographers are employed by planning departments, public works departments, transportation departments, law enforcement agencies, and departments of natural resources. In the private sector, Cartographers find work with engineering firms, construction firms, surveying companies, media companies, mapping companies, utilities, and software companies. Cartographers also work for academic institutions and nonprofit organizations. Some Cartographers are self-employed.

The job growth for Cartographers is expected to increase by 20 percent through 2016, according to the BLS. In addition, opportunities will become available as Cartographers retire or transfer to other positions. The BLS reports that a large number of Cartographers are expected to retire in the coming years.

Advancement Prospects

Mapmakers and research scientists can pursue management and administrative positions, such as becoming project leaders, department or program managers, and executive officers. Professors can advance in rank (assistant, associate, and full professor) as well as by obtaining job tenure.

Education and Training

Most employers require that candidate for entry-level mapmaking positions possess at least a bachelor's degree in cartography, geography, forestry, civil engineering, or another related field. Entry-level candidates for research scientist positions need either a master's or doctoral degree, depending on an employer's requirements. A doctorate is required to teach in academic institutions, conduct independent research, or advance to top management positions.

Experience, Skills, and Personality Traits

Employers prefer to hire candidates for entry-level positions who have one or more years of work experience. They may have gained experience through internships, research projects, employment, or postdoctoral training.

Cartographers must have fundamental skills in mathematics and computing, as well as in GIS and GPS technologies. In addition, they need effective interpersonal, organizational, analytical, and self-management skills. Some personality traits that successful Cartographers share are being imaginative, artistic, adaptable, detail oriented, accurate, precise, and patient.

Unions and Associations

Most Cartographers join professional societies to take advantage of professional services and resources such as networking opportunities and publications. Some associations that serve their interests are the Cartography and Geographic Information Society, the Cartography Specialty Group (part of the Association of American Geographers), and the American Geological Institute. See Appendix III for contact information.

Tips for Entry

1. Talk with various Cartographers to learn about the work they do.
2. Get as much training as possible (and keep updating your skills) in computer science, GIS, and GPS.
3. Contact professional and trade associations for information about scholarships, internships, fellowships, and employment.
4. Use the Internet to learn more about cartography. To get a list of relevant Web sites to read, enter the keyword *cartography* or *cartographers* in any search engine. For some links, see Appendix IV.

GEOGRAPHIC INFORMATION SYSTEMS (GIS) SPECIALIST

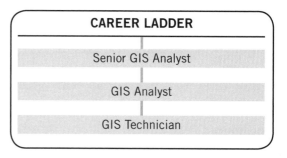

Position Description

Many issues and problems that individuals and organizations deal with involve location. For example, they may ask: What parts of the country are likely to face a drought in the next decade? What should be the boundaries of a state's new voting districts? What can be alternative routes for a parade? Is a health epidemic occurring in a city? Where should a new community college be built? Has the air quality in a region improved? What utility pipelines need servicing? Which crimes have occurred in a community during the last five years?

Today, many individuals and organizations utilize geographic information system (GIS) technology to help them solve problems and make critical decisions. GIS is a computer-based system that collects, stores, controls, analyzes, integrates, and displays spatial, or geographic, data. This technology allows users to assemble spatial data from various sources and formats (such as maps, satellite imagery, censuses, and data reports) so that they can examine and analyze the relationships between geographic features. GIS includes computer hardware, software, and other equipment as well as databases, the procedures for using the databases, and the practitioners, known as GIS Specialists, who work with the technology.

GIS Specialists work in government, academic, industrial, military, and nonprofit settings. They may hold staff or contractual positions. They provide technical support in virtually every field, including agriculture, urban planning, real estate, transportation, education, medicine, engineering, archaeology, natural resource management, environment, epidemiology, hydrology, meteorology, criminal justice, emergency services, and travel and tourism, among many others. GIS Specialists assist in mapping, scientific investigations, development planning, resource management, or other applications, depending on the projects.

Their primary role is to create, edit, and maintain GIS databases, as well as analyze databases to obtain the particular spatial and thematic information that is needed for projects. GIS Specialists integrate the data, and transform geographic information into maps and other decision-making tools.

In addition to being skilled in GIS technology, GIS Specialists are knowledgeable about cartography and cartographic techniques as well as computer programming and database management. They are also familiar with remote sensing, global positioning systems (GPS), and other geospatial technologies.

GIS Specialists are assigned multiple duties, which vary according to their position, experience, and skill level. They might perform such tasks as:

- compiling spatial data from field observations, censuses, maps, aerial photographs, satellite imagery, and other sources
- creating or editing spatial data
- inputting data into GIS systems
- converting maps, aerial photographs, and other materials into a digitized format
- analyzing and interpreting spatial data
- meeting with project managers and others to discuss project requirements
- creating digital maps, graphs, and other visuals
- preparing reports and other documentation
- operating and maintaining computer hardware, software, and other equipment such as digitizers, scanners, printers, cameras, and GPS receivers
- designing GIS applications
- providing GIS training to employees within their organization

Entry-level practitioners, usually known as GIS technicians, perform routine duties under the supervision and direction of experienced GIS specialists. As they gain experience and become more skilled, technicians advance to GIS analyst positions wherein they perform such complex duties as designing and maintaining GIS applications and databases, as well as supervising and training subordinate GIS staff.

Experienced GIS Specialists may specialize in various ways. For example, they may focus on programming or developing GIS software; concentrate in a specific type of mapping technology (such as remote sensing) or type of mapping (such as statistical mapping); or work in a particular subject matter, field, or industry. Some experienced practitioners become GIS managers who are responsible for planning, overseeing, and coordinating GIS activities for their organization.

GIS Specialists work alone as well as interact with various people on a daily basis. The job can be stressful during times when people need to meet deadlines.

GIS Specialists are employed full time or part time. They occasionally put in additional hours to complete tasks or to meet deadlines. Their work is usually done in office environments. Because the nature of their job requires working for long hours on a computer, they may be at risk of developing such health conditions as eyestrain, backaches, and carpal tunnel syndrome.

Salaries

Salaries for GIS Specialists vary, depending on such factors as their education, experience, position, employer, and geographical location. According to the Career Prospects in Virginia Web site, annual salaries ranged approximately from $30,000 to $40,000 for entry-level GIS Specialists, and from $50,000 to $80,000 for experienced professionals who possess advanced degrees. The Salary.com Web site reports the median base salary for entry-level GIS analysts (in May 2007) as being $36,408 per year, and for analysts at the specialist level, $74,152.

Employment Prospects

Geospatial technology is a fast growing industry, according to many experts. In 2004, the U.S. Department of Labor identified this industry as being one of the emerging industries with an insufficient number of skilled workers.

Opportunities are readily available for GIS Specialists (entry-level and experienced) in both the public and private sectors. For example, in the government, these specialists are employed in governmental planning departments, law enforcement agencies, natural resource management agencies, and public health departments. Other employers include educational institutions, public interest groups, architecture and engineering firms, petroleum exploration companies, environmental consulting firms, telecommunications companies, market research firms, real estate companies, and insurance companies. The demand for skilled GIS professionals is expected to increase as more organizations become aware of the benefits of utilizing geospatial technologies to help solve problems and make critical decisions.

Advancement Prospects

GIS Specialists can advance in various ways. They can rise through the ranks as technicians, analysts, project leaders, coordinators, and managers. They can also specialize by working in a particular field or industry. Those with entrepreneurial ambitions can pursue a consulting career. Alternatively, these specialists may become researchers and instructors in geographic information science. Individuals usually need a master's or doctoral degree to obtain top management, research, or college teaching jobs.

Education and Training

Educational requirements vary for the different positions. Depending on the employer, candidates for entry-level positions may need at least an associate or bachelor's degree in geography, geographical information science, cartography, or another related field. Employers may also accept applicants who have college degrees in other disciplines (such as urban planning or computer programming) with a concentration in GIS, or have GIS training and practical experience, or have completed a GIS certificate program.

As this book was being written, the most common way to obtain formal GIS training was for individuals to enroll in GIS certificate programs, which are offered by colleges and universities. Increasingly more schools are developing college degree programs in geographical information science, including professional master's degree programs.

Throughout their careers, GIS Specialists enroll in continuing education programs to update their skills and keep up with advancements in their fields.

Experience, Special Skills, and Personality Traits

Employers prefer to hire candidates for entry-level positions who have one or more years of practical experience in GIS. They may have gained their work experience through internships, employment, or volunteer work. Employers usually seek candidates for both entry-level and advanced positions who are familiar with the concepts and practices of their industry.

Because they must work well with colleagues, managers, staff, and others from diverse backgrounds, GIS Specialists need excellent interpersonal, communication, and customer service skills. Their work also requires that they possess effective computer, writing, problem-solving, organizational, and self-management skills. Being analytical, creative, flexible, honest, diplomatic, and enthusiastic are some personality traits that successful GIS Specialists share.

Unions and Associations

GIS Specialists can join professional associations to take advantage of professional resources and services such as networking opportunities, publications, and certification programs. Some national societies that serve the diverse interests of GIS professionals include the Geographic and Land Information Society, the Cartography and Geographic Information Society, the Urban and Regional Information Systems Association, and the Association of American Geographers. For contact information, see Appendix III.

GIS Specialists who are employed by government agencies may be members of unions.

Tips for Entry

1. What fields—environment, public health, urban planning, and so forth—interest you the most? Learn as much as you can about them and how GIS applications are used in those fields.

2. Many employers hire candidates who have proficient cartography, computer programming, and database management skills.

3. Apply directly to employers for whom you wish to work. If you apply in person, be sure to bring your résumé, as well as be ready for the possibility that you will be interviewed.

4. Do not assume that the duties and requirements for a particular job (such as GIS technician) are the same among all employers. Read a job announcement carefully to make sure that the position is really the one you seek and that you meet the qualifications to apply for it.

5. Learn more about the GIS field on the Internet. You might start by visiting these Web sites: GIS Lounge, http://gislounge.com, and Geospatial Information and Technology Association, http://www.gita.org. For more links, see Appendix IV.

MATHEMATICS

MATHEMATICIAN

Position Description

Mathematics has been described as being one of the oldest and most basic scientific disciplines. It is based purely on logic. It is the study of measurement, properties, and relationships of quantities and sets of people and things. Mathematicians use mathematical theory, algorithms, computational techniques, and computer technology to solve problems in physics, biological science, medicine, social science, engineering, business, economics, public health, education, manufacturing, and numerous other fields.

Mathematicians are involved in two general areas of study—theoretical mathematics and applied mathematics. Theoretical mathematicians investigate and test new mathematical theories as well as seek to establish connections between existing ideas. They explore axioms and learn what happens when mathematical rules are followed or not followed. They discover new mathematical patterns, reveal unknown relationships, develop new mathematical principles, and even create new kinds of mathematics.

Theoretical mathematicians usually work at research institutions or as professors in colleges and universities. They specialize in one or more mathematical areas throughout their careers. Some specialties include mathematical logic, number theory, discrete mathematics, algebraic geometry, graph theory, stochastic processes, game theory, probability and statistics, and computational mathematics. The findings of basic research have been used to further many scientific discoveries and technological achievements.

Applied mathematicians make up a larger group of mathematicians than the theoreticians. Applied mathematicians are involved in research and development in academic, government, business, industrial, nongovernmental, and nonprofit settings. They work on research teams that may engage in basic research, applied research, or product development. Their role is to utilize mathematical principles, algorithms, computational techniques, and computer models to solve specific problems in a research project. For example, applied mathematicians might address such questions as: What effects would certain drugs have on curing cancer? What is the most cost-effective way to produce canned vegetables? How many voters might approve a state bond to raise $500 million for new schools? What will the global climate look like in 50 years?

Applied mathematicians construct mathematical models on computers to help them solve problems. Mathematical models are equations that describe the components of a problem and their relationship to each other. The variables of an equation represent the components in the problem. By assigning different values to the variables, Mathematicians can create simulations to see how alternative solutions might work.

Applied mathematicians are often known by other job titles, such as research scientist or systems analyst, which describe their specific positions in an organization. Many applied mathematicians are professionals, such as engineers, physicists, and accountants, who frequently use mathematics on their job.

Mathematicians also work in the various branches of applied mathematics. Some of these professionals are:

- bioinformaticians, who manage and analyze biological data stored in computer databases
- cryptologists, who develop systems to encrypt or decode in formation
- statisticians, who analyze and interpret collections of numerical data
- actuaries, who examine the financial risk, uncertainties, and probabilities of future events for organizations
- operations research analysts, who examine problems related to the allocation of resources (people, equipment, facilities, and money) in organizations

Mathematicians work in offices and laboratories. They perform various duties, which may include designing research projects, reviewing scientific literature, analyzing and interpreting data, writing reports, meeting with colleagues, preparing presentations, and performing administrative tasks.

Mathematicians normally work on more than one research project at a time. Those who conduct independent research are usually responsible for seeking grants from the federal government and other sources to fund their research projects. This involves writing grant proposals that describe goals, methodologies, budgets, and other aspects about their proposed projects.

Many Mathematicians hold teaching appointments in colleges and universities. They are responsible for teaching courses along with conducting research. They also advise students as well as supervise students with their research projects. In addition, faculty perform administrative duties, produce scholarly work, and fulfill community service obligations. In some four-year colleges, professors may be appointed to only teach mathematics courses.

Many Mathematicians work more than 40 hours per week to complete their various tasks and to meet deadlines. They may be required to travel to meet with clients or attend seminars or conferences.

Salaries

Salaries for Mathematicians vary, depending on such factors as their education, experience, employer, and geographical locations. According to the May 2006 *Occupational Employment Statistics* survey by the U.S. Bureau of Labor Statistics (BLS), the estimated annual salary for most Mathematicians ranged between $43,500 and $132,190, and for most mathematics professors, between $31,580 and $103,330.

Employment Prospects

Mathematicians are employed by academic institutions, government agencies, research institutes, and non-profit organizations. They also work throughout the private sector in such organizations as computer service firms, computer and electronics manufacturers, energy companies, defense contractors, insurance companies, banks, financial services firms, transportation services, aerospace companies, pharmaceutical companies, and engineering research groups.

Competition for Mathematician opportunities is keen. Job openings generally become available as Mathematicians retire or transfer to other positions. According to the BLS, job growth for Mathematicians is expected to increase by 10 percent through 2016. Experts say that there is a continued demand for professionals who have a background in advanced mathematics.

Some experts say that opportunities for applied mathematicians are more plentiful than for theoretical mathematicians. Competition for theoretical research jobs is highly competitive. Applied mathematicians who have training or experience in the field in which they plan to work have the best job prospects.

With a background in mathematics, individuals can pursue careers as computer scientists, computer programmers, software developers, engineers, school teachers, financial analysts, economists, lawyers, physicians, and so on.

Advancement Prospects

Mathematicians with management and administrative interests can pursue advancement to such positions in any work setting. For example, research scientists in industry or government settings may advance by becoming project leaders, program directors, and executive officers. Professors receive promotional rankings as assistant professors, associate professors, or full professors.

Education and Training

Depending on the employer, Mathematicians must possess either a bachelor's or advanced degree in mathematics or a related field. The minimum requirement for an entry-level position in the federal government is a bachelor's degree. A master's or doctoral degree is required for most research positions in private industry, although employers may hire individuals with a bachelor's degree if they have qualifying work experience. Doctoral degrees are usually required to teach in universities and colleges, to conduct independent research, and to obtain top management positions.

Experience, Skills, and Personality Traits

In general, employers look for applicants who have relevant work experience. Entry-level applicants may have gained experience through research projects, internships, fellowships, or employment. Industry employers prefer candidates who are knowledgeable about related sciences and who have experience working in the employers' particular settings. Many employers prefer that Ph.D. applicants for research scientist positions have a few years of postdoctoral experience.

Mathematicians should be knowledgeable about computer programming and have excellent problem-solving skills. In addition, they should have strong writing, communication, interpersonal, and teamwork skills. Mathematicians must be able to work well with others and present ideas and solutions clearly to colleagues and others.

Being imaginative, intuitive, curious, persistent, logical, and flexible are some personality traits that successful Mathematicians share.

Unions and Associations

Mathematicians can join local, state, and national professional associations to take advantage of an array of services and resources such as education programs and networking opportunities. Some national societies that serve the different interests of Mathematicians are:

- Mathematical Association of America
- American Mathematical Society
- Society for Industrial and Applied Mathematics
- American Statistical Association
- Society of Actuaries
- Association for Women in Mathematics

Faculty members might join societies that serve academic interests such as the National Association of Scholars or the American Association of University Professors.

See Appendix III for contact information for all of the above organizations.

Tips for Entry

1. Talk with college professors, career counselors, and professionals in the various fields to learn about the different career options that are available in applied mathematics.
2. Many employers go to college and university job fairs and career days to recruit for entry-level positions.
3. Most professional societies have career development pages on their Web sites which may include job listings.
4. Many universities, corporations, research institutes, and other organizations post current vacancies as well as provide information about their application process and working environments.
5. Use the Internet to learn more about Mathematicians. Two Web sites you might visit are the Young Mathematicians Network, http://www.youngmath.org; and American Mathematical Society, http://www.ams.org. For more links, see Appendix IV.

STATISTICIAN

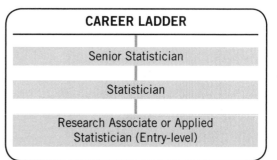

Position Description

Statistics is a branch of mathematics that involves the collection, organization, analysis, and interpretation of large masses of numerical, or statistical, data about a particular subject. For example, Statisticians might derive statistical data from reading test scores of all third graders in a state, measurements of the air temperature for a city over a 20-year period, answers from a salary survey of an organization's 5,000 members, or results from experiments done for a geophysics study. Statistical information is used by scientists, engineers, financial analysts, educators, policy makers, and many others for different reasons—to help solve problems, design projects, evaluate programs, make policy decisions, predict future events, and so on.

Statisticians work throughout the public and private sectors where they are involved in research and development. They might work alone or as part of a team—with other mathematicians, scientists, engineers, and others—on research projects. The projects may be concerned with basic research, applied research, or product development.

Statisticians are generally classified into two groups. One group is composed of theorists known as mathematical statisticians. They conduct research to gain new knowledge and understanding of statistics; and they utilize mathematical theory to design and improve analytical methods, sampling techniques, and computational approaches.

The second, and larger, group is made up of applied statisticians. These mathematicians use statistical principles and techniques to solve problems in diverse fields, such as biology, medicine, agriculture, education, public health, criminal justice, marketing, economics, engineering, and sports. For example, government statisticians might develop and analyze surveys that measure job growth or public transportation ridership, while Statisticians at a pharmaceutical company might evaluate the results of clinical trials to determine if new medications are safe.

Many applied statisticians specialize in a particular field, such as economics, agriculture, or biological sciences. Some Statisticians work as consultants. They may provide services to specific industries or specialize in particular statistical methods. In many work settings, applied statisticians are known by other job titles such as research scientist or research analyst. Some have professional designations that describe the specific area or field in which they work—marketing researcher, biostatistician, demographer, or quality control specialist, for example.

Whether they are theorists or applied mathematicians, Statisticians are responsible for producing statistical data that is accurate, unbiased, and trustworthy. Statisticians perform various duties, which vary according to their position, experience, and skills. For example, their tasks may involve:

- applying statistical methods to the design of research projects
- determining the methods to use for sampling, data collection, and data analysis
- designing experiments
- developing questionnaires according to project specifications
- providing instructions to staff who collect information
- monitoring experiments to ensure that desired information is correctly obtained
- organizing and processing data
- reviewing, interpreting, and supervising data
- developing new statistical software programs for studies
- keeping up with developments in their fields and updating their skills

Statisticians in universities and colleges are usually appointed as faculty members. Along with conducting research, they are responsible for teaching and advising students as well as supervising them with their research projects. In addition, faculty members are required to perform administrative duties, produce scholarly work, and fulfill community service obligations.

Statisticians work a 40-hour week, but often put in additional hours to complete their various tasks and meet strict deadlines. Some Statisticians travel on their job to meet with clients in their offices or to gather statistical data in the field.

Salaries
Salaries for Statisticians vary, depending on factors such as their education, experience, position, employer, and geographical location. The U.S. Bureau of Labor Statistics (BLS) reports in its May 2006 *Occupational Employment Statistics* (OES) survey that the estimated annual salary for most Statisticians ranged between $37,010 and $108,630.

Employment Prospects
According to the BLS May 2006 OES survey, about 19,660 Statisticians are employed in the United States. The largest employer, the federal government, employed about 20 percent of Statisticians. Statisticians are also hired by state and local government agencies, academic institutions, nonprofit groups, and nongovernmental organizations. Additionally, they find employment in many private industries, including the insurance, pharmaceutical, automobile, aerospace, chemicals manufacturing, scientific research and development services, and software manufacturing industries, among others.

In general, most opportunities become available as Statisticians retire or transfer to other positions. The BLS reports that job growth for Statisticians is expected to increase by up to 9 percent through 2016. However, this does not account for jobs with other job titles (such as market researcher or demographer) that require a statistics degree. According to many experts, opportunities for experienced Statisticians should continue to be favorable.

Job prospects should be good for Statisticians who have additional background or training in another field such as biological science, finance, engineering, or economics.

Many employers in industry hire qualified Statisticians for positions in quality control, systems analysis, business analysis, market research, operations research, software development, and other areas.

Advancement Prospects
Statisticians can advance to supervisory and management positions, as they gain more technical skills and experience. Having advanced degrees may improve chances for advancement opportunities. The top goal for some Statisticians is to become consultants.

Education and Training
For research positions, Statisticians usually need a master's or doctoral degree in statistics, mathematics, or another related field. Many entry-level positions in the federal government require only a bachelor's degree. To teach in four-year colleges and universities, Statisticians must possess a doctoral degree.

Experience, Skills, and Personality Traits
In general, employers look for candidates who have relevant work experience, preferably in their industry or work setting. Entry-level applicants may have gained experience through research projects, internships, fellowships, part-time employment, and so on. In addition, Statisticians need to be familiar with or knowledgeable about the subject matter with which they are working. For example, Statisticians in pharmaceutical firms must be familiar with pharmaceutical terminology and processes in order to handle the data.

Statisticians must have computer programming skills and be familiar with appropriate statistical software. Statisticians need strong communication skills, as they must be able to explain technical information to individuals without statistical backgrounds. In addition, Statisticians need excellent interpersonal and teamwork skills. Further, Statisticians should have good writing skills.

Being curious, well-organized, detail-oriented, methodical, and practical are some personality traits that describe successful Statisticians.

Unions and Associations

Statisticians join professional associations to take advantage of networking opportunities, job listings, education programs, and other professional services and resources. Some national societies that serve the interests of Statisticians are:

- American Statistical Association
- Institute of Mathematical Statistics
- Caucus for Women in Statistics
- International Biometric Society
- Mathematical Association of America
- American Mathematical Society
- Society for Industrial and Applied Mathematics

For contact information for these organizations, see Appendix III.

Tips for Entry

1. Are you thinking about a career as an applied statistician? To enhance your employability, take some courses in the field—such as biology, economics, or sociology—that interests you. Talk with Statisticians in the field for course recommendations.

2. You can find job listings for federal positions at the U.S. Office of Personnel Management Web site, http://usajobs.opm.gov. Some federal agencies also post employment opportunities, as well as career information at their Web sites. Some federal agencies you might check out include the U.S. Census Bureau, http://www.census.gov; the U.S. Bureau of Labor Statistics, http://www.bls.gov; the U.S. National Institutes of Health, http://www.nih.gov; and the U.S. Office of Justice Programs, http://www.ojp.usdoj.gov.

3. Use the Internet to learn more about Statisticians. One Web site to visit is for the American Statistical Association. Its URL is http://www.amstat.org. For more links, see Appendix IV.

OPERATIONS RESEARCH ANALYST

Duties: Analyze and solve complex operational problems within organizations; perform duties as required

Alternate Title(s): Decision Scientist, Management Analyst, Systems Analyst, Risk Analyst

Salary Range: $39,000 to $108,000

Employment Prospects: Good

Advancement Prospects: Good

Prerequisites:

    Education or Training—An advanced degree in operations research or related field

    Experience—Several years of work experience in operations research, systems analysis, or related fields

    Special Skills and Personality Traits—Computer, interpersonal, teamwork, writing, and communication skills; be energetic, self-motivated, hardworking, creative, tactful

CAREER LADDER

Senior Operations Research Analyst

Operations Research Analyst

Operations Research Analyst (Entry-level)

Position Description

Operations Research (OR) Analysts are applied mathematicians who study complex problems that are involved with the daily operations of organizations. They provide scientific analyses that managers use to make sound decisions about program planning, scheduling, staffing, job performance measurement, inventory control, pricing, facilities layout, systems design, distribution of goods or services, marketing, and other activities.

Operations research (OR) is an interdisciplinary field that incorporates mathematics, engineering, management, and psychology. The beginning of the OR field goes back to World War II when military planners wanted to base their decisions about military operations on scientific and mathematical principles and techniques. After the war, decision makers in industry found that OR methodologies could be applied to problems in their organizations.

Today OR is also known as management science. OR Analysts work in both the public and private sectors. They are involved in diverse areas, including criminal justice, protective service, the environment, health care, social services, transportation, energy policy, defense, natural resources management, communications, manufacturing, education, meteorology, and biological sciences.

The procedures that OR Analysts use are basically the same, regardless of their project or work setting. Their projects begin by analyzing the information that managers give them. OR Analysts define the problem in terms of the managers' goals and objectives and identify the details that they need to study. They also break down the problem into components that can be solved mathematically.

Their next step is to collect data. They read relevant materials and literature. They interview people who are involved in or affected by the issues being studied, asking for feedback about the problems as well as for suggestions for ways to solve them. OR Analysts talk to engineers and scientists, to managers and support staff, as well as to vendors and customers.

OR Analysts use various techniques to help them analyze and interpret the data, including statistics, stochastic, queuing theory, network analysis, and optimization. They select the OR methodology that most effectively addresses a problem and helps them find alternative solutions. For example, if an OR Analyst is addressing a question about how to keep lines flowing smoothly in supermarkets, he might use the queuing theory. If a problem involves scheduling bus routes for a city bus system, an OR Analyst might use the mathematical technique called network analysis. Sometimes OR Analysts use a combination of two or more methods to find solutions.

An OR Analyst's work involves constructing mathematical models, or mathematical equations that describe the behavior of the problems being studied. A mathematical equation describes the components of a problem and their relationship to each other. The variables of an equation represent the components in the problem. By assigning different values to the variables,

OR Analysts can create simulations to see how alternative solutions might work.

OR Analysts generally use computer programs to create their mathematical models. (They sometimes need to design a new program if one does not exist for their purposes.) With computer models, OR Analysts are able to run the program over and over, changing the values to examine what can happen under different circumstances.

Upon completion of their evaluations, OR Analysts prepare written or oral reports for management. They provide a comprehensive analysis as well as their recommendations for the suitable solutions. They present the information clearly and in language that nontechnical people can understand.

Some OR Analysts are generalists, while others specialize in particular OR methodologies. OR Analysts may work in a central OR department in an organization or be assigned to work in different departments.

OR Analysts work 40 hours a week. Many put in additional hours to meet deadlines.

Salaries

Salaries for OR Analysts vary, depending on such factors as their qualifications, employer, and geographical location. According to the May 2006 *Occupational Employment Statistics* (OES) survey by the U.S. Bureau of Labor Statistics (BLS), the estimated annual salary for most OR Analysts ranged between $38,760 and $108,290.

Employment Prospects

The BLS reports in its May 2006 OES survey that about 56,170 OR Analysts are employed in the United States. These professionals work for local and state government agencies as well as for the federal agencies and the U.S. Armed Forces. In the private sector, OR Analysts find employment in such diverse areas as transportation, telecommunications, computer and data processing services, banks, financial services, insurance, energy, manufacturing, retail, health care, and security. Many are employed by engineering and management services firms as well as by research and testing organizations that offer operations research consulting services.

Opportunities for experienced OR Analysts are strong, as managers are continually interested in improving the effectiveness and productivity of their organizations in order to stay competitive in their fields. However, the Bureau of Labor Statistics reports that few of the job openings are expected to have the title of Operations Research Analyst, but rather such titles as management analyst, systems analyst, and operations analyst.

Experienced operations research specialists with advanced degrees should have the best chances of finding employment. Opportunities are expected to be especially favorable in finance, manufacturing, transportation, telecommunications, and homeland security.

Advancement Prospects

OR Analysts with management and administrative ambitions can seek such positions in the different work settings. They can advance to top-level positions in the operations research departments as well as in other departments such as marketing. Some OR Analysts aspire to become independent consultants or to own consulting firms.

With additional experience and advanced degrees, OR Analysts can pursue academic careers, by teaching college students and by conducting independent research in operations management.

Education and Training

The minimum requirement for OR Analysts is a bachelor's degree in operations research, science management, mathematics, engineering, or another related field. Most employers prefer that candidates possess a master's or doctoral degree.

OR Analysts are expected to keep up with new developments in operations research and computer science. Many employers provide training for entry-level and experienced OR Analysts. Some employers offer education programs that pay for OR Analysts to enroll in appropriate courses at local colleges or universities.

Experience, Skills, and Personality Traits

In general, applicants should have several years of experience working in operations research, systems analysis, or related areas. In addition, they should have experience working in the industry to which they are applying.

OR Analysts must be computer literate and be able to use various software programs, including database collection and management programs. In addition, OR Analysts must be knowledgeable about computer programming and be able to develop software programs.

OR Analysts need strong interpersonal and teamwork skills, as they must be able to work well with others. In addition, they must have good writing and communication skills in order to present information clearly and persuasively.

Being energetic, self-motivated, hardworking, creative, and tactful are some personality traits that successful OR Analysts have in common.

Unions and Associations

Many OR Analysts belong to professional associations to take advantage of professional services and resources, such as networking opportunities, education programs, and professional publications. At the national level, the Institute for Operations Research and the Management Sciences serves the particular interests of OR Analysts. They are also eligible to join societies for mathematicians such as the Mathematical Association of America, the American Mathematical Society, the Society for Industrial and Applied Mathematics, or the Association for Women in Mathematics. See Appendix III for contact information.

Tips for Entry

1. Talk with OR Analysts in different work settings to get an idea of what areas may interest you.

Also ask them to recommend courses in other disciplines that may be useful for an OR career.

2. Take advantage of your college career center. Career counselors can help you find internship and employment opportunities, as well as help you build your job search techniques. College career centers usually offer services to alumni.

3. Learn more about the operations research field on the Internet. One Web site to visit is for the Institute for Operations Research and the Management Sciences at http://www.informs.org. For more links, see Appendix IV.

ACTUARY

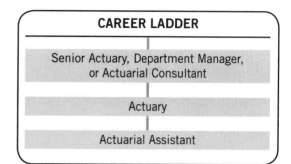

Special Skills and Personality Traits—Computer, project management, problem-solving, teamwork, interpersonal, and communication skills; be analytical, flexible, self-motivated, enthusiastic, and creative

Position Description

Actuaries are experts in identifying financial risk, uncertainties, and probabilities that could occur in the future. Using mathematics, statistics, and financial theory, Actuaries provide their employers with financial strategies and forecasts that can help them make important business decisions. Actuaries also help employers create programs that would be able to handle future financial loss.

Actuaries generally work in the insurance, pension plans, and financial investments industries. Insurance actuaries specialize in life, health, casualty, or workers' compensation insurance.

Actuaries work on a wide range of different projects, which vary depending on their experience and work setting. For example, they might:

- determine prices for products and services that their employers sell
- calculate potential profits and losses for a new product
- project the cost of a loss over a number of years
- determine the financial risk involved in a business merger or acquisition
- estimate the financial loss for an employer if a natural or man-made disaster should occur
- determine the amount of reserves needed to cover future losses
- appraise the current value of an organization, a particular program, or specific inventory

- design new products or programs
- establish rating guidelines and risk categories
- estimate future cash flows, earnings, taxes, assets, and liabilities
- develop investment strategies

Actuaries gather, analyze, and interpret data from various sources. They read numerical information, historical data, laws and regulations, and trends. They develop mathematical models to help them analyze problems. Actuaries then discuss their findings with executives, attorneys, marketing staff, and other employees.

Actuaries may provide expert witness testimony at court trials, depositions, administrative hearings, legislative hearings, and alternative dispute resolution hearings. For example, an Actuary might provide testimony about the value of a pension plan in a divorce case, while another Actuary might testify at an administrative hearing about how proposed regulation would affect business.

Actuaries are responsible for keeping up with current legislation, economic and social trends, and developments in their industry.

Actuaries work a standard 40-hour week.

Salaries

Salaries for Actuaries vary, depending on such factors as their experience, qualifications, employer, and geographical location. According to the May 2006 *Occupational*

Employment Statistics (OES) survey by the U.S. Bureau of Labor Statistics (BLS), the estimated annual salary for most Actuaries ranged between $46,470 and $145,600.

Employment Prospects

Some employers of Actuaries are insurance companies, banks, financial service firms, health maintenance organizations (HMOs), government agencies, corporations and actuarial consulting firms.

The BLS reports in its May 2006 OES survey that about 16,620 Actuaries are employed in the United States; and nearly half of them worked in the insurance carriers industry. This agency predicts that employment for Actuaries should increase by about 24 percent through 2016. In addition, openings will become available as Actuaries retire or transfer to other positions.

Advancement Prospects

Actuaries obtain professional status (on a voluntary basis) by passing a series of actuarial examinations that are administered by actuary associations. There are two professional levels. The first level is the Associate designation, which takes most Actuaries three to five years to achieve. The higher level is the Fellow designation, which takes a few more years to complete. The Casually Actuarial Society grants the professional credential to those in the property and casualty practices. The Society of Actuaries grants the credential to those who practice in life insurance, health insurance, finance, investments, or pension plans.

Actuaries can advance to supervisory, management, and executive positions, including positions in other departments. For example, insurance Actuaries might be appointed to managerial roles in the underwriting, accounting, or marketing departments. Actuaries can also follow a career path as independent consultants or business owners that provide actuarial services.

Education and Training

Many employers prefer to hire entry-level candidates who hold a bachelor's degree in mathematics, actuarial science, business, finance, statistics, or another related field. Employers may hire candidates with a nonmath degree if they have passed one or more actuarial examinations.

Employers provide on-the-job training for entry-level positions. Many employers have education programs to help Actuaries study for their actuarial examinations.

Experience, Skills, and Personality Traits

Requirements vary from employer to employer for entry-level positions. Employers often hire college graduates with little or no experience, if they can demonstrate strong mathematical and technical aptitudes as well as good business sense. Many employers prefer that candidates have completed one or more actuarial examinations.

Actuaries must have effective computer and project management skills. They also need strong problem-solving, teamwork, and interpersonal skills. Having communication skills is important for their job, too. They must be able to explain complex technical concepts in terms that are clearly understood. Some personality traits that successful Actuaries share are being analytical, flexible, self-motivated, enthusiastic, and creative.

Unions and Associations

Actuaries can join professional associations to take advantage of networking opportunities, education programs, and other services and resources. Some national societies that serve the interests of actuaries include the American Academy of Actuaries, the American Society of Pension Professionals and Actuaries, the Casualty Actuarial Society, the Conference of Consulting Actuaries, and the Society of Actuaries. See Appendix III for contact information.

Tips for Entry

1. As a college student, obtain internships to see if the actuarial field is right for you. Visit your college career center for help in finding internships.
2. You can enhance your employability for entry-level positions by passing one or more actuarial examinations while still in college.
3. Actuaries who practice in pension plans that are governed by federal laws must be licensed by the Joint Board for the Enrollment of Actuaries, part of the U.S. Internal Revenue Service. For specific information, visit its Web site at http://www.irs.gov/taxpros/actuaries/index.html.
4. Learn more about Actuary careers on the Internet. One Web site you might visit is called Be an Actuary. The URL is http://www.beanactuary.com. For more links, see Appendix IV.

CRYPTOGRAPHER

Duties: Study the science of cryptology; design and conduct research; develop systems to encrypt or decode information; perform duties as required

Alternate Title(s): Cryptanalyst, Cryptologist

Salary Range: $44,000 to $132,000

Employment Prospects: Good

Advancement Prospects: Good

Prerequisites:

Education or Training—A master's or doctoral degree required for research positions

Experience—Previous work experience required

Special Skills and Personality Traits—Communication, interpersonal, and teamwork skills; be curious, innovative, patient, and methodical

Position Description

Throughout time, individuals, companies, governments, and the military have passed on important details in code and ciphers so that only the intended recipients receive the information. Converting text into codes or ciphers is an art. It is also a science known as cryptology. Today, Cryptographers are involved in such critical activities as deciphering secret messages between criminals, devising code systems for national security, and creating codes to prevent hackers from viewing and retrieving vital data from computer systems.

Cryptographers utilize the principles and techniques of mathematics and computer science. They may be involved in one or both of the major areas of cryptology—cryptography and cryptanalysis—during their careers.

Cryptography is the science of converting data into and back from an unreadable format. Using algorithms, Cryptographers develop cryptosystems (or code systems) to protect information from being read by unauthorized parties. The process of translating data into codes is known as encryption, and the method of restoring coded data to its original language is called decryption. Cryptographers design cryptosystems so that only individuals with a secret key (an algorithm) can unravel the coded data.

Cryptanalysis is the science of analyzing codes and cryptosystems and unscrambling them without having prior knowledge of the codes or having the required secret keys. In more familiar terms, cryptanalysis is known as code breaking. Cryptanalysts generally look for errors or weaknesses in the algorithms, which make up the codes, or in the way that they have been implemented.

Cryptographers work in various settings. Many of them are research scientists who work in industrial, government, and academic environments. They conduct basic research to gain further knowledge and understanding about the different facets of cryptology, including topics related to the cryptographic infrastructure and standards for information systems. Cryptology researchers also are involved in applied research for practical and commercial purposes. They create and design new or improved cryptographic algorithms, architectures, and infrastructures as well as develop and improve cryptanalysis techniques for applications in information security, telecommunications, and other fields.

Some Cryptographers are engaged in making and breaking codes for the purposes of national security. These experts are usually employed by the military or by government agencies such as the National Security Agency (NSA) or the Central Intelligence Agency (CIA). Other Cryptographers are involved in information security for private corporations, government agencies, banks, retailers, schools, hospitals, and other establishments. They design encryption systems to protect data stored on computers from being accessed by unauthorized parties. They also develop cryptosystems to ensure the safe and secure transmission of confidential information such as credit card numbers, electronic money, business data, medical information, and e-mail messages over computer networks.

Depending on their projects, Cryptographers may work alone or collaborate with others as part of a team. Their duties vary according to their position, experience, and skills. Research scientists, for example, are responsible for generating ideas for new research projects, designing and conducting research projects, and writing and presenting technical reports of their findings and conclusions. Cryptographers also perform many of the same routine tasks regardless of their position. For example, they develop, study, and test theories; conduct research to gather information about a problem; analyze, design, and implement algorithms; encrypt messages, databases, or systems; and develop methods for handling cryptic messages and processes.

Academic researchers normally hold professorships at colleges and universities where they usually teach in the mathematics or computer science department. Along with performing scholarly research, they are responsible for teaching courses, advising students, supervising students' research projects, fulfilling community service, and performing administrative duties. Academic researchers are also responsible for seeking sufficient grants to fund their research projects and producing published works about their research.

Cryptographers, in all settings, typically put in long hours to complete their tasks and meet deadlines.

Salaries

Earnings for Cryptographers vary, depending on such factors as their education, experience, position, employer, and geographical location. A general idea of their salaries can also be gained by looking at what mathematicians earn. According to the May 2006 *Occupational Employment Statistics* survey by the U.S. Bureau of Labor Statistics, the estimated annual salary for most mathematicians ranged between $43,500 and $132,190. The Schools in the USA Web site (http://www.schoolsintheusa.com) reports that the average salary for cryptanalysts is $76,470 per year.

Employment Prospects

Some employers of Cryptographers include colleges and universities, banks, financial institutions, insurance companies, computer design companies, telecommunications companies, science and engineering firms, and research institutes. These specialists are also employed by the military, law enforcement agencies, and government agencies.

According to some experts in the field, the demand for Cryptographers is high. Opportunities are expected to grow through the years, as cryptology is playing an increasing role in information security due to the popular use of the Internet and wireless technologies for communication purposes.

With their training and background, Cryptographers can also pursue careers as information security professionals.

Advancement Prospects

As Cryptographers gain experience, they earn higher salaries, receive greater responsibilities, and are assigned to more complex and sophisticated projects. They can also advance to lead, supervisory, and management positions. Those with entrepreneurial ambitions can become independent consultants or start their own consulting firms.

Academicians are promoted in rank from instructor to assistant, associate, and full professor. They also advance by gaining tenure at their institution.

Education and Training

Minimally, individuals must hold a bachelor's degree in mathematics, computer science, or another related field. For research positions, individuals usually need a master's or doctoral degree in mathematics or computer science. To teach at four-year colleges and universities, individuals must possess a doctoral degree.

Throughout their careers, Cryptographers enroll in continuing education and training programs to update their skills and keep up with advancements in their fields.

Experience, Special Skills, and Personality Traits

Employers prefer to hire candidates for entry-level positions who have work experience in cryptology. They may have gained their experience through employment, internships, postdoctoral fellowships, or research projects. For research positions, many employers seek scientists who have strong publication records.

To be effective at their jobs, Cryptographers must have strong communication, interpersonal, and teamwork skills. Being curious, innovative, patient, and methodical are some personality traits that Cryptographers share.

Unions and Associations

Cryptographers may join professional associations to take advantage of networking opportunities, current research findings, publications, and other professional resources and services. Some societies that serve the diverse interests of these experts include the International Association for Cryptologic Research, the IEEE Computer Society's Technical Committee on Security and Privacy, the Association for Computing Machinery, and the Society for Industrial and Applied Mathematics. For contact information, see Appendix III.

Tips for Entry

1. As a high school student, read books and articles about cryptography to get an idea if it is a field that may interest you.

2. Future Cryptographers need a strong background in mathematics. Some experts recommend that college students take courses in number theory, algorithms, statistics, abstract algebra, and complexity theory.

3. As a college student, gain experience by obtaining an internship with companies or government agencies that are involved in cryptology. You might also volunteer or seek research assistantships with professors who are conducting cryptography research projects.

4. Use the Internet to learn more about cryptology and its applications in the real world. To get a list of relevant Web sites, enter any of these keywords into a search engine: *cryptography, cryptographers,* or *cryptanalysts.* For some links, see Appendix IV.

COMPUTER SCIENCE

COMPUTER SCIENTIST

Position Description

Computer Scientists are researchers and inventors. They are involved in the study and design of computers and computational processes. They are interested in understanding the foundations (algorithms and theories) upon which the operation and design of computers and computer systems are based. They are also concerned with understanding the computational processes for handling and managing large masses of information. Furthermore, they create computer hardware, software, and information technologies that are used in medicine, scientific research, biotechnology, agriculture, education, law, space travel, energy, protective services, business, finance, and other areas.

Computer Scientists engage in research and development in academic, government, and industrial settings. Their work involves developing mathematical models as well as building computational artifacts (such as computer chips, operating systems, computing programs, and robots) to analyze and test their theories. These scientists might perform basic research to pursue new knowledge and understanding of computing processes and computer systems. They might conduct applied research in which they take the results of basic research to develop technologies and processes that can solve general problems in various fields. Computer Scientists are also involved in product development. Working mostly in private companies, these researchers participate in the development of a wide range of consumer products.

Although it is a relatively young discipline, computer science has been evolving rapidly since its beginnings in the 1940s. As new computer technologies are discovered, new subdisciplines emerge. Research scientists typically focus their studies in one or more areas, such as computer theory and algorithms, computer architecture, programming languages, software engineering, operating systems, networking, database systems, information management, computer security, artificial intelligence, human and computer interaction, computational biology, scientific computing, computer graphics, and electronic commerce. In addition, these scientists conduct studies that are connected to research in other disciplines such as biology, economics, mechanics, physics, art, and medicine.

Academic researchers usually choose the types of projects that they wish to explore while government and industrial researchers generally conduct research that meets the missions of their employers. Many Computer Scientists work on team projects, collaborating with other Computer Scientists who are experts in their particular subdisciplines. They also work with other scientists, engineers, technologists, and technicians. Senior research scientists may be involved in leading team projects or research divisions.

Computer Scientists work in offices and laboratories. They perform a wide range of tasks that vary each day. For example, they design research projects, gather research data, read research studies, conduct experiments or develop models, analyze and interpret data, write reports, attend meetings, provide consulting services, and perform administrative tasks. Independent researchers are usually responsible for seeking out grants to fund their research projects.

Computer Scientists are expected to share the results of their research with their colleagues. They may write scientific papers or make presentations at scientific meetings. Some scientists develop Web sites to disseminate their research data. Further, Computer Scientists are responsible for keeping up with new technologies and developments. They read professional journals and books, enroll in workshops and seminars, attend professional conferences, network with colleagues, and so on.

Some Computer Scientists teach academic courses in computer science, electrical engineering, or other areas. In addition to doing research and teaching, full-time faculty members are responsible for producing scholarly work and performing administrative and community service duties.

Computer Scientists occasionally work long hours to compete various tasks and to meet deadlines.

Salaries

Salaries for Computer Scientists vary, depending on their education, experience, employer, geographical location, and other factors. According to the May 2006 *Occupational Employment Statistics* survey by the U.S. Bureau of Labor Statistics (BLS), the estimated annual salary for most research Computer Scientists ranged from $53,590 to $144,880, and from $32,130 to $108,780 for postsecondary computer science teachers.

Employment Prospects

Computer Scientists find employment in a variety of settings in the private and public sectors. Opportunities become available each year as Computer Scientists retire, advance to higher positions, or transfer to other occupations. In addition, new positions are created each year to meet the growing needs of employers. The BLS reports that employment growth for research computer scientists is expected to increase by 22 percent through 2016.

Advancement Prospects

Computer Scientists can advance to administrative and management positions as project leaders, program managers, and research division directors. Professors receive promotional rankings as assistant professors, associate professors, or full professors.

Computer Scientists with entrepreneurial ambitions may become independent consultants or owners of start-up companies that offer consulting or other computing services, produce computer hardware or software, or sell computer products.

Education and Training

Computer Scientists generally hold a master's or doctoral degree in computer science, computer engineering, or another related field. Industrial employers may hire candidates with only a bachelor's degree if they have several years of extensive experience. To teach in colleges and universities, conduct independent research, or to advance to top-level management positions, a doctoral degree is usually required.

Computer science students are trained in the basic concepts and techniques of computing, algorithms, and computer design. Doctorate programs in computer science normally take between four and six years to complete, which includes completing an independent research project.

Experience, Skills, and Personality Traits

Employers generally choose candidates who have previous work experience and have completed relevant research studies. Entry-level applicants may have gained experience through research projects, internships, or employment. Employers may require that candidates have completed a few years of postdoctoral training. Candidates for industry positions should have some related industry experience or a background in business or economics.

Computer Scientists have strong communication and writing skills as well as excellent analytical and interpersonal skills. In addition, they have good self-management skills—the ability to organize and prioritize tasks, meet deadlines, work independently, work well with others, and so on. Being analytical, detail-oriented, persistent, inquisitive, creative, and innovative are some personality traits that successful Computer Scientists share.

Unions and Associations

Various local, state, and national societies serve the different professional interests of Computer Scientists. They offer networking opportunities, education programs, certification programs, job listings, and other professional services and resources. Some professional associations that serve the general interests of Computer Scientists include the Association for Computing Machinery, the IEEE Computer Society, and the Association for Women in Computing. See Appendix III for contact information.

Tips for Entry

1. Take advantage of internship or work-study programs at your college. Ask your college adviser, professors, college career counselors, and others about available internship programs. Also contact companies or government agencies that you are interested in working for to learn about available programs.

2. Many employers recruit prospective candidates at college job fairs. Bring copies of your résumé, and be ready to handle job interviews. Also be sure to get business cards of recruiters so that you can contact them later for further information.

3. Read the classified ads of major newspapers, especially the Sunday edition. Job ads are sometimes placed in the business and technology sections as well. You can usually find major newspapers for your area at a library.

4. Learn more about the research world of Computer Scientists on the Internet. One Web site you might visit is for the Computing Research Association. Its URL is http://www.cra.org. For more links, see Appendix IV.

ARTIFICIAL INTELLIGENCE (AI) SCIENTIST

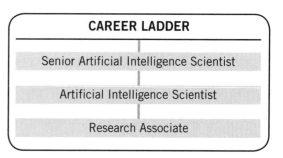

Position Description

Artificial intelligence (or AI) is the scientific study of computational models that describe human thinking processes. It is a young discipline that began during the 1950s. From the start, AI Scientists believed that it would be possible for computers to one day think and behave like human beings. Several decades later, man-made creatures with humanlike minds have not yet been invented. However, much of AI research has resulted in many practical applications that people use for work and pleasure. Some examples are word processing applications, operating systems software, computer games, automation systems in factories, voice-mail systems, Internet search engines, and e-mail filtering. Other examples are computer programs that allow cameras, kitchen appliances, medical diagnostic tools, vehicles, aircraft, robotic rovers, spacecraft, and other objects to perform tasks automatically.

Artificial intelligence is a multidisciplinary endeavor that combines knowledge from computer science, mathematics, electrical engineering, logic, neuroscience, biology, philosophy, linguistics, psychology, cognitive science, physics, and other disciplines. AI Scientists develop algorithms that explain specific characteristics of human intelligence, such as applying rules to make decisions, recognizing patterns, doing steps in logical order, or assessing how to improve task performance.

For example, an AI Scientist might develop algorithms that instruct a mobile robot to recognize obstacles in its path and go around them.

AI Scientists are engaged in research in academic, government, and industrial settings. Those who conduct basic research are interested in adding to the body of knowledge about artificial intelligence, which includes understanding how human intelligence works. They contribute new principles, methodologies, and technologies. Typically, they construct artifacts (such as computer systems) to test the validity of their theories. Their studies may require that they create new programming languages, software tools, standard designs, and methodologies.

Many AI Scientists are involved in applied research in which they seek practical uses for basic AI research. Many are part of research and development teams that create new or improved commercial products. Examples of such products include software packages, kitchen appliances, medical devices, animated films, service robots, and vehicles. Applied researchers typically specialize in a particular field or industry, such as biology, geology, nuclear physics, medicine, pharmaceuticals, agriculture, robotics, electronics, software engineering, architecture, manufacturing, military, aerospace, law, education, or entertainment.

AI Scientists generally work on several projects at a time. They work on solo projects as well as collaborate with others. Team projects may involve working with scientists and engineers from other disciplines.

Tasks for AI Scientists are varied each day. For example, they may read scientific literature; conduct experiments; meet with colleagues to discuss research projects; keep up with correspondence, phone messages, and e-mail; and work on scholarly articles or presentations. Senior researchers are involved in writing grant proposals, administering budgets, supervising research staff, and so on.

Many AI Scientists hold full-time teaching appointments at research universities. They are responsible for handling a variety of tasks involved with teaching, student advising, and research. In addition, they perform administrative and community service duties, as well as produce scholarly works for publication.

AI Scientists are expected to keep up with developments in their fields, as well as to update their skills. For example, they enroll in continuing education programs, read professional publications, and network with colleagues.

Salary

Salaries for AI Scientists vary, depending on their education, experience, employer, geographical location, and other factors. According to the May 2006 *Occupational Employment Statistics* survey, by the U.S. Bureau of Labor Statistics, the estimated annual salary for most research computer scientists (including AI Scientists) ranged between $53,590 to $144,880.

Employment Prospects

Many AI Scientists work for academic and government laboratories. Some are employed by large computer and robotics companies that have strong research and development departments.

As automation and robotics technologies are increasingly used in practical applications, opportunities for AI Scientists will grow accordingly. In general, most opportunities will become available as AI Scientists retire or transfer to other positions. Employers may create additional positions as their needs grow and funding is available.

Advancement Prospects

AI Scientists may advance to management and administrative positions as project leaders, program directors, and executive officers. Professors receive promotional rankings as assistant professor, associate professor, or full professor.

Education and Training

Advanced degrees are usually required for individuals to become AI Scientists. Most AI Scientists have earned a master's or doctorate in computer science, mathematics, or another related field. A doctoral degree is required to teach in academic institutions, conduct independent research, or advance to high-level management positions.

Experience, Skills, and Personality Traits

Job candidates are expected to have one or more years of work experience as well as research experience in areas in which their prospective employers specialize. Entry-level applicants may have gained experience through research projects, internships, employment, or teaching assistantships. Many employers expect candidates to have completed a few years of postdoctoral training.

AI Scientists need adequate computer programming and writing skills along with excellent problem-solving and analytical skills. They also need strong communication, interpersonal, and teamwork skills, as they must be able to work well with others and present their ideas clearly. Some personality traits that successful AI Scientists share are being imaginative, creative, curious, persistent, flexible, and self-motivated.

Unions and Associations

Many AI Scientists join professional associations to take advantage of networking opportunities, education programs, professional publications, and other professional resources and services. Two national societies that serve their interests are the Association for the Advancement of Artificial Intelligence and the Special-Interest Group on Artificial Intelligence (part of the Association for Computing Machinery). See Appendix III for contact information.

Tips for Entry

1. Talk with various AI Scientists to learn about their work, and how they gained entry into the field.
2. Not all graduate computer science departments have strong AI programs, nor are all AI programs alike. Do your research. Choose a program that offers the type of courses and research that interests you.
3. Use the Internet to learn more about artificial intelligence. One Web site you might visit is for the Association for the Advancement of Artificial Intelligence at http://www.aaai.org. For more links, see Appendix IV.

ROBOTICS RESEARCHER

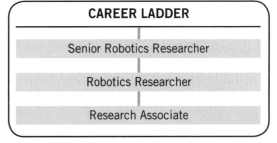
Position Description

Robotics Researchers are involved in the scientific study and practical application of robots. These are man-made machines that can move automatically and perform human tasks. Most robots have three main components—a computer that functions as a brain, a body made up of mechanical parts and devices, and sensors which give robots the ability to "see," "hear," "touch," "move," and so forth. Robots come in different shapes and forms. For example, some robots are box-shaped with moveable arms or other attachments, while other robots resemble insects, four-legged animals, and the human form. In recent years, researchers have been developing microscopic robots called nanobots.

Robotics Researchers study how robots work and how robots may be used. For the last several decades, Robotics Researchers have created increasingly more complex robots that have been used for various applications in many fields. Different types of robots are used to perform repetitive tasks, such as painting, welding parts, or assembling parts in factories. Robots also have been programmed to perform extremely difficult and dangerous tasks—such as exploring space, ocean floors, and volcanoes; locating and disposing bombs; examining extremely toxic environments; and performing routine inspections in such hard-to-reach places as heating ducts, pipes, and sewers. In addition, robots are

being used to help surgeons perform certain medical operations.

Robotics Researchers are involved in research and development in academic, government, and industrial laboratories. Basic researchers conduct studies to learn more about robots and robotic systems. They are interested in understanding the principles upon which robots and robotic systems work. They conduct studies without any specific purpose other than to learn and to add new knowledge to the robotics field.

Applied researchers use the results of basic research to solve practical problems or develop consumer products. They invent new types of robots and robotic systems as well as improve existing ones. The kinds of research that applied researchers conduct are usually defined by their employers.

Robotics Researchers are responsible for designing and conducting research projects. Their research involves applying principles and techniques from computer science, engineering, and mathematics. They sometimes build computer models that describe specific movements that researchers want robots to make.

Some Robotics Researchers apply artificial intelligence technologies to their projects, utilizing software programs that instruct robots or robotic systems to use human thinking processes to solve problems. For example, a robot might be programmed to recognize certain patterns around it or to automatically improve how well it performs its tasks by evaluating how well it had previously performed them.

Robotics Researchers typically collaborate with other scientists and engineers on research projects. Robotics Researchers also share the results of their research by writing scientific papers and making presentations at scientific conferences.

Researchers perform a variety of tasks each day, which might include reading research literature, analyzing and interpreting data, building computer models, writing reports, supervising assistants and technicians, preparing research grants, and performing administrative tasks.

Some Robotics Researchers work as full-time faculty members at research universities. In addition to conducting research, they teach and advise students in computer science or engineering departments, fulfill administrative tasks, and participate in community service.

Salaries

Salaries for Robotics Researchers vary, depending on their education, experience, employer, geographical location, and other factors. In general, they receive similar earnings as research computer scientists. The estimated annual salary for most of these professionals ranged between $53,590 to $144,880, according to the May 2006 *Occupational Employment Statistics* survey by the U.S. Bureau of Labor Statistics.

Employment Prospects

Robotics Researchers are employed by academic and government research laboratories. Many researchers, particularly robotics engineers, find employment in the robotics industry (which manufactures and sells robots) as well as in such industries as the automotive, medicine, electronics manufacturing and assembly, military, and service industries.

Most research opportunities become available as Robotics Researchers retire, advance to higher positions, or transfer to other positions.

Advancement Prospects

Robotics Researchers measure their success in various ways—through new discoveries and inventions, by earning higher pay, by gaining professional recognition, and so on.

Researchers with administrative and management ambitions can seek such positions. Those with entrepreneurial ambitions can become independent consultants or company owners.

Education and Training

Robotics Researchers hold a master's or doctoral degree in robotics, computer science, mechanical engineering, or another related field. A Ph.D. is usually required to teach in academic institutions, to conduct independent research, or to advance to high-level management positions.

Experience, Skills, and Personality Traits

Employers generally choose candidates who have work and research experiences related to the positions for which they apply. Candidates for industrial positions should have industrial experience or a background in business or economics. Entry-level applicants may have gained experience through research projects, internships, and employment. Employers may require that candidates completed a few years of postdoctoral training.

Robotics Researchers need strong analytical, problem-solving, and writing skills to do their work effectively. Having adequate skills in programming is also important. In addition, they must have excellent communication, interpersonal, and teamwork skills, as they must be able to work well with colleagues and others. Being creative, imaginative, innovative, curious, and persistent are some personality traits that successful Robotics Researchers share.

Unions and Associations

Robotics Researchers join professional associations to take advantage of professional services and resources such as networking opportunities, education programs, and professional publications. Two national societies are the IEEE Robotics and Automation Society and the American Society of Mechanical Engineers. See Appendix III for contact information.

Tips for Entry

1. In high school, take as many science and mathematics courses as you can. Also read about robotics and take advantage of opportunities to tinker with mechanical and electronic devices. For example, you might build robots from kits.
2. As a college student, seek internship opportunities in academic, government, or industrial laboratories to gain experience.
3. Learn more about robotics on the Internet. You might start by visiting Robot Information Central (by Arrick Robotics) at http://www.robotics.com/robots.html. For more links, see Appendix IV.

PROGRAMMER

Position Description

Computers affect our lives in so many ways every day. We use computers to perform our jobs, play video games, and look up information on the Internet. We use them to control and monitor numerous types of vital systems such as heating and air conditioning systems, security systems, waste management systems, and transportation systems. In addition, we use countless objects in which computers are embedded, such as watches, cell phones, appliances, electronic equipment, medical equipment, vehicles, and airplanes. Furthermore, companies, stores, restaurants, hospitals, government agencies, public utilities, factories, and various other organizations rely on computer networks to store, process, and manage vital information.

All computers are able to perform different types of functions because of instructions known as software or computer programs. In a sequence of logical steps, these programs tell computers how to identify, access, and process information as well as how to use the equipment that they control properly and accordingly. Computer professionals known as Programmers are responsible for developing the sequence of instructions for each task that a computer is designed to execute. For example, a task may be opening a file, calculating figures, tracking inventory, printing documents, controlling equipment, connecting to a network, or downloading files from the Internet.

Computer Programmers are not to be confused with software engineers. The latter often does programming

on their job, but that is not their primary responsibility. Software engineers are responsible for the overall process of designing and developing computer programs, of which computer programming is one phase.

Programmers are responsible for writing and testing computer programs. They may be engaged in developing new programs or modifying, updating, or expanding existing computer programs. In addition to being knowledgeable about algorithms and computers, these Programmers must be familiar with the subject matter of the application (such as finance or avionics) on which they are working. They generally work alone, but may work as part of a team under the supervision of a project manager.

Programmers begin a project by reviewing the specifications for a program, which is a detailed description about the goals and objective of the program that is usually prepared by a software engineer or a systems analyst. They use workflow charts and diagrams to help them identify the series of steps that an application must perform, as well as determine what each step must accomplish. They also consult with software engineers, systems analysts, and computer users as needed.

Instructions for computer programs are written in a certain computer language, such as Java, C++, Visual Basic, Prolog, HTML, Delphi, COBOL, or Visual Basic. Most Programmers know several computer languages, each used for a specific type of application. For example, Programmers might use COBOL for business applications, HTML for Web sites, or C++ for scientific programs. Programmers spend most of their time writing code, which is exacting work.

When Programmers finish writing instructions, they run tests to ensure that a program is accurate and produces the desired results. They look for any errors, which they call bugs, in the program. They may correct errors and retest the program, or report the problem to a software engineer. (This stage is generally known as testing and debugging.)

Programmers sometimes assist in preparing technical or user manuals for the applications on which they worked, by writing procedures or preparing graphs, tables, or other visual aids. Some Programmers are assigned to provide technical support to computer users in person, over the telephone, or through e-mail.

Programmers are involved in creating two types of software. Applications programmers develop software that performs a specific function, such as wordprocessing, graphic design, accounting, creating databases, or tracking inventory. These Programmers also work on computer games, educational software, and scientific and engineering programs.

Systems programmers, on the other hand, are responsible for developing programs (such as operating systems, database systems, and network systems) that maintain and control computers and computer systems. Many of them also act as technical advisers in their organizations, and assist systems analysts, applications programmers, and other personnel to resolve problems with computer systems.

Entry-level Programmers begin their careers doing routine work, under the supervision of senior Programmers. As they gain experience, Programmers are assigned increasingly complex tasks. They may specialize in certain computer languages, by performing specific functions, or by working on particular applications such as computer games or educational software. Some Programmers become involved in developing new computer languages and programming methods.

Programmers work in an office environment. Their work can be stressful, particularly when meeting deadlines or while working in the debugging phase of a project. They sit for long periods of time at a computer performing repetitive motions and are therefore at risk of developing eyestrain, back problems, and carpel tunnel syndrome.

Programmers work a standard 40-hour week, but put in additional hours as needed to meet deadlines or to resolve critical problems that occur after work hours. Some Programmers work on a temporary or contractual basis; such assignments may last for several weeks or months. Some are independent consultants who are expected to travel to a client's office to work.

Salaries

Salaries for Programmers vary, depending on various factors including their education, experience, position, employer, and geographical location. According to the May 2006 *Occupational Employment Statistics* (OES) survey, by the U.S. Bureau of Labor Statistics (BLS), the estimated annual salary for most Programmers ranged between $38,460 and $106,610. The "2006 *Computerworld* Salary Survey," reports that the annual average salary for programmers/analysts was $65,030 and for systems programmers, $80,690.

Employment Prospects

The BLS predicts that the job growth for Programmers is expected to fall slowly through 2016, decreasing by 4 percent. However, opportunities will continue to become available as Programmers are promoted, transfer to other occupations, retire, or leave the workforce. According to the BLS May 2006 OES survey, an estimated 396,020 Programmers are employed in the United States. Nearly 30 percent of them worked in the computer systems design and related services industry which employs the greatest number of these professionals. Programmers also work in various industries, including insurance, education, government, finance, telecommunications, and software publishing industries, among others.

Many employers outsource routine programming jobs to contractors. Increasingly, these jobs are being outsourced overseas to China, India, Bulgaria, and other countries where labor costs are low. Due to the constant advancement of technologies, job opportunities in the United States will continually be favorable for experienced Programmers who are knowledgeable about current programming languages and techniques. Some areas in which there is a strong demand for advanced Programmers include client/server programming, wireless applications, multimedia technology, intranet and Internet applications, expert systems, and cybersecurity.

Advancement Prospects

With additional experience and training, applications programmers may become systems programmers. Those who work in either position can become systems analysts. Programmers with administrative and managerial positions can be promoted to lead, supervisory, and management positions. Entrepreneurial Programmers can pursue careers as independent consultants or start their own software companies.

By obtaining further education, training, or experience, Programmers can pursue other computing careers by becoming software engineers, network administrators, information security specialists, research computer scientists, or computer science instructors.

Education and Training

Employers generally prefer to hire candidates for entry-level positions who possess a bachelor's degree in computer science, information systems, mathematics, or another related field. Many employers will hire candidates with a college degree in another field, or with only a high school diploma, if they have training with the programming languages and tools in which they would work.

Novice Programmers learn on the job, working under the supervision and guidance of experienced Programmers. Employers usually provide formal training programs to employees to update their skills in the newest computer technologies, languages, and applications.

Experience, Special Skills, and Personality Traits

Employers seek candidates for entry-level positions who have experience working with various programming languages and tools. College graduates may have gained their experience through volunteer work, internships, or employment.

Besides technical skills, Programmers need excellent teamwork, problem-solving, and communication skills. Additionally, they must have effective self-management skills, including the ability to work independently, understand and follow directions, prioritize multiple tasks, and handle stressful situations. Some personality traits that successful Programmers share include being analytical, detail-oriented, creative, patient, persistent, and cooperative.

Unions and Associations

Many Programmers join local, state, or national societies to take advantage of networking opportunities and other professional services and resources. Two national associations that serve the general interests of Programmers are the Association for Computing Machinery and the IEEE Computer Society. For contact information, see Appendix III.

Programmers who work in government agencies usually belong to a union.

Tips for Entry

1. As a high school student, take computer-programming courses. If none are available at your school, consider enrolling in courses offered at a community college or center.

2. Many employers prefer to hire Programmers who possess business skills and have general work experience related to their operations.

3. To enhance their employability, many Programmers acquire certification from hardware and software manufacturers. Many of them also voluntarily obtain professional certification granted by recognized organizations such as the Institute for Certification of Computing Professionals.

4. Contact prospective employers directly about job openings. Many companies, agencies, and other organizations list vacancies at their Web sites.

5. Use the Internet to learn more about the computer-programming field. You might start by visiting the Free Programming Resources Web site at http://www.freeprogrammingresources.com. For more links, see Appendix IV.

INFORMATION SECURITY SPECIALIST

CAREER PROFILE

Duties: Plan, develop, coordinate, and implement security measures for protecting information systems and the information stored in those systems; perform duties as required of position

Alternate Title(s): Computer Security Specialist, Information Systems Security Specialist; a title that reflects a particular position such as Security Auditor or Data Security Administrator

Salary Range: $39,000 to $97,000

Employment Prospects: Good

Advancement Prospects: Good

Prerequisites:

  Education or Training—Bachelor's degree usually preferred

  Experience—Extensive computing experience and several years of experience in information security

CAREER LADDER

Information Security Manager

Information Security Analyst/Engineer

Information Security Administrator

Special Skills and Personality Traits—Interpersonal, teamwork, communication, conflict management, presentation, problem-solving, troubleshooting, writing, project management, and self-management skills; be analytical, detail-oriented, creative, self-motivated, honest, dependable, flexible, positive, and patient

Position Description

Today, almost every organization—whether it is a small business, a corporation, a school, a hospital, a public utility, a factory, a government agency, a nonprofit group, or another establishment—stores and processes all of its information assets on computers and computer networks. Accounting records, financial reports, physical inventories, invoices, payroll files, customer data, and employee records are a few examples of vital information that an organization manages on its computer systems. The protection of these assets is critical, hence organizations employ Information Security Specialists to safeguard their complex information systems and the data stored on them.

Information Security Specialists, also known as computer security specialists, are responsible for uncovering and resolving security problems in an organization's information systems. This includes hardware, software, databases, internal and external networks, telecommunication technologies, the procedures for running the information systems, and the people who work on these systems. It is these specialists' job to ensure the confidentiality, reliability, and availability of all aspects of an organization's information systems. They devise various strategies to guarantee that only authorized parties

access an organization's information systems and that they are able to gain entry to the resources and services to which they are permitted. These specialists also plan, coordinate, and execute security measures to prevent unauthorized changes, destruction, or disclosure of information and technology by parties whether they are from within or without an organization. For example, they install security software or implement password authentication programs that keep unauthorized users from accessing a particular software program, computer, or network.

Information Security Specialists are responsible for different aspects of information security. They may be involved in monitoring networks for security breaches, designing modified or new technologies, developing plans for emergency situations, investigating computer crimes, managing security staffs, or other activities. The following are just a few of the different specialists that work in information security:

- Information security administrators develop, implement, and maintain the security systems that detect, prevent, contain, and deter security risks.
- Information security architects design, plan, build, test, and implement the technology needed to safe-

guard computer systems as well as the data stored in those systems.

- Security software engineers create new computer applications to protect information assets.
- Cryptographers design solutions to encrypt and decrypt electronic data so that only parties with the proper authority are able to read the information.
- Information security analysts evaluate computer security systems to identify security risks and recommend strategies for improving systems.
- Information system auditors evaluate computer systems to determine whether they protect and maintain the integrity of data adequately, effectively, and efficiency as well as comply with organizational policies and governmental laws and regulations.
- Disaster recovery specialists design, test, implement, and update policies and procedures to ensure uninterrupted access to critical data systems when an emergency or disaster (such as a fire, storm, or power outage) occurs.
- Computer security incident response specialists plan, develop, and implement procedures and protocols during security threats such as virus attacks.
- Privacy officers develop and implement standards, policies, and procedures to ensure compliance with laws governing the privacy, confidentiality, and security of an individual's information (such as health or financial information).
- Information security managers are responsible for the daily administration and management of information security operations.
- Computer forensics specialists seek, identify, extract, and document evidence stored in computers for criminal investigations.

Information Security Specialists apply scientific and engineering principles and techniques. Their jobs require them to be knowledgeable about computer hardware, software, and networks as well as be familiar with a variety of networking technologies. They must also have a thorough understanding of computer programming and be skilled in risk management. These specialists must also be able to communicate technical information clearly and concisely, as they work with all levels of employees in an organization.

Information Security Specialists perform various duties, which vary with the different positions. For example, some of their tasks may include:

- meeting with managers and staff to discuss security needs
- training computer users about ways to use their organization's computer systems securely

- formulating security plans, procedures, policies, or protocols
- testing computer systems to make sure security measures are working effectively
- investigating security breaks
- monitoring computer systems for vulnerabilities
- making recommendations for new hardware and software
- installing and modifying security software programs
- writing reports that document security procedures
- conducting research on current security threats
- attending workshops to update their skills and knowledge about developments in the information security field

Information Security Specialists work in well-maintained offices. The nature of their job can be stressful, particularly when working with people who are angry or frustrated with computer problems. They spend long periods of time sitting in front of computer terminals performing repetitive motions; hence they are at risk of developing eyestrain, back problems, and carpal tunnel syndrome.

Information Security Specialists work a 40-hour week, but sometimes put in additional hours to complete tasks. They may be on call to work evenings and weekends to handle emergency situations. In some organizations, specialists are assigned to different work shifts. Consultants may be required to travel to other cities and spend several days or weeks working at a client's office.

Salaries

Salaries for Information Security Specialists vary, depending on such factors as their position, education, experience, employer, and geographical location. These specialists are categorized as network and computer systems administrators by the U.S. Bureau of Labor Statistics (BLS). According to its May 2006 *Occupational Employment Statistics* survey, the estimated annual salary for this occupation ranged between $38,610 and $97,080. The "2006 *Computerworld* Salary Survey" reported that Information Security Specialists earned an average of $76,087 per year.

Employment Prospects

Information security is a fast-growing field, which started in the 1980s. The need for Information Security Specialists is expected to be favorable for years to come due to such reasons as the continual development of new and complex technologies, the round-the-clock access to the Internet, the growth of e-commerce, and the increase in computer crime. In addition, increasingly more companies and organizations are storing and processing important data on computers and thus seek specialists to ensure the protection of their electronic information and computer systems.

The BLS reports that employment of network and computer systems administrators is predicted to increase by 27 percent through 2016. Many of these jobs are expected to be in the information security field. Additionally, Information Security Specialists will be needed to replace those who advance to higher positions, transfer to other jobs, retire, or leave the workforce for various reasons.

Advancement Prospects

Information Security Specialists advance by earning higher incomes as well as by pursuing opportunities in technical and management areas that interest them. To advance to high-level management positions, specialists may need to possess a college degree in information security or another related field as well as a master's degree in business administration.

Individuals with entrepreneurial ambitions can start their own security consulting firms.

Education and Training

To gain entry into this field, individuals must have extensive computer training, which may have been gained through technical schools, community colleges, universities, hardware and software vendors, or training institutes. Individuals should have training in such areas as programming, operating systems, data structures, quality assurance, cryptology, data communications, and information systems management.

In general, employers prefer to hire Information Security Specialists who possess at least a bachelor's degree in computer science, management information science (MIS), information security, or another related field. Many employers will hire candidates with some or no college background if they have extensive computer security experience as well as hold relevant vendor-specific and professional certifications.

The number of educational programs in information security is growing as more people express interest in a career in this field.

Experience, Special Skills, and Personality Traits

Employers typically hire Information Security Specialists who are highly experienced in computing and have several years of experience in computer security. Strong candidates are also able to demonstrate to prospective employers that they have an understanding of security issues related to the computer systems that employers use.

Because Information Security Specialists work with colleagues, managers, computer users, and many others, they need to have effective interpersonal, teamwork, communication, conflict management, and presentation skills. Their job also requires that they have excellent problem-solving, troubleshooting, writing, project management, and self-management skills. Being analytical, detail-oriented, creative, self-motivated, honest, dependable, flexible, positive, and patient are some personality traits that successful Information Security Specialists have in common.

Unions and Associations

Information Security Specialists can join professional associations to take advantage of professional resources and services such as professional publications, certification, training programs, and networking opportunities. Some national societies that serve the interests of this profession are ISACA, Information Systems Security Association, Computer Security Institute, High Technology Crime Investigation Association, IEEE Computer Society, and ASIS International. For contact information, see Appendix III.

Tips for Entry

1. Check out Web sites of professional associations for job listings.
2. Maintain a clean record. You must be able to obtain a security clearance to work for a federal government agency or for a company that does contractual work with the federal government.
3. To enhance their employability, many Information Security Specialists obtain certification from professional organizations. For a list of certification programs, visit the Information Systems Security Association Web site at http://www.issa.org.
4. Keep up with the latest technologies.
5. Use the Internet to learn more about the field of information security. You might start by visiting the SANS Institute Web site at http://www.sans.org. For more links, see Appendix IV.

TECHNICAL SUPPORT SPECIALIST

Position Description

We use computers every day for various purposes at work, school, and home. When we have trouble with our computers, many of us seek experts generally known as Technical Support Specialists for help. These men and women have the knowledge, training, and expertise to resolve the variety of issues that may occur with computer hardware, software, systems, and networks. For example, they might troubleshoot such problems as these: a software program that keeps crashing, a computer that will not boot up from sleep mode, a mouse that is working improperly; a computer that does not upload Web sites completely, or a network of computers that has been infected by a virus.

Technical Support Specialists work in a wide range of settings. Many of them work for manufacturers of software and hardware products, computer stores, software vendors, computer services, Internet services, and computer repair shops. These specialists provide technical advice and assistance to their employer's customers, who may be individuals or organizations. Many other Technical Support Specialists are hired as in-house staff at private companies, government agencies, schools, universities, hospitals, utilities, manufacturers, and other types of establishments and institutions. These specialists provide support to the various computer users within their organizations.

Most Technical Support Specialists are responsible for providing customer service on a daily basis. Computer users might contact these specialists in person, over the telephone, by e-mail, or through the Internet (such as online help systems or interactive discussion forums). With each inquiry, the specialists try to obtain a clear description of the problem from the computer users. They then diagnose and troubleshoot the problem to identify its cause and to determine the best solution for fixing the problem. This may involve running tests, monitoring systems, reading technical manuals, and conferring with senior technicians, supervisors, computer engineers, or others.

Technical Support Technicians then make the necessary adjustments to correct the problems. They may reinstall software, perform minor repairs, or replace parts or software, according to design or installation specifications. They may also demonstrate to computer users what steps they need to take should the same problems occur again.

When Technical Support Specialists do not have direct access to a computer, they direct the computer users on how to fix the problem. Either orally or through written instructions, the specialists walk the computer users through each step that they must perform. These specialists usually deal with computer users with little or no technical experience; hence the specialists must be able to explain technical concepts in language that can be easily understood.

Besides troubleshooting problems, many Technical Support Specialists provide other types of technical assistance to computer users. For instance, they might install software and operating systems, set up new hardware, create online accounts, secure computer systems from hackers, or teach computer users how to use new software or hardware.

Technical Support Specialists are expected to maintain an accurate and complete record of each problem that they help to solve. They also write reports about the problems to help computer programmers, designers, software engineers, and others with developing new or improved products.

Many in-house technical specialists perform other responsibilities related to the daily operation of their organization's computer systems and networks. Their duties may include:

- maintaining software, hardware, and systems to ensure they are working properly
- evaluating computer systems and software to determine if they need to be upgraded or expanded to meet their organization's goals and policies
- researching, testing, evaluating, and recommending new software and hardware for purchase
- modifying software to meet the needs of their organization
- developing training manuals for software and computer systems
- keeping track of software licenses and hardware warranties

All Technical Support Specialists are expected to stay up to date with new technologies. They read trade magazines, attend professional and trade conferences, and network with colleagues.

These specialists work in offices or computer labs. Many help-desk technicians work in call centers. With the advancement of technologies, increasingly more specialists are able to provide technical support from a remote location.

These technicians may work alone or as part of a team. Because they spend long periods of time sitting in front of computer terminals performing repetitive motions, they are at risk of developing eyestrain, back problems, and carpal tunnel syndrome. Their work can sometimes be stressful, when they must work with computer users who are frustrated, angry, rude, or unpleasant.

These specialists usually work a 40-hour week. They put in additional hours as needed to handle technical problems. Some of them are assigned on a rotating basis to be available evenings or weekends to handle technical problems that may occur. Consultants may be required to spend several days or months working at their client's office.

Salaries

Salaries for Technical Support Specialists vary, depending on such factors as their education, experience, position, employer, and geographical location. According to the *2006 ASP Tech Support Salary Survey* by the Association of Support Professionals, median salaries in the software industry ranged from $35,000 for the least-skilled support technicians to $112,500 for senior support executive officers. The U.S. Bureau of Labor Statistics (BLS) reports in its May 2006 *Occupational Employment Statistics* (OES) survey that the estimated annual salary for Technical Support Specialists ranged between $25,290 and $68,540.

Employment Prospects

According to the BLS May 2006 OES survey, about 514,460 computer support specialists were employed in the United States. The highest level of employment of these specialists was in the computer systems design and related services industry. Technical Support Specialists are employed in all industries, from start-up firms to established companies. Some employers include educational institutions, government agencies, banks, financial services, insurance companies, hospitals, health care facilities, administrative and support services companies, computer hardware and software manufacturers, and wholesale and retail vendors of computers, office equipment, appliances, and home electronic equipment.

In recent years, increasingly more U.S. firms have been outsourcing routine support work, particularly overseas to countries where labor costs are lower. However, numerous opportunities for Technical Support Specialists will continue to be available in the United States. There will remain a need for in-house technical staff, as companies throughout the different industries are constantly developing and expanding their computer systems that involve more complex and sophisticated technologies.

According to the BLS, the job growth for computer support specialists in the United States is expected to increase by 13 percent throughout 2016. In addition, opportunities will become available to replace specialists who are promoted, transfer to other jobs, or leave the workforce for various personal reasons. Some experts state that opportunities are strongest for college graduates who possess the most current skills, are well versed in the latest technologies, and have practical work experience.

Advancement Prospects

Technical Support Specialists usually begin their career working as help-desk technicians. As they gain experience, they are assigned higher-level tasks and greater responsibilities. They may advance in any number of ways, depending on their ambitions. For example, those interested in consulting, administration, or management can pursue such positions. With additional training, these specialists can pursue other career paths by becoming systems analysts, network administrators, software engineers, or research computer scientists.

Education and Training

Educational requirements for entry-level positions vary among employers. Some of them require that candidates possess a bachelor's degree in computer science, information systems, or another related field, while others require an associate degree in a computer field. Employers may hire candidates who have a college degree in a noncomputer field or who only have some college background if they have the appropriate skills as well as several years of practical experience.

Employers typically provide Technical Support Specialists with training in the different technical areas in which they would be giving support. Employees may go through in-house training programs or attend training sessions given by vendors, private training firms, or academic institutions.

Experience, Special Skills, and Personality Traits

Employers prefer to hire candidates for entry-level positions who have one or more years of practical work experience with computers. They may have gained experience through employment, internships, or volunteer work. In addition, employers seek candidates who are knowledgeable about the computer systems and software that they would be supporting, as well as are familiar with the employer's industry in which they would work.

To work well at their job, Technical Support Specialists need excellent analytical, problem-solving, and writing skills. They also must have outstanding listening, communication, and interpersonal skills, as they must be able to effectively deal with customers, co-workers, managers, and others from diverse backgrounds. Having strong teaching and customer service skills is also essential. Being polite, honest, calm, empathetic, articulate, dependable, flexible, and self-motivated are some personality traits that successful specialists share.

Unions and Associations

Technical Support Specialists may join professional associations to take advantage of networking opportunities, job listings, and other professional services and resources. Two national societies that serve the particular interests of these professionals are HDI (formerly known as the Help Desk Institute) and the Association of Support Professionals. For contact information, see Appendix III.

Specialists who work in government agencies usually belong to a union.

Tips for Entry

1. Develop your writing and communication skills by taking such classes as composition, business or technical writing, drama, speech, or public speaking.
2. Some Technical Support Specialists got their first job by applying for an in-house support position within their company.
3. To enhance their employability, many specialists obtain certification offered by vendors, manufacturers, and/or professional organizations.
4. Use the Internet to learn more about the computer technical support field. You might start by visiting these Web sites: HDI, http://www.thinkhdi.com and Association of Support Professionals, http://www.asponline.com. For more links, see Appendix IV.

AGRICULTURAL SCIENCE AND FOOD SCIENCE

HORTICULTURAL SCIENTIST

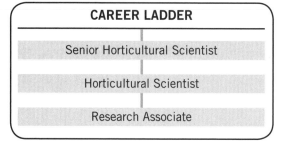

Position Description

Horticulture, a branch of agriculture, is the science of growing edible and ornamental plants for gardens and landscaping. These include vegetables, fruits, herbs, spices, flowers, potted plants, shrubs, trees, ground covers, and turfgrass. Most horticultural crops are grown commercially in greenhouses and nurseries, as well as on farms and in orchards.

Many technical and professional occupations are available in the field of horticulture. Those who are involved in conducting research are Horticultural Scientists. They understand how plants grow and know the most effective methods for growing them. They are trained in botany, genetics, biochemistry, plant pathology, plant physiology, soil science, entomology, and other biological and physical science disciplines. In addition, Horticultural Scientists have an understanding of the commercial value of horticultural crops and are knowledgeable about federal and state regulations related to horticultural matters.

Horticulture is divided into different specialties. Horticultural Scientists might specialize in one or more of the following areas:

- olericulture—the study of cultivating vegetable crops
- pomology—the growth and production of nut and fruit crops
- viticulture—the science of growing grape vines
- floriculture—the production and use of flowers and foliage plants

- ornamental horticulture—the use and management of trees, shrubs, and other plants grown for decorative purposes
- turfgrass science—the study of grasses for functional, recreational, and ornamental purposes

Horticultural Scientists work in academic, industrial, government, and nongovernmental settings. Some Horticultural Scientists conduct basic research for the sole purpose of adding new knowledge and understanding to their fields. Others are involved in applied research, addressing specific problems or issues which are usually determined by their employers. Applied researchers also are part of research teams engaged in the development of new commercial products or services.

Horticultural researchers are engaged in a variety of projects. They study ways to improve the nutritional value, quality, or crop yield of different plants. They develop new plant varieties through the use of seeds, tissue cultures, grafting, and other scientific methods. They seek out new or improved techniques for producing, harvesting, processing, storing, or marketing horticultural crops. Further, they seek solutions to manage pests, control weeds, treat plant diseases, and protect the environment.

Most academic scientists are employed as faculty at four-year colleges and universities. Along with conducting research, they are responsible for teaching courses to undergraduate and graduate students. Most professors are required to perform administrative duties and community service as well as produce scholarly works.

At land-grant universities, some Horticultural Scientists receive appointments from Cooperative Extension offices. (These local and state offices provide free educational programs in agriculture, economic development, and other topics to communities.) These Horticultural Scientists conduct independent research studies as well as applied research projects on topics that concern local industry. In addition, they provide public service to farmers, growers, local industry, professional horticulturists, and amateur gardeners. For example, they perform such activities as providing technical information and advice, conducting educational programs, and publishing technical bulletins.

Many Horticultural Scientists in the research arena are research assistants and technicians. They provide scientists with technical support. They perform a variety of duties that may include conducting experiments and tests, analyzing data, writing reports, handling and caring for greenhouse plants, maintaining laboratory equipment and facilities, and performing routine administrative tasks.

Horticultural Scientists perform their studies in offices, laboratories, and greenhouses. They also conduct field work in test fields and gardens, which are usually part of research facilities. Their work occasionally exposes them to fertilizers, pesticides, and other chemicals that may be harmful.

Salaries

Salaries for Horticultural Scientists vary, depending on such factors as their education, experience, employer, and geographic location. The U.S. Bureau of Labor Statistics (BLS) reports in its May 2006 *Occupational Employment Statistics* survey that the estimated annual salary for most plant scientists ranged between $33,650 and $93,460, and for most postsecondary agricultural science instructors, between $41,440 and $118,180.

Employment Prospects

Horticultural Scientists are employed by seed, chemical, fertilizer, and other companies in private industry. Many find employment in the government, particularly within the various agencies of the U.S. Department of Agriculture and with state agricultural research stations. They also work for colleges and universities where many hold faculty positions. Opportunities usually become available as individuals retire, transfer to other positions, or enter other professions.

According to the BLS, employment for agricultural scientists overall is predicted to increase by 7 to 13 percent through 2016. Opportunities are expected to be favorable for academic positions due to the large number of faculty members expecting to retire in the next few years.

Research horticulturists can seek other occupations in which to use their training, such as vocational horticultural instructor, extension educator, nursery manager, plant breeder, vineyard manager, landscape designer, floral arts designer, golf course superintendent, plant inspector, environmentalist, arborist, seed company sales representative, botanical illustrator, and horticultural therapist.

Advancement Prospects

Experienced researchers become team leaders and project managers as well as specialists in their areas of interest. They can also advance to such administrative and management positions as department administrator, program manager, and executive officer. Professors receive promotional rankings as assistant professors, associate professors, or full professors.

Those with entrepreneurial ambitions strive to become independent consultants and owners of consulting firms, nurseries, seed companies, landscaping firms, or other horticulture-related business.

Education and Training

A bachelor's degree in horticulture, agricultural science, or a related field is the minimum requirement for research assistant and technician positions; but many employers prefer candidates with a master's degree. Horticultural Scientist positions in industry or government usually require a master's or doctoral degree.

A Ph.D. is generally required for Horticultural Scientists to teach in universities and four-year colleges, to obtain top management positions, or to conduct independent research.

Experience, Skills, and Personality Traits

Employers typically choose candidates for entry-level positions who have related work and research experience, which may have been gained through student research projects, internships, fellowships, and employment. Ph.D. candidates for research scientist positions are usually expected to have a few years of postdoctoral experience.

Horticulturists need basic computer skills for their work. They also need excellent communication, writing, and interpersonal skills to do their work effectively. They should have strong self-management skills such as being able to work independently, organize and prioritize tasks, and meet deadlines. Being creative, enthusiastic, persistent, and flexible are a few personality traits that research Horticulturists share.

Unions and Associations

Many Horticultural Scientists join local, state, and national professional associations to take advantage of education programs, professional certification, networking opportunities, and other professional services and resources. Some national societies include the American Society for Horticultural Science, the Botanical Society of America, and the American Society of Agronomy. See Appendix III for contact information.

Tips for Entry

1. If you are a high school student, start gaining knowledge and experience in horticulture. For example, you might read books and magazines about plants; raise a vegetable or flower garden; join a garden club or horticultural society; get a part-time job with a local nursery, garden center, seed company, landscaping firm, or gardening service; or volunteer in the gardening or landscaping department of a public park, zoo, or botanical garden.

2. While in college, take advantage of research assistant opportunities at your college or apply for internships with government agencies and private employers. You can learn about positions from your college career center as well as from your academic adviser and professors.

3. Contact employers with whom you would like to work to find out about current and future job vacancies. A few days after submitting a résumé or job application, contact the prospective employer and ask when you could come in for a job or information interview.

4. You can learn more about horticulture on the Internet. One Web site you might visit is for the American Society for Horticultural Science. Its URL is http://www.ashs.org. For more links, see Appendix IV.

CROP SCIENTIST

CAREER PROFILE

Duties: Study the growth and management of field crops; design and conduct research projects; perform duties as required

Alternate Title(s): Agronomist, Research Scientist, Crop Specialist

Salary Range: $34,000 to $118,000

Employment Prospects: Good

Advancement Prospects: Good

Prerequisites:

    Education or Training—A master's or doctoral degree in crop science or a related field

    Experience—Work and research experience required

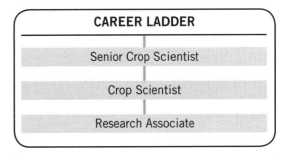

CAREER LADDER

Senior Crop Scientist

Crop Scientist

Research Associate

Special Skills and Personality Traits—Organizational, writing, communication, teamwork, interpersonal, and self-management skills; enthusiastic, objective, inquisitive, open-minded, and adaptable

Position Description

Crop Scientists study the growth and management of field crops—corn, wheat, barley, rice, millet, potatoes, dry beans, legumes, alfalfa, vetch, sunflowers, flax, cotton, sugarcane, turfgrass, and so on. The different field crops are grown to produce food for people all over the world. Field crops are also produced for a variety of nonfood uses, including fibers, feed for livestock, and ground cover for roadsides, parks, athletic fields, golf courses, and home lawns. Some field crops (such as corn) are grown to produce alternative sources of energy. Many field crops are used as raw materials in various industrial applications such as paints, solvents, adhesives, lubricants, cosmetics, dyes, pharmaceuticals, packaging materials, and building materials.

Crop science, also called agronomy, is a branch of agricultural science. Crop Scientists are concerned with conducting studies that help farmers and growers produce high-quality crops more efficiently and economically. Crop Scientists are also interested in helping farmers make decisions that not only serve to increase the yields of their crops but also conserve natural resources and protect the environment.

Crop Scientists are involved in research and development in such areas as crop production, crop yield, genetics, breeding, physiology, plant disease, weed control, and pest control. They develop new crop varieties that are more suitable for particular locations, study new uses for specific crops, and investigate the feasibility of introducing alternative crops to an area. Additionally, Crop Scientists develop new principles, methods, and technologies that are relevant to crop systems for small and large farms. Further, they are involved with studying environmental issues that are related to crop production, such as soil erosion, pesticide contamination of water sources, damaged ecosystems, and conservation of natural resources.

Their research is highly scientific and technical. They apply principles of biological sciences, chemistry, and physics to their quest for knowledge and solutions to problems. They have a fundamental understanding of soils, climates, and plant science, which includes genetics, plant breeding, cell biology, and plant physiology. Many Crop Scientists are skilled in biotechnology, which are techniques that use cells or tissues to create new or improved products. Crop Scientists also use such research tools as computers, satellites, electron microscopes, geographic information systems (GIS), geographical positioning system (GPS) technology, and remote sensing equipment.

Crop Scientists often work on projects with soil scientists, microbiologists, entomologists, geneticists, meteorologists, agricultural engineers, and other scientists. They sometimes collaborate on projects with scientists from other countries.

Crop Scientists' work involves designing and managing research projects. They perform various duties, such as conducting experiments, interpreting and analyzing data, preparing reports, and performing administrative tasks. They conduct research in laboratories and greenhouses, as well as outdoors in experimental fields.

Along with conducting research, many Crop Scientists perform duties in education. For example, some Crop Scientists teach agricultural courses in colleges and universities, while others coordinate and teach education programs in Cooperative Extension offices. (These local and state offices provide free educational programs in agriculture, economic development, and other topics to communities.) Many Crop Scientists provide consulting and technical support services to farmers, growers, agribusinesses, and government agencies, among others.

Crop Scientists are expected to share research results with colleagues, farmers, professional societies, and others. They write articles, or scientific papers, which are published in scientific journals. Some make presentations at scientific meetings that are sponsored by professional associations. Others build Web sites to disseminate their research data as well as to provide practical information related to the production, handling, and marketing of crops.

Crop Scientists who conduct independent research are usually responsible for obtaining research grants from the federal government and other sources to fund their projects.

All Crop Scientists are responsible for keeping up with new developments in their field. They attend professional meetings and conferences, read professional journals and books, network with colleagues, and so on.

Traveling to other states and countries may be required of those who offer consulting services. Crop Scientists might also travel out-of-state or abroad to attend professional conferences and meetings.

Salaries

Salaries for Crop Scientists vary, depending on such factors as their education, experience, and geographic location. According to the May 2006 *Occupational Employment Statistics* survey by the U.S. Bureau of Labor Statistics (BLS), the estimated annual salary for most plant scientists ranged between $33,650 and $93,460, and for most postsecondary agricultural science instructors, between $41,440 and $118,180.

Employment Prospects

Crop Scientists are employed by government agencies, agricultural research stations, universities, and nongovernmental organizations. They also work for agribusinesses, agrochemical companies, seed companies, agricultural consulting firms, and other private companies. Some Crop Scientists are independent consultants.

In general, most opportunities become available as Crop Scientists retire, transfer to other positions, or leave the job market entirely. Employers create additional positions to meet their growing needs.

With a background in crop science, individuals can pursue other careers, including commodity broker, crop chemist, climatologist, environmental specialist, farmer, farm manager, agricultural lawyer, plant breeder, agricultural teacher, or extension agent.

Advancement Prospects

Crop Scientists with administrative or management ambitions can advance to such positions as project leader, program manager, laboratory director, or executive officer. Professors receive promotional rankings as assistant, associate, or full professors.

Education and Training

Employers generally require that Crop Scientists hold a master's or doctoral degree in crop science, agronomy, or another related field. Employers may hire candidates with a bachelor's degree if they have extensive qualifying experience.

A doctoral degree is usually required to teach in universities and four-year colleges, conduct independent research, or obtain top management positions.

Experience, Skills, and Personality Traits

Employers generally choose candidates who have a few years of related work and research experience. Entry-level applicants may have gained experience through research projects, internships, postdoctoral training, and employment. Hands-on farm experience is not generally necessary, but having such experience can be an advantage.

Crop Scientists need strong organizational, writing, and communication skills to do their work effectively. They must also have teamwork and interpersonal skills, along with self-management skills, such as being able to work independently, organize and prioritize work, and handle stressful situations.

Being enthusiastic, objective, inquisitive, open-minded, and adaptable are a few personality traits that successful Crop Scientists share.

Unions and Associations

The American Society of Agronomy and the Crop Science Society of America are two national societies that serve the particular interests of Crop Scientists. They offer networking opportunities, professional certification, education programs, and other professional services and resources. See Appendix III for contact information.

Tips for Entry

1. Before enrolling in a crop science program, be sure that its mission and philosophy are compatible with yours. Also check that they offer courses which interest you and that there are professors with whom you would like to study and possibly do research projects. In addition, find out what kinds of opportunities for practical training are available.

2. Many organizations post job listings on their Web sites. They also provide information about the selection process. Some employers allow applicants to complete applications or submit résumés online.

3. Use the Internet to learn more about crop science. To get a list of relevant Web sites enter one of these keywords in a search engine: *crop science, crop scientists,* or *agronomy.* For some links, see Appendix IV.

SOIL SCIENTIST

CAREER PROFILE

Duties: Study soils and soil environments; design and conduct research projects; perform duties as required

Alternate Title(s): Agronomist, Research Scientist

Salary Range: $34,000 to $118,000

Employment Prospects: Good

Advancement Prospects: Good

Prerequisites:

    Education or Training—A bachelor's or advanced degree in soil science or related field required

    Experience—Previous work and research experience required

    Special Skills and Personality Traits—Analytical, problem-solving, communication, writing, team-

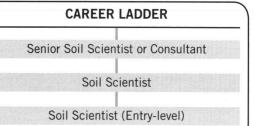

CAREER LADDER

Senior Soil Scientist or Consultant

Soil Scientist

Soil Scientist (Entry-level)

work, and interpersonal skills; enthusiastic, persistent, detail-oriented, and self-motivated

    Special Requirements—State licensure or certification may be required

Position Description

Soil is an essential—and precious—natural resource, which takes thousands of years to form from rock through wind and water erosion. About 25 percent of the Earth's surface is made up of dry land, and only about half of that holds soil suitable for food production.

Soil Scientists specialize in the study of soils and soil environments. They are experts in understanding the biology, microbiology, morphology, classification, chemistry, and physics of different soils. Soil Scientists work with crop scientists and other agricultural scientists to seek ways to increase crop production while still conserving natural resources and protecting the environment.

Most Soil Scientists are involved in research work in academic, government, and industrial settings. They cover such diverse topics as soil decomposition, soil fertility, water erosion, pesticides, the effects of tillage or crop rotation, water management, and waste management. Basic researchers conduct studies that are aimed at gaining new understanding and knowledge about the properties and behaviors of the various soils, soil conservation, and soil management. Applied researchers, on the other hand, work on solving specific issues. For example, they might find ways to repair contaminated soil or to improve the quality of soil in a particular location. Applied researchers also develop new technologies and management practices that can improve crop yields, conserve natural resources, or protect the environment.

Soil Scientists perform their research in offices and laboratories as well as in the field. Increasingly Soil Scientists are integrating electronic and information technologies—such as remote sensing, Geographic Positioning System (GPS), and geographic information systems (GIS)—into their work. Many Soil Scientists also work with computer models to analyze and interpret data.

Soil Scientists typically work on several research projects at a time, and often collaborate on projects with fellow scientists and engineers. Their research work involves conducting experiments and tests, analyzing and interpreting research data, reading scientific literature, and writing reports. Soil Scientists who conduct independent research are usually responsible for obtaining grants from the federal government and other sources.

Soil Scientists share information about their research with colleagues and others by writing scientific papers for professional journals, making presentations at professional meetings, or building Web sites to disseminate research data.

Some Soil Scientists offer consulting and technical services to farmers, engineers, landscape designers, land developers, environmentalists, government agencies, and others. They provide decision makers with information about the suitability of soils in a location for particular uses or about the impact of specific activities on the land—including agricultural production, landscape design, erosion control, forest products, mine reclamation, and site restoration. Soil Scientists might provide these services as independent consultants or as staff employees.

Many Soil Scientists are employed as full-time professors or adjunct instructors by colleges and universities. They teach courses about soil classification, soil mapping, soil biophysics, water management, agricultural ecology, and other subjects. Depending on the institution, soil science faculty may teach in agriculture, botany, geography, geology, engineering, and other departments. Full-time faculty are responsible for conducting independent research projects, advising students, producing scholarly work, and performing community service and administrative duties.

Soil Scientists who work in government settings may perform educational duties along with research and technical service duties. For example, they might conduct workshops for farmers or develop educational materials about management practices suitable for their locations.

Soil Scientists often work long days in order to complete their tasks or meet deadlines. Many travel frequently to other cities, states, or countries.

Salaries

Salaries for Soil Scientists vary, depending on such factors as their education, experience, and geographic location. According to the May 2006 *Occupational Employment Statistics* survey by the U.S. Bureau of Labor Statistics (BLS), the estimated annual salary for most soil scientists ranged between $33,650 and $93,460, and for most postsecondary agricultural science instructors, between $41,440 and $118,180.

Employment Prospects

Government agencies, academic institutions, agricultural research stations, and nonprofit organizations are all employers of Soil Scientists. In addition, these scientists are employed by commercial farms, land appraisal firms, chemical companies, fertilizer firms, and various agribusiness companies. Some work for consulting firms in such areas as agriculture, environmental science, and engineering. Some scientists are independent consultants.

According to the BLS, employment of Soil Scientists is expected to increase by 8 percent through 2016. In addition to job growth, opportunities become available as scientists retire, transfer to other positions, or leave the workforce for other reasons.

With a background in soil science, individuals can pursue other careers, such as becoming soil surveyors, farmers, farm managers, extension agents, park rangers, foresters, geologists, and environmental specialists.

Advancement Prospects

Soil Scientists advance in their careers in various ways, depending on their career path, ambitions, and interests. Those interested in management and administrative work can find opportunities in any work setting. Those with entrepreneurial ambitions can become independent consultants or owners of consulting firms. Professors receive promotional rankings as assistant, associate, or full professor.

Education and Training

To enter this field, Soil Scientists need at least a bachelor's degree in soil science, agronomy, natural resources management, environmental studies, earth science, or another related field. Many employers require that candidates have at least a master's degree. A Ph.D. is usually required to teach in four-year colleges and universities, conduct independent research, or hold top management positions.

Entry-level Soil Scientists typically work under the training and supervision of experienced Soil Scientists for the first few years of their careers.

Special Requirements

Soil Scientists who provide services that involve the health, safety, and welfare of the general public may be required to be licensed or certified as professional soil scientists. Some employers prefer to hire licensed professionals. Many Soil Scientists obtain licensure on a voluntary basis to enhance their employability. Further, entry-level applicants may be required to register as soil scientists-in-training, which leads to professional registration.

Licensure requirements vary from state to state. For information, contact the appropriate board of professional licensure where you wish to practice.

Experience, Skills, and Personality Traits

Employers generally choose candidates for entry-level positions who have related work and research experience, which may have been gained through research projects, internships, employment, or postdoctoral training. Many employers look for applicants who have field experience. Employers typically prefer candidates who are familiar with their business or industry.

In order to do their work effectively, Soil Scientists must have excellent analytical and problem-solving skills. They also need strong communication and writing skills, as well as teamwork and interpersonal skills. Being enthusiastic, persistent, detail-oriented, and self-motivated are a few personality traits that successful Soil Scientists have in common.

Unions and Associations

Many Soil Scientists join local, state, or national societies to take advantage of professional services and resources such as education programs, professional certification, and networking opportunities. The Soil Science Society of America, the Association of Women Soil Scientists, the National Society of Consulting Soil Scientists, and the American Society of Agronomy are some national societies that serve the interests of Soil Scientists. See Appendix III for contact information.

Tips for Entry

1. As a college student, gain experience by obtaining an internship or work-study position, or by becoming a research assistant with a professor whose work interests you.

2. Many trade and professional associations post listings for local, state, and nation-wide job openings on their Web sites. Be sure to check out agricultural, geology, and environmental science associations as well as those specifically organized for Soil Scientists.

3. Use the Internet to learn more about Soil Scientists. Two Web sites you might visit are Soil Science Society of America, http://www.soils.org; and National Resources Conservation Service (part of the USDA), http://www.nrcs.usda.gov. For more links, see Appendix IV.

ANIMAL SCIENTIST

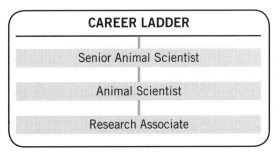

Position Description

Animal science, an applied science, is a branch of agriculture. It is the study of animals that are used as sources of food and fiber as well as of animals that are used for work, play, or companionship. Traditionally, animal science is known as the study of livestock animals—beef cattle, dairy cows, poultry, sheep, swine, and horses. (In some locales, this discipline is known as animal husbandry.) Today, this discipline includes the study of goats, buffalo, emus, ostriches, llamas, and other exotic species.

Additionally, this discipline includes the study of aquaculture, or fish and shellfish—such as trout, salmon, catfish, tilapia, shrimp, and oysters—that are farmed in natural and controlled environments. Further, animal science embraces the study of dogs, cats, reptiles, aquarium fish, rodents, and other small animals that serve as household pets.

Animal Scientists are interested in two broad areas of research. One area is the study of the animals themselves. Animal Scientists inquire into the welfare and well-being of the animals. These scientists investigate topics that concern the reproduction; growth and development; genetics; nutrition; care; and management of animals.

The other general area of study is food and fiber production. Animal Scientists engage in studies that help provide high-quality products—such as meat, eggs, dairy products, and wool—at affordable prices to consumers. These scientists research topics involving food or fiber production, processing, handling, and quality control.

Animal Scientists apply principles of the biological, physical, and social sciences to their research studies. They conduct research in academic, government, and industry settings. Some Animal Scientists are involved in basic research. They conduct research for the sole purpose of adding new knowledge—theories and technologies—to their discipline. Other Animal Scientists conduct applied research. They apply the findings of basic research to develop useful products or find solutions to problems in animal production, animal management, or food processing.

Animal Scientists sometimes collaborate on projects with colleagues in their field as well as with other scientists, such as physiologists and geneticists. Animal Scientists might also work with agricultural engineers, technicians, managers, and other professionals.

Animal Scientists' research involves designing and overseeing research projects. They perform various duties, such as conducting experiments, interpreting and analyzing data, preparing reports, and doing administrative tasks. Senior researchers and principal investigators may perform supervisory and management duties. Animal Scientists who conduct independent research are usually responsible for obtaining grants from the federal government and other sources to fund their projects.

Typically, Animal Scientists exchange research information with their colleagues. They might write articles, or scientific papers, which are published in scientific journals. Some might make presentations at scientific meetings that are sponsored by professional associations.

Some Animal Scientists are employed as university and college professors. Along with teaching courses in animal science, they may teach classes in other disciplines in which they specialize, such as nutrition, physiology, or genetics. Academic scientists juggle various tasks each day. Their duties include conducting independent research, preparing for and teaching courses, advising students, supervising student research projects, producing scholarly works, performing administrative duties, and participating in community service.

Animal Scientists are also employed as technicians and research assistants. They provide research scientists with technical support. Their duties include conducting experiments, making observations, analyzing data, writing reports, handling and caring for lab animals, maintaining laboratory equipment and facilities, and completing routine administrative tasks.

All Animal Scientists are responsible for keeping up with new developments. They attend professional meetings and conferences, read professional journals and books, network with colleagues, and so on.

Animal Scientists work in offices and laboratories. In addition, they may spend some of their time conducting research in feedlots, dairies, barns, or other animal facilities.

Salaries

Salaries for Animal Scientists vary, depending on such factors as their education, experience, employer, and geographic location. According to the May 2006 *Occupational Employment Statistics* survey by the U.S. Bureau of Labor Statistics (BLS), the estimated annual salary for most Animal Scientists ranged between $31,540 and $81,430, and for most postsecondary agricultural science instructors, between $41,440 and $118,180.

Employment Prospects

Animal Scientists are employed by colleges and universities; government agencies and laboratories; agricultural research stations; food and meat processing companies; biotechnology firms; agribusinesses; and so on.

The BLS reports that employment of Animal Scientists is expected to increase by 10 percent through 2016. In addition to job growth, openings will become available as Animal Scientists retire, transfer to other jobs, or advance to higher positions. According to some experts, opportunities are expected to be favor-

able for academic positions due to the large number of faculty members predicted to retire in the next several years.

With a background in animal science, individuals can qualify for positions in a number of areas. For example, they can become extension agents, farm managers, livestock producers, aquaculturists, feedlot operators, animal breeders, meat inspectors, horse trainers, dog trainers, animal caretakers, veterinary assistants, and market forecasters. They can also find employment in such positions as quality control specialist, sales representative, manager, and public relations specialist with food processing companies, feed manufacturers, animal breed companies, pharmaceutical companies, trade associations, and other organizations. With additional training and education, individuals can become vocational agricultural teachers, veterinarians, animal behaviorists, or medical doctors.

Advancement Prospects

Research scientists can advance to administrative and management positions, by becoming project leaders, program managers, laboratory directors, executive officers, and so on. Professors receive promotional rankings as assistant professor, associate professor, or full professor.

Education and Training

A bachelor's degree in animal science or a related field is the usual minimum requirement for research assistant and technician positions. Some employers prefer to hire candidates who hold master's degrees. Research scientists must possess a master's degree or a Ph.D. A Ph.D. is required to teach in universities and four-year colleges, conduct independent research, or obtain top management positions.

Experience, Skills, and Personality Traits

Requirements vary for the different positions as well as among various employers. For entry-level positions, employers generally choose candidates who have related work and research experience. This may have been gained through research projects, internships, fellowships, and employment. Ph.D. candidates for research scientist positions may be required to have a few years of postdoctoral experience.

Animal Scientists need adequate computer, writing, and communication skills to do their work effectively. They should also have strong teamwork and interpersonal skills along with excellent self-management skills, such as being able to work independently, organize and prioritize work, and handle stressful situations.

Some personality traits that successful Animal Scientists share are being curious, creative, persistent, analytical, and flexible.

Unions and Associations

Many Animal Scientists join professional associations at the local, state, and national levels. These societies offer a variety of services and resources, such as professional certification, education programs, and networking opportunities, to help Animal Scientists with their professional development. Some national professional societies that serve the interests of different Animal Scientists are the American Society of Animal Science, the American Dairy Science Association, the American Meat Science Association, and the Poultry Science Association. See Appendix III for contact information.

Tips for Entry

1. As a middle school or high school student, start learning about animal science. Read books about different livestock animals. Check out local 4-H clubs or other youth groups to see what they might offer. Also visit dairy farms, poultry farms, cattle ranches, and petting zoos. If possible, raise a domestic animal.

2. If you are a college student, gain valuable experience by working as an intern or becoming a research assistant to a professor in whose work you are interested.

3. Professional journals, such as the *Journal of Animal Science*, usually carry advertisements for internship and employment opportunities.

4. Learn more about animal science on the Internet. Here are a few Web sites to visit: American Society of Animal Science, http://www.asas.org; and Virtual Livestock Library (Oklahoma State University), http://www.ansi.okstate.edu/library. For more links, See Appendix IV.

AGRICULTURAL TECHNICIAN

Duties: Provide technical support to agricultural scientists and engineers involved in research and development; perform duties as required

Alternate Title(s): Laboratory Technician, Research Assistant; Horticulture Technician, Animal Science Technician, Extension Associate, or another title that reflects a specialty or occupation

Salary Range: $21,000 to $49,000

Employment Prospects: Good

Advancement Prospects: Good

Prerequisites:

    Education or Training—Minimally, a high school diploma; on-the-job training

    Experience—Work experience preferred

CAREER LADDER

Senior Agricultural Technician

Agricultural Technician

Agricultural Technician (Entry-level)

Special Skills and Personality Traits—Computer, writing, communication, interpersonal, teamwork, self-management, analytical, and problem-solving skills; detail-oriented, organized, self-motivated, persistent, flexible, honest, and dependable

Position Description

Agricultural Technicians provide technical support and assistance to scientists and engineers who engage in research in the various areas of agriculture, including crop science, soil science, dairy science, food science, aquaculture, and horticulture, among other fields. These technicians are involved in various aspects of research and development, from basic research to applied research to the development of new and improved agricultural products and processes. They participate in the study of a wide range of agricultural topics and issues. For example, they may be part of projects that seek to:

- improve the yield and quality of crops
- understand the properties and behaviors of soils
- manage pests and weeds naturally
- increase the resistance of livestock to disease
- breed animals or plants for specific characteristics
- determine how certain foods affect the behavior or physical health of animals
- design improved techniques for producing horticultural crops
- develop new seeds, animal feed, agricultural machinery, or other agricultural products
- investigate the responses of livestock to different range management practices
- conserve soil or other type of natural resource

Agricultural Technicians work in both the public and private sectors. They assist agricultural researchers in academic institutions, nongovernmental research institutes, and governmental agencies such as the U.S. Department of Agriculture and the U.S. Cooperative State Research, Education, and Extension Service. Agricultural Technicians also work in research and development laboratories in biotechnology firms, seed companies, food processing companies, farm equipment manufacturers, and other private companies.

These technicians apply science and mathematic principles and techniques to solve problems, while working under the direction of scientists, engineers, supervisors, and managers. Agricultural Technicians utilize various scientific equipment and instruments, such as incubators, drying ovens, weight meters, temperature gauges, and spectrometers. They also use computers and such technologies as geographic information systems (GIS) and global positioning systems (GPS) tools. In addition they operate farming equipment and machinery, such as hand and power tools, animal husbandry equipment, chemical sprayers, tractors, cultivators, mowers, hay balers, and trucks.

Agricultural Technicians conduct their work in offices and laboratories. They may be assigned to work in greenhouses, at research farms, or at such outdoor locations as rivers, lakes, and ocean shores. They perform a variety of fundamental tasks, regardless of whether they are working with plants or animals. They are responsible for keeping accurate records of field and laboratory data. They collect samples (such as soil, plant, or insect specimens) as well as prepare samples, solutions, and media for experiments and tests. They monitor experiments or tests, and collect and analyze experimental or test data as well. These technicians are responsible for preparing data summaries, analyses, and reports that document research findings and results. In addition, they maintain an inventory of supplies for laboratory and field operations, and make purchases as needed. Furthermore, Agricultural Technicians perform minor construction, maintenance, and repair of agricultural facilities and equipment.

These technicians also perform duties that are specific to their positions. Those who work on research farms are responsible for establishing and maintaining plots in fields, orchards, or vineyards. They prepare the soil and plant seeds, as well as cultivate, irrigate, fertilize, harvest, and store crops. Some Agricultural Technicians work in nurseries or greenhouses where they assist with horticultural research. They perform such tasks as pollinating plants; propagating plants; testing plants for insect, disease, and weed control; and collecting, caring for, and germinating seeds.

Agricultural Technicians who are involved in animal science research may be responsible for laboratory animals, livestock, exotic species (such as buffalo or ostriches), aquaculture (which may include any variety of fish or shellfish), or companion animals (such as dogs, cats, and parakeets). They perform such tasks as monitoring the nutritional requirements of animals; feeding, watering, and taking care of them; administering vaccinations accordingly; maintaining the proper level of environmental controls and temperatures; and keeping the enclosures and cages where animals live sanitary and clean.

Entry-level technicians typically perform simple routine tasks under the tutelage of experienced technicians and scientists. As Agricultural Technicians gain experience, they are assigned more complicated duties in which they exercise independent judgment. Their work is checked by superiors for progress and conformance with established requirements and policies. Senior technicians may be responsible for completing administrative duties, and may be assigned to lead or supervisory positions in which they oversee the work of junior technicians, farm laborers, and other staff members.

Agricultural Technicians perform physical work that requires the ability to lift and carry objects weigh-ing 50 pounds or more. They frequently stand, walk, climb, bend, and stoop as they work. They may work in a dusty environment or outdoors in varying weather conditions. Their tasks may require them to work with toxic chemicals, heavy equipment, or machinery with exposed moving parts. Hence, they must follow strict safety procedures and wear protective clothing and equipment.

These technicians work a 40-hour week, but they often put in additional hours to complete their tasks, such as monitoring experiments, harvesting crops, or preparing reports. Some of them work irregular hours, including early mornings, evenings, late nights, and weekends.

Salaries

Salaries for Agricultural Technicians vary, depending on such factors as their education, experience, job duties, employer, and geographic location. According to the May 2006 *Occupational Employment Statistics* survey by the U.S. Bureau of Labor Statistics (BLS), the estimated annual salary for most Agricultural Technicians ranged between $20,850 and $49,270. Those who were employed in the scientific research and development services industry earned an estimated annual mean salary of $36,080, while those who worked in colleges, universities, and professional schools earned an estimated annual mean salary of $33,810.

Employment Prospects

In the private sector, Agricultural Technicians are employed in the agricultural, food processing, biotechnology, environmental protection, and scientific research and development services industries, among others. They also find employment in academic institutes, nonprofit organizations, and government agencies such as the U.S. Department of Agriculture and state fish and wildlife departments.

The BLS reports that employment of Agricultural Technicians is expected to increase by 7 percent through 2016. Opportunities are reported to be strongest in the biotechnology, the food processing, and the scientific research and development services industries. In addition to job growth, openings will become available as technicians advance to higher positions, transfer to other jobs, or leave the workforce for various reasons.

With their training and background, Agricultural Technicians can seek employment in nonresearch positions. For example, they may work as technical farm workers for farms and ranches where they oversee the growing and harvesting of crops, or assist in animal breeding, nutrition, and disease control. A few other positions include sales representatives for seed, fertilizer, and other companies; farm machinery mechanics; field agents for food processing and packaging companies; field representatives for farmers, growers, or cooperatives; and agricultural inspectors for local, state, or federal government agencies.

Advancement Prospects

Agricultural Technicians may advance in various ways, depending on their interests and ambitions. Many technicians measure their success through job satisfaction, by assuming greater responsibilities, and by earning higher wages. With additional training, laboratory technicians may advance to research assistant and research associate positions. Individuals with supervisory or managerial ambitions can pursue such positions, for which they may be required to obtain additional education and training. Those working in private industry may pursue opportunities in other areas such as sales, technical service, technical writing, or marketing.

Some technicians choose to continue their education to become research scientists, engineers, or educators, or to work in other professions that interest them.

Education and Training

Minimally, entry-level applicants must have a high school diploma or general equivalency diploma. Depending on the position and an employer's requirements, applicants may also be required to have one or two years of vocational training or possess an associate degree in agricultural technology or another related field. Some positions, such as extension associates, which perform more complex duties, are required to possess a bachelor's degree in an appropriate field.

Entry-level technicians are typically given on-the-job training, as they work under the guidance of experienced engineers. Employers may also provide employees with formal classroom training.

Throughout their careers, Agricultural Technicians enroll in continuing education programs to update their skills and keep up with advancements in their fields.

Experience, Special Skills, and Personality Traits

Employers generally prefer to hire entry-level candidates who have one or more years of practical experience relevant to the position for which they apply.

Recent college graduates may have gained experience through internships, work-study programs, research assistantships, employment, or volunteer work.

Agricultural Technicians need strong computer, writing, and communication skills. They must have excellent interpersonal and teamwork skills, as they would be working with scientists, managers, and others from diverse backgrounds. Self-management, analytical, and problem-solving skills are also essential. Being detail-oriented, organized, self-motivated, persistent, flexible, honest, and dependable are some personality traits that successful Agricultural Technicians have in common.

Unions and Associations

Some Agricultural Technicians are members of a labor union that represents them in contract negotiations for better wages and working conditions. The union also handles any grievances that union members have against their employers.

Agricultural Technicians can join professional associations at the local, state, or national level that serve their particular interests. By joining a society they may take advantage of networking opportunities, continuing education programs, current research findings, and other professional services and resources.

Tips for Entry

1. As a high school student, gain valuable experience by participating in 4-H or the FFA (formerly Future Farmers of America), enrolling in agricultural courses at your school, or taking advantage of educational programs offered by your local extension program.
2. Contact local extension offices, farm bureaus, trade associations, and chambers of commerce for job leads.
3. For some positions, applicants are required to hold a valid driver's license. Employers sometimes hire candidates without a license, on the condition that they obtain a license within a certain time period.
4. Part-time, seasonal, or temporary jobs can sometimes lead to offers for permanent positions.
5. Use the Internet to learn more about the field of agricultural research. To get a list of relevant Web sites to view, enter the keywords *agricultural research* into a search engine. For some links, see Appendix IV.

FOOD SCIENTIST

CAREER PROFILE

Duties: Engage in research and development or production of food products; design and conduct research projects; perform duties as required

Alternate Title(s): Food Technologist; a title that reflects a specific occupation such as Food Chemist, Quality Assurance Specialist, or Product Development Scientist

Salary Range: $30,000 to $97,000

Employment Prospects: Good

Advancement Prospects: Good

Prerequisites:

Education or Training—A bachelor's or advanced degree in food science or related field

Experience—Requirements vary for the different positions

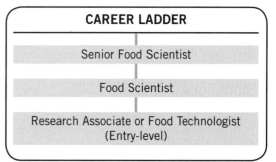

CAREER LADDER

Senior Food Scientist

Food Scientist

Research Associate or Food Technologist (Entry-level)

Special Skills and Personality Traits—Communication, problem-solving, critical thinking, writing, computer skills, and interpersonal skills; be creative, curious, outgoing, tenacious, instinctive, and self-motivated

Position Description

Food Scientists are involved in the research, development, and production of packaged, canned, and frozen food products. Their role is to make sure that these products are healthy, safe, tasty, and attractive. Food Scientists, however, are not chefs, nutritionists, home economists, or food service professionals. They are trained scientists in food science, a branch of agriculture. They apply the principles and techniques of chemistry, microbiology, physics, engineering, and other scientific disciplines to study the nature of foods as well as to develop and produce new food products that meet the needs and desires of consumers.

Many Food Scientists work in academic and government settings, where they conduct basic research to gain new knowledge and understanding about the composition and properties of different foods—meats, fish, dairy products, grains, vegetables, and fruits. They also study ingredients, such as food additives, alternative sweeteners, and fat substitutes, that are added to food products.

Food Scientists examine how foods behave under certain conditions, such as when they are being preserved, frozen, or cooked over high heat. They also investigate why and how different foods decompose and spoil. In addition, they study how the quality, wholesomeness, and safety of foods may be improved for consumption.

Many academic Food Scientists hold appointments as full-time faculty members. In addition to doing research, they teach courses to undergraduate and graduate students. They also advise students, supervise student research projects, perform administrative duties, produce scholarly work, and fulfill community service obligations.

Food Scientists who work in the food industry are usually known as food technologists. They apply the findings of basic research to the creation, preservation, processing, packaging, storage, and distribution of safe and nutritious food products. Some food technologists work for food processing companies that make various types of food products—beverages, soups, breads, baked goods, frozen dinners, lunch meats, canned fruits and vegetables, packaged salads, cheeses, ice cream, candies, cakes, sauces, condiments, and so on. Other food technologists work for food ingredient companies which make spices, flavors, stabilizers, thickeners, preservatives, and other key ingredients needed for food products.

Industrial Food Scientists specialize in the different areas of product development and production. Those who are responsible for creating new or improved products are called product development scientists. Their role is to develop formulas (or recipes) that preserve the flavor, appearance, texture, and nutritional value of the ingredients in the food products.

Many industrial Food Scientists are employed as quality assurance specialists or quality control scientists. They are responsible for determining the quality of ingredients and food products. They check raw foods to make sure they are fresh and conform to specifications. These scientists also monitor production lines to ensure that the regulations and standards set by the government, by the food industry, and by employers are being followed. Other food technologists specialize in package development, production management, safety, marketing, technical sales, or management.

All Food Scientists are expected to keep up with constantly changing developments and new technologies. They might read scientific journals and books, attend professional conferences and meetings, network with colleagues, enroll in continuing education programs, and so forth.

Food Scientists conduct their work in test kitchens or laboratories that are set up like kitchens. They use ovens, microwaves, blenders, hand food processors, and other cooking equipment.

Salaries

Salaries for Food Scientists vary, depending on their education, experience, geographic location, and other factors. The U.S. Bureau of Labor Statistics (BLS) reports in its May 2006 *Occupational Employment Statistics* survey that the estimated annual salary for most Food Scientists ranged between $29,620 and $97,350.

Employment Prospects

Most research Food Scientists work for academic institutions, state and federal government agencies and laboratories, and independent research institutes. Some researchers are employed by international organizations and work in other nations. Food technologists are employed by food processors, food ingredient companies, food equipment manufacturers, food store chains, and other companies.

Employment of Food Scientists is expected to increase by 10 percent through 2016, according to the BLS. In addition to job growth, openings will become available as Food Scientists retire, transfer to other jobs, or advance to higher positions.

The food industry is one of the largest industries in the world and continues to expand as the population grows. Each year over thousands of new food products are introduced into the market, although only a very small percentage of these products become established. Opportunities for Food Scientists are expected to continue growing throughout the decade to keep pace with consumer demands for safe, healthy, and convenient food products.

Advancement Prospects

Food Scientists can advance in any number of ways, depending on their interests. Those with administrative and management ambitions can advance to such positions as program manager, research director, department administrator, or executive officer. Professors receive promotional rankings as assistant professor, associate professor, or full professor. Food Scientists can also become independent consultants or business owners.

Many Food Scientists pursue advancement by earning higher pay; receiving higher-level responsibilities; conducting independent research projects; and receiving professional recognition.

Education and Training

Food Scientists possess a bachelor's or advanced degree in food science, food chemistry, or another related field.

Specific educational requirements vary with different positions. A bachelor's degree is the minimum requirement for most industrial positions. At many companies, the minimum requirement for their research and development positions is a master's degree. A doctorate is typically needed in order to conduct independent research teach in universities and colleges, or advance to high-level positions.

Experience, Skills, and Personality Traits

Requirements vary among employers. In general, candidates must have relevant work experience and be able to demonstrate that they have the appropriate knowledge and experience for the jobs in which they are applying. Entry-level applicants may have gained experience through internships, research assistantships, fellowships, and employment.

For industrial positions, candidates should have a basic understanding of business principles as well as an awareness of consumer demands.

To perform well in their work, Food Scientists need effective communication, problem-solving, and critical thinking skills. They must also have strong writing and computer skills. In addition, they need excellent interpersonal skills in order to work well with scientists, engineers, managers, technicians, and others.

Some personality traits that successful Food Scientists share are being creative, curious, outgoing, tenacious, instinctive, and self-motivated.

Unions and Associations

Many Food Scientists join local, state, or national societies to take advantage of networking opportunities and other professional services and resources. Some professional associations that serve the interests of Food Scientists are the Institute of Food Technologists, the Society of Flavor Chemists, and the American Chemical Society. See Appendix III for contact information.

Tips for Entry

1. As a high school and college student, gain experience in food research or technology by obtaining part-time employment, internships, research assistantships, or work-study positions in academic, government, or industrial settings.

2. Knowing yourself is part of accomplishing a successful job hunt. Would you be able to describe your weaknesses and strengths, if asked in a job interview? Could you clearly and briefly state your career interests and goals? If not, take the time to think about them, and write them out.

3. The Agricultural Research Service, part of the United States Department of Agriculture (USDA), posts job openings and information about working with the service at their Web site, http://www.ars.usda.gov.

4. Learn more about food science on the Internet. Two Web sites you might visit are Institute of Food Technologists, http://www.ift.org; and Center for Food Safety and Applied Nutrition, (U.S. Food and Drug Administration) http://www.cfsan.fda.gov. For more links, see Appendix IV.

FOOD SCIENCE TECHNICIAN

CAREER LADDER

Senior Food Science Technician

Food Science Technician

Food Science Technician (Entry-level)

Special Skills and Personality Traits—Writing, computer, communication, critical-thinking, problem-solving, organizational, self-management, interpersonal, and teamwork skills; honest, reliable, detail-oriented, flexible, and cooperative

Position Description

Have you ever wondered who comes up with all the different cereals, canned soups, frozen foods, fruit drinks, and other food products that are sold in grocery stores? Did you ever wonder who determines that products are tasty and safe enough to eat, or who decides how products should be made and packaged?

The applied science of developing, processing, and packaging food products is called food science. The Food Science Technician is one of the many occupations in this field. The job of these technicians is to provide technical support and assistance to food scientists, technologists, and engineers in the areas of research and development and production of food products. Food Science Technicians, and all other food technology personnel, are responsible for ensuring that all packaged, canned, and frozen foods are tasty, safe, and healthy for consumption. They also make sure that the design and manufacture of products are in compliance with laws and regulations.

Food Science Technicians work under the direction of scientists and engineers in industrial, government, nongovernmental, and academic settings. They may assist basic researchers who conduct studies to advance knowledge and understanding about the composition and properties of foods, what causes different foods to spoil, how foods behave under different methods of processing, food safety, and various other topics.

Many Food Science Technicians are part of applied research projects in which investigators utilize the findings of basic research to solve problems in food processing, preservation, packaging, distribution, and other areas. Food Science Technicians are members of development teams that are involved in creating new or improved food products for commercial purposes.

Many other Food Science Technicians work in various areas of production where they monitor manufacturing processes and machinery as well as participate in establishing production and packaging standards. Food Science Technicians also play a role in maintaining quality control. They check that raw ingredients are fresh and stored under proper conditions. They test products for proper amounts of ingredients, purity, nutritional value, flavor, appearance, and other critical parameters. They also assist in making sure processed food products meet government regulations as well as their company's quality standards.

Food science incorporates various disciplines, including biology, microbiology, biochemistry, chemical engineering, and statistics, among others. Hence, Food Science Technicians are knowledgeable about the application of fundamental science and mathematical principles and techniques. Their work also requires that they operate a variety of sophisticated laboratory equipment and instruments, such as thermometers, scales, balances, microscopes, pH meters, and distilling equipment. In addition, these technicians utilize computer technology, including database, spreadsheet, and word processing software, in the performance of their responsibilities.

Food Science Technicians perform various tasks each day, which vary according to their experience, skill level, and position. Some of their general duties include:

- performing physical, chemical, sensory, and other standardized tests on food, beverages, or ingredients
- monitoring experiments
- examining biological samples to identify cells structures, bacteria, or other materials
- analyzing, recording, and compiling results of tests or experiments
- keeping accurate and detailed records and logs of their work activities
- preparing reports and paperwork
- maintaining inventory of laboratory supplies
- setting up, cleaning, sterilizing, and maintaining laboratory equipment and instruments
- staying up to date with current laws and regulations

Entry-level technicians typically perform simple routine tasks under the guidance of experienced technicians and scientists. As Food Science Technicians gain experience, they are assigned more complicated duties in which they exercise independent judgment. Their work is checked by superiors for progress and conformance with established requirements and policies. Senior technicians may be responsible for completing administrative duties, and may be assigned to lead or supervisory positions in which they oversee the work of junior technicians and other staff members.

Food Science Technicians work primarily in offices and laboratories. Those who are involved in the production process may work in plants. They often stand or sit for long periods of time. They follow strict safety procedures and wear protective clothing and equipment while handling hazardous chemicals or toxic materials.

These technicians usually work a 40-hour week, but put in additional hours as needed to complete tasks and meet deadlines. Some technicians are assigned to work shifts, which may require them to work nights or weekends.

Salaries

Salaries for Food Science Technicians vary, depending on such factors as their education, experience, job duties, and geographic location. The U.S. Bureau of Labor Statistics (BLS) reported in its May 2006 *Occupational Employment Statistics* survey that the estimated annual salary for most Food Science Technicians ranged between $20,850 and $49,270.

Employment Prospects

Food Science Technicians are employed by such private companies as food processors, food ingredient companies, and food equipment manufacturers. They also work for government agencies, nongovernmental research institutes, and academic research laboratories. In addition to working in research and development, production technology, and quality control, Food Science Technicians can find employment as food inspectors for state and federal government agencies that regulate the food processing industry.

According to the BLS, employment of Food Science Technicians is predicted to increase by 7 percent through 2016. In addition to job growth, opportunities will become available as technicians retire, advance to higher positions, or transfer to other jobs.

Advancement Prospects

Many Food Science Technicians measure their success through job satisfaction, by earning higher wages, and by assuming greater responsibilities. With additional training, laboratory technicians may advance to research assistant and research associate positions. Those working in private industry may pursue opportunities in other areas such as sales, technical service, technical writing, or marketing. Individuals with supervisory or managerial ambitions can pursue such positions, for which they may be required to obtain additional education and training. Some technicians choose to continue their education to become research scientists, engineers, or educators, or to work in other professions that interest them.

Education and Training

Education requirements vary among employers. Minimally, entry-level applicants need a high school diploma or general equivalency diploma. However, many employers require that candidates have also acquired vocational training or completed college course work in food processing, laboratory science, or related fields. Some employers prefer to hire entry-level candidates who possess an associate degree in applied science or another related field, while others seek candidates who possess a bachelor's degree in chemistry, biology, or food science. Some employers hire candidates with a bachelor's degree in another field, if they have completed course work in science and mathematics.

Entry-level technicians typically receive on-the-job training. Some employers also provide their employees with formal classroom instruction.

Throughout their careers, Food Science Technicians enroll in workshops, seminars, and courses to update their skills and knowledge.

Experience, Special Skills, and Personality Traits

Employers generally prefer to hire entry-level candidates who have one or more years of practical experience in the food or agricultural industry that is relevant to the position for which they apply. They may have gained experience through employment, work-study programs, research assistantships, or volunteer work.

To perform their various tasks well, Food Science Technicians need strong writing, computer, and communication skills. They must also have excellent critical-thinking, problem-solving, organizational, and self-management skills. Additionally, they need effective interpersonal and teamwork skills, as they must be able to work well with scientists, engineers, managers, and others from diverse backgrounds. Being honest, reliable, detail-oriented, flexible, and cooperative are some personality traits that successful technicians share.

Unions and Associations

Some Food Science Technicians are members of a labor union that represents them in contract negotiations for better wages and working conditions. The union also handles any grievances that union members have against their employers.

These technicians can join professional associations to take advantage of networking opportunities, continuing education, professional certification, and other professional services and resources. One national society that serves the interests of food technology personnel is the Institute of Food Technologists. For contact information, see Appendix III.

Tips for Entry

1. As a high school student, you can prepare for a career as a Food Science Technician by taking courses in chemistry, biology, and mathematics.
2. Contact employers directly about current and future job openings.
3. Ask friends and family members as well as former co-workers, supervisors, and teachers for leads to job openings.
4. Use the Internet to learn more about the field of food science and technology. You might start by visiting these Web sites: The Institute of Food Technologists, http://www.ift.org; and The World of Food Science, http://www.worldfoodscience. org. For more links, see Appendix IV.

MEDICAL SCIENCE

MEDICAL SCIENTIST

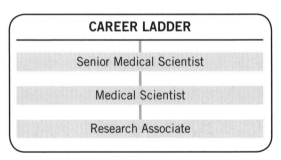

management, and problem-solving skills; persistent, independent, curious, flexible, and enthusiastic

Special Requirements—Physician-scientists must be licensed; board certification in medical specialty or sub-specialty may be required

Position Description

Medical Scientists are biomedical researchers. They engage in research that advances medicine and benefits human health. Their research has resulted in medical tests, techniques, methodologies, therapies, devices, and equipment that medical doctors and specialists use to diagnose, treat, and cure their patients. In addition, Medical Scientists have conducted research that has produced general guidelines for leading healthy lives from infancy to old age. Further, Medical Scientists have provided policy makers with the necessary information to make laws and public policies that ensure the safety and quality of health and health services.

Medical Scientists work in academic, government, industrial, and nongovernmental settings. Many biomedical researchers are molecular biologists, biophysicists, physiologists, microbiologists, geneticists, ecologists, and other scientists who are trained in the different biological sciences. Some researchers, known as physician-scientists, are medical doctors, dentists, veterinarians, or medical specialists such as dermatologists, pediatricians, medical oncologists, surgeons, and psychiatrists.

Medical Scientists perform their work in laboratories and offices, as well as in clinical settings such as hospitals. Depending on their research, they may be involved in examining cells, tissues, or organs; manip-

ulating genetic matter; creating computer models; or conducting interviews or surveys. They also devise experiments or tests that may use greenhouse plants, lab animals, or human subjects.

Medical Scientists are engaged in various areas of biomedical research. Some Medical Scientists conduct basic research. They do not direct their studies toward finding specific solutions to biomedical problems. Their concern is to advance knowledge and understanding of biological systems and diseases. They study such questions as: How do genes function? How does a virus affect living organisms? How do cancer cells grow? What may cause cells to resist disease?

Some Medical Scientists are involved in translational research, or applied research. They specifically conduct studies that translate knowledge gained through basic research, and sometimes from clinical research. Their objectives are to discover medical solutions for the diagnosis, prevention, or treatment of diseases. They work on the development of new and improved vaccines, medicines, medical devices, diagnostic tools, methodologies, medical procedures, instrumentation, and so on. Further, they seek ways to improve the quality of health and health services.

Other Medical Scientists are involved in clinical research. These researchers test the safety and effectiveness of vaccines, therapies, new combinations of drugs, medical devices, and surgical procedures on volunteer patients. The tests, or clinical trials, are done in three phases, in which Medical Scientists gather information about whether a treatment, methodology, or other variable will work, and about the risks that may be involved. The clinical trials take place in hospitals or other clinical settings. Because the research is patient-oriented, most Medical Scientists in these studies are physicians. Those clinical researchers who are not physicians collaborate with medical doctors who deal directly with the patients.

Medical Scientists also conduct other types of biomedical research. Some are engaged in prevention research, in which they examine how people may avoid contracting a particular disease. Some Medical Scientists are involved in outcomes research. They study the results that particular medical interventions or health-care practices have upon patients' lives. Other Medical Scientists are interested in health services research, in which they cover topics related to the delivery of health-care services.

Medical Scientists are usually involved with more than one study at any given time. They often collaborate on projects with other medical scientists, biological scientists, engineers, and other science professionals.

Medical Scientists fulfill a variety of duties each day. They perform such tasks as designing research projects, conducting experiments, recording experimental data, reviewing research literature, analyzing and interpreting data, writing reports, meeting with colleagues, and performing administrative tasks. Many Medical Scientists, particularly senior scientists, are responsible for supervising and training clerical staff, research assistants, and lab technicians. Independent researchers are responsible for seeking grants to fund new research projects as well as for raising funds to continue current studies.

In addition, Medical Scientists present the results of their research work to the scientific community. They write articles which they submit to scientific journals as well as make presentations at scientific conferences. Their research findings may also be posted on the Internet.

Many Medical Scientists teach in colleges, universities, and medical schools. They may be employed as adjunct instructors or be appointed to full-time positions. Along with their research and teaching duties, full-time faculty in research institutions are responsible for advising students, supervising students with their research projects, performing administrative duties, fulfilling community service obligations, and producing scholarly work.

Medical Scientists occasionally work evenings and on weekends to perform their experiments, write reports, complete administrative tasks, attend meetings, and so on.

Salaries

Salaries for Medical Scientists vary, depending on such factors as their experience, employer, and geographic location. According to the May 2006 *Occupational Employment Statistics* (OES) survey by the U.S. Bureau of Labor Statistics (BLS), the estimated annual salary for most Medical Scientists ranged between $35,490 and $117,520.

Employment Prospects

Medical Scientists are employed by colleges and universities as well as by medical schools, teaching hospitals, and medical centers. Medical Scientists also find employment in the military, in government agencies, and at research institutes. In addition, Medical Scientists work in private industries, such as the biotechnology and pharmaceutical industries.

The BLS reports that employment of Medical Scientists should grow by 20 percent through 2016. In addition, job openings will become available as professionals transfer to other jobs or retire. Although opportunities are expected to be favorable, job competition is strong, particularly for basic research positions.

Advancement Prospects

Medical Scientists can advance to supervisory, managerial, or administrative positions in any work setting. For example, they can become a project leader, program manager, division director, or executive officer. Those with entrepreneurial ambitions can become independent consultants or owners of companies that provide medical services—such as research and testing—or that develop and produce medical products.

Education and Training

Employers require that Medical Scientists have a doctoral degree (Ph.D.), doctor of medicine degree (M.D.), or a doctor of osteopathy degree (D.O.). Medical Scientists who perform clinical research, which deals directly with patients, are usually required to have an M.D. or D.O.

Most Medical Scientists earn their doctoral degrees in biological science disciplines. Others obtain their doctorates in biomedical engineering, epidemiology, public health, mathematics, psychology, organic chemistry, or another related field.

Several years of intensive study are required of students who aim to become Medical Scientists. Students first complete a bachelor's degree program (about four to five years) and then a master's degree program (about one to two years). A Ph.D. program, which is several years long, includes advanced classroom studies and lab research training as well as completion of a dissertation that involves original research. Ph.D. graduates typically complete several years of postdoctoral training to gain further research experience in their fields.

The educational path for physician-scientists varies. One path is the completion of a dual degree (M.D./Ph.D.) program, which is offered at many medical schools. (Students usually enter medical school after completion of bachelor's degrees in premedicine or a science field.) M.D./Ph.D. programs normally take between seven to nine years. In general, students first complete the first two years of clinical study. During the next three to five (or more years), they do their graduate work in their chosen fields. After they have completed their dissertations, they then finish the last two years of medical school.

Those aspiring to work in clinical research complete three or more years of graduate medical education, more commonly known as residency, in a medical specialty such as internal medicine. If they wish to specialize in a subspecialty, such as cardiovascular disease, they complete another one to three more years of training.

Special Requirements

Physician-scientists must be licensed physicians in the states where they practice. Licensure requirements vary from state to state. For specific information, contact the medical licensing board in the state where you wish to practice.

Many employers prefer to hire physician-scientists who are board-certified in a specialty, such as internal medicine, or a subspecialty (for example, infectious diseases and medical oncology are subspecialties of internal medicine). Board certification is usually through one of the various member boards that are recognized by the American Board of Medical Specialties and the American Medical Association.

Experience, Skills, and Personality Traits

Medical Scientists typically have previous work and research experience related to the positions for which they are applying. Many employers prefer that Medical Scientists have several years of postdoctoral experience in their research areas.

Medical Scientists must be able to express themselves clearly and succinctly to different groups of people from diverse backgrounds and with various levels of technical expertise. Therefore, they need excellent writing, communication, interpersonal, and teamwork skills. In addition, having strong self-management and problem-solving skills are important to accomplishing their objectives.

Successful Medical Scientists have several personality traits in common, such as being persistent, independent, curious, flexible, and enthusiastic.

Unions and Associations

Many Medical Scientists belong to professional associations that serve their particular professions as microbiologists, pathologists, epidemiologists, cardiovascular surgeons, medical oncologists, pediatricians, and so on. Physician-scientists may join medical societies such as the American Medical Association. (See Appendix III for contact information.) Professional associations provide Medical Scientists with networking opportunities, education programs, certification programs, and other professional services and resources.

Tips for Entry

1. As a high school student, start learning about biomedical research. For example, you might talk with professionals as well as read books and periodicals related to medicine, health, and science.

2. If you are interested in working for the federal government, contact the U.S. Office of Personnel Management (OPM). You may find a local office through your telephone directory. Or go to the OPM Web site, http://usajobs.opm.gov.

3. The federal government sponsors the Medical Scientist Training Program (MSTP) that pays tuition for students enrolled in a combined M.D./Ph.D. program. To learn about the MSTP program, go to this Web page at the National Institute of General Medical Sciences Web site, http://www.nigms.nih.gov/Training/Mechanisms.

4. Use the Internet to learn more about biomedical researchers. To get a list of relevant Web sites, enter one of these keywords into a search engine: *medical scientists, physician scientists*, or *biomedical research*. For some links, see Appendix IV.

PATHOLOGIST

Duties: Study and diagnose human disease; design and conduct research projects; perform duties as required

Alternate Title(s): Clinical Pathologist, Forensic Pathologist, Pediatric Pathologist, or other title that reflects a specialty

Salary Range: $45,000 to $146,000+

Employment Prospects: Good

Advancement Prospects: Good

Prerequisites:

Education or Training—Medical degree; residency training

Experience—Requirements vary for the different positions

Special Skills and Personality Traits—Diagnostic, investigative, communication, writing, interper-

sonal, and self-management skills; detail-oriented, analytical, creative, and honest

Special Requirements—Physician licensure; board certification in specialty and subspecialty may be required

Position Description

Human pathology is both the scientific study of disease and the practice of laboratory medicine, which is the diagnosis of disease through the examination of cells, tissues, and bodily fluids. Human Pathologists are trained as medical doctors, but unlike other physicians, they do not examine patients to assess the status of their health. Instead, they study the specimens that have been extracted from patients to determine if they have diseases or show early signs of diseases. Pathologists make their diagnoses and summarize the results in reports, which are given to the patients' doctors. Other physicians also consult with Pathologists for advice and suggestions for treating diseases.

Working in laboratories, Pathologists apply principles and techniques from anatomy, biochemistry, physiology, microbiology, molecular biology, genetics, and other biological sciences to study and diagnose diseases. Depending on their interests, Pathologists are engaged in practicing laboratory medicine or conducting biomedical research. Some Pathologists are involved in both areas.

The study and practice of pathology is divided into two specialties—anatomical pathology and clinical pathology—and each is divided further into subspecialties. Some Pathologists practice in both specialties, while others concentrate in one area.

In anatomic pathology, Pathologists make diagnoses based on analyzing specimens by gross (what is visible

to the eye), microscopic, or molecular examination. Subspecialties include:

- surgical pathology—the analysis and diagnosis of specimens, particularly cancerous samples, that have been removed in surgery
- cytopathology—the examination of cells for early signs of disease; the specimens have been scraped from tissues or collected with a fine needle
- autopsy pathology—the internal and external examination of dead bodies to determine the cause of death
- forensic pathology—the medico-legal investigation into the cause and manner of death of individuals

Clinical pathology is the practice of laboratory medicine where various chemical, biological, molecular, and other types of tests are performed on specimens received from patients' doctors. Clinical pathologists are generally responsible for overseeing medical labs, supervising lab personnel, and ensuring that lab analyses and findings are accurate and reliable, as well as completed in a timely manner.

Some of the subspecialties in clinical pathology include:

- clinical chemistry—the biochemical analysis of hormones, enzymes, antibodies, proteins, drugs, and other substances in bodily fluids

- hematology—the analysis of blood cells and bone marrow to determine the morphology of blood cells, how well blood may be clotting, and if there are any abnormalities in blood cell counts
- microbiology—the examination of specimens to identify microorganisms (such as bacteria) that can cause infections as well as to determine the most effective drugs to treat infections
- molecular pathology—the use of DNA testing to diagnose and monitor the spread of disease
- immunology—the analysis of the amount of antibodies being made by the body to fight infections or diseases
- blood banking (or transfusion medicine)—the collection, storage, processing, and testing of donated blood and blood products

Many Pathologists dedicate themselves to working in one of the various subspecialties of anatomical and clinical pathology. In addition, Pathologists may specialize by studying diseases that affect specific organs, such as ocular pathology (eye diseases) or that occur within a particular population, such as pediatric pathology (childhood diseases).

Pathologists who engage in research development work in academic, government, industrial, and other settings. Many conduct basic research to gain new knowledge and understanding about the pathology of different diseases. They are interested in learning about the nature of different diseases, their causes, how they develop and progress, and how diseases affect the human body. Research Pathologists are also engaged in applied research. They apply the findings of basic research to develop new and improved diagnostic techniques and tests for the different diseases.

Research pathologists typically collaborate on projects with other Pathologists and scientists. Principal investigators are usually responsible for seeking grants to fund new and current research projects.

Research pathologists perform a variety of duties each day. Some tasks might include planning research projects, conducting experiments, analyzing and interpreting data, writing reports, reading literature, meeting with colleagues, preparing articles or presentations about research, and performing administrative tasks. Pathologists use a variety of sophisticated tools and methods in their work. These include electron microscopy, computer models, biochemical analysis, cell culture, molecular genetic techniques, and experimental animals.

Academic researchers normally hold faculty appointments in medical schools. In addition to doing research, academic pathologists teach courses in their specialties to medical students as well as train pathology residents. Their duties also include producing scholarly works for publication, performing administrative duties, and fulfilling community service obligations. Many academic pathologists continue to provide pathology services to physicians.

Pathologists are responsible for keeping up with new developments in their specialties as well as in the field of pathology in general. They attend professional meetings and conferences at the local, state, national, and international levels. They also read professional books and journals, enroll in workshops and seminars, and network with colleagues.

Salaries

Salaries for Pathologists vary, depending on such factors as their experience, employer, and geographic location. According to the May 2006 *Occupational Employment Statistics* survey by the U.S. Bureau of Labor Statistics, the estimated annual salary for most physicians (not listed by specialty) ranged between $45,160 and $145,600.

At the Explore Health Careers.org Web site (http://www.explorehealthcareers.org), sponsored by the American Dental Education Association, starting annual salaries for newly certified Pathologists ranges between $120,000 and $150,000.

Employment Prospects

Pathologists are employed by hospitals, clinics, and other medical facilities as well as by commercial medical laboratories. They also find employment in medical schools, government agencies (such as the U.S. Food and Drug Administration), the military, and research institutes. In addition, they work in private industries, particularly in the biotechnology and pharmaceutical industries.

Because the practice and study of pathology is essential to human health, there shall be a continual need for Pathologists. Most opportunities will become available as individuals retire or transfer to other positions. Employers will create additional positions to meet growing needs, as long as funding is available.

Advancement Prospects

Pathologists can advance to administrative and management positions in medical laboratories, research organizations, medical schools, and professional societies.

Education and Training

To become a Pathologist, medical training is necessary. Students first complete four years of medical school to earn either a doctor of medicine degree (M.D.) or doctor of osteopathy degree (D.O.). This is followed by several years of residency training, also known as general medical education. Residents first complete one year of general medical training and then three years of residency in either anatomical or clinical pathology. Those who choose to be trained in both specialties, must complete another two years of training in the second specialty. For example, residents may first complete their training in clinical pathology, and then fulfill training in anatomical pathology. To practice in a subspecialty, individuals must complete a one- or two-year fellowship program.

Many research Pathologists have earned a doctoral degree in pathology, in a biomedical science, or in another related field. Some schools offer dual-degree programs that allow students to earn both an M.D. and a Ph.D.

Special Requirements

Pathologists must be licensed to practice medicine in the United States, its territories, or the District of Columbia where they wish to practice. Employers may require that Pathologists be board-certified by the American Board of Pathology or the American Osteopathic Board of Pathology.

Experience, Skills, and Personality Traits

Job requirements vary with the different employers. In general, they look for Pathologists with previous work experience that is pertinent to the positions for which they are applying. They may have gained experience through employment, residencies, or postdoctoral training.

Research pathologists are expected to have excellent diagnostic and investigative skills as well as strong communication and writing skills so they can present information clearly. They should also have effective interpersonal skills as they will work and deal with various people from diverse professions and backgrounds. Additionally, Pathologists must have adequate self-management skills, including the ability to handle stressful situations, meet deadlines, organize and prioritize multiple tasks, and work independently. Being detail-oriented, analytical, creative, and honest are some personality traits that successful Pathologists share.

Unions and Associations

Many Pathologists are members of professional associations that serve their particular interests. These organizations offer various professional services and resources such as continuing education, professional publications, current research information, and networking opportunities. Some national societies are:

- American Society for Clinical Pathology
- American Society for Investigative Pathology
- Association for Molecular Pathology
- Association for Pathology Informatics
- College of American Pathologists
- Society for Cardiovascular Pathology
- Society for Pediatric Pathology
- United States and Canadian Academy of Pathology

In addition, Pathologists may join the American Medical Association and other professional associations that serve the general interests of physicians.

For contact information for any of the above organizations, see Appendix III.

Tips for Entry

1. Talk with Pathologists to learn more about their jobs as well as about their education and training.
2. As a high school or college student, you might get a part-time job or internship at a clinical laboratory to get an idea of the work that is done there.
3. To learn about fellowships and permanent positions, contact professional societies. Many societies have Web sites where they post information about fellowships they sponsor as well as links to other organizations. Many also post job listings.
4. Many Pathologists voluntarily obtain board certification to enhance their employability.
5. Use the Internet to learn more about human pathology and medical Pathologists. You might start by visiting the Intersociety Committee on Pathology Information, http://www.pathology training.org. For more links, See Appendix IV.

PHARMACOLOGIST

Position Description

Pharmacologists are involved in the scientific study of drugs and how they affect biological systems. They investigate such questions as: How do drugs alter the processes of cells? How can a certain disease be managed with drugs? What side effects can occur when taking a particular drug?

These scientists study the properties of various drugs, both beneficial and harmful. They investigate drug actions—the mechanisms that cause drugs to work in biological systems—and they examine how biological systems handle drugs. Furthermore, Pharmacologists are involved in developing new or improved synthetic drugs for therapeutic purposes.

Pharmacologists are often confused with pharmacists. However, pharmacology and pharmacy are two separate disciplines within the pharmaceutical sciences. Pharmacologists are scientific investigators who work in academic, government, nongovernmental, or industrial research laboratories, while pharmacists prepare and dispense medicines to physicians and patients in health-care facilities and pharmacies. Pharmacologists supply the information that pharmacists use to provide physicians and patients advice about the selection and use of drugs.

Pharmacology is a multidisciplinary field, in which Pharmacologists apply principles and techniques of analytical chemistry, biochemistry, cellular biology, molecular biology, genetics, immunology, medicinal chemistry, microbiology, pathology, and physiology.

Pharmacology is generally divided into two areas of study. Some Pharmacologists are involved in pharmacodynamics, which examines how drugs work in and affect biological systems. Other Pharmacologists do research in pharmacokinetics, which studies how the body handles drugs and chemicals.

Many Pharmacologists also specialize in one of the subdisciplines of pharmacology, such as:

- cardiovascular pharmacology—the study of how drugs affect the heart, the vascular system, and other life systems that regulate the cardiovascular function
- neuropharmacology—the study of how drugs affect the brain and nervous system
- psychopharmacology—the study of the effect of drugs on mood and human behavior
- molecular pharmacology—the application of molecular biology to study how drugs work at the cellular and molecular levels
- chemotherapeutics—the development of chemical agents that can destroy or inhibit the growth of parasites or diseased cells without seriously hurting the host cells
- clinical pharmacology—the study of therapeutic and toxic actions of drugs in humans
- toxicology—the study of toxic effects of drugs as well as chemicals that are potentially environmental, industrial, or household hazards
- veterinary pharmacology—the research and development of drugs to address health problems in animals

Pharmacologists are engaged in different types of research and development. Those who conduct basic research are interested in gaining new knowledge and understanding about the properties of drugs and their interactions in biological systems. Other Pharmacologists apply the findings of basic research to find practical solutions to drug, chemical, and hormone-related problems that affect human health. These applied researchers typically work on the development of new or improved drug therapies and medicinal products.

Some Pharmacologists specialize in clinical research, which involves the final stages of development of new drugs or new uses for existing drugs. They study the effectiveness of experimental therapies on human subjects, who are volunteer patients. Because drugs are administered to patients, clinical Pharmacologists are either medical doctors or they collaborate with physicians who work directly with patients.

Pharmacologists usually work on more than one research project at a time, and often collaborate on projects with other Pharmacologists and scientists from other disciplines. Pharmacologists share information about their research by writing articles (or scientific papers) for scientific journals or by giving presentations at scientific conferences.

Pharmacologists work in laboratories and offices, while performing a variety of tasks each day. Some of their duties might include designing research projects; formulating hypotheses; conducting experiments; developing computer models to test theories; studying scientific literature; analyzing and interpreting data; writing reports; meeting with colleagues; and performing administrative tasks. Senior researchers or principal investigators perform supervisory and management tasks. In addition, independent investigators are responsible for obtaining research grants to fund their new and ongoing research projects.

Many Pharmacologists hold academic appointments at colleges and universities. They may teach undergraduate, graduate, medical, nursing, dental, or pharmacy courses. Full-time professors are responsible for advising students, supervising student research projects, and performing administrative tasks. They are also required to publish scholarly work and fulfill community service obligations.

Salaries

Salaries for Pharmacologists vary, depending on their experience, employer, geographic location, and other factors. According to the May 2006 *Occupational Employment Statistics* survey by the U.S. Bureau of Labor Statistics, the estimated annual salary for most medical scientists, including Pharmacologists, ranged between $35,490 and $117,520.

Employment Prospects

Pharmacologists are employed in various settings, including government agencies, nongovernmental organizations, research institutes, academic institutions, and hospitals. They also find work in private industries, particularly the pharmaceutical and biotechnology industries.

Opportunities are available in both the public and private sectors for Pharmacologists to develop and test numerous new drugs, which have been identified as having the potential to treat various diseases. According to some experts in the field, the job outlook for Pharmacologists should be favorable for the coming years. This is partly due to fewer students entering the field of pharmacology during the last few decades.

Advancement Prospects

Pharmacologists with management or administrative ambitions can advance to such positions in any work setting. Professors receive promotional rankings as assistant professor, associate professor or full professor.

Education and Training

Employers usually hire applicants for research scientist positions who possess a doctoral degree. Some employers prefer that applicants for clinical research or medical school teaching appointments possess a medical degree.

Pharmacologists typically need a doctorate to conduct independent research, advance to top managerial positions, or to teach in colleges and universities.

Ph.D. graduates normally complete one or more years of postdoctoral training before obtaining permanent positions.

Some schools offer dual-degree programs in which students can earn an M.D. and a Ph.D. in pharmacology or another related field.

Experience, Skills, and Personality Traits

Employers generally choose candidates who have previous work and research experience related to the jobs for which they are applying. Entry-level applicants may have gained experience through research projects, internships, fellowships, or part-time employment. Many employers require that Ph.D. applicants have a few years of postdoctoral experience.

Pharmacologists need strong analytical, writing, and communication skills to succeed at their work. They also need excellent teamwork and interpersonal skills, as they must be able to work well with scientists, technicians, administrators, patients, and others. Mathematics and statistics skills are also essential. Being enthusiastic, organized, flexible, diligent, and creative are some personality traits that successful Pharmacologists share.

Unions and Associations

Many Pharmacologists join professional associations to take advantage of professional services and resources such as education programs, certification programs, and networking opportunities. Some national societies that serve the different interests of Pharmacologists include the American Society for Pharmacology and Experimental Therapeutics; the American College of Clinical Pharmacology; the American Society for Clinical Pharmacology and Therapeutics; the American Association of Pharmaceutical Scientists; and the American Psychological Association Division of Psychopharmacology and Substance Abuse. For contact information, see Appendix III.

Tips for Entry

1. Gain experience during your undergraduate years by obtaining an internship or research assistantship.
2. Check with professional associations, government agencies, research institutes, companies, and universities for job listings. They may provide job hot lines or have postings on their Web sites.
3. Clinical Pharmacologists may be required to be licensed physicians as well as be board-certified by the American Board of Clinical Pharmacology.
4. Learn more about Pharmacologists on the Internet. You might start by visiting the American Society for Pharmacology and Experimental Therapeutics Web site at http://www. aspet.org. For more links, see Appendix IV.

PHARMACEUTICAL CHEMIST

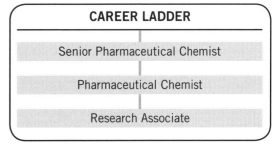

Position Description

Tens of thousands of pharmaceutical drugs are used every day to help people lead healthy lives. These include medicines that physicians use to diagnose, treat, and prevent a wide range of health disorders and diseases, including allergies, infections, eczema, arthritis, pneumonia, tuberculosis, diabetes, cancer, HIV/AIDS, and cardiovascular disease, to name a few. Pharmaceutical drugs also consist of over-the-counter remedies that people take to ease muscle pains, stop nausea, lessen stuffy noses, relieve insect bites, and treat other minor health symptoms. In addition, pharmaceutical drugs include those medications that are used to address other diverse health issues such as depression, drug addiction, obesity, birth control, sexual dysfunction, and baldness. Pharmaceutical drugs include medicines prescribed by physicians as well as nonprescription drugs.

Developing and producing new medications is a long process, which can take as long as 14 years or more. Among the many professionals who are involved in their creation are Pharmaceutical Chemists. They are experts in the discovery and design of new pharmaceuticals, the chemical compounds used as active ingredients in medicinal, or pharmaceutical, drugs. The goal of these scientists is to find the right combination of chemical substances that can effectively destroy a particular virus, bacterium, or other pathogen that causes an infection, illness, or disease in the human body. Once they obtain a potential drug compound, Pharmaceutical Chemists continue to test and alter the compound until it effectively heals the affected cells and causes few side effects. Originally, medicines were made from nature—plants, animals, bacteria, molds, and minerals. With the advancements of science and technology, Pharmaceutical Chemists have been able to create synthetic drugs that copy or improve upon natural substances.

Pharmaceutical Chemists are not to be confused with pharmacists or pharmacologists. The former are professionals who prepare and dispense drugs and other medications to patients, while the latter are scientists who study drugs and how they affect biological systems. Pharmacologists often work alongside Pharmaceutical Chemists on research projects.

Pharmaceutical Chemists work in industrial, academic, and government settings where they perform research and development. Their work requires that they have a firm grasp of both chemistry and biological processes. They apply the principles and techniques of various disciplines, including organic chemistry, biochemistry, analytical chemistry, biology, pharmacology, and toxicology, among others. These scientists comprehend the chemistry of drugs as well as how pharmaceuticals interact with and are delivered to the body's biological systems. In addition, they are knowledgeable about the diseases or health conditions with which they are working. In other words, they understand what causes a particular disease or health condition, how it affects the body, and what treatments have been used to diagnose, cure, or prevent it.

Many Pharmaceutical Chemists are part of development teams in industrial laboratories that engage in designing brand new pharmaceutical drugs or improving drugs already on the market so that they are less toxic and more effective therapeutically.

In the discovery stage, Pharmaceutical Chemists are responsible for identifying chemical substances that have the desired biological properties needed for a new drug. This typically involves screening hundreds, and sometimes thousands, of compounds that may come from natural or synthetic sources. Traditionally, Pharmaceutical Chemists find potential compounds by synthesizing sets of compounds in the laboratory. Today, increasingly more Pharmaceutical Chemists use a variety of advanced technologies, such as computer simulation and molecular modeling to help them narrow down the countless number of chemical combinations.

These chemists are also involved in selecting, designing, synthesizing, modifying, and testing compounds until they find the precise compounds to act as the active ingredients in potential drugs. They look for compounds that exhibit the best absorption rate and the ability to target the diseased or infected cells most efficiently. They also seek compounds that consist of the most potent and least toxic combination of chemical substances. Promising compounds are then developed into drugs, which undergo an extensive testing process in the laboratory. The process is long, risky, and difficult, as well as costly.

Pharmaceutical Chemists are concerned with other areas of research and development. Some chemists engage in conducting basic research to further knowledge and understanding about topics involved in designing and developing drugs. For example, they might investigate how drugs are transported to certain parts of the body; examine how drugs affect the body at the molecular level; or study the chemistry of new sources of potential drugs, such as marine organisms or microorganisms. Basic researchers generally do not seek practical purposes with their research, but the results of their findings are often applied by other scientists in finding solutions to problems in their areas of interest. For example, applied researchers might be concerned with developing new methods of drug delivery to the body, designing better techniques to determine the safety and potency of drugs in the pharmacies or stores, or improving drug-manufacturing processes.

Depending on the nature of the research, Pharmaceutical Chemists work alone or with scientists from other disciplines, including biologists, pharmacologists, toxicologists, virologists, biochemists, organic chemists, and computational chemists, among others.

Industrial research teams are responsible for developing new drug products that can be produced efficiently and cost-effectively for their employers.

Pharmaceutical Chemists perform general research tasks that are the same regardless of their setting or the type of research they perform. Some of their duties include designing and conducting research projects; planning and executing experiments and tests; reading scientific literature; collecting, analyzing, and interpreting experimental or test data; preparing reports of their findings and conclusions; keeping up with the latest technologies and advancements; and completing administrative tasks. Independent researchers are also responsible for seeking grants to fund their research projects. Senior researchers and principal investigators may have supervisory and managerial responsibilities as well.

Researchers typically share and exchange information with other scientists. Many write papers about their findings and conclusions for scientific journals, as well as give presentations at scientific conferences.

Most academic researchers hold professorships at colleges and universities where they teach undergraduate and graduate students in materials sciences, chemistry, physics, or other subjects. These researchers are responsible for teaching courses, advising students, supervising students' research projects, producing scholarly work, fulfilling community service, and performing administrative duties.

Salaries

Salaries for Pharmaceutical Chemists vary, depending on such factors as their experience, employer, industry, and geographic location. According to the May 2006 *Occupational Employment Statistics* survey by the U.S. Bureau of Labor Statistics (BLS), the estimated annual salary for most chemists ranged between $35,480 and $106,310, and for most chemistry professors, between $36,160 and $116,910.

Employment Prospects

The pharmaceutical industry is the major employer of Pharmaceutical Chemists. These chemists also find employment in biotechnology firms, chemical manufacturing companies, and private consulting firms, among others in the private sector. Additionally, they work for government agencies such as the U.S. Food and Drug Administration (FDA), the U.S. Department of Agriculture, and the U.S. National Institutes of Health. Some Pharmaceutical Chemists are employed by nonprofit research institutes, hospitals, and academic research laboratories. Others are employed as faculty members in colleges and universities, where they may hold teaching appointments in more than one science department.

Job openings generally become available as Pharmaceutical Chemists transfer to other jobs, advance to higher positions, or retire.

Opportunities for Pharmaceutical Chemists should be favorable for the coming years because of the continuing demand for both prescribed and over-the-counter drugs, regardless of whether the economic conditions of the country are strong or weak. The BLS reports that the pharmaceutical and medicine manufacturing industry is among the fastest growing manufacturing industries in the United States. The number of jobs overall in this industry is expected to increase by 24 percent through 2016. Most jobs are found in California, Texas, Illinois, Indiana, Pennsylvania, New York, New Jersey, and North Carolina.

Advancement Prospects

Many Pharmaceutical Chemists measure their success by making important discoveries, through job satisfaction, and by earning professional recognition among their peers. Those with management and administrative ambitions can pursue such positions in government, industrial, and academic laboratories. Entrepreneurial individuals might choose to become independent consultants or start up their own companies.

Academicians can advance in rank from instructor to assistant, associate, and full professor, as well as gain job tenure at their institution.

Education and Training

Employers generally hire candidates for research scientist positions who possess a master's or doctoral degree in organic chemistry, pharmaceutical chemistry, or another related field. Some industrial employers hire applicants with only an undergraduate degree in organic chemistry or another related field, if they have many years of on-the-job training in designing and developing pharmaceutical drugs. In general, bachelor degree holders are qualified to apply for research assistant and technician positions.

Pharmaceutical Chemists usually need a doctorate to teach in academic institutions, conduct independent research, or advance to top management positions.

Throughout their careers, Pharmaceutical Chemists enroll in continuing education programs to update their skills and keep up with advancements in their fields.

Experience, Special Skills, and Personality Traits

Employers generally seek candidates who have work experience as well as have completed research work relevant to the positions for which they apply. Entry-level applicants may have gained their experience through internships, work-study programs, student research projects, or employment. Many employers prefer to hire Ph.D. applicants who have a few years of postdoctoral experience.

To succeed in their work, Pharmaceutical Chemists need strong writing and communication skills. They must be able to work well with colleagues, managers, and others from different backgrounds; thus, they need excellent teamwork and interpersonal skills. In addition, they should have effective critical-thinking, problem-solving, and self-management skills. Being flexible, imaginative, innovative, persistent, and meticulous are some personality traits that successful Pharmaceutical Chemists share.

Unions and Associations

Many Pharmaceutical Chemists join professional associations to take advantage of networking opportunities, job listings, and other professional services and resources. Two national societies that serve their interests include the American Chemical Society and the American Association of Pharmaceutical Scientists. For contact information, see Appendix III.

Tips for Entry

1. As an undergraduate student, obtain an internship in a pharmaceutical laboratory to determine how much you might like working in such a setting.
2. Learn as much as you can about a potential employer before you go to your job interview. You can often learn much about an organization by visiting its Web site.
3. Many industrial employers prefer to hire candidates who have a strong background in organic chemistry.
4. Many employers accept job applications and résumés through the Internet.
5. Learn more about Pharmaceutical Chemists on the Internet. You might start by visiting the American Association of Pharmaceutical Scientists Web site at http://www.aapspharmaceutica.com. For more links, see Appendix IV.

IMMUNOLOGIST

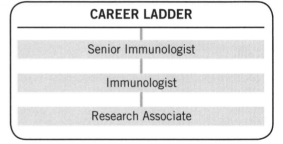

Position Description

Immunology is the scientific study of the body's immune system—the group of cells and organs (such as the thymus, spleen, and lymph glands) that work together to protect the body from illnesses and diseases ranging from colds to life-threatening diseases. When bacteria, viruses, fungi, or other parasites infect the body, the immune system naturally attacks and kills them while leaving healthy tissues alone. Usually, once invaded by a particular pathogen, the body becomes immune to future infections. When the body's immune system misbehaves, diseases can occur. Thus, immunology plays an important role in the diagnosis, treatment, and cure of many diseases. The medical scientists who specialize in this field are known as Immunologists. They are experts in the characteristics, structure, function, interactions, and disorders of the immune system.

Immunologists work in academic, government, nongovernmental, and industrial settings. They engage in a wide range of biological and medical research projects that are dedicated to improving the health of humans. (Research scientists who focus on animal healthcare are called veterinary immunologists.) Clinical immunologists are physicians who diagnose and treat patients with immunological disorders, including allergies, asthma, leukemia, and HIV, among others. These medical specialists, generally known as allergists/immunologists, maintain private practices or work in hospitals and clinics.

Immunology is a broad biomedical science that encompasses a wide range of topics. Some Immunologists study how different parts of the immune system respond to infections. For example, mucosal immunologists focus on the surfaces of the respiratory or gastrointestinal organs, or other sites where most pathogens enter the body. Other Immunologists conduct investigations into diseases that are specifically connected to disorders of the immune system. These include:

- hypersensitivity disorders or allergic conditions (such as asthma, hay fever, and eczema)—the immune system responds to such harmless substances as dust, pollen, or mold, causing damage to the body's tissues
- autoimmune diseases (such as lupus, diabetes, and rheumatoid arthritis)—the immune system attacks the body's tissues because it cannot distinguish the body from the foreign substances that are invading the body
- immunodeficiency diseases (such as AIDS and severe combined immunodeficiency disease)—the immune system fails to respond properly to infections, which causes individuals to develop infections frequently

Immunologists might work alone or collaborate with other scientists on research projects. Some are part of research teams that examine specific diseases such as cancer or heart disease. Some Immunologists develop vaccines and other therapies to protect humans from various diseases. Others engage in transplantation immunology studies to seek ways to help the immune system to accept, rather than reject, organ transplants.

Some Immunologists participate in research involving infectious diseases that can spread quickly among large populations of people. For example, avian (or bird) flu, West Nile virus, HIV/AIDS, tuberculosis, and malaria are some infectious diseases that have caused great concern in recent years. Immunologists are also part of research teams that seek ways to destroy a disease completely. In addition, Immunologists are among research scientists who work in the field of bioterrorism. These scientists assist in the development of strategies to protect communities from diseases (such as anthrax and smallpox) that may be released intentionally by criminals.

Like other medical scientists, Immunologists engage in different areas of biomedical research and development. Some Immunologists conduct basic research to gain further knowledge and understanding about the immune system in their areas of interest. They seek answers to such questions as: How do immune cells and molecules develop? Why is it difficult for the immune system to recognize that tumor cells are foreign to the body? How do different pathogens evolve? How did the immune system evolve in the human body? How do pathogens interact with host cells? What are the factors that cause a particular allergy?

Other Immunologists conduct applied research. They are interested in utilizing findings of fundamental research to solve problems in their specialties. Applied researchers also participate in the development of new or improved vaccines, diagnostic tests, medicine, and other medical products and therapies.

Some Immunologists are involved in clinical research. They work with volunteer patients to test the safety and effectiveness of vaccines, diagnostic tests, drugs, and other products. For example, Immunologists might conduct clinical trials on the treatment of an autoimmune disease using gene therapy. Clinical researchers who work directly with patients must be physicians, otherwise they collaborate with medical doctors.

The research work of Immunologists involves analyzing blood and tissues for various purposes such as for detecting antibodies, measuring levels of immune cells, monitoring immunodeficiencies, or diagnosing allergies. They use a number of immunological techniques and tools in conducting their experiments or tests, such as microscopy, cell culture (growing cells under laboratory conditions), flow cytometry, immunohistochemistry, molecular cloning, and microarrays. Immunologists might utilize animals for their scientific research; for example, they use chicken eggs for producing vaccines or work with animal models, which are animals that have contracted the disease that they are investigating.

Immunologists perform various duties that are similar to other research scientists. For example, they plan and conduct research projects, design experiments and tests, analyze and interpret experimental or testing data, read scientific literature, prepare reports and correspondence, meet with research team members, and supervise research technicians and assistants. Immunologists also formally present the results of their research work to colleagues through presentations at professional conferences, as well as in published scientific papers. Independent researchers are responsible for seeking grants from the federal government and other sources to finance their projects.

Many academic researchers hold part-time or full-time faculty appointments in various biological science or medical science departments. Along with teaching and research duties, full-time academicians are responsible for advising students, supervising student research projects, fulfilling community service obligations, producing scholarly work, and performing administrative tasks.

Immunologists generally work long hours, including evenings and weekends, to monitor experiments, write reports, and perform their various tasks.

Salaries

Salaries for immunology researchers vary, depending on such factors as their experience, employer, and geographic location. According to the May 2006 *Occupational Employment Statistics* survey by the U.S. Bureau of Labor Statistics, the estimated annual salary for most medical scientists, including Immunologists, ranged between $35,490 and $117,520. Immunologists who are practicing physicians typically earn higher incomes.

Employment Prospects

Immunologists are employed by research laboratories in academic, government, and nonprofit settings. They also work in the private sector, particularly in the biotechnology and pharmaceutical industries. Academic positions may be found in medical schools as well as in the various biological sciences departments of colleges and universities. Immunologists who continue to provide patient care may be employed in private practices, medical clinics, or hospitals.

Because immunology plays an essential role in maintaining human health as well as in seeking treatments to disease, opportunities for experienced immunology researchers will continually be favorable. However, job competition is high, especially for basic research positions. In general, positions become available as Immunologists transfer to other jobs or retire. Employers may create additional positions to meet growing needs, as long as funding is available.

Advancement Prospects

Many Immunologists measure their success by making important discoveries, through job satisfaction, and by earning professional recognition among their peers. Those with management and administrative ambitions can pursue such positions in government, industrial, and academic laboratories. Entrepreneurial individuals might choose to become independent consultants or start up their own companies.

Academicians can advance in rank from instructor to assistant, associate, and full professor, as well as gain job tenure at their institutions.

Education and Training

Many research immunologists possess a doctoral degree in immunology, microbiology, molecular biology, biochemistry, or another related field. Some researchers hold a medical (M.D.) degree, and some have earned both degrees upon completion of a joint Ph.D. and M.D. program, with an emphasis in immunology.

Physician-researchers who wish to provide patient care as allergists/immunologists must complete two years of fellowship training in allergy and immunology from an accredited program.

Throughout their careers, Immunologists enroll in continuing education programs and training programs to update their skills and keep up with advancements in their fields.

Special Requirements

Physicians must be licensed to practice medicine in the United States.

Allergists/immunologists are usually board-certified in internal medicine or pediatrics as well as in the medical specialty of allergy and immunology. Being board-certified by a recognized medical organization is not a requirement to become licensed physicians. Some employers may require that physicians be certified in their specialties, however. Many physicians obtain certification on a voluntary basis.

Experience, Special Skills, and Personality Traits

Employers generally seek candidates who have previous work and research experience, which they may have gained through employment, student research projects, residencies, or postdoctoral training. Many employers prefer to hire Ph.D. applicants who have a few years of postdoctoral experience. Strong candidates would have a background in immunology and be familiar with the subject matter that they would be researching. In addition, they are experienced in the research methods that they would be performing. For example, an employer may prefer to hire Immunologists who have experience working with animal models.

To work well with colleagues and others from diverse backgrounds, Immunologists must have excellent communication, interpersonal, and teamwork skills. They also need strong organizational skills as well as self-management skills, such as the ability to work independently, meet deadlines, and prioritize and manage multiple tasks. Being self-motivated, creative, persistent, enthusiastic, and flexible are some personality traits that successful Immunologists have in common.

Unions and Associations

Many Immunologists belong to professional associations to take advantage of networking opportunities, continuing education, professional publications, and other professional resources and services. Some national societies that serve the diverse interests of this profession include:

- American Association for the Advancement of Science
- American Association of Immunologists
- American Society for Histocompatability and Immunogenetics
- American Society for Reproductive Immunology
- Association of Medical Laboratory Immunologists
- Clinical Immunology Society
- Society for Mucosal Immunology

For contact information for the above organizations, see Appendix III.

Tips for Entry

1. Keep up with developments in your areas of interest, as well as in immunology in general. Be flexible, and be willing to take advantage of unexpected opportunities that come your way.

2. Many employers choose job candidates who have a strong publishing record.

3. While still in a Ph.D. program, participate in student or professional organizations. Take the time to meet new people at scientific conferences.

4. Use the Internet to learn more about the field of immunology. To obtain a list of relevant Web sites, enter any of these keywords into a search engine: *immunology, clinical immunology,* or *immunologists.* For some links, see Appendix IV.

EPIDEMIOLOGIST

CAREER PROFILE

Duties: Study human health and disease; plan and conduct research projects; perform duties as required

Alternate Title(s): Environmental Epidemiologist, Cancer Epidemiologist, or another title that reflects a specialized area

Salary Range: $37,000 to $87,000

Employment Prospects: Fair

Advancement Prospects: Good

Prerequisites:

　Education or Training—Advanced degree in epidemiology, public health, or related field; a medical degree may be required

　Experience—Previous work experience required

CAREER LADDER

Senior Epidemiologist

Epidemiologist

Epidemiologist Trainee

Special Skills and Personality Traits—Organizational, reasoning, writing, communication, interpersonal, and teamwork skills; curious, flexible, logical, innovative, and patient

Position Description

Epidemiology is the scientific study of human health and disease. Often known as "disease detectives," Epidemiologists identify health problems and hazards in communities, locally, nationwide, locally, and throughout the world. They study the patterns and causes of diseases that occur within certain populations of people, communities, or geographical regions. They examine what causes a disease to occur within a location or a population of people, why some people contracted the disease, and why others did not. Epidemiologists also recommend solutions for preventing the disease and controlling it from spreading further.

Epidemiologists investigate sudden outbreaks of infectious diseases as well as examine the risk factors that lead to chronic diseases, such as cancer, arthritis, or HIV/AIDS. Epidemiologists also conduct research on a wide range of health issues such as birth defects, developmental disabilities, infant mortality, teenage suicides, violent behavior, injury control, occupational health, and environmental hazards. For example, Epidemiologists might seek answers to questions such as these: What is causing workers at a workplace to become ill with the same symptoms? What caused so many guests at a wedding reception to get *E. coli* food poisoning? What are the risk factors for cardiovascular disease among women between the ages of 40 and 65? What are the reasons for the increasing number of obese children in the United States?

Epidemiologists also conduct prevention research, in which they study ways to prevent people from contracting a certain injury, illness, or chronic disease. Epidemiologists also perform outcomes research, in which they examine the patterns and delivery of treatments for a particular disease and the effects of these treatments on the patients.

The results of epidemiological studies help public health authorities, government officials, and lawmakers develop policies, strategies, and interventions that prevent or control disease. Further, they help other public health specialists develop general guidelines that promote good mental and physical health practices for people of all ages and backgrounds.

Epidemiologists usually specialize in one or more areas of research. The list is long and varied and new specialties are continually being added. Some specialties are cardiovascular epidemiology, cancer prevention epidemiology, infectious disease epidemiology, molecular epidemiology, reproductive epidemiology, psychiatric epidemiology, and environmental epidemiology. Some Epidemiologists focus their research work on developing new epidemiological methodologies.

Epidemiologists may work on studies alone or collaborate with colleagues, scientists, and public health specialists. Many Epidemiologists work closely with the news media in order to inform the general public of critical health news.

Epidemiologists conduct their studies by gathering information from a sampling of people who are part of the population whom they are studying. The most common methodology is collecting data through surveys and interviews with people. Another methodology is observing people over a period of time to gather pertinent information. Some researchers choose to conduct experiments in which they provide or withhold substances from people to determine the toxic or beneficial effects of the substances. Some Epidemiologists work in the laboratory examining blood samples for viruses or bacteria.

Epidemiologists' duties vary, depending on their position and experience. For example, senior Epidemiologists are usually responsible for designing, planning, and managing research projects. Many Epidemiologists hold full-time faculty positions in colleges, universities, and medical schools. Along with conducting epidemiological studies, they teach and advise students and perform other duties that are required of their academic appointments.

Some general tasks that Epidemiologists perform include

- recruiting people for project surveys and interviews
- analyzing and interpreting research data
- reviewing and analyzing medical and scientific reports
- preparing written or oral presentations about research projects and results
- providing consultative services to policy makers, educators, health-care providers, the general public, and public health specialists
- developing informational materials related to the prevention and control of disease
- attending meetings and conferences
- performing administrative tasks, such as writing correspondence and reports

Many Epidemiologists travel to other cities, states, and countries to gather research data, attend professional meetings, and make presentations. Their work may require them to spend several days or weeks at a location.

Salaries

Salaries for Epidemiologists vary, depending on such factors as their education, experience, employer, and geographic location. According to the May 2006 *Occupational Employment Statistics* survey by the U.S. Bureau of Labor Statistics (BLS), the estimated annual salary for most Epidemiologists ranged from $36,920 to $87,300.

Employment Prospects

Epidemiologists are employed by local and state public health departments, government agencies, colleges and universities, medical schools, research institutes, health organizations, HMOs, pharmaceutical companies, and biotechnology firms.

The BLS reports that job competition is generally high because the number of jobs is limited. Most opportunities become available as Epidemiologists advance or transfer to other positions or retire. Employers create additional staff positions to meet their growing needs, as funding becomes available.

Advancement Prospects

Administrative and management positions are available to Epidemiologists in any work setting. They can advance to such positions by becoming a project coordinator, program manager, director, or executive officer.

Education and Training

Educational requirements vary for different positions. In general, Epidemiologists are required to possess either a master's or doctoral degree in epidemiology, public health, or another related field. Some employers hire candidates with a bachelor's degree in biological sciences, health sciences, social sciences, or other disciplines if they have qualifying work experience.

Those interested in becoming medical epidemiologists need a medical degree (M.D.) or doctor of osteopathy degree (D.O.) in addition to a master's degree in public health with an emphasis in epidemiology. A doctorate is the usual requirement for teaching in academic institutions, advancing to high-level management positions, and conducting independent research.

Many students entering graduate programs in epidemiology have a bachelor's degree in the biological sciences. Others hold an undergraduate degree in sociology, psychology, or another discipline.

Experience, Skills, and Personality Traits

In general, employers look for candidates who have previous work experience that is relevant to the positions for which they are applying. Entry-level candidates should have at least one year of qualifying work experience, which may have been gained through internships, work-study programs, summer employment, or postdoctoral training.

Having strong organizational, reasoning, writing, and communication skills is essential for Epidemiologists to perform their work well. In addition, they need excellent interpersonal and teamwork skills, as they must be able to handle working with people from different backgrounds. Being curious, flexible, logical, innovative, and patient are a few personality traits that successful Epidemiologists have in common.

Unions and Associations

Various local, state, regional, and national societies serve the diverse interests of Epidemiologists. These organizations offer Epidemiologists many professional resources and services such as networking opportunities, job listings, education programs, and professional publications. A few of the many professional associations at the national level are:

- American Academy of Pediatrics—Section on Epidemiology
- American College of Epidemiology
- American College of Preventative Medicine
- American Public Health Association—Epidemiology Section
- Association for Professionals in Infection Control and Epidemiology
- Society for Epidemiologic Research

For contact information see Appendix III.

Tips for Entry

1. As a high school student, start exploring the different career options available to Epidemiologists. For example, you might contact different professional societies for information, read about the various subfields, talk with Epidemiologists, or visit an epidemiology lab at a nearby university.
2. Contact professional associations for information about internship, fellowship, and other training programs that they might sponsor.
3. Gain work experience by doing internships in different work settings or volunteering to work on research projects with professors.
4. For some Epidemiologist positions candidates must possess physician or registered nurse (R.N.) licenses.
5. Use the Internet to learn more about the field of epidemiology. To get a list of relevant Web sites, enter the keyword *epidemiology* or *epidemiologists* into a search engine. For some links, see Appendix IV.

MEDICAL PHYSICIST

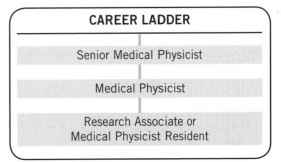

Position Description

Medical physics, a branch of applied physics, is devoted to solving biomedical problems. It involves the application of physical tools (such as radiation, ultrasound, heat, lasers, and magnetic fields) to the diagnosis and treatment of human diseases and health problems.

This discipline is made up of several specialties, which include:

- radiation oncology physics—the application of radiation to treat diseases such as cancer
- diagnostic imaging physics—the use of medical imaging systems (such as X rays, ultrasonic radiation, magnetic resonance imaging, and computerized tomography scans) to diagnose illnesses and injuries inside the body
- medical nuclear physics (or nuclear medicine)—the use of radioactive isotopes for diagnosing and treating patients
- medical health physics—the safe and proper application of radiation for diagnosis or treatment purposes

Medical Physicists are generally engaged in three activities: scientific research, clinical practice, and teaching. In their capacities as research scientists, Medical Physicists conduct studies in academic, government, industrial, and nongovernmental laboratories. They often collaborate on projects with medical doctors, scientists, engineers, and others.

Medical Physicists engage in various types of research and development. Some of them conduct basic research to gain further knowledge and understanding in medical physics. They develop new theories relevant to biomedical processes, diagnostic techniques, radiation delivery systems, radiation therapy, and so on. Like other physicists, Medical Physicists may emphasize a theoretical or experimental approach in their studies. Theoretical researchers create computer models to analyze whether the results of experiments (which may be done by other physicists) fulfill the predictions of physics theories. Experimental Medical Physicists design and run experiments and make careful observations and measurements to explain what happened in the experiments.

Some Medical Physicists are involved in applied research or translational research. By using the results of basic medical physics research, they develop new or improved tools, methodologies, and approaches for more accurate, precise, and safe diagnostic and therapeutic uses. For example, Medical Physicists might develop new techniques for imaging internal organs or participate in the design of improved radiotherapy treatment. Still other Medical Physicists participate in clinical research. They study the results of experimental techniques and therapies that are tested on human subjects, who are volunteer patients.

Many Medical Physicists are involved in the practice of medical physics. They provide clinical services and consultation in hospitals, medical clinics, and other health-care facilities. As health-care practitioners, Medical Physicists work closely with physicians, nurses, radiologists, and other technical staff. They collaborate in the planning and delivery of radiation treatments for patients. They also monitor procedures and equipment to ensure that the proper and safe dosages of radiation are delivered appropriately to patients.

Medical Physicists also provide consultation for the optimal use of the various diagnostic imaging systems. They make sure that equipment is properly installed and in working order, and that it meets government regulations and standards. They also develop accurate, safe, and proper diagnostic and treatment procedures and protocols. Furthermore, they provide essential education to medical staff, patients, and the general public on radiation safety. Medical Physicists may be involved in performing other services or supervising other staff members.

Most Medical Physicists are involved in teaching. Some are adjunct instructors or full-time professors in colleges and universities, teaching physics and medical physics courses in undergraduate and graduate programs. Others hold teaching appointments in medical schools and teaching hospitals where they train medical students, medical residents, and medical technologists (such as radiology and nuclear medicine technologists) in the proper use of radiation for the diagnosis and treatment of patients.

In general, Medical Physicists divide their time among research, clinical service, and teaching. Their involvement in each area varies, depending on their education, interests, workplace, and other factors. For example, Medical Physicists who work in academic institutions mostly do research and teaching activities, while those working in nonteaching hospitals and medical clinics are more involved in clinical practice.

Salaries

Salaries for Medical Physicists vary, depending on their experience, education, geographic location, and other factors. The U.S. Bureau of Labor Statistics reports in its May 2006 *Occupational Employment Statistics* survey that the estimated annual salary for physicists, in general, ranged between $52,070 and $143,570. According to the July 2006 issue of *Medical Imaging*, the average annual salary of Medical Physicists who responded to its survey was $139,664.

Employment Prospects

Medical Physicists work in hospitals, cancer treatment centers, and other medical care facilities. They also are employed by government agencies, industry, research institutes, academic institutions, and consulting firms.

Job opportunities for Medical Physicists are highly favorable, particularly for therapeutic specialists. This trend is expected to continue for the coming years, partly due to the low number of Medical Physicists graduating each year as well as the large number of Medical Physicists who are becoming eligible for retirement.

Advancement Prospects

Administrative and management positions are available for Medical Physicists in any work setting. Those with entrepreneurial ambitions can become independent consultants as well as owners of consulting firms or companies that provide clinical services to health-care practitioners and medical-care facilities.

Education and Training

Most employers require that Medical Physicists hold a master's or doctoral degree in medical physics, physics, radiation biology, or another related field. Doctoral degrees are usually required for Medical Physicists to conduct independent research, teach in universities and colleges, or advance to executive level positions.

Upon earning their academic degrees, graduates usually obtain medical physics residencies to gain practical experience in clinical service.

Those interested in a research career usually work one or more years in postdoctoral positions to get additional training in their research areas.

Special Requirements

Some states require that clinical Medical Physicists hold valid licensure to practice. For specific information, contact the professional licensing agency in the state where you wish to practice.

Hospital, clinics, and medical centers may require that clinical Medical Physicists be board-certified by a recognized organization such as the American Board of Medical Physics or the American Board of Radiology.

Experience, Skills, and Personality Traits

Job requirements vary with the different employers. They generally hire candidates who have work experience related to the positions for which they are applying. Entry-level applicants may have gained experience through internships, research assistantships, residency programs, and postdoctoral training.

Because Medical Physicists work with medical doctors, scientists, engineers, patients, and others, they must have excellent communication, interpersonal, and teamwork skills. In addition, they should have strong analytical and self-management skills. Being flexible, adaptable, logical, and inquisitive are some personality traits that successful Medical Physicists share.

Unions and Associations

Many Medical Physicists join one or more professional associations to take advantage of networking opportunities, professional certification, education programs, and other professional services and resources. Professional associations are available at the local, state, national, and international level. Some national societies that serve the different interests of Medical Physicists include the American College of Medical Physics, the American Association of Physicists in Medicine, the American College of Radiology, the Health Physics Society, the Biophysical Society, and the American Physical Society. See Appendix III for contact information.

Tips for Entry

1. As an undergraduate, gain experience through internships or work-study programs. You might also volunteer to work with a professor who is conducting research that interests you.
2. When you are doing a job search, remember to contact professors, colleagues, college career counselors, medical practitioners, scientists, and others whom you know for job leads.
3. Learn more about Medical Physicists on the Internet. You can start by visiting these Web sites: American Association of Physicists in Medicine, http://www.aapm.org; and American College for Medical Physics, http://www.acmp.org. For more links, see Appendix IV.

MEDICAL TECHNOLOGIST

Position Description

Medical Technologists are among the many professionals who work in the background to provide patients with essential health care. These scientists work in medical (or clinical) laboratories where they perform diagnostic and therapeutic tests on specimens including blood, bodily fluids, DNA, and tissues that have been drawn or extracted from patients. The results of such tests help physicians to diagnose, monitor, treat, and prevent diseases. For example, lab tests can provide physicians with information to identify the cause of infections in patients; detect if patients are at risk of particular health conditions (such as anemia or low-blood sugar); confirm that patients have cancer, AIDS, diabetes, or other diseases; determine if female patients are pregnant; establish a match between blood or organ donors and recipients; and uncover drug abuse by patients.

Medical Technologists work in clinical laboratories that may be part of hospitals, medical clinics, or physician's offices. They are also employed by commercial laboratories that offer their services to physicians locally, regionally, statewide, or nationally.

Some technologists work in academic, government, or industrial laboratories where they are part of research and development (R&D) teams in such areas as medical science, biotechnology, pharmaceuticals, food science, or chemistry. They may be engaged in basic research projects that advance knowledge and understanding in a particular subject, or in applied research projects in which they are involved in solving specific problems or in developing new or improved products. Other Medical Technologists work in forensic laboratories (also known as crime laboratories) where they perform tests on evidence in criminal investigations. Furthermore, Medical Technologists are employed by local, state, or federal public health agencies where they assist in the monitoring and prevention of contagious diseases.

In some facilities, Medical Technologists are called clinical laboratory scientists or clinical lab technologists. More commonly, they are known as lab techs or med techs, but they should not be confused with medical technicians who also play an important role in clinical laboratories. Medical technicians perform routine laboratory tests that are less complex than those conducted by Medical Technologists, because they have less training than technologists.

Medical laboratories are generally divided into different disciplines. Medical Technologists may be responsible for conducting tests in one, several, or all areas. Some of these areas are:

- clinical chemistry lab, where blood and other bodily fluids are analyzed for their chemical and hormonal contents

- microbiology lab, where specimens are tested for bacteria, viruses, and other microbes that may be the cause of infections
- hematology lab, where blood counts and other investigations of blood samples are performed
- histology lab, where samples of organs (such as heart and liver) are processed and prepared for microscopic slides, which will be examined by other lab professionals
- molecular biology lab, where genetic testing is conducted on DNA, RNA, or other cell samples to identify infections or disease
- immunology lab, where specimens are tested for antibodies, which respond to bacteria, viruses, or other infectious agents
- cytology lab, where cells are studied for evidence of cancer
- blood bank lab, where donated blood is tested for safety and matches are made between blood donors and recipients

As they gain experience, Medical Technologists might specialize in a particular type of lab work. Some might choose to work in specific types of settings such as blood bank, forensic, or medical research laboratories.

Medical Technologists work under the supervision and direction of pathologists who are physicians trained to analyze specimens and interpret any alterations that may appear in the cells or tissues. Technologists follow strict procedures and protocols as they conduct different laboratory tests. They are expected to complete tests in a timely manner, as well as perform tests that meet high standards to ensure the accuracy and reliability of test results.

These clinical laboratory scientists utilize the principles and techniques of chemistry, biology, and mathematics in the performance of their jobs. They operate sophisticated and complex equipment and instruments, including computers, microscopes, cell counters, and automated equipment, among others. They perform a variety of duties, which vary according to their skills and experience. Their tasks may include:

- collecting, receiving, and processing specimens
- preparing specimens, reagents, and supplies for tests
- performing chemical, microscopic, biological, hematological, immunologic, bacteriological, or other tests
- analyzing and interpreting test results
- reviewing data to ensure the information is accurate and precise

- reporting test findings to pathologists, other physicians, or research scientists
- entering test analyses and findings into computer databases
- setting up, cleaning, and maintaining laboratory equipment and instruments, including adjusting and repairing them
- helping in the development of laboratory policies and procedures

Senior technologists may be assigned managerial tasks. They supervise, train, and direct the work of lab assistants, technicians, junior-level technologists, and other personnel in one or more laboratory sections. They may also be responsible for such duties as implementing new test procedures, performing quality-control checks in their laboratories, and evaluating new lab equipment.

Medical Technologists work in clean and well-lighted laboratories. Their duties may require them to stand for long periods of time, as well as be exposed to unpleasant sights and odors from blood, mucus, stools, polyps, and other bodily fluids and tissues. To ensure their safety from toxic fumes and potential life-threatening diseases, these laboratory scientists wear protective clothing and equipment while working.

Medical Technologists typically work a 40-hour week. In large hospitals or private laboratories that operate 24 hours a day, technologists are assigned to shifts, which may include working evening or night hours, as well as weekends and holidays. In some laboratories, employees are on call to work at night or on weekends in the event of emergencies.

Salaries

Salaries for Medical Technologists vary, depending on such factors as their education, experience, employer, and geographic location. According to the May 2006 *Occupational Employment Statistics* (OES) survey by the U.S. Bureau of Labor Statistics (BLS), the estimated annual salary for most of these technologists ranged between $34,660 and $69,260.

Employment Prospects

The BLS reports in its May 2006 OES survey that an estimated 160,760 Medical Technologists were employed in the United States. About 60 percent of them work for general medical and surgical hospitals.

In addition to hospitals, technologist opportunities are available in commercial medical labs, physician's offices, fertility centers, blood banks, veterinary clinics, public health agencies, forensic labs, and research and development laboratories in academic, government, and industrial settings.

The job outlook is strong for this occupation, and should continue for years due to the increase in population and demand for health care services. According to the BLS, employment of Medical Technologists is expected to increase by 14 percent through 2016. In addition to job growth, technologists will be needed to replace those who retire, transfer to other jobs, or leave the workforce for various reasons.

As this book was being written, some experts in the field reported a shortage of qualified professionals, and expressed concern about the decline in student enrollment in clinical laboratory science.

Advancement Prospects

Medical Technologists can advance in various ways, depending on their ambitions and interests.

As they gain experience, they are assigned greater responsibilities and earn higher wages. They may become specialists in blood banking, chemistry, microbiology, medical informatics, cancer research, or another area. They can also pursue supervisory and managerial positions, which may require obtaining an advanced degree. In industrial settings, they may choose to transfer their skills and knowledge to occupations in marketing, sales, technical service, quality assurance, or another field.

With their background, Medical Technologists can further their studies in health or medicine to become registered nurses, physician assistants, physicians, dentists, public health administrators, research scientists, college professors, or other professions that interest them.

Education and Training

To enter the medical technology field, individuals minimally need a bachelor's degree and one year of training in a clinical laboratory. Their usual route is to earn a bachelor's degree in medical technology (or clinical laboratory science). Medical technology degree programs include academic course work in chemistry, biological sciences, microbiology, mathematics, statistics, and clinical laboratory medicine. In addition, students complete a one-year practicum (or internship) in a clinical laboratory, where they work full time performing diagnostic testing under the supervision of laboratory personnel.

Employers also hire applicants with bachelor's degrees in life science disciplines, as long as they hold a certification of completion from a medical technology program.

Special Requirements

California, New York, Florida, and several other states require Medical Technologists to be licensed or registered by the appropriate state regulatory agency. To learn about requirements in the area where you wish to practice, contact the state department of health.

Some employers prefer to hire candidates who possess professional certification, such as the clinical laboratory scientist (CLS) credential granted by the American Society for Clinical Pathology (ASCP). Professional certification is obtained on a voluntary basis. Upon successful completion of an accredited medical technology program, individuals are eligible to apply for certification offered by the ASCP, the National Credentialing Agency for Laboratory Personnel, and other recognized professional organizations.

Experience, Special Skills, and Personality Traits

Employers hire candidates for entry-level positions who have at least one year of clinical laboratory experience. Recent medical technology graduates may have gained their experience through the completion of their required practicum.

Medical Technologists need excellent analytical, problem-solving, interpersonal, teamwork, and self-management skills to perform well at their job. They also must have effective customer-service, communication, writing, and computer skills. In addition, these professionals need proficient motor skills, including hand-eye coordination and manual dexterity. Being calm, self-motivated, flexible, organized, precise, and detail-oriented are some personality traits that successful Medical Technologists share.

Unions and Associations

Many Medical Technologists belong to professional associations to take advantage of education programs, professional certification, networking opportunities, and other professional services and resources. Some of the national societies that serve this general population are the American Medical Technologists, the American Society for Clinical Pathology, and the American Society for Clinical Laboratory Science. Professional organizations are also available for the different specialists in this field, such as the American Association for Clinical Chemistry, Association of Genetic Technologists, National Society for Histotechnology, and the American Society for Histocompatability and Immunogenetics. For contact information, see Appendix III.

Tips for Entry

1. As a high school student, talk with your guidance counselor or a human resources officer at your local hospital (or private medical laboratory) about your interest in clinical laboratory science. Try to arrange a visit to a lab, or obtain a part-time or volunteer position at the lab.

2. Employers generally prefer to hire applicants who have completed a medical technology program that is accredited by a recognized organization such as the National Accrediting Agency for Clinical Laboratory Sciences.

3. Some employers hire medical technicians to technologist positions if they have completed relevant on-the-job training, as well as have a combination of qualifying work experience and education.

4. To enhance their employability, many Medical Technologists obtain certification in their areas of specialty from recognized professional organizations.

5. Use the Internet to learn more about Medical Technologists. To obtain a list of relevant Web sites, enter any of these key words into a search engine: *medical technologists, medical technology,* or *clinical laboratory scientists.* For some links, see Appendix IV.

MEDICAL TECHNICIAN

Duties: Conduct routine clinical laboratory tests on cells, tissue, and bodily fluids for various purposes; perform other duties as required

Alternate Title(s): Clinical Laboratory Technician, Medical Laboratory Technician; Histotechnician or another title that reflects a particular specialty

Salary Range: $22,000 to $50,000

Employment Prospects: Excellent

Advancement Prospects: Fair

Prerequisites:

Education or Training—An associate degree usually required

Experience—Previous work experience preferred

Special Skills and Personality Traits—Interpersonal, teamwork, self-management, computer, writing, communication, and problem-solving skills; analytical, self-motivated, detail-oriented, accurate, reliable, honest, and dedicated

Special Requirements—A state license may be required

CAREER LADDER

Senior Medical Technician or Medical Technologist

Medical Technician

Medical Technician (Entry-level) or Laboratory Assistant

Position Description

Medical laboratory technicians, or Medical Technicians, work in clinical laboratories in hospitals, medical clinics, doctors' offices, blood banks, research institutes, and other settings. Their job is to perform various types of chemical, biological, microscopic, bacteriological, and other lab tests on specimens—such as cells, tissues, or bodily fluids—that have been extracted from patients. The results of these tests are used for different purposes. They help physicians detect, diagnose, and treat diseases or other health conditions such as pregnancy, vitamin deficiencies, and drug abuse. Clinical laboratory tests can also help physicians to find matches between blood or organ donors and recipients, public health agencies to monitor contagious diseases within communities, crime labs to examine evidence in criminal investigations, or medical scientists to conduct clinical research.

Clinical laboratories are usually divided into several smaller laboratories, such as the clinical chemistry, microbiology, molecular biology, hematology, and immunology laboratories. Like all clinical laboratory professionals, Medical Technicians are responsible for conducting laboratory tests accurately, efficiently, and in a timely manner. Depending on their experience, training, and skill level, they may be trained to conduct tests in one, some, or all of the disciplines in their lab. For example, Medical Technicians may be assigned to:

- perform blood cell counts
- analyze bodily fluids for chemical or hormone contents
- examine tissue samples for bacteria, viruses, or other parasites that may be the cause of infections
- assess cell samples for signs of cancer or another disease
- type blood cells for transfusions
- perform genetic testing on DNA samples to identify a particular disease

Some Medical Technicians specialize in a particular discipline and hold job titles that reflect their responsibilities. For instance, phlebotomy technicians collect blood samples directly from patients; histology technicians prepare slides of tissue samples, which will be examined by pathologists or technologists; and blood bank technicians collect, type, and prepare blood and its components for transfusions.

Medical Technicians are often confused with medical laboratory technologists (or medical technologists) who work alongside them. Both technicians and technologists execute lab tests and analyses. Technologists have more education and training than technicians and therefore assigned more complex tests and laboratory procedures to perform. Technicians are generally delegated to complete routine tasks, which they perform under the supervision and direction of technologists, pathologists, or laboratory managers.

Medical Technicians perform a variety of tasks, which vary according to their experience and skill levels. Some general tasks include:

- collecting samples of blood or other bodily fluids for tests
- preparing cell, tissue, or bodily fluid samples for testing
- assisting technologists, physicians, or scientists with special projects
- analyzing test results
- recording test data
- making sure tests and experiments are performed to specifications
- providing physicians, scientists, or appropriate personnel with test results
- sterilizing lab instruments
- entering laboratory data and results into computer databases
- keeping lab logs and record books up to date
- setting up, adjusting, maintaining, and cleaning lab equipment and instruments
- troubleshooting problems in the laboratory

Medical Technicians work in clean and well-lighted laboratories. They utilize computers as well as operate sophisticated laboratory instruments and equipment, such as microscopes, cell counters, and automated analyzers. They often stand or sit for long periods of time, and wear protective clothing and equipment for safety purposes.

These technicians normally work 40 hours per week. Employees of hospitals and private laboratories may be assigned to work regular or rotating shifts that may include working evenings, weekends, or holidays. In some laboratories, technicians are on call to work at night or on weekends in the event of emergencies.

Salaries

Salaries for Medical Technicians vary, depending on such factors as their education, experience, employer, and geographic location. The estimated annual salary for most of these technicians ranged between $21,830 and $50,250, according to the May 2006 *Occupational Employment Statistics* (OES) survey by the U.S. Bureau of Labor Statistics (BLS).

Employment Prospects

The BLS reports in its May 2006 OES survey that an estimated 144,710 Medical Technicians were employed in the United States. Over 40 percent of them are employed by general medical and surgical hospitals. These technicians are also hired by physicians' offices, private medical and diagnostic laboratories, blood banks, public health agencies, government agencies, research institutes, academic institutions, and industrial research laboratories, among others.

The job outlook for Medical Technicians is strong, and should continue to be favorable for years to come, partly due to the increase in population and demand for health care services as well as to the lack of qualified technicians. According to the BLS, employment of Medical Technicians and technologists is expected to increase by 14 percent through 2016. In addition to job growth, technicians will be needed to replace those who retire, transfer to other jobs, or leave the workforce for various reasons.

Advancement Prospects

In general, Medical Technicians advance by earning higher wages, through job satisfaction, and by being assigned more complex responsibilities. By earning a bachelor's degree in medical technology (or getting on-the-job training), they can become medical technologists. As technologists, they have more advancement options, such as becoming lab specialists or pursuing supervisory and managerial positions.

Education and Training

Educational requirements for entry-level Medical Technicians vary among employers. Minimally, applicants must have a high school diploma or general equivalency diploma. Many employers prefer to hire candidates who have completed formal training in clinical laboratory science. For example, they may have earned an associate degree or certificate in a medical laboratory technician program from a two-year college. Vocational and technical schools, hospitals, and the military also offer laboratory technician programs. These programs provide students with an academic foundation in clinical laboratory science, as well as practical experience.

Throughout their careers, Medical Technicians enroll in continuing education to update their skills and keep up with advancements in their fields.

Special Requirements

New York, Montana, and several other states require Medical Technicians to be licensed or registered by the appropriate state regulatory agency. To learn about requirements in the area where you wish to practice, contact the state department of health.

Experience, Special Skills, and Personality Traits

In general, employers prefer to hire candidates for entry-level positions who have some experience working in clinical laboratories. They may have gained their experience through volunteer work, employment, internships, or work-study programs.

To perform well at their job, Medical Technicians must have effective interpersonal, teamwork, and self-management skills. They also need strong computer, writing, communication, and problem-solving skills. Some personality traits that successful Medical Technicians share include being analytical, self-motivated, detail-oriented, accurate, reliable, honest, and dedicated.

Unions and Associations

Medical Technicians can join professional associations to take advantage of networking opportunities, professional certification, training programs, and other professional services and resources. For example, many of these technicians are members of such national societies as the American Society for Clinical Laboratory Science, the American Society for Clinical Pathology, or the American Medical Technologists. Specialists may belong to societies that serve their particular fields, such as the American Society of Phlebotomy Technicians, the National Society for Histotechnology, and the American Association of Bioanalysts. For contact information, see Appendix III.

Tips for Entry

1. Employers like to hire candidates who demonstrate manual dexterity and have normal color vision.
2. Some employers prefer to hire candidates who possess professional certification granted by a recognized organization such as the American Society for Clinical Pathology or the National Credentialing Agency for Laboratory Personnel. Professional certification is obtained on a voluntary basis.
3. When doing a job search, take advantage of your school's job placement office or career center. Most, if not all, schools continue to provide job assistance to alumni.
4. Being persistent is part of finding a job you want. If prospective employers do not have current openings, ask how long they will keep your application on file. Check back regularly to see if a position has become available, and remind them when you had completed your application.
5. Use the Internet to learn more about clinical laboratories. To obtain a list of relevant Web sites, enter either of these keywords—*clinical laboratories* or *medical laboratories*—into a search engine. For some links, see Appendix IV.

ENVIRONMENTAL PROTECTION AND CONSERVATION

ENVIRONMENTAL SCIENTIST

Position Description

Environmental Scientists are involved with the protection of the environment and the conservation of air, water, land, and other natural resources. They study how human activities affect the health of the environment. They investigate and monitor such environmental problems as air pollution, water pollution, toxic waste sites, contamination of water supplies, global climate changes, destruction of ecosystems, population growth, endangerment of plant and animal species, depletion of natural resources, and public health and safety. In addition, Environmental Scientists develop solutions and manage programs that help prevent, control, or treat environmental problems at local, regional, and global levels.

Environmental science is a multidisciplinary field that integrates principles and techniques from the biological, physical, and earth sciences (or geosciences). Environmental Scientists therefore include biologists, oceanographers, health scientists, chemists, geologists, hydrologists, ecologists, foresters, and agronomists, among others.

Many Environmental Scientists specialize in a particular area. Some specialties are air quality management, groundwater protection, hazardous waste management, solid waste management, wetlands protection, energy, industrial hygiene, land conservation, and fishery and wildlife management.

Environmental Scientists work in academic, government, industrial, nonprofit, and nongovernmental settings. They hold different types of positions. Many of them are involved in research and development. Some scientists conduct basic research to gain new knowledge and understanding about air, water, and soil environments as well as about the impact of human activities on the natural environment and the various environmental conditions. Their research also contributes to the creation of environmental laws and policies.

Other Environmental Scientists are involved in applied research. They use the findings of basic research to develop practical solutions to specific environmental problems. They design new or improved technologies and practices that can help with the prevention or remediation of environmental problems as well as with the management of natural resources. For example, Environmental Scientists might develop conservation practices to protect drinking water supplies, design innovative technologies to reduce pollution emissions in refineries, or devise new methods to clean up contaminated sites.

In industrial research labs, many Environmental Scientists are involved in the development of new products, by studying ways to create products that are less harmful to the environment. Other researchers are concerned with improving production processes and investigate ways to reduce the amount of waste that enters the environment.

Not all Environmental Scientists work in research and development. Many of them fulfill other primary responsibilities as managers, inspectors, technicians, and specialists. For example, Environmental Scientists may be responsible for:

- performing lab analyses of water, soil, and air samples to identify sources of pollutants or contaminants
- designing and managing programs and systems for the protection or restoration of air quality, water supplies, and land areas
- conducting assessments of proposed projects—such as construction sites, housing developments, stream alterations, offshore drilling, or pesticide use—to determine their impact on the environment
- monitoring the toxicity of air, water, and soil at specific sites, in communities, or in regional areas
- performing resource surveys of specific plant or animal species in wetlands, forests, and other ecosystems
- inspecting environmental systems and facilities to ensure that companies, businesses, agencies, and other organizations are compliant with local, state, and federal laws
- responding to emergency spills of hazardous wastes
- conducting investigations into environmental violations, which includes such tasks as gathering and preparing evidence and providing testimony as expert witnesses

Many Environmental Scientists are consultants who offer environmental services to government agencies, businesses, manufacturers, farmers, developers, hospitals, and others. Consultants may be independent contractors or employees of environmental consulting firms. They are hired by clients to perform specific jobs, such as conducting environmental assessments of proposed construction projects, overseeing the cleanup of toxic sites, or making sure that clients are in compliance with environmental regulations. Environmental consultants are expected to continually generate new business for their firms.

Many Environmental Scientists are involved in environmental education, as employees of government agencies. Some Environmental Scientists develop and coordinate public educational outreach programs. Some of them provide technical assistance to companies, hospitals, manufacturers, and others to help them generate less waste and prevent pollution.

Additionally, many Environmental Scientists are adjunct instructors and full-time professors at colleges and universities. Many full-time faculty members are responsible for conducting research projects along with teaching courses, advising students, and performing other required duties.

Environmental Scientists work in offices, laboratories, and in the field. Their field work may be performed at lakes or rivers, by coastlines, on mountains, or in forests. Depending on the nature of their project, they may be required to be away from home for several days or weeks at a time.

Many Environmental Scientists are frequently exposed to toxic chemicals, thus they follow certain procedures to keep health and safety hazards to a minimum. Certain tasks may require them to wear special clothing, respiratory protection masks, or other safety equipment.

Salaries

Salaries for Environmental Scientists vary, depending on such factors as their education, experience, occupation, employer, and geographic location. According to the May 2006 *Occupational Employment Statistics* survey by the U.S. Bureau of Labor Statistics (BLS), the estimated annual salary for most Environmental Scientists ranged between $34,590 and $94,670; and for most postsecondary environmental science instructors, between $32,890 and $119,260.

Employment Prospects

Job opportunities for Environmental Scientists exist at local, state, national, and international levels. The need to address environmental problems and comply with environmental laws and regulations should contribute to a growing demand for Environmental Scientists. However, the job market for Environmental Scientists is sensitive to changes in environmental policies. For example, job opportunities may shrink when environmental regulations are loosened or repealed.

The BLS reports that the employment of Environmental Scientists is expected to grow by 25 percent through 2016. In addition to job growth, openings will become available as professionals transfer to other jobs or retire.

With their backgrounds, Environmental Scientists can pursue other careers in the environmental field. For example, they can become high school teachers, environmental policy analysts, lobbyists, environmental advocates, landscape architects, surveyors, park rangers, environmental journalists, and environmental health specialists.

Advancement Prospects

Environmental Scientists may advance in any number of ways, depending on their ambitions and interests. They can become technical specialists as well as pursue such supervisory and managerial positions as supervisors, project leaders, program managers, directors, and executive officers. Professors can advance in rank, as well as receive tenure. Scientists with entrepreneurial ambitions can become independent practitioners or owners of firms that offer environmental consulting or technical services.

Education and Training

A bachelor's degree is usually required of candidates applying for such positions as environmental regulatory specialists, environmental technicians, and research associates. Some employers require that candidates have a master's degree. A master's or doctoral degree is normally required for anyone interested in research, consulting, and management positions. For a candidate to teach in universities and colleges, advance to top management positions, or conduct independent research, a doctorate is the typical requirement.

A bachelor's and advanced degree may be earned in environmental science or a related discipline in the biological sciences, physical sciences, or geosciences. For example, many Environmental Scientists hold a degree in ecology, biology, chemistry, geology, geography, meteorology, hydrology, agronomy, or soil science. Some Environmental Scientists have earned their undergraduate degree in science or nonscience disciplines, then obtained an advanced degree in environmental science.

Experience, Skills, and Personality Traits

Employers typically hire candidates who have previous work experience related to the positions for which they are applying. Entry-level applicants may have gained experience through research projects, internships, fellowships, or employment. Many employers expect Ph.D. applicants to have worked one or more years in postdoctoral positions. Environmental consultants are typically midlevel and senior level scientists in their field, which includes experience in research, project management, and technical leadership.

Environmental Scientists should have strong technical skills, including some experience with data analysis, computer modeling, remote sensing, geographic information systems (GIS), and global positioning system (GPS) technology. In addition, they need excellent interpersonal, teamwork, and communication skills as well as strong technical writing and problem-solving skills.

Being creative, positive, energetic, dedicated, flexible, and detail-oriented are some personality traits that successful Environmental Scientists share.

Unions and Associations

Professional associations for Environmental Scientists are available at local, state, national, and international levels. They offer their members the opportunity to network with colleagues as well as provide various professional services and resources such as education programs, professional certification, and current research data. Some societies that serve the different interests of Environmental Scientists include the National Association of Environmental Professionals, the Air and Waste Management Association, the Soil and Water Conservation Society, and the Water Environment Federation. See Appendix III for contact information.

Tips for Entry

1. While you are an undergraduate, seek out internships or work-study positions with environmental consulting firms, government agencies, conservation groups, and other organizations. If you are interested in a research career, you can also gain experience through research assistantship positions.

2. Some sources of environmental job listings are professional associations, environmental organizations, college career centers, and environmental publications. Many groups have phone job banks or post job vacancies at their Web sites.

3. Keep in mind that job ads for Environmental Scientist may reflect the type of specialists that employers want, such as environmental chemist, soil scientist, or hydrologist. Also be aware that a job title can refer to different positions. Therefore, carefully read job descriptions to make sure they are positions that you qualify for as well as jobs that you want.

4. Use the Internet to learn more about the environmental field. You might start by visiting the U.S. Environmental Protection Agency Web site at http://www.epa.gov. For more links, see Appendix IV.

ENVIRONMENTAL CHEMIST

Position Description

Environmental Chemists play an important role in the protection of the environment and in the conservation of natural resources. They study and seek solutions to a wide range of environmental problems, such as air pollution, water pollution, hazardous waste disposal, contaminated groundwater, and damaged ecosystems.

Environmental Chemists use the principles and techniques of chemistry, biochemistry, and other related sciences to examine the chemical compounds of pollutants and contaminants found in the air, water, and soil. They study the composition and reactions of toxic substances, as well as study the fates of those substances—where they end up in the environment—and how they are transported there. In addition, Environmental Chemists examine how toxic substances affect the air, water, and soil environments.

Environmental Chemists work in public and private settings. Many of them are responsible for providing lab analyses to public works (such as wastewater treatment plants), regulatory agencies, refineries, chemical plants, industrial plants, and research labs, among others. Their primary duty is to analyze soil, water, and air samples from industrial sites, waste treatment centers, water supplies, contaminated sites, and other locations. They may be asked to:

- identify and measure the amount of contaminants within samples
- estimate the exposure and effects of environmental contamination on humans and other living organisms
- assess the potential risk of pollution or contamination to the environment and public health
- monitor industrial processes or wastewater and, if necessary, incorporate appropriate chemical treatments to correct any problems
- test air, water, and soil samples to make sure that operations or processes are in compliance with local, state, and federal environmental laws and regulations

Many Environmental Chemists are members of teams that respond to emergencies such as oil spills or sudden discharges of toxic substances into water supplies. Some government-employed Environmental Chemists assist in collecting evidence to prosecute violators of environmental regulations. Government employees also might develop safety regulations or provide technical advice to companies, the general public, and others regarding hazardous waste disposal and treatment methods.

Many Environmental Chemists are involved in conducting research in academic, government, industrial, and other private research labs. Some conduct basic research to gain new knowledge and understanding about toxic chemicals, the effects of pollutants on the environment and on human health, the way human activities affect the chemistry of the biosphere, and so on. They study such questions as: What happens to certain toxic compounds when they dissolve in water? How does the atmosphere carry pollutants? What is the rate of global oxygen depletion? What happens to pesticides in the environment?

The results of basic research often lead to the development of practical applications for solving environmental problems. For example, Environmental Chemists might discover new industrial processes that reduce pollutants, invent new recycling technologies, develop ways to decontaminate toxic waste sites, or create better methods of treating and storing hazardous wastes.

Research environmental chemists conduct studies in various areas, such as toxicology, hydrogeology, oceanography, and health and safety. They often collaborate on projects with environmental engineers, other environmental scientists, and scientists from other disciplines. Researchers also develop new technologies and methods for detecting, measuring, and analyzing pollutants and toxic substances.

Environmental Chemists are involved in a variety of tasks, which vary each day. They perform such tasks as collecting samples in the field, setting up tests or experiments, recording data, developing computer models to analyze and interpret data, writing reports, attending meetings, and performing administrative duties. Senior chemists may perform supervisory and managerial duties.

Many Environmental Chemists teach courses in chemistry or environmental studies in colleges and universities, as adjunct lecturers or as full-time faculty members. Full-time professors juggle research, teaching, and other responsibilities each day. In addition, they are required to produce scholarly works on a regular basis.

Environmental Chemists perform controlled tests and experiments in the laboratory as well as conduct studies in the field. Their fieldwork may involve traveling to isolated areas, such as forests and wilderness areas.

They follow specific safety procedures while handling chemicals to keep health and safety hazards to a minimum. They may be required to wear protective clothing, respiratory masks, and other safety equipment.

Salaries

Salaries for Environmental Chemists vary, depending on such factors as their education, experience, employer, and geographic location. The starting salaries for Environmental Chemists with a doctoral degree is typically higher than for those with a master's or bachelor's degree.

According to the May 2006 *Occupational Employment Statistics* survey by the U.S. Bureau of Labor Statistics, the estimated annual salary for most chemists, including Environmental Chemists, ranged between $35,480 and $106,310.

Employment Prospects

Environmental Chemists work for government agencies and laboratories, colleges and universities, and nonprofit and nongovernmental research institutes. They also find employment in various industries, such as the chemical, pharmaceutical, mining, and pulp and paper industries. Many Environmental Chemists are independent consultants or are employed by environmental consulting firms.

The BLS reports that the employment of environmental scientists is expected to increase by 25 percent through 2016. In addition to job growth, openings will become available as professionals transfer to other jobs or retire.

Opportunities for qualified Environmental Chemists, in particular, should remain favorable for years to come. This is due to the need of companies, government agencies, and other organizations to monitor and reduce environmental pollutants and contaminants; to manage environmental protection and conservation plans; and to comply with complex environmental laws and regulations.

Advancement Prospects

Many Environmental Chemists measure their success by being able to conduct independent research, by making discoveries or inventions, by earning higher incomes, and through gaining professional recognition. Those with managerial ambitions can pursue such positions as project leader, program manager, and program director.

Education and Training

Depending on the position, employers require that Environmental Chemists hold a bachelor's or advanced degree in chemistry. Employers sometimes accept degrees in other disciplines, if candidates have a minimum number of hours of course work in chemistry as well as qualifying experience.

To teach at the university level, conduct independent research, or advance to top management posts, a doctorate is generally required.

Employers usually provide formal and on-the-job training to new employees.

Special Requirements

Federal or state laws may require that employees complete appropriate certification programs, if they are to perform certain types of lab analyses, such as wastewater analysis or hazardous materials analysis. To learn about certification for specific occupations, contact the U.S. Environmental Protection Agency or the state department of health or state department of natural resources in the state where you plan to work.

Experience, Skills, and Personality Traits

Job applicants generally need one or more years of work experience performing chemical analyses. Recent graduates may have gained experience through internships, work-study programs, employment, or research assistantships. In addition, applicants should be knowledgeable about the environmental issues with which they will be working. They should also be able to understand and use the terminology of biology, geology, ecology, mineralogy, genetics, water chemistry, and other disciplines.

To do their work effectively, Environmental Chemists need strong communication, interpersonal, and teamwork skills. They should also have excellent analytical and organizational skills. Being curious, patient, persistent, flexible, creative, and detail-oriented are some personality traits that successful Environmental Chemists share.

Unions and Associations

Environmental Chemists can join local, state, or national societies to take advantage of professional services and resources such as education programs, professional certification, job listings, and networking opportunities. Many of them join the Division of Environmental Chemistry, part of the American Chemical Society. They also become members of societies that serve the general interests of chemists, such as the American Institute of Chemists and the American Association for the Advancement of Science.

In addition, Environmental Chemists are eligible to join professional associations that serve the interests of professionals working in a particular field. For example, the National Ground Water Association, the Water Environment Federation, and the Air and Waste Management Association are some such societies. See Appendix III for contact information.

Tips for Entry

1. As a college student, gain experience by obtaining internship(s) with government agencies or private employers and by doing volunteer work with environmental organizations.
2. To enhance their employability, as well as to gain training and background in the field, many chemistry students take some courses in environmental science.
3. Use the Internet to learn more about environmental chemistry. To get a list of relevant Web sites, enter the keywords *environmental chemistry* or *environmental chemists* in a search engine. For some links, see Appendix IV.

ENVIRONMENTAL PLANNER

Position Description

Environmental Planners help decision makers adopt land-use plans that offer economic and social benefits for people as well as preserve natural environments. They contribute to the process of developing land-use plans for communities, companies, organizations, and individuals. These plans are formal documents that outline how areas of land, such as a city, region, or park, would be used and developed through the years. The plans provide goals, objectives, and strategies for various purposes, such as public works, transportation, housing, commercial sites, industry, agriculture, recreation, and open space.

Environmental Planners provide environmental analyses of existing conditions and future trends for land areas. They evaluate the environmental impact of current and proposed uses of land areas. They address such environmental issues as air pollution, water quality management, solid waste management, toxic waste disposal, traffic congestion, urban sprawl, and habitat conservation.

Their investigations involve collecting, organizing, and analyzing information about natural resources and land-use patterns. (This consists of all the uses—such as housing, agriculture, or open space—for a specific area of land.) Planners analyze and interpret statistical data about physical, social, and economic factors. They also seek feedback from land developers, conservationists, property owners, residents, and other interested parties.

Environmental Planners review alternative solutions to environmental problems and make recommendations. They prepare reports and present them to decision makers, who may decide to adopt or modify the solutions. These solutions then become the environmental plans, which may be integrated with comprehensive land-use plans.

Environmental Planners also assist in the implementation of land-use plans by developing environmental programs that meet planning objectives. For example, municipal Environmental Planners might formulate plans that include cleaning up brownfields (abandoned and contaminated properties), building a new sewage treatment facility, and planting more trees in neighborhoods. Environmental Planners submit reports to decision makers about their proposed programs. They also develop strategies to make sure their programs can be realized.

Environmental planning is a complicated and multifaceted process. Some Environmental Planners are involved with all aspects of environmental planning. Others focus on working in a particular service such as conducting environmental impact studies or developing environmental programs and policies. Some planners specialize in planning for a specific geographical area—a town, region, or watershed, for example. Other planners prefer to work on particular issues such as public transportation, flood management, or water quality management

Environmental Planners apply principles and techniques of environmental science, economics, and other disciplines to their work. In addition, they follow standard planning processes. They are also familiar with environmental laws, and are responsible for making their plans compliant with appropriate regulations.

Environmental Planners usually work a 40-hour week. Many work evenings and on weekends to attend meetings or public hearings. Environmental Planners spend some time in the field to inspect and document land conditions.

Salaries

Salaries for Environmental Planners vary, depending on such factors as their education, experience, and geographic location. According to the May 2006 *Occupational Employment Statistics* survey by the U.S. Bureau of Labor Statistics, the estimated annual salary for most urban and regional planners ranged between $35,610 and $86,880.

Employment Prospects

Environmental Planners are employed by local, state, and federal government agencies; planning and design firms; real estate development companies; and environmental law firms. They also find employment with companies and organizations that own and manage land.

Professional planners, in general, will continually be needed to address transportation, land use, development, environmental issues, and other problems that come with the growth of communities and regions. Most job openings are expected to be created to replace planners who retire, transfer to other positions, or leave the job force entirely. Employers will create additional positions to meet growing needs, as long as resources are available.

Advancement Prospects

Managerial and administrative positions available to Environmental Planners include project leader, planning supervisor, planning manager, and program director. An advanced degree is usually required for candidates to obtain management positions.

Many Environmental Planners pursue advancement by receiving greater responsibilities, earning higher pay, and gaining professional recognition.

Education and Training

Minimally, Environmental Planners must possess a bachelor's degree in environmental studies, planning, business, public administration, or a related field. Some employers require that Environmental Planners hold a master's degree in planning, with emphasis in environmental planning, land use planning, landscape architecture, or another related field.

Experience, Skills, and Personality Traits

Employers typically seek candidates who have work experience relevant to the positions for which they are applying. Many employers require that entry-level applicants have at least one year of planning experience, which may have been gained through internships, employment, or work-study programs. Candidates should be knowledgeable about the environmental issues that they would be addressing, as well as be familiar with environmental laws and regulations.

Environmental Planners should have strong analytical, communication, writing, computer, research, and presentation skills. Having excellent interpersonal and teamwork skills is also important, as they must be able to work well with people from diverse backgrounds. Some personality traits that successful Environmental Planners share are being energetic, innovative, creative, farsighted, pragmatic, and flexible.

Unions and Associations

Many Environmental Planners join professional associations to take advantage of networking opportunities, training programs, and other professional services and resources. Two national societies that serve the interests of these planners are the American Planning Association and the National Association of Environmental Professionals. For contact information, see Appendix III.

Tips for Entry

1. As a high school student, gain experience by volunteering with an environmental organization.
2. Gain experience by obtaining an internship with a local government planning office or planning firm.
3. Familiarity with geographic information systems (GIS) is highly desirable.
4. Use the Internet to learn more about the planning field. Two Web sites you might visit are Cyburbia http://www.cyburbia.org; and Planetizen: The Planning and Development Network, http://www.planetizen.com. For more links, see Appendix IV.

ENVIRONMENTAL TECHNICIAN

CAREER PROFILE

Duties: Provide technical support to environmental scientists, specialists, engineers, and managers in the areas of environmental protection, conservation, and remediation; perform duties as required

Alternate Title(s): Water Quality Technician, Hazardous Materials Technician, or another title that reflects a particular occupation

Salary Range: $24,000 to $61,000

Employment Prospects: Excellent

Advancement Prospects: Good

Prerequisites:

    Education or Training—Educational requirements vary with the different employers

    Experience—Previous practical experience preferred

    Special Skills and Personality Traits—Math, computer, writing, communication, problem-solving, decision-making, self-management, teamwork, and interpersonal skills; reliable, self-motivated, detail-oriented, patient, honest, persistent, and flexible

    Special Requirements—State license or certification may be required

CAREER LADDER

Senior Environmental Technician

Environmental Technician

Environmental Technician (Entry-level)

Position Description

Environmental Technicians engage in the protection of the environment as well as the conservation of air, water, land, and other natural resources. Their role is to provide technical assistance to environmental scientists, specialists, engineers, and managers in government, industrial, academic, and nongovernmental settings.

Because environmental science is such a broad field, Environmental Technicians perform a wide range of activities related to preventing, controlling, and fixing environmental problems. Many technicians perform tests to measure pollutant levels in the air, water, or soil; to analyze materials for the presence of contaminants; to determine sources of pollution; or to assess the compliance of companies and other organizations with pollution standards. Some technicians investigate complaints about pollution problems at factories and industrial sites, or study the impact of noise levels at industrial sites, airports, roadways, and public areas on residential areas and protected natural sites.

Some Environmental Technicians work at wastewater treatment plants where they assist in cleaning, purifying, and neutralizing water for human consumption; while other technicians work at waste disposal and treatment facilities where they are involved in the proper disposal of solid or hazardous waste as well as monitoring sites for leaking storage containers. Other technicians are responsible for identifying and removing hazardous materials (such as lead, asbestos, or toxic spills), and others have the duty of testing for radiation and developing ways to prevent exposure to radiation.

Many Environmental Technicians assist researchers who conduct basic studies about how human activities affect the health of people, animals, and the environment, or who use findings of basic research to develop solutions to various environmental problems. Technicians are also part of research and development teams that design new or improved technologies, practices, and processes that can help with the management of natural resources or the prevention or remediation of environmental problems.

Additionally, some Environmental Technicians participate in examining workplaces to determine how ventilation, lighting, noise, equipment, and other conditions may affect the health, comfort, and efficiency of employees. Furthermore, many technicians assist scientists and specialists in such areas as land management, wetlands protection, and fishery and wildlife management that involve protecting and conserving natural resources. Groundwater monitoring, recycling, regulatory inspections, public health, forensic investigations, and cleanups of emergency spills are just a few of the various other areas in which Environmental Technicians are involved.

These technicians apply science, engineering, and mathematics principles and techniques to their work, which they perform under the direction of scientists, specialists, and managers. Environmental Technicians are knowledgeable about the policies, standards, laws, and regulations that govern the area (such as air-pollution control or solid waste management) in which they work. They operate complex instruments and equipment, such as microscopes, and environmental sampling and monitoring equipment.

They perform a variety of tasks, which vary according to their job, experience, and skill level. They may be assigned such general tasks as:

- carrying out field surveys for environmental studies
- collecting samples of materials for tests or experiments
- preparing samples for testing and analysis
- conducting field or laboratory tests
- monitoring experiments
- recording and tabulating test or experimental data
- analyzing and interpreting experimental data or test results
- preparing correspondence, reports, and paperwork
- reviewing technical documents for completeness and accuracy
- maintaining computer files
- assisting in inspections of facilities, industrial sites, or workplaces
- setting up, adjusting, calibrating, troubleshooting, cleaning, and maintaining equipment and instruments

Entry-level technicians typically perform simple routine tasks under the supervision of scientists and experienced technicians. As Environmental Technicians gain experience, they are assigned more complicated duties in which they exercise independent judgment. Their work is checked by superiors for progress and conformance with established requirements and policies. Senior technicians may be responsible for completing administrative duties, and may be assigned to lead or supervisory positions in which they oversee the work of junior technicians and other staff members.

Environmental Technicians might perform their tasks indoors in offices, laboratories, or industrial plants, or outdoors in forests or parks, on rangelands or mountain tops, along rivers and ocean shores, or in other remote areas. They wear protective clothing and equipment and follow strict safety procedures to minimize health hazards due to toxic chemicals and materials.

Environmental Technicians are hired for full-time, part-time, temporary, or seasonal positions. They may be required to work early mornings, nights, and weekends. All technicians put in additional hours as needed to complete tasks or to handle emergencies.

Salaries

Salaries for Environmental Technicians vary, depending on such factors as their education, experience, position, employer, and geographic location. According to the May 2006 *Occupational Employment Statistics* survey by the U.S. Bureau of Labor Statistics (BLS), the estimated annual salary for most Environmental Technicians ranged between $23,600 and $60,700.

Employment Prospects

Environmental Technicians are hired by government agencies at the local, state, and federal levels, including environmental, public works, public health, natural resources, fish and wildlife, and other departments. They also find employment with academic institutions and laboratories, research institutes, and nongovernmental organizations. Additionally, they work in a variety of private industries such as the chemical manufacturing, agriculture, food processing, biotechnology, and pharmaceutical and medicine manufacturing industries. Furthermore, these technicians are employed by private testing laboratories as well as professional, scientific, and technical firms that offer environmental consulting or technical services.

According to the BLS, employment of environmental science and protection technicians is expected to increase by 28 percent through 2016. In addition to job growth, Environmental Technicians will be needed to replace those who retire, transfer to other jobs, or leave the workforce for various reasons.

Advancement Prospects

Environmental Technicians may advance in various ways, depending on their interests and ambitions. Many technicians measure their success through job satisfaction, by assuming greater responsibilities, and by earning higher wages. Technicians may also specialize by working in a particular area, such as air-pollution control, water resources management, solid-waste management, industrial hygiene, or land management. Senior technicians can pursue lead and supervisory positions. To obtain managerial positions, technicians may need to complete a bachelor's or advance degree.

With additional training, laboratory technicians may advance to research assistant and research associate positions. (A bachelor's degree may be required as well.) Those working in private industry may pursue opportunities in other areas such as sales, technical service, technical writing, or marketing.

Some technicians choose to continue their education to become research scientists, engineers, or educators, or to work in other professions that interest them.

Education and Training

Educational requirements for entry-level positions vary with the different employers, as well as with the different occupations. Employers may hire applicants with a high school diploma or general equivalency diploma if they have one or more years of vocational training or on-the-job training related to the positions for which they apply. In general, most employers require that applicants minimally possess either an associate or bachelor's degree in environmental science, biology, chemistry, geology, or another related field.

Novice technicians are given on-the-job training in which they work under the guidance and supervision of experienced Environmental Technicians. Some employers also provide their workers with formal classroom instruction.

Throughout their careers, Environmental Technicians enroll in workshops, seminars, and courses to update their skills and knowledge.

Special Requirements

Environmental Technicians may be required to be licensed or certified by the state in which they work, if they are involved in overseeing wastewater treatment facilities, working around hazardous materials, or operating certain types of equipment. Employers may hire candidates on the condition that they obtain the appropriate license or certification within a certain time period.

Experience, Special Skills, and Personality Traits

Employers generally prefer to hire entry-level candidates who have one or more years of practical experience that is relevant to the position for which they apply. They may have gained their experience through internships, work-study programs, research assistantships, volunteer work, or employment.

Environmental Technicians need strong math, computer, writing, and communication skills for their job. In addition, they must have adequate problem-solving, decision-making, self-management skills, teamwork, and interpersonal skills. Some personality traits that successful Environmental Technicians share include being reliable, self-motivated, detail-oriented, patient, honest, persistent, and flexible.

Unions and Associations

Some Environmental Technicians are members of a labor union that represents them in contract negotiations for better wages and working conditions. The union also handles any grievances that union members have against their employers.

Environmental Technicians can join professional associations at the local, state, or national level that serve their particular interests. By joining a society they may take advantage of networking opportunities, continuing education programs, professional certification, and other professional services and resources.

Tips for Entry

1. Read each job announcement carefully to make sure you understand the responsibilities and duties of a position, and whether it is a job that interests you and for which you are qualified.

2. Some Environmental Technicians obtain professional certifications to enhance their employability.

3. Take advantage of college job placement offices and career centers, as well as state unemployment offices for information about current job listings.

4. Sometimes an employer will allow applicants to substitute relevant work experience for one or more years of the educational requirement.

5. Use the Internet to learn more about the field of environmental science. You might start by visiting ECO World at http://www.ecoworld.com. For more links, see Appendix IV.

FORESTER

CAREER PROFILE

Duties: Primary responsibilities vary according to position: manage forest lands, conduct research, provide consulting services, teach, or provide educational outreach; perform duties as required of position

Alternate Title(s): Forest Scientist; Procurement Forester, Urban Forester, Extension Forester, or other title that reflects a specific position

Salary Range: $33,000 to $75,000

Employment Prospects: Fair

Advancement Prospects: Good

Prerequisites:

Education or Training—A bachelor's or advanced degree in forestry, biology, or a related field

Experience—Forest management experience required

Special Skills and Personality Traits—Communication, interpersonal, teamwork, conflict management, writing, computer, presentation, and self-management skills; diplomatic, honest, flexible, ethical, innovative, energetic, and self-motivated

Special Requirements—Professional licensure or registration may be required

CAREER LADDER

Senior Forester or Supervisory Forester

Professional Forester

Forester Trainee

Position Description

Foresters are involved in the science, art, and practice of conserving and managing forest lands and all the natural resources contained in those wooded areas. They oversee public forest lands as well as forested properties owned by companies, organizations, and individuals. Forest lands are used for various purposes, such as timber production, watershed protection, shelter for endangered plant and animal species, recreational activities, and cattle grazelands.

Foresters perform a variety of roles. They are managers, advisers, consultants, researchers, and educators. Regardless of their role, Foresters apply scientific, economic, and social principles and techniques to the care and control of forest lands.

A large number of Foresters, also known as professional foresters, are involved in the management of public and private forest lands. They develop management plans, or long-term strategies, for achieving the land-use objectives of public agencies or private owners. Some Foresters focus on the management of specific natural resources, such as wildlife management or watershed management.

Professional Foresters perform a variety of duties that are specific to their positions. Some duties might include conducting forest inventory, appraising timber, designing reforestation (planting and growing of trees) operations, developing harvest plans, supervising logging operations, surveying wildlife populations, designing forest roads, and protecting forests from fire, disease, and insect infestations.

Public forest lands may be under municipal, state, or federal jurisdiction. (Foresters who manage forest ecosystems within metropolitan environments are often known as urban foresters.) Along with forest management, these Foresters perform such duties as planning and overseeing special forest programs, developing forest policies and regulations, enforcing natural resources ordinances, designing recreational areas, and providing technical support to the general public.

Some Foresters in state government are service foresters. Their role is to provide forestry assistance to private landowners within the counties that they are assigned to cover. They give out technical information about silviculture (the development and care of trees), cutting practices, state forestry laws and regulations, and other topics. These foresters may conduct general assessments of private properties to give owners an idea of the potential uses for their land. In addition, they inform landowners about forestry programs and forest management practices that may fit their particular needs, as well as recommend consultants who can help landowners develop management plans.

Industrial foresters are responsible for managing timberlands owned by sawmills, pulp mills, and other private companies in the forest industry. In addition, they make sure that all state and federal government laws, regulations, and specifications are being followed.

Other industrial foresters, called procurement foresters, are responsible for purchasing timber from private landowners and overseeing the process of removing timber from their lands. Procurement foresters perform such duties as taking inventory of the timber on the property, appraising the value of the timber, negotiating purchasing contracts with landowners, and working with subcontractors to remove timber.

Many Foresters are private consultants who offer any number of services to private landowners. For example, they may develop forest management plans, administer timber sales for landowners, supervise the harvesting of timber, oversee reforestation, conduct forest inventory, and provide assessments of damaged property.

Research foresters, or forest scientists, conduct research in government and academic settings. Some of them perform basic studies to advance knowledge and understanding about forests, forest ecosystems, and forest management. Other researchers conduct applied research to find solutions to particular problems, such as prevention of forest fires or the maintenance of urban forests. Researchers also develop new forest management practices and technologies. They work in laboratories as well as in the field, including in experimental forests.

Many forest scientists are adjunct instructors or full-time professors in forestry programs at colleges and universities. Full-time professors juggle research and teaching responsibilities with administrative and community service duties. They are also expected to produce scholarly works about their research projects.

Some Foresters, known as extension foresters, work for state cooperative extension programs at land-grant universities. These foresters provide technical advice and educational outreach programs to local forest landowners. They provide landowners, the forestry community, and the general public with new technical information from university forestry departments as well as from research and experiment stations run by the USDA Forest Service. (USDA is the U.S. Department of Agriculture.)

Depending on their projects, Foresters work alone or as part of teams, which may include other Foresters, forestry technicians, natural resources professionals (such as ecologists, and soil scientists), landscape architects, engineers, and others. Their work requires them to meet regularly with landowners, loggers, government officials, conservation groups, and the general public.

Foresters take advantage of developing technologies to assist them with their jobs. They use computers extensively, both in the field and in the office. Special software, such as geographic information systems (GIS) software, helps them gather, analyze, store, and retrieve information they need for their work. They also use photogrammetry and remote sensing for mapping large forest areas and for detecting widespread trends regarding forest and land use.

Most Foresters spend time working outdoors in all seasons and weather conditions. Their work can be physically demanding and dangerous; for example, many Foresters assist with fighting fires. In addition, Foresters sometimes work in isolated areas, which may require walking long distances through wetlands and wildernesses.

Foresters sometimes work during evenings and on weekends to complete tasks, attend meetings and conferences, and participate in other work-related activities and programs.

Salaries

Salaries for Foresters vary, depending on such factors as their education, experience, employer, and geographic location. The U.S. Bureau of Labor Statistics reports in its May 2006 *Occupational Employment Statistics* survey that the estimated annual salary for most Foresters ranged from $33,490 to $74,570.

Employment Prospects

The federal government is the largest employer of Foresters. Many of them are employed by the USDA Forest Service, the Bureau of Land Management, the National Park Service, and the military. Some other employers of Foresters include municipal and state government agencies, forest products manufacturing companies, forestry consulting firms, scientific research and development services, academic institutions, and conservation organizations. Many Foresters are self-employed as independent consultants.

Foresters are concentrated in the western and southeastern regions of the U.S. where most forests are found, but opportunities are available throughout the country. Competition for both entry-level and experienced positions is high. Most opportunities are created to replace Foresters who retire or transfer to other positions. Some experts predict an increased demand for professional Foresters in the coming years, as a large number of Foresters start reaching retirement age.

Depending on their backgrounds, training, and interests, Foresters can seek employment as park rangers, environmental educators, wildlife managers, landscape gardeners, environmental analysts, hydrologists, timber sales administrators, science writers, and lobbyists.

Advancement Prospects

Foresters with administrative and management ambitions can pursue supervisory, managerial, and executive-level positions. The highest ambition for some Foresters is to become a self-employed consultant or business owner. Many Foresters realize advancement through job satisfaction, higher pay, assignments of choice, and professional recognition.

Education and Training

A bachelor's degree in forestry, natural resource management, biology, or another related field is the minimum requirement for a candidate to become a professional Forester. A master's or doctoral degree is usually required for one to become a forest scientist. To teach in colleges and universities and to conduct independent research, a candidate should have a doctorate degree.

Many employers prefer to hire candidates who hold a forestry degree from a forestry school, accredited by the Society of American Foresters, which is the governing authority for curricula standards in forestry.

Special Requirements

Some states require that Foresters be licensed or registered to practice their profession. Licensure or registration requirements vary from state to state. For specific information, contact the professional licensure board in the state where you would like to practice.

Experience, Skills, and Personality Traits

Job requirements differ for the various types of positions that are available. In general, employers look for candidates who have previous forest management experience related to the position for which they are applying. Recent graduates may have gained experience through summer employment, volunteer work, internships, research assistantships, and so on. Candidates should have a strong understanding of forestry-related policy issues, laws, and regulations.

Because Foresters must be able to work well with various people, they need effective communication, interpersonal, and teamwork skills. Adequate conflict management skills are also helpful. In addition, Foresters need strong writing, computer, and presentation skills, as well as strong self-management skills.

Some personality traits that successful Foresters share are being diplomatic, honest, flexible, ethical, innovative, energetic, and self-motivated.

Unions and Associations

Foresters might join professional associations to take advantage of networking opportunities, professional certification, education programs, and other professional services and resources. Some national societies are the Society of American Foresters, the Association of Consulting Foresters of America, and the Forest Stewards Guild. See Appendix III for contact information.

Tips for Entry

1. While you are still in high school and college, gain experience working in forestry or conservation during summer breaks. Apply for jobs with parks, government agencies, private companies, or conservation groups. Contact employers in early spring about summer employment opportunities.

2. Many government agencies, such as the USDA Forest Service, offer student employment programs to college students. To find out if a local, state, or federal agency has such programs, contact it directly or visit its Web site on the Internet.

3. To improve your opportunities, be willing to relocate to other states or regions.

4. Private-sector employers generally look for candidates who are knowledgeable about economics and business.

5. Learn more about Foresters on the Internet. Two Web sites you might visit are USDA Forest Service, http://www.fs.fed.us; and Society of American Foresters, http://www.safnet.org. For more links, see Appendix IV.

RANGE SCIENTIST

CAREER PROFILE

Duties: Study, manage, conserve, and protect range-lands; perform duties as required of position

Alternate Title(s): Range Manager, Range Conservationist, Range Management Specialist, Range Ecologist, Restoration Ecologist

Salary Range: $30,000 to $80,000

Employment Prospects: Fair

Advancement Prospects: Good

Prerequisites:

Education or Training—A bachelor's or advanced degree in range science, biology, or a related field

Experience—Previous work experience required

Special Skills and Personality Traits—Interpersonal, teamwork, communication, writing, and self-management skills; creative, inquisitive, observant, adaptable, detail-oriented, and analytical

CAREER LADDER

Senior Range Scientist or Program Manager

Range Scientist

Range Scientist (Entry-level)

Position Description

Range Scientists are involved in the study, management, conservation, and protection of rangelands and the natural resources found on them. Rangelands are ecological systems dominated by grasses, shrubs, and other natural vegetation. In the United States, millions of acres of rangelands cover the country as grasslands (such as prairies), savannas, shrub lands, tundra, alpine meadows, wetlands, and deserts. These rangelands are owned by the public as well as by private individuals and companies. (Public rangelands may be under the jurisdiction of municipal, state, or federal government agencies.)

Rangelands are used for a variety of purposes. They produce forage for grazing by cattle and other livestock animals and provide browsing for wildlife. Rangelands also supply humans with water, minerals, energy resources, and other precious natural resources. In addition, rangelands are natural systems that produce oxygen for all living things as well as reduce carbon dioxide in the air. Rangelands are home to diverse wildlife habitats, including those of threatened and endangered species. Further, rangelands provide open space and places for hiking, camping, fishing, hunting, and other recreational activities.

A large number of Range Scientists, usually known as range managers, are involved in the practice of range management. They develop and administer management plans that outline how rangelands are to be used, improved, and maintained. These plans meet the specific goals of public agencies or private owners. Range managers try to get the maximum use out of rangelands without harming them. For example, a management plan might define grazing seasons, the number of animals allowed to forage in certain range areas, types of vegetation to plant for foraging, methods for controlling toxic plants, practices for protecting land from fires and pest damages, and strategies to restore damaged lands.

Range managers are also responsible for overseeing and monitoring the progress of all conservation, restoration, and construction projects on the lands they manage. They make sure that management practices comply with all appropriate laws and regulations. In addition, they conduct investigations to define and solve problems as they arise. Many range managers help with fighting fires on range lands and provide emergency help after floods, mudslides, and tropical storms.

Responsibilities vary with the different range managers. Some work for government agencies. Their duties include:

- administering grazing and cropland leases for use of public lands

- monitoring the activities of landowners to ensure they are complying with appropriate laws and regulations
- providing technical assistance to landowners
- coordinating outreach educational programs that offer the latest information about range management practices and technologies
- reviewing proposed legislation
- explaining policies, rules, and regulations to the public, legislators, and special-interest groups
- conducting hearings or meetings regarding disputes affecting public lands

Many Range Scientists are involved in conducting research in academic and government settings. Some of them conduct basic research to gain additional knowledge and understanding of the structure and processes of rangeland ecosystems as well as the different natural resources found on rangelands. Other Range Scientists conduct applied studies to develop new management practices and technologies for reducing soil erosion, improving water quality, enhancing wildlife habitats, restoring damaged ecosystems, and so forth.

As researchers, Range Scientists' duties include planning research projects, designing and conducting experiments, gathering data, reviewing research literature, analyzing and interpreting data, writing reports, meeting with colleagues, and performing administrative duties. They also share the results of their research through articles published in professional journals and presentations given at professional conferences. Some researchers are responsible for obtaining grants to fund their new or ongoing projects.

Many academic researchers are full-time professors. In addition to their research duties, they are responsible for teaching undergraduate or graduate courses, advising students, and supervising student research projects. They are also expected to produce scholarly works on a regular basis as well as perform administrative duties and community service.

Range Scientists work from time to time with other scientists (such as foresters, hydrologists, and soil scientists), administrators, and technicians. Many Range Scientists deal with government officials, special-interest groups, the general public, and others on a regular basis.

Range Scientists work in offices and laboratories as well as in the field. Fieldwork is done in all types of weather, and sometimes Range Scientists are required to work in isolated areas. These scientists typically spend more hours working outdoors during the early years of their careers.

Salaries

Salaries for Range Scientists vary, depending on such factors as their education, experience, employer, and geographic location. According to the May 2006 *Occupational Employment Statistics* survey by the U.S. Bureau of Labor Statistics, the estimated annual salary for most conservation scientists, including Range Scientists, ranged between $29,860 and $80,260.

Employment Prospects

Range Scientists are employed by government agencies at the federal, state, and local levels. Most federal Range Scientists are employed in the various agencies of the U.S. Department of Agriculture and the U.S. Department of the Interior. Range Scientists also find employment with ranches, preserves, environmental consulting firms, forestry-related companies, and academic institutions. Some Range Scientists are self-employed as consultants.

Job opportunities generally become available as Range Scientists retire or leave their positions for other reasons. Employers create additional positions to meet growing needs. New opportunities in the public sector depend on available funding.

With their backgrounds, Range Scientists can also qualify for other occupations, such as ranch manager, park ranger, natural resources specialist, watershed manager, forester, agronomist, environmental educator, science writer, lobbyist, and conservation activist.

Advancement Prospects

Range Scientists can advance to administrative and management positions, such as program manager and director. In general, Range Scientists measure their success in individual terms. For example, they may realize advancement through pay increases, by receiving choice assignments, or by earning professional recognition from their peers.

Education and Training

A bachelor's degree in range science, range management, biology, ecology, or another related discipline is the minimum requirement needed to become a Range Scientist. A master's or doctoral degree is usually required for research positions. To teach in universities and colleges, conduct independent research, or hold top management positions, a doctoral degree is required.

Range Scientists continue developing their own professional growth through independent study, enrollment in education and training programs, and networking with colleagues.

Experience, Skills, and Personality Traits

Employers typically choose candidates who have work experience related to the position for which they are applying. Entry-level candidates may have obtained experience through employment, internships, research projects, or postdoctoral training. Candidates are expected to be knowledgeable about rangeland ecosystems.

In general, Range Scientists need strong interpersonal, teamwork, communication, and writing skills. They should also have excellent self-management skills, including the ability to organize and prioritize tasks, handle stressful situations, and work independently. Being creative, inquisitive, observant, adaptable, detail-oriented, and analytical are a few personality traits that successful Range Scientists share.

Unions and Associations

Most Range Scientists join local, state, or national societies to take advantage of professional services and resources such as education programs, professional certification, and networking opportunities. One national association that serves rangeland professionals is the Society for Range Management. Other national societies that many Range Scientists join are the American Forage and Grassland Council, the American Society of Agronomy, and the Ecological Society of America. See Appendix III for contact information.

Tips for Entry

1. As a college student, gain experience through internship, work-study, or summer employment programs that offer placements with private or public sector employers. Talk with your college adviser or a college career counselor for assistance in finding such programs.

2. Check out the Web sites of state and federal agencies where you might be interested in working. Along with learning about an agency's activities, you may find job listings as well as information about recruitment and application processes.

3. Use the Internet to learn more about the range management field. Two Web sites you might visit for more information are Rangelands West, http://ag.arizona.edu/agnic; and USDA Forest Service Rangelands, http://www.fs.fed.us/rangelands. For more links, see Appendix IV.

NATURAL RESOURCES TECHNICIAN

Duties: Provide technical support to scientists, specialists, and managers in the management, conservation, and protection of natural resources; perform duties as required

Alternate Title(s): Biological Technician, Environmental Technician; Conservation Technician, Forestry Technician, Wildlife Technician, or another title that reflects a particular occupation

Salary Range: $22,000 to $49,000

Employment Prospects: Fair

Advancement Prospects: Good

Prerequisites:

Education or Training—Educational requirements vary with the different employers

CAREER LADDER

Senior Natural Resources Technician

Natural Resources Technician

Natural Resources Technician (Entry-level)

Experience—Work experience preferred

Special Skills and Personality Traits—Communication, interpersonal, teamwork, writing computer, self-management skills; detail-oriented, honest, ethical, cooperative, dedicated, and self-motivated

Position Description

Natural Resources Technicians provide technical support and assistance to scientists, managers, and specialists who are responsible for the management, conservation, and preservation of natural resources on public and private lands. Natural resources include air, soil, minerals, water supplies, ground water, plants, forests, fish, and wildlife, among others.

Natural Resources Technicians are involved in a wide range of supportive activities concerning water supplies, forests, rangelands, parks, recreation areas, wildlife refuges, fisheries, and other natural resources. They help professionals and managers implement projects and programs; respond to water quality, erosion control, and other issues; and carry out management plans for wildlife and natural areas. These technicians may be assigned such responsibilities as:

- restoring and caring of forests, prairies, wetlands, or other natural areas
- performing forestry work—for example, collecting seeds, or thinning or pruning
- monitoring streams, rivers, and lakes for water quality
- providing the general public with information about conservation projects or programs
- investigating land management problems
- conducting wildlife census
- observing fish in hatcheries for signs of disease
- capturing, transporting, and releasing fish or wildlife

- designing equipment for fisheries and wildlife programs (for example, fish traps or bird nesting structures)
- leading tours of natural areas
- enforcing park policies, regulations, and laws
- fighting forest fires
- building roads, facilities, and recreational areas

Natural Resources Technicians also assist biologists and other scientists to conduct research projects. These technicians may be involved in basic research, in which scientists are interested in extending knowledge and understanding about natural resources. These technicians are also part of applied research teams that utilize the findings of basic research to solve problems or develop new or improved practices and technologies for managing, preserving, and restoring natural resources.

Many Natural Resources Technicians hold job titles—such as conservation technician, forestry technician, park technician (or ranger aide), wildlife technician, and watershed technician—that specifically refer to the area in which they work.

Natural Resources Technicians apply science and mathematics principles and techniques to complete their tasks, under the general direction of scientists, specialists, and managers. These technicians are knowledgeable about the natural resources (such as fish, wildlife, soil, water resources) with which they work, including their identification, care, and handling. They are also familiar with the laws, rules, and regulations pertaining to the area of resource conservation and protection in which they work. Many of them use computers and such technologies as geographic information systems (GIS) and global positioning system (GPS) tools. In addition, they utilize various scientific instruments and equipment, power tools, and equipment (such as chain saws and mowers) used for maintaining buildings and landscapes. Some technicians drive trucks, all-terrain vehicles, boats, tractors, and road-building equipment such as backhoes and bulldozers.

Natural Resources Technicians perform a wide range of tasks each day under general supervision. Some are specific to their position; for example, forestry technicians may be assigned such duties as estimating the amount of trees in a forest, inspecting trees for disease or infestation, building roads through forest lands, and explaining land management activities to the public. Natural Resources Technicians also perform many general tasks, such as:

- gathering and preparing specimens for experiments, tests, or analyses
- collecting field and laboratory data
- conducting tests on samples for specific purposes (for example, testing water for quality)
- compiling technical data for studies, reports, or surveys
- analyzing and interpreting data, and providing scientists with written summaries of findings
- preparing reports, correspondence, and paperwork
- maintaining records, files, and databases for projects
- repairing and maintaining instruments and equipment
- maintaining buildings, facilities, grounds, and/or roads

Entry-level technicians typically perform simple routine tasks under the guidance of scientists and experienced technicians. As Natural Resources Technicians gain experience, they are assigned more complicated duties in which they exercise independent judgment. Their work is checked by superiors for progress and conformance with established requirements and policies. Senior technicians may be responsible for completing administrative duties, and may be assigned to lead or supervisory positions in which they oversee the work of junior technicians, seasonal staff, or volunteers.

Natural Resources Technicians generally work outdoors in all types of weather conditions. Some of them travel to remote locations where they may live and work for several days or weeks. Some technicians, such as forestry technicians, live where they work.

Some Natural Resources Technicians perform duties that involve contact with the general public. For example, park technicians may have the task of collecting camping or day-use fees from park patrons, or forestry technicians may provide assistance to private landowners.

The work of these technicians can be physically demanding. They frequently walk, stand, bend, and stoop as they work; and they often lift or carry objects and equipment that may weigh up to 50 pounds or more. Their tasks may require them to work with toxic chemicals, heavy equipment, or machinery with exposed moving parts. Hence, they follow strict safety procedures and wear protective clothing or equipment.

Natural Resources Technicians are hired to part-time, full-time, temporary, or seasonal positions. They put in overtime hours as needed to complete tasks and handle emergency situations. Some technicians work irregular hours, and their hours can vary according to the weather and the seasons.

Salaries

Salaries for Natural Resources Technicians vary, depending on such factors as their education, experience, position, employer, and geographic location. Specific salary information for this occupation is unavailable. However, the estimated annual salary for most forest and conservation technicians ranged from $22,450 to $49,380, according to the May 2006 *Occupational Employment Statistics* survey by the U.S. Bureau of Labor Statistics.

Employment Prospects

Many Natural Resources Technicians are employed by local, state, and federal government agencies, including public utility districts, park systems, natural resources departments, forestry services, and others. These technicians are also hired by nonprofit and nongovernmental organizations as well as by academic institutions and private establishments such as ranches, logging companies, forest products manufacturers, and environmental consulting firms.

Job competition is strong because of the popularity of natural resources careers. Individuals with the most education and practical experience have a better advantage of obtaining jobs that they desire. In general, job opportunities become available as Natural Resources Technicians transfer to other jobs, advance to higher positions, or leave the workforce for various reasons.

Advancement Prospects

Many Natural Resources Technicians measure their success through job satisfaction, by assuming greater responsibilities, and by earning higher wages. Individuals with managerial ambitions can pursue lead and supervisor positions, but those are limited. With additional training, laboratory technicians may advance to research assistant and research associate positions. Those working in private industry may pursue opportunities in other areas such as sales, technical service, or marketing.

Some technicians choose to continue their education to become scientists, engineers, educators, or natural resources managers.

Education and Training

Educational requirements vary with the different employers, as well as with the different positions. For some entry-level positions, applicants need at least an associate degree in natural resources, forestry technology, or another related discipline. For other entry-level positions, the minimum requirement is a bachelor's degree in natural resource management, forestry, botany, ecology, or another related field. Employers may hire applicants who possess a high school diploma or general equivalency diploma, if they have completed one or more years of specialized training through vocational programs or employment. For example, applicants may have worked as forestry, ranger, or natural resources aides.

Entry-level Natural Resources Technicians receive on-the-job training. They work under the guidance and supervision of scientists, natural resources managers, or senior technicians.

Experience, Special Skills, and Personality Traits

Work requirements vary with the different employers. In general, employers prefer to hire entry-level candidates who have one or more years of practical experience relevant to the position for which they apply. Recent college graduates may have gained experience through work-study programs, internships, research projects, or employment. Many employers seek applicants who have experience or skills operating various hand and power tools and such equipment as mowers, chain saws, trucks, and tractors.

Natural Resources Technicians must be able to work well with others; thus, they need excellent communication, interpersonal, and teamwork skills. They also need strong writing and computer skills as well as effective self-management skills, such as the ability to work independently, prioritize multiple tasks, follow and understand instructions, and handle stressful situations. Some personality traits that successful technicians share include being detail-oriented, honest, ethical, cooperative, dedicated, and self-motivated.

Unions and Associations

Some Natural Resources Technicians belong to a labor union that represents them in contract negotiations for better wages and working conditions. The union also handles any grievances that union members have against their employers.

These technicians can join professional associations to take advantage of networking opportunities, continuing education programs, job listings, and other professional services and resources. The Society of American Foresters and the Society for Range Management are examples of two societies that Natural Resources Technicians are eligible to join.

Tips for Entry

1. Many Natural Resources Technicians started their career by working in one or more seasonal positions. They worked for several months out of the year, usually anywhere between February and November.
2. You can gain valuable experience by doing volunteer work with a government agency, such as the U.S. National Park Service, or by joining a nonprofit conservation group and participating in its activities.
3. Be sure to submit your job applications by the deadlines. Although employers may continue accepting late applications, they usually give first priority for consideration to those applicants who sent in their applications on time.
4. Use the Internet to learn more about the field of natural resources. To get a list of relevant Web sites to view, enter any of these key words into a search engine: *natural resources, natural resources management,* or *natural resources technicians.* For some links, see Appendix IV.

OPPORTUNITIES IN GOVERNMENT

FEDERAL SCIENTIST

Duties: Study a particular area of interest, such as fisheries or air quality; conduct research and development or perform other work activities; perform duties as required of position

Alternate Title(s): Research Scientist, Staff Scientist; a title that reflects specific specialty such as Hydrologist, Microbiologist, Chemist, or Astronomer

Salary Range: $26,000 to $75,000 for entry-level positions

Employment Prospects: Good

Advancement Prospects: Good

Prerequisites:

Education or Training—Undergraduate or advanced degree

Experience—Work experience not generally required for entry-level positions

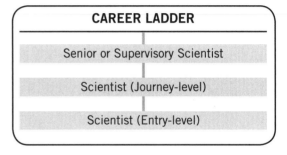

Special Skills and Personality Traits—Communication, writing, problem-solving, self-management, interpersonal, and teamwork skills; creative, curious, persistent, flexible, cooperative, and self-motivated

Special Requirements—U.S. citizenship; a security clearance may be required

Position Description

About 200,000 life, physical, mathematical, computer, and social scientists are employed by the executive branch of the U.S. government. Along with other employees, Federal Scientists contribute to the implementation and enforcement of federal laws, which is the constitutional duty of the executive office headed by the President of the United States. These scientists work in the various executive departments, including the Department of Agriculture, the Department of Energy, the Department of Transportation, the Department of Defense, the Department of Health and Human Services, and the Department of Homeland Security, among others. Many of them also work for such independent executive agencies as the Environmental Protection Agency and the National Aeronautics and Space Administration.

Federal Scientists are employed to fulfill different roles in the various executive departments and agencies. Probably the most familiar role is that of research scientists who contribute to the advancement of scientific principles and technologies. Through their research, they help to serve and protect the American public and their interests domestically and abroad, as well as to conserve and safeguard America's natural resources and its environment. Federal research scientists engage in research and development that fulfills the particular

mission, goals, and objectives of their agencies. They conduct research in public health, food safety, animal health, biotechnology, energy efficiency, pollution control, conservation, climate change, telecommunications, national defense, and space exploration, among many other areas.

Research scientists are involved in different types of studies. They conduct basic research to further scientific knowledge and understanding of phenomena and of observable facts. Through basic research, they seek to discover new ideas, concepts, and approaches without any particular purpose in mind. For example, biomedical researchers might investigate how molecular and cellular components of tissues behave; geologists might examine the processes that occur when volcanoes erupt; or astrophysicists might study the composition of matter in space.

The results of basic research are used in applied research projects. In such projects, research scientists conduct research that is focused on finding solutions to specific problems. For example, Federal Scientists in different agencies undertake research projects that address diverse issues of public concern, such as making public transportation systems more safe and efficient, enhancing the income of small farmers; creating affordable and sustainable means of space exploration; improving the quality of water supplies; stopping the spread of

West Nile virus or other communicable diseases; and protecting archival records from deterioration.

Federal research scientists also engage in the development of new or improved technologies, processes, methodologies, systems, or materials for practical uses. For example, chemists might design improved techniques for examining physical evidence; physicists might invent X-ray machines to study minuscule biological structures; computer scientists might develop new software algorithms for satellite surveillance systems; or medical scientists might create improved diagnostic tests for a rare disease.

Research and development is just one of many primary activities that Federal Scientists may be hired to perform. Many Federal Scientists are applied scientists who use the principles and techniques of their disciplines to perform other professional and scientific work. For example, atmospheric scientists might predict weather; chemists might analyze and interpret physical evidence from crime scenes; conservation scientists might manage rangelands; and wildlife biologists might provide technical assistance to airports regarding wildlife hazards. Some Federal Scientists work as technicians and research assistants who provide technical support to research scientists. In general, nonresearch Federal Scientists may be involved in such work activities as:

- collecting, processing, and analyzing data
- performing tests and analyses on specimens, samples, or products
- monitoring and evaluating operational programs
- managing natural resources
- enforcing regulations
- training scientific and technical personnel
- administering technical programs
- providing technical assistance and consulting to specific groups of people (for example: other government agencies, farmers and ranchers, or the general public)

Federal Scientists engage in various tasks each day, which vary according to their position, experience, and skill levels. They perform duties that are specific to their specialty and position. Most, if not all, Federal Scientists perform general research tasks on their job, such as:

- planning and implementing research projects
- designing and conducting experiments or tests
- reading scientific journals and other research literature
- collecting, analyzing, and interpreting data

- forming conclusions on findings and making recommendations based on findings
- meeting with colleagues to discuss projects
- maintaining work logs and records
- preparing reports, correspondence, and paperwork
- presenting research findings and conclusions at meetings and conferences
- making sure that work complies with standards, policies, laws, and regulations
- using a variety of laboratory instruments and techniques
- staying up to date with current developments and technologies in their disciplines

Federal Scientists primarily work in offices and laboratories. Many scientists perform some of their duties in outdoor locations. For example, agricultural scientists might visit experimental farms to monitor crops, geologists might carry out experiments in wilderness areas, environmental chemists might collect water samples at various streams; and oceanographers might conduct studies in the middle of oceans.

Federal Scientists work a 40-hour week, but put in additional hours as needed to complete their various tasks. Many of them are on a flexible schedule, which allows them to establish the hours they work. Some scientists travel to other locations, including remote ones, to conduct fieldwork, attend meetings, or perform other duties.

Salaries

Annual salaries for Federal Scientists vary, depending on such factors as their education, experience, position, and pay grade. Most Federal Scientists earn a salary based on the pay scale known as the general schedule (GS), which has several levels and steps. The starting salaries for entry-level scientists may begin as low as the GS-5 level and as high as the GS-12 level, depending on their position and qualifications. For example, entry-level research scientists with a Ph.D. can usually earn a salary starting at the GS-11 or GS-12 level. In 2008, the annual basic pay for the GS-5 to GS-12 levels ranged from $26,264 to $75,025. Employees in metropolitan areas, such as New York, Los Angeles, and Washington, D.C., earn additional pay for living in an area where the cost of living is higher.

Employment Prospects

According to the May 2006 *Occupational Employment Statistics* survey by the U.S. Bureau of Labor Statistics, about 132,000 life, physical, and social scientists and 79,270 computer and mathematical scientists were employed by the federal government.

The Department of Defense and the National Institutes of Health are the two largest employers of Federal Scientists. Other executive departments and agencies that employ a significant number of scientists include the Department of Agriculture, the Department of Human and Health Services, the National Aeronautics and Space Administration, the Department of Interior, and the Environmental Protection Agency. Although headquarters for all government agencies are in Washington D.C., Federal Scientists work throughout the United States and its territories. Some scientists are assigned to work in embassies or defense installations in other countries.

In general, opportunities become available when Federal Scientists advance to higher positions, retire, or resign. Agencies will create additional positions, as long as funding is available. Job vacancies throughout the federal workforce are expected to increase in the coming decade due to the large number of employees who will become eligible for retirement.

Advancement Prospects

All federal employees advance within their pay schedule until they reach the full-performance level for their occupation. These are considered noncompetitive promotions. Upon reaching their full-performance level, employees compete for further promotions. Along with pay increases, many Federal Scientists measure success through job satisfaction, by performing assignments of choice, and through professional recognition.

Federal Scientists may advance to supervisory or managerial positions, from project, lead, and supervisory positions to executive-level management positions. They may also choose to move into other areas within their agency, such as policy analysis, grant applications review, or scientist recruitment and training.

Education and Training

Educational requirements for entry-level positions may include a bachelor's or an advanced degree in a specific discipline. To enter at specific level on the GS-schedule, applicants must have the following minimum educational requirements:

- GS-5: a bachelor's degree in an appropriate discipline, with a minimum number of credits in specific subjects; for example, candidates for wildlife biologist positions may qualify at this level by possessing a bachelor's degree in biological science along with completing a specific number of semester hours in wildlife subjects (such as ornithology, animal ecology, or wildlife management), zoology, and botany

- GS-7: a bachelor's degree plus one year of full-time graduate study
- GS-9: a master's degree, or two years of graduate study
- GS-11: a doctoral degree, or three years of graduate study leading to a doctorate

Candidates may also qualify by meeting the required combination of education and experience, which varies with the different positions.

Novice employees typically receive on-the job training, while working under the guidance and direction of experienced scientists, as well as receiving formal instruction.

Throughout their careers, Federal Scientists enroll in workshops, seminars, courses, and training programs to update their skills and keep up with advancements in their fields.

Special Requirements

The federal government usually requires that applicants for full-time positions be U.S. citizens.

Applicants for positions that handle sensitive or classified materials must normally undergo a security clearance. This involves a thorough background check of such areas as an applicant's employment, credit, and criminal history.

Experience, Special Skills, and Personality Traits

For entry-level positions, work experience is generally not required of applicants, as long as they have met the educational requirements for the entry-level positions for which they apply. Having practical experience that is relevant to the positions for which they apply may enhance their chances of obtaining employment. They may have gained experience through internships, work-study programs, fellowships, student research projects, or employment.

Federal Scientists must have effective communication, writing, problem-solving, and self-management skills. They also need excellent interpersonal and teamwork skills, as they must be able to work well with colleagues, managers, technicians, and others on various research projects. Being creative, curious, persistent, flexible, cooperative, and self-motivated are some personality traits that successful Federal Scientists have in common.

Unions and Associations

Many Federal Scientists join professional associations to take advantage of networking opportunities, continuing education, professional certification, and other professional resources and services. A few examples of the various scientific societies that serve the interests of different scientists are the American Society for Microbiology, the Society for Integrative and Comparative Biology, the American Chemical Society, the American Geophysical Union, the American Institute of Physics, the American Mathematical Society, the Institute of Food Technologists, and the Society of American Foresters. For contact information, see Appendix III.

Tips for Entry

1. Most federal agencies participate in the Student Temporary Employment Program, which offers jobs, internships, and work-study positions to high school, undergraduate, and graduate students. Many openings can be found at the Studentjobs.gov Web site at http://www.studentjobs.gov. You can also directly check for openings with individual agencies where you would like to work.

2. Many federal agencies send job announcements to college career centers, and recruit applicants at college careers fairs.

3. Check Web sites of the agencies where you would like to work for job postings as well as information for postdoctoral fellowships. Many agencies allow applications and résumés to be submitted online. In addition, visit the USAJobs.gov Web site, http://www.usajobs.gov, which is an up-to-date database of most positions that are available throughout the federal government.

4. To learn more about working with the federal government, visit the U.S. Office of Personnel Management Web site at http://www.opm.gov. To learn about the types of research that are performed by Federal Scientists, visit Science.gov, http//www.science.gov.

CRIMINALIST

CAREER PROFILE

Duties: Analyze, identify, and interpret evidence collected at crime scenes; prepare reports about findings; provide expert witness testimony; perform duties as required

Alternate Title(s): Forensic Scientist, Crime Laboratory Analyst; a title that reflects a specialty such as Forensic Chemist, DNA Analyst, Firearms and Toolmark Examiner, or Questioned Document Examiner

Salary Range: $28,000 to $73,000 or more

Employment Prospects: Good

Advancement Prospects: Fair

Prerequisites:

    Education or Training—A bachelor's degree in chemistry, biology, forensic science, or a related field; on-the-job training

    Experience—One or more years of crime lab or related experience

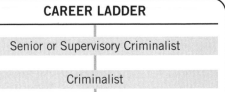

CAREER LADDER

Senior or Supervisory Criminalist

Criminalist

Criminalist Trainee

Special Skills and Personality Traits—Mathematical, computer, problem-solving, writing, communication, presentation, interpersonal, teamwork, and self-management skills; honest, patient, detail-oriented, objective, diligent

Special Requirements—Peace officer certificate may be required

Position Description

Criminalists help law enforcement officers solve crimes. Their job is to analyze, identify, and interpret physical evidence that has been collected at crime scenes. Using scientific methods and principles, Criminalists attempt to prove that crimes have taken place, to reconstruct what occurred at the crime scene, and to identify crime suspects and victims.

Criminalists are also called forensic scientists. They are often confused with criminologists. Both professions are part of the same field—criminology, or the study of the causes of crime. However, Criminalists work in forensic or crime laboratories performing lab analyses on physical evidence. Criminologists, on the other hand, usually work in academic settings, conducting research about crime and criminal behavior.

Many people also get Criminalists mixed up with crime scene investigators (more popularly known as CSIs). Both groups perform work involving physical evidence. CSIs work at crime scenes where they are responsible for collecting and processing all types of physical evidence—including fingerprints, bloodstains, hair, fibers, glass fragments, drugs, computer files, documents, soil, and tire tracks, among others. Although Criminalists may collect evidence, their primary role is to examine evidence in the laboratory, where they

conduct chemical, microscopic, comparative, and other complex laboratory analyses on various items of physical evidence.

Depending on their experience and the needs of their labs, Criminalists may be assigned to conduct analyses on one or more types of evidence. Some of the more common forensic disciplines include:

- serology—the analysis of blood and other bodily fluids
- DNA analysis—the identification and testing of individuals' DNA samples
- forensic chemistry—the identification and analysis of unknown chemical substances, gun powder residue, explosives, and other chemical products
- imprint and impression evidence—the examination of footprints, tire markings, and other two- or three-dimensional impressions
- latent prints—the identification and comparison of hidden impressions from fingers, palms, or feet
- drug chemistry—the analysis of blood and other body fluids and tissues for the presence of controlled substances
- trace evidence—the examination of hairs, fibers, soils, glass fragments, and other small particles of physical evidence

- firearms and toolmarks—the examination of guns and other weapons and tools
- questioned documents—the examination of wills, checks, invoices, currency, correspondence, and other documents to determine if they are counterfeit or forgeries or if any alterations have been made to the documents
- computer forensics—the recovery and analysis of data in computers

Criminalists may also be trained in other forensic areas, such as toxicology, blood splatter analysis, forensic anthropology, video analysis, audio analysis, or crash reconstruction.

Before performing any tests on an item, Criminalists find out what needs to be known about the evidence and get an idea of the significance of the item. They sometimes visit crime scenes to get a better sense of what they are dealing with. Criminalists can then determine what type of data they need to obtain and the best methods to use.

Criminalists next perform their tests. They sort, compare, or identify the evidence, developing useful information for the investigation or trial. They analyze and interpret the test results. They then prepare formal reports that describe in detail their findings and that explain the methods they used to obtain the results. Their reports need to be clear, concise, and easily understood by law enforcement officers, attorneys, judges, and juries.

If needed, Criminalists provide expert witness testimony at depositions and trials. They may appear as witnesses for the prosecution or for the defense. They answer legal issues related to their particular examinations on physical evidence or on crime lab techniques.

Criminalists are expected to perform their duties accurately and correctly. They follow strict procedures at all times to maintain the chain of custody for all physical evidence that they handle. This includes writing about everything that they do to physical evidence so as to ensure that it has not been tampered with or contaminated. If the chain of custody is broken for a piece of physical evidence, it will usually not be admitted as testimony in court trials.

Criminalists are responsible for keeping up with current information and updating their skills as new technologies and methodologies emerge. Many Criminalists are involved in developing new or improved methodologies and techniques for their areas of forensic investigations.

To ensure their safety, Criminalists follow strict lab procedures for operating lab equipment, handling chemicals, and performing tests. They also wear protective clothing to protect themselves from exposure to disease, odors, fumes, and chemicals.

Criminalists may be civilian employees or law enforcement officers. Entry-level Criminalists work under the guidance and supervision of experienced staff for several months to two or three years, depending on the area of forensic investigation. During this developmental phase, Criminalists focus on learning analytical skills as well as laboratory rules, standards, procedures, and practices.

As they gain experience and knowledge, they receive more complex assignments and are able to exercise greater levels of authority. After several years, Criminalists usually reach the journey level and are competent in one or more forensic disciplines. They are assigned sensitive and highly technical casework, and may assist in training laboratory staff.

Criminalists mostly work indoors in clean, well-lit, and ventilated laboratories. They operate a variety of instruments and machines, such as lights, cameras, microscopes, and spectroscopes for recording, measuring, and testing evidence.

They work 40 hours a week, and put in additional hours as needed to complete tasks and meet deadlines. Some Criminalists are on call 24 hours a day. Sworn officers are also on stand-by alert to assist with law enforcement matters at any time of the day.

Salaries

Salaries for Criminalists vary, depending on such factors as their experience, education, employer, and geographic location. According to the May 2006 *Occupational Employment Statistics* survey, by the U.S. Bureau of Labor Statistics (BLS), the estimated annual salary for most forensic science technicians ranged between $27,530 and $73,100.

Employment Prospects

Most Criminalists are employed by crime labs which are part of local, state, or federal law enforcement agencies. Other Criminalists work in private laboratories as well as in academic laboratories that offer services to law enforcement agencies on a contractual basis.

In general, job openings become available as individuals retire, transfer to other jobs, or advance to higher positions. Job growth in this field is predicted to increase by 31 percent through 2016, according to the BLS. Many experts in the field report that there is a continuous backlog of work in most laboratories; consequently, there is a need for experienced Criminalists. Many public laboratories are unable to hire enough Criminalists due to lack of funding, but as finances become available they may create additional positions.

Advancement Prospects

Criminalists can advance in any number of ways, depending on their ambitions and interests. They can become technical specialists in a particular area such as ballistics or blood splatter analysis. They can rise through the administrative and managerial ranks as technical leaders, unit supervisors, managers, and lab directors. Managerial opportunities are usually better in large laboratories that have several levels of management.

Individuals with entrepreneurial ambitions can become independent practitioners or owners of forensic firms that offer consulting or technical services. Criminalists can also pursue opportunities as instructors and researchers in higher education institutions. To advance to higher positions or to obtain teaching jobs, they may be required to possess a master's or doctoral degree.

Law enforcement officers have additional advancement opportunities. They can rise through the ranks as detectives, sergeants, lieutenants, and so on, up to chief of police. They can also seek positions in other special details that interest them, such as their agency's bomb squad, SWAT team, or K9 unit. In addition, they can pursue supervisory and managerial positions.

Education and Training

Employers generally require that applicants for entry-level positions possess a bachelor's degree in chemistry, biochemistry, biology, or another discipline within the physical sciences or natural sciences. A bachelor's degree in forensic science may be acceptable. Employers may hire applicants without a bachelor's degree for such positions as latent fingerprint examiner or fire examiner if they have enough years of qualifying experience.

Entry-level Criminalists typically complete a training period that may last several months to a few years, depending on the type of analysis that they are hired to perform. Some crime labs cross train employees in several forensic disciplines. Novice Criminalists work under the guidance and supervision of experienced Criminalists.

For sworn officer positions, Criminalists must complete three to six months or more of basic training at a law enforcement academy. They study various subjects such as law, investigative procedures, self-defense, use of firearms, and first aid.

Throughout their careers, Criminalists enroll in continuing education programs and training programs to update their skills and keep up with advancements in their fields.

Special Requirements

In agencies in which Criminalists are law enforcement officers, applicants must possess a basic peace officer standards and training certificate. These agencies may hire candidates without a certificate on the condition they complete the necessary law enforcement academy program to obtain the certificate.

Law enforcement officers must successfully complete annual training to maintain their certification.

Experience, Special Skills, and Personality Traits

Most crime labs choose candidates who have previous work experience. Entry-level candidates may have gained experience through internships, employment, research assistantships, or other positions in analytical, research, or crime laboratories. Employers may allow candidates to substitute advanced degrees for at least one year of work experience. Successful candidates are able to demonstrate their knowledge about appropriate lab procedures and handling of lab instruments and equipment, as well as their knowledge about proper procedures for handling and processing physical evidence.

In general, Criminalists need strong mathematical and computer skills. To do their various duties (such as interpreting tests, preparing reports, and testifying as expert witnesses), Criminalists must have excellent skills in problem-solving, writing, communication, and presentation. Having interpersonal and teamwork skills are also essential. Further, Criminalists need strong self-management skills, including the ability to work independently, handle stressful situations, meet deadlines, and organize and prioritize tasks.

Some personality traits that successful Criminalists share are being honest, patient, detail-oriented, objective, and diligent.

Unions and Associations

Many Criminalists are members of professional societies at the local, state, regional, national, and international levels that serve their particular interests. These societies offer various professional services and resources such as continuing education, professional certification, publications, job listings, and networking opportunities. Some professional associations include:

- American Academy of Forensic Sciences
- International Association of Bloodstain Pattern Analysts

- American Society of Questioned Document Examiners
- Association of Firearm and Toolmark Examiners
- Society of Forensic Toxicologists

For contact information, see Appendix III.

Tips for Entry

1. In high school or college, get an idea if becoming a Criminalist is right for you. Read books and articles about the criminalistic field. Contact professionals for more information. Attend court trials to listen to Criminalists give expert witness testimony.

2. While in college, you can gain experience working in crime labs through internship or work-study programs. Contact crime labs directly about available opportunities for students.

3. Some experts in the field suggest that students obtain a bachelor's degree in a physical or natural science in their field of interest, and then get a master's degree in forensic science.

4. Law enforcement officers must usually serve one or more years as patrol officers before they can apply for positions in their agency's crime lab.

5. Learn more about the criminalistics field on the Internet. Two Web sites you might visit are American Academy of Forensic Sciences, http://www.aafs.org; and Zeno's Forensic Site, http://forensic.to/forensic.html. For more links, see Appendix IV.

SCIENCE AND TECHNOLOGY (S&T) POLICY ANALYST

Special Skills and Personality Traits—Research, analytical, quantitative, writing, communication, interpersonal, and teamwork skills; well-organized, creative, objective, and self-motivated

Position Description

Policy makers in government, private companies, academia, and nongovernmental organizations make decisions related to science and technology every day. They vote on legislation, make policies, and address problems that concern natural resources, energy, nuclear waste disposal, biotechnology, pharmaceuticals, agriculture, infrastructure protection, space programs, and science education, among many other areas.

Science and Technology (S&T) Policy Analysts play an important role in helping policy makers create the most effective science and technology policies. They provide policy makers with analyses of the issues and problems they must address as well as offer alternative solutions. For example, analysts employed by Congress might analyze budget and policy issues related to proposed legislation on biotechnology research.

Policy analysts are given assignments which they must complete and deliver in a timely matter. They sometimes receive assignments that require a short turnaround time. Analysts begin by finding out what the policy maker wants to accomplish. For example, a legislator may need to vote on a bill on funding genetic research. Policy analysts must learn the conceptual framework or vision that a policy maker wishes to take. Analysts then define and shape the research to meet the decision maker's objectives. They perform their work objectively at all times. They do not inject their own concepts or beliefs into their assignments.

Analysts next collect data that addresses an assignment. They conduct research alone or with the help of research assistants and associates. They search databases and read appropriate literature. They also conduct interviews with subject matter experts, when necessary. They review, analyze, and interpret data and determine the major issues, costs, benefits, and other interests of their clients.

Policy analysts prepare reports that are accurate and comprehensive, yet short and clear. They present their reports orally or in written form. The memorandums, reports, or verbal briefs are presented in language that elected officials and managers can understand and use when they present the information to others.

Many S&T Policy Analysts are scientists, mathematicians, and engineers from different disciplines. Some have changed careers, while others continue working as research scientists, professors, and administrators and perform policy analysis on a consulting basis.

Salaries

Salaries for S&T Policy Analysts vary, depending on their education, experience, employer, and other factors. Specific salary information for this occupation is unavailable, but they generally earn salaries similar to operations research analysts. The estimated annual salary for most operations research analysts ranged between $38,760 and $108,290, according to the U.S. Bureau of Labor Statistics in its May 2006 *Occupational Employment Statistics* survey.

Employment Prospects

Science and technology policy is a young but growing field. Many S&T Policy Analysts work in the Washington, D.C., area.

In government, S&T Policy Analysts work for executive and legislative branches as well as for government agencies, mostly at the state and federal levels. They are also employed by research and policy institutes, nongovernmental organizations, professional and trade associations, public-interest organizations, academic institutions, and private companies. Policy analysts can find employment in other countries that need assistance with addressing various science and technology policy issues.

According to some experts in the field, job opportunities are favorable for individuals who have a strong science or engineering background. Traditionally, S&T Policy Analysts usually did not have any technical background, but due to the rapid growth in technology, employers seek analysts who can help them make sound decisions in many areas.

Advancement Prospects

S&T Policy Analysts can advance to senior positions such as project leader and program administrator. Those with policy-making ambitions can achieve an executive officer position, such as executive director or vice president. S&T Policy Analysts can also become independent consultants and consulting firm owners. Policy analysts often move back and forth between academia, government, industry, and other types of employers as they pursue their careers.

Education and Training

A master's or doctoral degree in science or engineering is generally required of candidates to gain employment as an S&T Policy Analyst. Many employers also hire candidates who hold a master's degree in science and technology policy, public policy, public administration, economics, or another related field. Those

interested in a career in higher education should possess a doctoral degree.

Experience, Skills, and Personality Traits

In general, candidates should have experience in or substantive knowledge about a particular area such as space exploration, natural resources, or telecommunications. They should also have a background in policy science and be familiar with issues affecting policies in their fields of interest. Having experience working with legislators and executive officers is preferred by many employers.

S&T Policy Analysts must have excellent research, writing, analytical, and quantitative skills. Additionally, they need superior communication skills and must be able to present complex technical concepts to nontechnical people. Strong interpersonal and teamwork skills are also necessary. Some personality traits that successful analysts share are being well organized, creative, objective, and self-motivated.

Unions and Associations

Many S&T Policy Analysts belong to scientific societies—such as the American Association for the Advancement of Science—that serve their field of interest. They are also eligible to join the Association for Public Policy Analyses and Management, which serves the general interests of policy professionals and institutions. By joining professional societies, S&T Policy Analysts can take advantage of networking opportunities and other professional resources and services. (For contact information for the above groups, see Appendix III.)

Tips for Entry

1. To learn more about public policy, talk with professionals in the field. You might also enroll in a public policy course to get an idea if this area interests you.

2. Gain first-hand experience by completing an internship in science and technology policy. Opportunities are available with professional societies, public interest organizations, Congress, state legislatures, and research institutes.

3. Use the Internet to learn more about science and technology policy. You might start by visiting the U.S. Office of Science and Technology at http://www.ostp.gov. For more links, see Appendix IV.

OPPORTUNITIES IN INDUSTRY

RESEARCH SCIENTIST

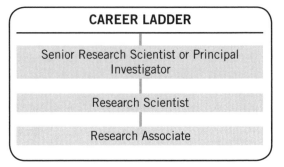

Special Skills and Personality Traits—Leadership, teamwork, interpersonal, writing, communication, presentation, and self-management skills; enthusiastic, creative, dedicated, analytical, and flexible

Position Description

Many scientists of various disciplines are involved in research and development in private industry. They work for small start-up companies as well as established corporations in the pharmaceutical, biotechnology, agriculture, food processing, chemical, computer hardware, electronics, aerospace, and telecommunications industries, among many others. These Research Scientists support the mission of their employers to create products for commercial purposes.

Industrial Research Scientists are mostly involved in product development. They apply the principles and techniques of their scientific discipline (such as chemistry, physics, materials science, or molecular biology) to the generation of new or improved products. Research Scientists are also involved in applied research, which is the utilization of their scientific knowledge to solve specific problems such as ways to improve manufacturing processes. On occasion, these scientists conduct basic research to gain new knowledge and understanding that may help them with their applied research and product development.

Research Scientists from different disciplines work together on research projects, along with engineers, technicians, project managers, and others. Research Scientists perform duties that are specific to their specialty in addition to general tasks such as:

- planning research projects
- organizing their work schedules

- designing and conducting experiments
- analyzing and interpreting data
- reading scientific journals and other research literature
- meeting with colleagues to discuss projects
- preparing written reports
- operating scientific instrumentation
- supervising research assistants and technicians, who provide administrative and research support
- making sure that work is in compliance with company policies, industry protocols, laws, and regulations
- keeping detailed notes and records about the work they perform
- keeping up with developments and technologies in their fields

Research Scientists work in laboratories and offices. Researchers may perform some of their assignments in the field. These researchers work a 40-hour schedule, but put in additional hours as needed to complete their tasks.

Salaries

Salaries for Research Scientists vary, depending on their education, experience, discipline, industry, and geographic location. The U.S. Bureau of labor Statistics (BLS) reports—in its May 2006 *Occupational Employment Statistics* survey—the following estimated salaries for most of these scientists:

- food scientists—$29,620 to $97,350
- chemists—$35,480 to $106,310

- computer scientists—$53,590 to $144,880
- environmental scientists—$34,590 to $94,670
- geologists—$37,530 to $93,930
- mathematicians—$43,500 to $132,190
- materials scientists—$41,810 to $118,670
- microbiologists—$35,460 to $108,270
- physicists—$52,070 to $143,570

Employment Prospects

In general, job prospects for qualified Research Scientists are favorable. Opportunities are especially strong in such areas as biotechnology, nanotechnology, pharmaceuticals, and defense and security, according to the BLS. The job market for Research Scientists usually falls and rises with the economy. During healthy periods, more jobs are generally available. Companies may reduce or shut down research operations when they are experiencing funding problems.

Most job openings are created to replace individuals who retire, transfer to other positions, or resign. Employers will create additional positions to fit growing needs for their companies.

Advancement Prospects

Scientists can advance to supervisory, managerial, and executive positions. For example, they can become principal investigators, program managers, laboratory directors, department managers, and executive directors. Research Scientists usually require doctorates to obtain top management positions.

Education and Training

Most industrial Research Scientists possess a doctorate in their discipline such as microbiology, molecular biology, biochemistry, toxicology, physics, or geology. Some employers hire Research Scientists with a master's degree, as long as they have qualifying experience.

Experience, Skills, and Personality Traits

Employers normally hire candidates who have work and research experience related to the positions for which they are applying. Experience may have been gained through student research projects, internships, fellowships, and employment. Ph.D. candidates may be required to have several years of postdoctoral experience.

Industrial Research Scientists are expected to have excellent leadership, teamwork, and interpersonal skills, as they must be able to work well with people from various backgrounds. In addition, Research Scientists have good writing, communication, and presentation skills. They also have strong self-management skills, including the ability to follow directions, work efficiently and independently, organize and prioritize tasks, and meet deadlines. Being enthusiastic, creative, dedicated, analytical, and flexible are some personality traits that Research Scientists have in common.

Unions and Associations

Many Research Scientists belong to professional associations that serve the interests of their particular disciplines. By joining these societies, they can take advantage of such professional services and resources as networking opportunities, continuing education programs, professional certification, and publications.

Tips for Entry

1. Contact companies with whom you would like to work to find out about internship, fellowship, and employment opportunities.
2. Attend career fairs sponsored by colleges or community organizations. Along with learning about job openings, take advantage of learning more about companies from their representatives.
3. Are your job skills lacking? Get help from your college career center. Counselors are available to help you fill out applications and prepare résumés more effectively. They can also help you prepare for job interviews and offer other resources for your use.
4. Use the Internet to learn more about companies where you would like to work. To see if a company has a Web site, enter its name in any search engine.

RESEARCH ASSOCIATE

Position Description

In private industry, Research Associates work closely with scientists to help them achieve the goals and objectives of their various research projects, which fulfill the commercial missions of their employers. As are the scientists under whose direction they work, Research Associates are trained in a particular field of life science, physical science, earth science, computing science, mathematics, or engineering. They are expected to apply scientific principles and techniques, as well as company policies and procedures to solve a wide array of complex problems on the laboratory bench or in field studies.

Research Associates participate in various types of research projects. In industry, a great number of them work on product development teams that engage in research to create commercial products and services. Some Research Associates assist scientists with applied research to find solutions to problems that had been encountered during the research and development or production phases. For example, scientists may be concerned with issues regarding the quality control, manufacturing, or packaging of products. Research Associates may also be part of basic research projects that scientists conduct to gain knowledge about phenomenon that can be utilized in other research projects. In performing basic or applied research, associates may discover new scientific ideas or invent new technologies.

Some Research Associates work in the area of clinical research. These professionals assist in testing the safety and effectiveness of pharmaceutical drugs, medical devices, surgical procedures, vaccines, therapies, methodologies, and equipment used to diagnose, treat, and cure diseases and health conditions. Clinical tests, also known as clinical trials, are performed on actual patients.

Research Associates work on research and development teams that are composed of scientists, technicians, research assistants, project managers, and others. As team members, Research Associates contribute to achieving the goal and objectives of their projects. For example, they assist with the development of new methods and technologies that can help their projects advance successfully.

While under the direction of scientists, Research Associates are responsible for conducting specific experiments or tests. They assist in the development, design, and execution of their assigned experiments and tests, as well as with the analysis and reporting of the data collected from them. They perform such tasks as:

- developing standard operating procedures for performing experiments or tests
- conducting experiments or tests, while following specific protocols and procedures

- monitoring their assigned experiments or tests
- troubleshooting problems as they occur
- operating, testing, calibrating, and maintaining laboratory and scientific equipment
- making sure experiments and tests are in compliance with protocols and company policies as well as with relevant laws and regulations
- keeping detailed and accurate logs and records of observations, data, and findings
- conducting literature searches on pertinent research topics
- examining and interpreting experimental or test data by utilizing scientific principles and statistical analysis techniques
- writing technical reports that describe in detail their findings

Research Associates may be asked to contribute to scientific papers as well as participate in presentations at scientific conferences. Some senior associates supervise laboratory technicians and research assistants.

Research Associates may perform tasks that expose them to dangerous chemicals, biological agents, equipment with moving parts, or other hazards. Hence, they must follow strict safety procedures and wear protective clothing and equipment. Some associates perform physical work where they need to lift and carry objects weighing 50 pounds or more.

Research Associates mostly work in laboratories and offices. Those involved in field studies might work in a dusty environment or in remote locations in varying weather conditions. Research Associates generally work a 40-hour week. When needed, they put in additional hours to monitor experiments and complete other tasks.

Salaries

Salaries for Research Associates vary, depending on such factors as their education, experience, employer, industry, and geographic location. Specific salary information for this profession is unavailable, but their earnings are similar to those of science technicians. The U.S. Bureau of Labor Statistics reported the following estimated annual salaries for most of these science technicians in its May 2006 *Occupational Employment Statistics* survey:

- agricultural and food technicians, $20,850 to $49,270
- biological technicians, $23,670 to $57,890
- chemical technicians, $24,560 to $60,120
- environmental technicians, $23,600 to $60,700

Employment Prospects

Opportunities for Research Associates are available in a variety of industries, including, among others, the biotechnology, pharmaceutical, medical devices, agricultural, food processing, aerospace, automotive, electronics, computing, and telecommunications industries. In addition to working in the private sector, Research Associates are employed by government agencies, research institutes, and colleges and universities.

In general, job openings become available when individuals advance to higher positions, transfer to other occupations, or leave the workforce for various reasons. Employers will create additional positions to meet growing needs, as long as funding is available. Job prospects are strongest in the biotechnology, the pharmaceutical and medicine manufacturing, the food processing, and the scientific research and development services industries.

Advancement Prospects

Research Associates advance according to their interests and ambitions. As they gain experience, they may become technical specialists or pursue supervisory and managerial positions. They may choose to move into production, quality control, marketing, sales, or another area within their company; or they may seek research jobs in government, academic, or other research settings.

After 15 or more years on the job, Research Associates in some companies may be appointed to positions as research scientists. Some Research Associates return to school to obtain the appropriate advanced degrees to become research scientists, college professors, or high-level administrators.

Many technicians measure their success through job satisfaction, by assuming greater responsibilities, and by earning higher wages.

Education and Training

Depending on the employer, candidates must have either a bachelor's or master's degree in an appropriate science discipline. For example, biotechnology companies hire Research Associates who have college degrees in biology, molecular biology, microbiology, biochemistry, chemistry, or other related fields.

Employers may hire candidates for entry-level Research Associate positions with associate degrees, as long as they have extensive experience as laboratory technicians or research assistants.

Novice Research Associates typically receive on-the-job training, which involves performing routine tasks under the direction and supervision of research scientists and experienced Research Associates.

Throughout their careers, Research Associates enroll in workshops, seminars, and courses to update their skills and knowledge.

Experience, Special Skills, and Personality Traits

Employers generally prefer to hire entry-level candidates who have one or more years of work experience relevant to the position for which they apply. Candidates, for example, may have worked in research assistant positions. Recent college graduates may have gained experience through internships, work-study programs, research assistantships, or employment. Strong candidates would have experience performing the research methods and applications in which they would be working. For example, candidates for biotechnology positions should have practical experience performing basic molecular biology techniques.

To perform their various tasks efficiently, Research Associates must have effective organizational, analytical, problem-solving, time-management, and teamwork skills. Having strong writing and computer skills is also important. In addition, they need excellent communication and interpersonal skills, as they must be able to work well with scientists, managers, and others from diverse backgrounds. Being creative, innovative, detail-oriented, cooperative, hardworking, persistent, flexible, and self-motivated are some personality traits that successful Research Associates have in common.

Unions and Associations

Research Associates can join professional associations that serve their particular interests to take advantage of networking opportunities, continuing education programs, job listings, professional publications, and other professional services and resources. These societies are available at the local, state, national, and international levels. For a list of scientific societies, see Appendix III.

Tips for Entry

1. While in college, gain experience by obtaining a research assistant position on campus. Check with your professors as well as with your department secretary and the college job placement office about available positions.

2. Job titles can mean different occupations for different employers. At some companies, Research Associates are fellowship positions held by postdoctoral researchers. Hence, read job announcements carefully and thoroughly to ensure you meet the qualifications.

3. Many employers list their job vacancies with Web sites that are dedicated to employment in their particular industry, such as biotechnology, pharmaceuticals, or agriculture.

4. Contact your current and former employers for job referrals.

5. Use the Internet to learn about the private industry in which you would like to work. To find relevant Web sites, enter the name of the industry (such as *biotechnology industry*) into a search engine.

SCIENCE TECHNICIAN

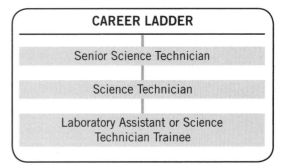

Position Description

In private industry, Science Technicians play an important role in developing and producing products and services that meet customers' satisfaction. Their job is to provide technical support and assistance to scientists and engineers as they solve problems in research, production, operations, and program administration. As with professionals, these technicians are trained in different fields, including biology, microbiology, molecular biology, biotechnology, agriculture, food science, chemistry, environmental science, and so on.

Science Technicians' responsibilities vary, depending on the area in which they work. As members of research teams, Science Technicians engage in these different types of research and development:

- product development research to create new or improved consumable products and services
- applied research to create or modify procedures, methodologies, or technologies to solve research or production problems
- basic research to gain new scientific knowledge that can be applied to solving problems or inventing products and services
- clinical research to test the safety and effectiveness of medical therapies, methodologies, and equipment used to diagnose, treat, and cure diseases and health conditions on actual patients

Research technicians assist scientists with their laboratory experiments, field studies, or clinical trials. They perform such tasks as preparing solutions and compounds for experiments; collecting specimens for testing; monitoring experiments or tests; assembling, analyzing, and interpreting experimental or test data; keeping detailed records; preparing technical summaries and reports; and maintaining laboratory equipment and facilities.

Science Technicians are also involved in the manufacturing of new and existing products. They monitor production processes to ensure that products are being manufactured according to product specifications, company procedures, and industry standards. Additionally, Science Technicians verify the quality of raw materials, products, and processes. They also make sure that raw materials and production processes comply with all governmental laws and regulations that govern their particular industries. Some Science Technicians provide support in their companies' waste management operations and other activities related to environmental regulatory compliance.

Entry-level technicians typically perform basic routine tasks, and work under the close supervision of scientists, technologists, or senior technicians. As they gain experience, they are assigned increasingly complicated duties. For example, experienced Science Technicians sometimes conduct experiments or tests independently, and provide scientists with reports of their results to review.

Many Science Technicians work in offices, laboratories, or plants. Some technicians work outdoors to perform some of their tasks. For example, agricultural technicians may be assigned to care for plants growing in fields or in greenhouses. Some technicians are required to travel to remote locations, such as wilderness areas and seashores, and work there for several days or weeks at a time.

Science Technicians may be exposed to dust, noise, toxic chemicals, infectious agents, extremes in temperature, or other hazards. To prevent risks, technicians are required to follow safety procedures, such as wearing respiratory masks while handling toxic chemicals.

Science Technicians work a 40-hour work schedule. Some of them work irregular hours, including evenings and weekends. Research technicians may be assigned to work rotating shifts in order to monitor experiments. Production technicians may be assigned to day, evening, or night shifts.

Salaries

Salaries for Science Technicians vary, depending on their education, experience, industry, and geographic location. According to the May 2006 *Occupational Employment Statistics* survey by the U.S. Bureau of Labor Statistics (BLS), the estimated annual salary for most of these Science Technicians ranged as follows:

- agricultural and food science technicians, $20,850 to $49,270
- biological technicians, $23,670 to $57,890
- chemical technicians, $24,560 to $60,120
- environmental science and protection technicians, $23,600 to $60,700
- geological and petroleum technicians, $22,020 to $88,150
- nuclear technicians, $42,550 to $89,240

Employment Prospects

Science Technicians are employed in many industries, including biotechnology, biomedicine, agriculture, food processing, chemicals, petroleum, energy, aerospace, and communications, among others.

The BLS reports that overall employment of Science Technicians is projected to increase by 12 percent through 2016. In addition to job growth, technicians will be needed to replace those who retire, advance to higher positions, transfer to other occupations, or leave the workforce for various reasons.

Job prospects are expected to be strongest in the biotechnology, pharmaceutical and medicine manufacturing, food processing, and scientific research and development services industries. However, the job market typically reflects the health of the economy. Fewer job openings and more layoffs for Science Technicians can be expected during economic downturns.

Advancement Prospects

Science Technicians may advance in various ways, depending on their interests and ambitions. Many technicians measure their success through job satisfaction, by assuming greater responsibilities, and by earning higher wages.

Some technicians pursue supervisory and managerial positions, for which they may need to transfer to other companies. Additional education may be required for technicians to advance to these positions. Industrial technicians may also pursue opportunities in other areas such as sales, technical service, technical writing, or marketing.

Education and Training

Requirements vary with the different employers. Science Technicians need at least a high school diploma or a general equivalency diploma. Many employers also require that Science Technicians possess an associate degree in an applied science or science-related technology, or have at least two years of specialized training. Some employers prefer to hire Science Technicians who have a bachelor's degree in an appropriate science discipline. For example, chemical technicians may be required to possess bachelor's degrees in chemistry or biochemistry.

Many technical and community colleges offer certificate and associate degree programs which combine instruction in scientific principles and theory with practical applications in laboratory settings. Most associate degrees are designed to fulfill general education requirements for four-year colleges and universities. Thus, students are able to transfer easily to a four-year college or university.

Employers typically provide entry-level technicians with on-the-job training. Many Science Technicians enroll in training programs and continuing education courses throughout their careers in order to maintain and update their knowledge and skills.

Experience, Skills, and Personality Traits

Employers generally prefer to hire entry-level candidates who have one or more years of work experience relevant to the position for which they apply. They especially seek candidates who have laboratory experience. Applicants may have gained experience through internships, training programs, or employment.

To do well in their work, Science Technicians need strong organizational, analytical, and observation skills. Having good computer, writing, and communication skills is also essential. In addition, they need effective interpersonal and teamwork skills, as they must be able to work well with scientists and others. Being adaptable, self-motivated, reliable, accurate, detail-oriented, curious, and creative are some personality traits that successful Science Technicians have in common.

Unions and Associations

Science Technicians are eligible to join science societies that serve their particular disciplines. For example, chemical technicians may join the American Chemical Society and food science technicians may belong to the Institute of Food Technologists. By joining professional associations, they can take advantage of networking opportunities, education programs, and other professional resources and services. For contact information for these associations, please see Appendix III.

Tips for Entry

1. In high school, take as many science and mathematics courses as you can.
2. Some two-year colleges offer internship and work-study programs which place students at local companies. Check with your college career center to see what is available.
3. To enhance your employability and advancement prospects, continue to update your technical skills.
4. Contact employers directly about permanent and temporary job openings. Also learn about jobs through your college career center as well as your state employment office.
5. Use the Internet to learn more about Science Technicians. To get a list of relevant Web sites, enter the keyword *science technician* in a search engine. For some links, see Appendix IV.

PROJECT MANAGER

Duties: Plan, direct, and coordinate the activities of company projects; perform duties as required

Alternate Title(s): Project Director, Project Manager/Consultant

Salary Range: $60,000 to $146,000

Employment Prospects: Good

Advancement Prospects: Good

Prerequisites:

Education or Training—A bachelor's degree in a technical or scientific discipline

Experience—Several years of experience in the scientific discipline and industry in which one would be working

Special Skills and Personality Traits—Leadership, teambuilding, interpersonal, communication

organizational, analytical, problem-solving, writing, self-management, and computer skills; energetic, enthusiastic, honest, dependable, flexible, and creative

CAREER LADDER

Senior Project Manager

Project Manager

Assistant Project Manager

Project Coordinator or Project Scheduler

Position Description

Project Managers plan, administer, and coordinate projects that companies initiate for research and development, production, and other purposes. For example, Project Managers may direct projects that involve developing new products or services; improving existing products; conducting basic research for new ventures; improving manufacturing processes; launching the sale of new products; or constructing facilities.

Project Managers oversee projects from beginning to end. They work closely with scientists and engineers, as well as with business managers to plan the direction of the project. The project team defines the purpose and goals of their project and they integrate scientific and technical objectives with company strategies and business goals. The team also establishes administrative policies and procedures, and determines the resources—such as money, staff, equipment, and materials—that are needed for their project. Potential risks that may occur during the various project stages are identified.

Project Managers act as liaisons between project members and the senior, or higher-level, management of their companies. Project Managers are responsible for the success or failure of projects that they direct. However, most Project Managers have no authority to make any decisions regarding the scientific or techni-

cal direction of the projects. Their role is to control the cost, time, and quality of the projects.

Project Managers develop project schedules that outline the required sequences of steps for completing the projects. In addition, they are in charge of allocating resources. For example, they coordinate all the purchasing or leasing of machinery and equipment, interface with vendors to make sure their materials conform to industrial standards, oversee the contracting of outside professional services, and supervise the hiring and training of new or temporary employees for the projects.

Project Managers perform various duties to assure that projects run smoothly, by applying project management methods and technologies as well as by meeting deadlines and staying within budget constraints. Some of their tasks include:

- coordinating work schedules of team members
- monitoring the progress of individual team members to ensure they are meeting project goals
- evaluating project-related issues and providing recommendations for solving problems
- confirming that projects are in compliance with appropriate procedures, protocol, and regulations
- providing progress reports to team members and senior managers
- scheduling, directing, and leading project team meetings

- meeting with contractors, subcontractors, vendors, and material suppliers
- preparing required forms, reports, and paperwork

Most Project Managers are involved in two or more projects at a time. They may run a project alone or lead a project management team, which would entail delegating tasks to assistants such as coordinators, schedulers, and assistant project managers. Project Managers report to technical project sponsors, who are usually the scientists or engineers that conceptualized the projects.

Project Managers work mostly in offices. Some may work in laboratories or in industrial plants, depending on the nature of the projects.

Project Managers work a regular 40-hour week, but they often work evenings and on weekends to complete tasks and meet project deadlines. Many Project Managers feel stressed as they are expected to complete projects with short deadlines or within tight budgets. Some Project Managers are required to be available 24 hours a day.

Salaries

Salaries for Project Managers vary, depending on various factors, including their education, experience, level of responsibility, industry, employer, and geographic location. The U.S. Bureau of Labor Statistics reports in its May 2006 *Occupational Employment Statistics* survey that the estimated annual salary for most natural resources managers ranged between $60,300 and $145,600.

Employment Prospects

Project Managers are employed throughout private industry. They may be hired to staff positions or as independent contractors. These professionals also work for firms that offer project management services to various industries.

Job opportunities for experienced Project Managers should continue to be favorable for years to come, as companies continually need personnel to manage new projects. However, most openings become available as Project Managers transfer to other positions, retire, or leave the workforce.

The demand for Project Managers vary with the different industries. Job opportunities should be better in those areas that are experiencing growth, such as biotechnology and pharmaceuticals. However, the job market generally goes up and down with the economy. For example, when the economy is on a downturn, companies tend to put projects on hold and lay off workers or hire fewer people.

Advancement Prospects

As Project Managers gain experience, they are assigned to manage larger and more complex projects. They can rise to senior project management positions as unit managers and division managers. Those with higher managerial ambitions can pursue administrative positions as executives.

Project Managers can become technical specialists, consultants, or researchers. They can also seek nontechnical positions in sales, marketing, human resources, or another area in their company. Entrepreneurial individuals can become self-employed consultants or owners of technical or consulting firms.

Education and Training

Depending on the employer, candidates may be required to have a bachelor's or advanced degree in a scientific or technical discipline related to the type of projects they would be managing. For example, Project Managers in technology usually hold a degree in computer science, electrical engineering, or other related fields. Some employers prefer to hire Project Managers with an advanced degree. Many employers hire candidates who have a bachelor's or master's degree in business administration, as long as they have qualifying experience.

Most companies provide training to new Project Managers, which may include either formal instruction or on-the-job training, or both.

Throughout their careers, Project Managers enroll in workshops, seminars, and courses to update their skills and knowledge.

Experience, Skills, and Personality Traits

Employers typically hire Project Managers who have experience or are familiar with the industry and discipline in which they would be working. Project Managers also have an understanding of business and financial principles. Most Project Managers in scientific and engineering fields have several years of work experience as scientists, engineers, technologists, technicians, or in other positions. They also have a few years of experience working on technical projects.

Project Managers must have excellent leadership, teambuilding, interpersonal, and communication skills, as they must be able to inspire people to work well together and focus on completing projects. Additionally, Project Managers need effective organizational, analytical, problem-solving, self-management, and writing skills. They also need strong computer skills, including experience working with word processing, spreadsheet, project management, and other software.

Being energetic, enthusiastic, honest, dependable, flexible, and creative are some personality traits that successful Project Managers share.

Unions and Associations

Project Managers can join professional associations to take advantage of professional resources and services, such as training programs, publications, current research studies, and networking opportunities. Many Project Managers belong to the Project Management Institute, a national society. (For contact information, see Appendix III.) Additionally, local or regional societies that serve the interests of Project Managers are available in many areas.

Tips for Entry

1. As a college student, you might gain experience by obtaining an internship or work-study position in project management. Talk with your adviser or a college career counselor for assistance in finding such positions.

2. Early in your career, let your supervisor know about your interest in project management. Together, discuss your career goals and how you can gain experience to become a Project Manager.

3. To enhance your employability, you might complete a project management certificate program through a college or university continuing education program.

4. Many Project Managers have gained experience through support project management roles, such as by being a project coordinator, project scheduler, or assistant project manager.

5. Use the Internet to learn more about project management. One Web site you might visit is for the Project Management Institute. Its URL is http://www.pmi.org. For more links, see Appendix IV.

QUALITY PROFESSIONAL

CAREER PROFILE

Duties: Inspect, test, and audit raw materials, manufacturing processes, and products for quality requirements; responsibilities vary with the different positions; perform duties as required of position

Alternate Title(s): Quality Control Technician, Quality Control Engineer, Quality Control Analyst, Quality Assurance Manager, Quality Control Auditor, or other title that reflects a specific position

Salary Range: $43,000 to $191,000

Employment Prospects: Good

Advancement Prospects: Good

Prerequisites:

Education or Training—A bachelor's degree in engineering or a scientific discipline for most positions

CAREER LADDER

Quality Manager

Quality Specialist (such as Quality Control Engineer)

Quality Technician or Quality Analyst

Experience—Experience in quality control preferred; previous experience related to position

Special Skills and Personality Traits—Math, writing, communication, computer, interpersonal, teamwork, and self-management skills; flexible, meticulous, detail-oriented, and observant

Position Description

The term *quality* in manufacturing means that products have all the characteristics required to meet customer satisfaction and that they are free of any defects or deficiencies. Manufacturers employ Quality Professionals to ensure that quality is being monitored throughout all product development and manufacturing phases. Quality Professionals also guarantee that the quality of the products, the raw materials used for making them, and the manufacturing processes all comply with company and industrial standards. In addition, Quality Professionals are involved with monitoring the quality of other aspects of a company's performance such as employee training programs, customer service, and information systems.

Quality operations are divided into two units—quality assurance and quality control. The quality assurance staff is responsible for developing and monitoring policies, procedures, and programs which ensure that the requirements of quality are being fulfilled. The quality control staff, on the other hand, is responsible for the day-to-day inspections of raw materials, packaging, and products during production processes. They check for unsatisfactory performance and can request that work be redone, materials or products be thrown out, or production be stopped until corrections have been made.

Most manufacturers employ various types of Quality Professionals—technicians, specialists, engineers, and managers. They may work in either the quality control or quality assurance units. Quality technicians are usually entry-level personnel. Quality control technicians inspect and test raw materials, samples, parts, or finished products, while quality assurance technicians conduct audits on products to make sure they meet appropriate levels of quality. All technicians keep accurate records of their test or audit data. They also evaluate the data and prepare reports of their findings.

Quality control analysts are responsible for the inspection of raw materials (such as food ingredients, chemicals for drugs, plastics, or packaging materials) before they can be used. Following standard operating procedures, they perform lab analyses on raw materials, and report any abnormalities. These analysts are also responsible for documenting their tests and evaluations.

Quality engineers ensure the quality standards during the production process. They often work closely with manufacturing engineers and technicians. Their duties vary, depending on their experience, position, and other factors. Some duties that they might perform include:

- inspecting and testing products during the production processes

- performing quality audits on finished products
- applying quality control standards
- inspecting, testing, and evaluating the precision and accuracy of production equipment
- developing quality control standards for processing raw materials into products
- conducting audits to confirm that processes are in compliance with company specifications and industrial standards
- preparing documentation

Quality assurance auditors are responsible for examining the activities of production and quality control departments. They assure that these departments are in compliance with in-house and industrial standards. They may also be responsible for confirming that their companies are meeting regulatory requirements for standard manufacturing practices.

Quality managers are responsible for planning, developing, and implementing quality activities and programs. They also supervise quality technicians, engineers, specialists, and others. Some quality managers are in charge of particular units. For example, quality control managers are responsible for product quality on their shifts, while quality assurance managers oversee the full life cycle of specific product lines. Other quality managers are in charge of quality departments, being responsible for planning, directing, and administering all quality programs. These managers, sometimes known as directors of quality operations, are usually members of company management teams which develop and implement company policies and operating procedures.

Depending on their positions, Quality Professionals may work in offices, in laboratories, or at production sites. Quality Professionals generally work a 40-hour week. Many of them work evening or night shifts.

Salaries
Salaries for Quality Professionals vary, depending on such factors as their education, experience, position, employer, and geographic location. Quality control engineers and managers typically make higher earnings than technicians. According to a 2006 salary survey by *Quality Digest*, annual salaries for Quality Professionals ranged from $43,007 for techinicans to $90,524 for directors. (These figures are for respondents who did not possess certification from the American Society for Quality.)

Employment Prospects
Quality Professionals are employed in practically all industries, such as the automotive, aviation, defense, medical devices, pharmaceuticals, biotechnology, chemicals, petroleum, telecommunications, computer hardware, computer software, environmental, energy, and food processing industries.

Most openings become available as Quality Professionals transfer to other positions or retire. Employers will create additional jobs to fit growing needs as long as resources are available.

The need for qualified Quality Professionals should continue to remain favorable due to the importance that manufacturers assign to the productions and delivery of high-quality products to customers. Keep in mind that during economic downturns, companies may have fewer jobs available and may also lay off employees.

Advancement Prospects
Quality Professionals with managerial and administrative aspirations can rise through the ranks as team leaders, project leaders, supervisors, managers, and executives.

Options vary for the different Quality Professionals. For example, quality technicians can usually rise to the supervisor level. With further education, they can become quality engineers.

Education and Training
Educational requirements vary with the different positions. Some employers prefer that candidates for quality assurance positions hold a master's degree in engineering or business administration, with a concentration in quality management. A bachelor's degree in engineering or science discipline is the minimum requirement for quality engineers, analysts, auditors, and managers. Many employers prefer to hire candidates with an advanced degree to these positions.

The minimum requirement for quality technicians varies with the different employers. Some employers hire qualified candidates with high school diplomas or general equivalency diplomas. Others require candidates to have an associate's or bachelor's degree.

Employers typically provide training for new employees.

Experience, Skills, and Personality Traits
Requirements vary with the different positions. Usually the higher the position, the more years of experience are needed. For example, a biotechnology firm may require two to five years of experience for quality control analyst positions. Many Employers prefer to hire candidates who have one or more years of experience in quality control. They also look for applicants who have work experience related to the positions for which they are applying.

In general, Quality Professionals should have strong math, writing, and communication skills. Having adequate computer skills is also essential. In addition, they need excellent interpersonal and teamwork skills as well as self-management skills, such as the ability to organize and prioritize tasks, handle stressful situations, and work independently. Being flexible, meticulous, detail-oriented, and observant are some personality traits that Quality Professionals share.

Unions and Associations

Many Quality Professionals are members of the American Society for Quality and other local, state, or national professional associations. (For contact information, see Appendix III.) By joining these societies, they can take advantage of training programs, professional certification, current research data, networking opportunities, and other professional services and resources.

Tips for Entry

1. Gain experience by obtaining a part-time job, summer job, or internship in quality control.
2. Read job descriptions carefully, as job titles differ from one company to the next.
3. Take advantage of resources such as state employment offices, career centers, professional associations, and Internet job banks to learn about job openings for Quality Professionals.
4. Before taking a job offer, be sure you understand how the quality department is structured and what kind of career advancement opportunities are available to you. Be sure to ask a prospective employer before taking any job offer.
5. Use the Internet to learn more about the quality control/assurance field. One Web site where you might start is American Society for Quality, http://www.asq.org. For more links, see Appendix IV.

REGULATORY AFFAIRS SPECIALIST
(HEALTH CARE PRODUCTS)

CAREER PROFILE

Duties: Confirm that companies in the health-care product industry are in compliance with all appropriate laws and regulations; assist companies with obtaining permits, licenses, and approvals for marketing new products; perform duties as required

Alternate Title(s): Regulatory Affairs Associate, Regulatory Affairs Manager

Salary Range: $43,000 to $55,000

Employment Prospects: Good

Advancement Prospects: Good

Prerequisites:

    Education or Training—A bachelor's degree in a science or health field preferred

    Experience—Previous industry work experience; experience or familiarity with regulatory affairs preferred

CAREER LADDER

Regulatory Affairs Manager

Senior Regulatory Affairs Specialist

Regulatory Affairs Specialist
(or Associate)

Special Skills and Personality Traits—Negotiation, organizational, writing, computer, statistical, communication, presentation, interpersonal, and teamwork skills; inquisitive, tactful, friendly, detail-oriented, diligent, pragmatic

Position Description

In the United States, all products that would be used for treating medical conditions or diseases must first be approved by the U.S. Food and Drug Administration (FDA) before they can be sold. These include pharmaceutical drugs (prescriptions as well as over-the-counter remedies), biologic products (such as plasma), and medical devices, among others. Professionals known as Regulatory Affairs (RA) Specialists play an important role in bringing safe and effective health care products to domestic and international consumers. These specialists act as regulatory resources for their companies.

RA Specialists are responsible for making sure that companies in the pharmaceutical, biomedical device, and other industries comply with the wide array of laws and regulations that govern the development, manufacturing, processing, and marketing of health care products. Additionally, these specialists are involved with obtaining product approval from regulatory agencies for new products.

RA Specialists also help their companies seek FDA approval for performing clinical studies on health care products. These studies involve testing the products on human subjects to further study their safety and effectiveness. The results from these studies would be presented to the FDA to obtain approval for marketing their products.

RA Specialists are usually assigned to provide support to several projects at a time. They are responsible for understanding, interpreting, and applying laws, regulations, guidelines, and guidance from different regulatory agencies. They advise scientists, engineers, project managers, and others about pertinent requirements which need to be followed. RA Specialists are also responsible for tracking and documenting changes in regulations and guidelines that relate to their assigned projects. They inform appropriate personnel who have the authority to make the changes needed for companies to be in compliance.

RA Specialists may be involved with certain phases or the whole life cycle of a project—from product development to the marketing of the final product. They interact with the different departments, such as the research and development, manufacturing, quality control, packaging, and advertising departments. For example, RA Specialists might work with quality professionals to verify that manufacturing processes are in compliance with regulations.

Regulatory Affairs Specialists perform a wide range of duties, which vary according to their skill levels and experience. Some of their duties may include:

- preparing and filing applications for licenses, permits, and product registrations required for commercial distribution of products
- gathering and assembling information for regulatory submissions
- reviewing technical documents for regulatory submissions
- acting as company liaison with regulatory affairs personnel in other countries
- negotiating submission issues with FDA reviewers for product approvals
- preparing regulatory reports
- assisting with inspections and audits from the FDA and other regulatory agencies
- helping to establish and maintain standard procedures and polices to assure continued compliance in all work areas
- training new company employees about regulatory requirements as well as industrial standards and protocols

Some RA Specialists also perform the role of quality professional in their company.

RA Specialists work under the guidance and supervision of RA managers. In some companies, RA Specialists are known as regulatory affairs associates.

Regulatory Affairs Specialists generally work a 40-hour week. Some may be required to travel to other countries to meet with regulatory agencies.

Salaries

Salaries for RA Specialists vary, depending on such factors as their experience, education, job duties, employer, and geographic location. According to Salary.com, in August 2007, entry-level RA Specialists earned a median base annual salary of $49,210. Salaries for this profession, per Salary.com, ranged from $43,356 to $54,621.

Employment Prospects

Health care Regulatory Affairs Specialists are employed in the biotechnology, pharmaceutical, and biomedical device industries. They may also find employment with companies that manufacture cosmetics, nutritional products, and veterinary products. Many also work as consultants for firms that offer regulatory affairs services.

Most opportunities become available as individuals retire, transfer to other positions, or leave the workforce. Additional openings are created by employers as their needs grow.

Job prospects for RA Specialists should continue to be favorable, as companies need experienced personnel to help them stay up to date with complex laws and regulations.

Advancement Prospects

RA Specialists can rise through the ranks as senior specialist, manager, and director. Moving from one company to the next may be required in order for a specialist to obtain higher level positions. In large companies, they can become promoted to vice president of regulatory affairs operations or other executive offices. Those with entrepreneurial ambitions can start up their own consulting firms.

A master's or doctoral degree may be required for higher-level positions.

Education and Training

In general, Regulatory Affairs Specialists must possess a bachelor's degree, preferably in the science or health care field. A bachelor's degree in engineering is also acceptable for positions in the medical devices industry. Some employers may require that RA Specialists hold an advanced degree in the sciences or in regulatory affairs.

Entry-level Specialists receive on-the-job training. Many also receive formal instruction through outside sources, such as training seminars sponsored by RA organizations or continuing education RA programs.

Throughout their careers, RA professionals enroll in training and educational programs to keep up with new developments in their areas as well as to update their skills.

Experience, Skills, and Personality Traits

Employers generally prefer to hire RA professionals who have private industry experience as research scientists, clinical researchers, quality professionals, production scientists, and so on. Candidates for entry-level RA associate positions should have at least one year of work experience within the industry to which they are applying. Employers also prefer that entry-level candidates have experience in or are familiar with regulatory affairs.

RA Specialists need excellent negotiation, organizational, and writing skills as well as proficient computer and statistical skills. Having excellent communication, presentation, interpersonal, and teamwork skills is also important for their work.

Being inquisitive, tactful, friendly, detail-oriented, diligent, and pragmatic are some personality traits that successful RA Specialists share.

Unions and Associations

Many RA Specialists belong to the Regulatory Affairs Professionals Society, a national association that provides networking opportunities, training programs, professional certification, and other professional services and resources. For contact information, please see Appendix III.

Tips for Entry

1. Early in your career, let your supervisor know about your interest in regulatory affairs. Together, discuss your career goals and how you can gain experience to eventually enter this field.

2. To enhance your employability, take courses in regulatory affairs offered by colleges and universities, or by professional associations.

3. Use the Internet to learn about job vacancies for regulatory affairs positions. For example, you can access online job banks, such as Medzilla.com, http://www. medzilla.com; and Monsters.com, http://www.monsters.com. Also check out job listings at Web sites of professional associations. In addition, many companies have Web sites on which they post current job vacancies as well as other recruitment information.

4. Learn more about the field of regulatory affairs on the Internet. Some Web sites you might visit are Regulatory Affairs Professionals Society, http://www.raps.org; and U.S. FDA Office of Regulatory Affairs, http://www.fda.gov/ora. For more links, see Appendix IV.

PATENT AGENT

Duties: Prepare patent applications; prosecute patents in the U.S. Patent and Trademark Office (USPTO); perform other duties as required

Alternate Title(s): Patent Analyst

Salary Range: $31,000 to $146,000

Employment Prospects: Good

Advancement Prospects: Fair

Prerequisites:

Education or Training—Bachelor's or advanced degree in an engineering or a science discipline; on-the-job training

Experience—Have work experience in a science or technical field; experience in or familiarity with patent law

Special Skills and Personality Traits—Writing, analytical, communication, and interpersonal

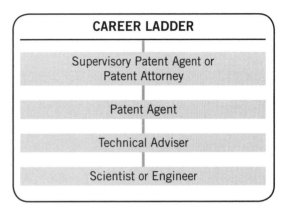

skills; curious, detail-oriented, organized, and flexible

Special Requirements—Must be registered to practice before the USPTO

Position Description

Patent Agents help companies obtain patents for new inventions that they own, such as medicines, computer hardware, devices, equipment, chemical processes, plant varieties, shoe designs, and compositions of matter. Patents are legal documents that protect the property rights of invention owners. Patent holders are able to sell their patented inventions exclusively. That means that no one else may make, use, sell, or import such inventions unless the patent holders first give their permission. In the United States, the U.S. Patent and Trademark Office (USPTO) has the authority to issue U.S. patents.

Patent Agents are involved with the preparation of patent applications, upon which the granting of patents is based. A patent application consists of a detailed description—including drawings—of an invention that describes how the invention is made and used. The application also includes the set of claims to the invention, which defines the territory of use that belongs exclusively to the inventors. Patent Agents work closely with inventors to draft the applications so that they are technically and legally clear. In companies, Patent Agents work with the research scientists who made the inventions.

Patent Agents who are registered to practice patent law before the USPTO can represent companies in the patent application process. (This is also known as the prosecution of patents.) As registered Patent Agents,

they can file patent applications, respond to formal correspondence (called office actions) from the USPTO, meet with examiners to discuss the merits of their clients' inventions, and make sure all deadlines are met. Patent Agents also counsel their clients on the progress of their applications.

Although registered Patent Agents can practice law before the USPTO, they are not lawyers. They cannot represent clients or practice patent law in federal or state courts. It is also unlawful for Patent Agents to provide any legal services other than the prosecution of patents with the USPTO. For example, Patent Agents cannot provide legal advice, negotiate licenses to use patented inventions, represent clients in court litigation, or file patent appeals in courts.

Patent Agents work a standard 40-hour week, but sometimes put in additional hours to meet deadlines and complete tasks.

Salaries

Salaries for Patent Agents vary, depending on factors such as their education, experience, and geographic location. Specific salary information for this occupation is unavailable, but a general idea of their earnings can be gained by looking at what other legal professionals earn. According to the May 2006 *Occupational Employment Statistics* survey by the U.S. Bureau of Labor Statistics, the estimated annual salary for most professionals within the legal occupation category ranged between $31,290 and $145,600.

Employment Prospects

Many Patent Agents are employed by law firms and corporate law departments. They work in various industries, such as the computer, biotechnology, pharmaceuticals, chemical, food manufacturing, agriculture, and telecommunications industries. Some Patent Agents are solo practitioners while others are members of firms that offer patent prosecution services.

The demand for qualified Patent Agents should remain constant for years because individuals and organizations continually create new inventions. Staff positions generally become available as Patent Agents transfer to other jobs, retire, or leave the occupation for other careers.

Advancement Prospects

Opportunities for supervisory and management positions are limited, and Patent Agents usually need to obtain such positions with other employers. Many Patent Agents realize advancement through job satisfaction and by earning higher incomes. Some Patent Agents set up independent practices.

Some Patent Agents enter law school to earn a juris doctor degree and become intellectual property attorneys.

Education and Training

In order to be eligible for the USPTO bar examination, Patent Agents must possess a bachelor's degree in engineering or a physical or natural science allowed by the USPTO. Employers may require that Patent Agents possess a master's or doctoral degree. Some employers may prefer that candidates hold a law degree in addition to a bachelor's or advanced degree in science or engineering.

Patent Agents typically receive on-the-job training.

Special Requirements

To practice before the U.S. Patent and Trademark Office, Patent Agents must be registered. This requires passing an entrance bar examination that covers patent law and USPTO procedures. USPTO bar applicants must also pay appropriate fees and fulfill other requirements. For more information, visit the USPTO Web site at http://www.uspto.gov.

Experience, Skills, and Personality Traits

In general, employers hire candidates who have previous work experience in the science or technology fields in which they would be practicing. They also have experience in or are familiar with patent law.

Many scientists and engineers first become technical advisers to patent lawyers in law firms and corporate law departments. As technical advisers, they gain experience by preparing patent applications and becoming familiar with patent law and USPTO procedures. After one or two years in these positions, they are usually ready to pass the USPTO examination to become registered Patent Agents.

Patent Agents need excellent writing skills, as they often prepare patent applications that are 30 or more pages long with detailed technical explanations. Analytical, communication, and interpersonal skills are also essential for their jobs. Being curious, detail-oriented, organized, and flexible are some personality traits that successful Patent Agents share.

Unions and Associations

Many Patent Agents join local, state, and national professional associations in the industries in which they serve. Patent Agents are also eligible to join the National Association of Patent Practitioners. (For contact information, see Appendix III.) By joining professional associations, Patent Agents can take advantage of networking opportunities and other professional services and resources.

Tips for Entry

1. As a college student, find out if patent law might interest you by obtaining an internship or getting a part-time job with law firms or corporate law departments that emphasize patent or intellectual property law.

2. Learn about technical adviser or patent agent positions through contacts that you have made with patent practitioners. You can also learn about openings through professional societies that serve the interests of patent practitioners.

3. Some employers provide educational programs to help technical advisers study for the USPTO entrance bar examination.

4. Former USPTO examiners who wish to become registered Patent Agents may be able to waive the examination if they have worked several years with the USPTO.

5. Learn more about Patent Agents on the Internet. Two Web sites to visit are for the United States Patent and Trademark Office, http://www.uspto.gov; and the National Association of Patent Practitioners, http://www. napp.org. For more links, see Appendix IV.

MARKET RESEARCH ANALYST

CAREER PROFILE

Duties: Conduct market studies; design research projects; write reports; perform other duties as required

Alternate Title(s): Market Analyst, Market Research Specialist

Salary Range: $32,000 to $113,000

Employment Prospects: Good

Advancement Prospects: Good

Prerequisites:

Education or Training—An advanced degree in marketing, business administration, or a related field

Experience—Marketing experience preferred

Special Skills and Personality Traits—Research, problem-solving, writing, presentation, computer,

CAREER LADDER

```
           Marketing Manager
                  |
        Market Research Analyst
                  |
    MBA Student, Marketing Research
        Associate, or Scientist
```

mathematics, statistics, interpersonal, and teamwork skills; curious, patient, persistent, creative, analytical, detail-oriented

Position Description

In business, Market Research Analysts conduct studies about how well products and services perform in the marketplace. They gather and analyze both statistical data as well as opinions from customers. With their findings, companies can make knowledgeable business and marketing decisions. For example, a medical supplies manufacturer might base its decision to change the packaging for its bandages because of the results of a market research study.

Many Market Research Analysts work in marketing departments in companies in various industries. Many others work in firms that offer market research services to companies and other organizations.

Like scientists, market researchers conduct their investigations in a thorough and methodical manner. First, they define the issues or questions that they must study. For example, Market Research Analysts might be asked to provide information about any of the following:

- the characteristics, dynamics, and trends of particular markets in specific geographical locations
- the needs, tastes, buying habits, purchasing power, and other characteristics of potential customers
- the products, sales, and marketing methods of the competition
- the reactions of customers to new products or services
- methods and strategies to bring products or services into particular markets

- potential sales for new products or services, or for existing ones in new markets

Next, Market Research Analysts design their research plans. They devise research methods and procedures that best suit their purposes. They also create any surveys, questionnaires, and other tools that they may need to solicit opinions from customers.

Market Research Analysts then collect and organize the data. They review statistical information gathered from surveys and questionnaires. They also read relevant materials from various sources, such as sales data from companies or demographic data from government agencies. In addition, their studies might require them to read materials about their competition. Market Research Analysts might also conduct one-on-one interviews or moderate small focus groups with targeted audience members, or direct and supervise trained interviewers.

These market researchers evaluate and interpret the data. They measure numerical data as well as appraise attitudes of people who have been interviewed. These analysts make recommendations based on their findings, and prepare written reports and statistical charts. They make sure that they have interpreted all technical information accurately and correctly, and present such information in language that is clearly understood by nontechnical individuals.

Depending on their projects, Market Research Analysts work alone or as part of a research team comprised of statisticians, information technology specialists, interviewers, and other marketing specialists.

Market Research Analysts work 40 hours a week, but often put in additional hours to complete their various tasks and to meet deadlines.

Salaries

Salaries for Market Research Analysts vary, depending on such factors as their education, experience, employer, and geographic location. The U.S. Bureau of Labor Statistics (BLS) reports in its May 2006 *Occupational Employment Statistics* survey that the estimated annual salary for most Market Research Analysts ranged between $32,250 and $112,510.

Employment Prospects

Some employers of Market Research Analysts are marketing research firms, management consulting firms, and advertising companies. Companies in finance, insurance, biotechnology, pharmaceuticals, biomedicine, information technology, computer and data processing, agriculture, health care, and other industries also employ Market Research Analysts. In addition, they work for government agencies, nongovernmental organizations, political campaign groups, and international organizations (such as the United Nations).

The job outlook for qualified Market Research Analysts is strong since they provide organizations with valuable information that they need to stay competitive. According to the BLS, employment of these market researchers is expected to increase by 20 percent through 2016. In addition, opportunities will become available as professionals retire, advance to higher positions, or transfer to other jobs. Opportunities are expected to be better in marketing research firms, as increasingly more companies outsource marketing research services rather than employ full-time staff.

Advancement Prospects

As they gain appropriate experience, Market Research Analysts can apply for positions in other marketing areas such as sales, brand (or product) management, business development, sales, purchasing, or distribution. Market Research Analysts with management and administrative ambitions can advance to become marketing managers and executives. In some organizations, a doctoral degree is required for top marketing positions. Those with entrepreneurial desires can become independent contractors or start up their own marketing research firms.

Education and Training

Employers generally hire candidates with advanced degrees in marketing, business administration, statistics, economics, or another related discipline. In biotechnology, computer manufacturing, and other technical industries, employers prefer to hire candidates who have a bachelor's or advanced degree in science or engineering combined with a master's degree in business administration.

Entry-level Market Research Analysts receive on-the-job training, which involves working under the guidance of experienced market researchers. Some employers also provide novices with normal formal classroom instruction.

Throughout their careers, Market Research Analysts enroll in workshops, seminars, and courses to update their skills and knowledge.

Experience, Skills, and Personality Traits

In general, employers prefer to hire candidates who have marketing experience, particularly in the industry in which they would be working. Many employers hire scientists for market research positions with little or no experience, as their scientific training matches the duties they would fulfill as Market Research Analysts.

Market Research Analysts are expected to have excellent research, problem-solving, writing, and presentation skills. They must have strong computer skills and be proficient in mathematics and statistics. They also need effective interpersonal and teamwork skills, as they must work well with others from different backgrounds.

Being curious, patient, persistent, creative, analytical, and detail-oriented are some personality traits that successful Market Research Analysts share.

Unions and Associations

Market Research Analysts might join such professional associations as the Marketing Research Association, the American Marketing Association, and the Qualitative Research Consultants Association. These national societies, as well as those at the local and state levels, offer networking opportunities, training programs, job listings, and other professional services and resources. For contact information, see Appendix III.

Tips for Entry

1. As a college undergraduate, get an idea if the marketing field is right for you by obtaining a part-time job or internship position with a marketing firm, advertising agency, public relations firm, or

company marketing department. If you are a science major, you might try to obtain a position in the industry in which you would like to work.

2. Talk with marketing researchers who have changed from science and engineering careers. Ask them about their work, how they made the transition, how they got their jobs, what courses they might recommend, and so forth.

3. Contact companies directly about job openings that are currently available or may be available soon. Many firms list current vacancies on their Web sites.

4. Before going to a job interview, learn as much as you can about the prospective employer and the position. Also practice your interviewing skills by doing a mock interview with a job counselor or friend.

5. Use the Internet to learn more about the field of marketing research. To get a list of other Web sites, enter the keywords *marketing research* or *market research analyst* in a search engine. For some links, see Appendix IV.

TECHNICAL WRITER

CAREER PROFILE

Duties: Develop and produce scientific, technical, or clinical materials, such as manuals, help systems, reports, and Web sites; perform duties as required

Alternate Title(s): Technical Communicator, Information Developer, Documentation Specialist

Salary Range: $36,000 to $92,000

Employment Prospects: Good

Advancement Prospects: Good

Prerequisites:

Education or Training—A bachelor's degree in any field

Experience—Have related work experience, or training, or background in one's subject matter

Special Skills and Personality Traits—Computer, writing, research, presentation, communication, interpersonal, teamwork, and self-management skills; creative, diplomatic, self-motivated, analytical, organized, flexible, and enthusiastic

CAREER LADDER

Senior Technical Writer or Independent Contractor

Technical Writer

Junior or Assistant Technical Writer

Position Description

Technical Writers develop written materials and multimedia works about scientific, medical, or technical subjects for their employers or clients. These materials are used by various organizations for training, reference, information, and other purposes. For example, Technical Writers might be assigned to:

- produce operating manuals for equipment, machinery, computer hardware, or other products
- develop help systems that are integrated into software and Web sites to assist users
- create in-house materials such as employee handbooks, training materials, and employee newsletters
- prepare project proposals and business plans
- write scientific, technical, or clinical reports
- create promotional materials (such as brochures, press releases, and magazine articles) about company products, services, projects, or employees
- develop company Web sites, which may include writing codes and designing Web pages

Technical Writers may be permanent employees, temporary workers, or independent contractors. They create materials on a work-for-hire basis. In others words, they do not own the final products. Those belong to their employers or clients who can take full credit for them. Their clients can also make further changes to them or discard them if they do not like the finished products.

Technical Writers carefully plan and organize each project before they begin writing. They first define the scope of the project by answering such questions as these: What is the purpose of the product? Who will use it? How will it be used? What is the subject matter? How should it be presented? What format should be used?

Once they have established a working outline of the project, writers gather information about the subject matter. They interview scientists, technicians and others for relevant information, as well as read literature about the subject matter. If they are writing instructions about a product or procedure, they observe how it works, and sometimes learn how to use it themselves. Throughout their projects, Technical Writers meet with experts to discuss ideas and clarify information.

Technical Writers write a first draft of their work, following specific formats and guidelines. They are responsible for writing copy that presents scientific or technical concepts in a clear and logical matter. They express concepts clearly and accurately in language that can be understood by readers who may be unfamiliar with the subject matter or are less technically minded. Many Technical Writers produce diagrams and other visual aids to help reinforce the information they are presenting.

Technical Writers submit drafts to their employers or clients for review. The writers do one or more revisions to incorporate any changes that are requested. Technical Writers may be also involved in the design and production of the final product.

Technical Writers often work long and irregular hours, which may include working on weekends to meet deadlines.

Salaries

Salaries for Technical Writers vary, depending on such factors as their education, experience, employer, and geographic location. According to the May 2006 *Occupational Employment Statistics* survey by the U.S. Bureau of Labor Statistics, the estimated annual salary for most Technical Writers ranged between $35,520 and $91,720.

Employment Prospects

Many staff openings become available as Technical Writers retire, transfer to other positions, or leave the work-force. The job market for Technical Writers is expected to be strong through the coming years due to the continuing development of new technology and scientific discoveries. However, the rate of job growth is dependent on the health of the economy. For example, when the economy is in a downturn, there are fewer job openings and more layoffs for Technical Writers.

Advancement Prospects

Technical Writers can advance to supervisory and managerial positions as team leaders, project managers, and department supervisors. For many writers, their highest ambition is to become successful independent contractors.

Most Technical Writers realize advancement by earning higher incomes, receiving more complicated assignments, and being recognized for the quality of their work.

Education and Training

Employers normally require that Technical Writers possess at least a bachelor's degree, which may be in any field. Many Technical Writers hold a bachelor's or advanced degree in English, communications, engineering biology, chemistry, physics, computer science, or another related discipline.

Many Technical Writers complete technical writing or technical communication programs sponsored by colleges, universities, and professional societies.

Employers usually provide on-the-job training to entry-level employees.

Experience, Skills, and Personality Traits

Employers generally hire Technical Writers who have previous work experience related to the position for which they are applying. Many employers hire candidates without experience for entry-level positions as long as they have appropriate technical training or backgrounds in the subject matter about which they would be writing.

Along with having expert writing, research, and presentation skills, Technical Writers need strong computer skills, including the ability to use publishing, Web development, word-processing, and other software. These professionals also need effective interpersonal and teamwork skills, as they must be able to work well with many people from diverse backgrounds. In addition, these writers need excellent self-management skills.

Some personality traits that successful Technical Writers have in common are being creative, diplomatic, self-motivated, analytical, organized, flexible, and enthusiastic.

Unions and Associations

Many Technical Writers join professional associations to take advantage of networking opportunities, training programs, and other professional services and resources. Two national societies that serve their interests are the Society for Technical Communication and the National Writers Union. Technical Writers also join societies that serve their particular fields, such as the IEEE Professional Communication Society. For contact information on these organizations, see Appendix III.

Tips for Entry

1. To gain practical experience, consider working with temporary agencies.
2. Many Technical Writers learn about jobs through networking with colleagues.
3. Bring a portfolio of your work to your interviews to show prospective employers or clients.
4. Use the Internet to learn more about Technical Writers. To get a list of relevant Web sites to read, enter any of these keywords into a search engine: *technical writers, technical writing,* or *technical communication.* For some links, see Appendix IV.

SALES REPRESENTATIVE

CAREER PROFILE

Duties: Promote and sell products directly to customers in the field; build and maintain a customer base; perform duties as required

Alternate Title(s): Sales Engineer, Manufacturer's Agent; Pharmaceutical Sales Representative or other title that reflects a specific field

Salary Range: $33,000 to $122,000

Employment Prospects: Good

Advancement Prospects: Good

Prerequisites:

    Education or Training—A bachelor's or advanced degree in science, mathematics, or engineering discipline

    Experience—Several years of sales experience; technical background desirable

CAREER LADDER

Sales Manager

Senior Sales Representative

Junior Sales Representative

Special Skills and Personality Traits—Interpersonal, communication, leadership, organizational, problem-solving, self-management, math, and computer skills; pleasant, enthusiastic, trustworthy, diplomatic, persuasive, persistent, self-motivated, creative, and flexible; can handle rejection

Position Description

Sales Representatives of technical and scientific products are responsible for generating and increasing sales of products for manufacturers and wholesale distributors. They work in the field, promoting products directly to customers—which may be manufacturers, retail establishments, educational institutions, hospitals, government agencies, and other organizations. For example, Sales Representatives in the medical device industry might promote sales to hospitals, medical health centers, HMOs, physicians, and other health-care practitioners.

Sales Representatives are experts about the products that they sell. They are comfortable with discussing scientific concepts and using the technical language of their customers. Many Sales Representatives have technical training. Some of them, in fact, have switched from careers as research scientists, technologists, technicians, engineers, and health-care practitioners. Those with engineering backgrounds are sometimes known as sales engineers.

Sales Representatives are assigned to cover geographical regions, or territories, which may consist of several cities, counties, states, and even foreign countries. They are responsible for building up and maintaining a customer (or client) base within their territories. They are also expected to meet with a certain number of customers each day. To find new customers, Sales Representa-

tives follow up leads they obtain from customers, local chambers of commerce, professional and trade associations, and others.

Sales Representatives usually make their initial contact with prospective customers through phone calls or e-mails. They introduce themselves and their products, and schedule appointments to meet with them in person. Sales Representatives do research about potential customers before contacting them, so they can discuss how their products may meet the customers' needs. Meetings are usually brief. Sales Representatives show their products and demonstrate or explain how they can be useful to a customer's business.

Making a sale can take several weeks or months. Sales Representatives leave catalogs with their potential customers. These catalogs describe the products, including their prices, availability, and other attractive features. Sales Representatives may also give customers samples of their products to try out. Sales Representatives follow up their initial meetings with e-mails, phone calls, and additional visits.

For many Sales Representatives, their goal is to establish trusting, long-term relationships with customers for their repeat business. These sales professionals become familiar with their clients' needs and provide them with valuable information that may be useful for developing their businesses. Many Sales Representatives take customers out to lunch or dinner. Some of them occasionally entertain their customers at sports events or other entertainment venues.

Sales Representatives perform a wide range of duties. For example, they:

- schedule appointments with customers
- take sales orders as well as negotiate sales contracts
- help customers with problems regarding products and sales deliveries
- prepare sales reports, expense account forms, and other required paperwork
- attend company sales meetings to review sales performance and discuss sales goals
- participate in trade shows, professional conferences, and conventions to promote products and make new contacts
- monitor how well their competition is doing in sales
- keep up with new developments and technologies in their industries

Some Sales Representatives are responsible for installing products, training customers' employees, or providing maintenance service for products. Many Sales Representatives are involved in developing new products, marketing strategies, or promotional programs for their companies.

In some companies, Sales Representatives (without technical backgrounds) and subject-matter experts work together. The Sales Representatives perform the regular sales duties, while the experts describe the products, answer technical questions, and assist customers with any problems or concerns.

Some Sales Representatives work on a contractual basis as independent sales agents. They are hired either directly by the manufacturers themselves or by agencies known as manufacturers' agents firms. Independent sales agents often sell different, but complementary, product lines for two or more manufacturers within the industry.

Sales Representatives work long days and irregular hours. They arrange their own schedules, and often work in the evenings and on weekends to meet with customers. Most Sales Representatives frequently travel by automobile or airplane and sometimes stay away from home for several days or weeks at a time.

Salaries

Earnings for Sales Representatives vary, depending on various factors. These include an individual's qualifications, ambition, and sales ability; the type of employer and industry; the products or services being sold and the demand for them in a geographical location; and

the general well-being of the economy. Their earnings may also vary from year to year.

Sales Representatives may receive income based on salary, commission, or a combination of both salary and commission. The U.S. Bureau of Labor Statistics reports in its May 2006 *Occupational Employment Statistics* survey that the estimated annual salary for most Sales Representatives who sell technical and scientific products ranged between $33,410 and $121,850.

Many companies reward outstanding job performances with monetary bonuses and/or gifts such as free vacation trips. Sales Representatives may be reimbursed for such expenses as meals, lodging, transportation, and home office costs. Many employers provide Sales Representatives with company cars.

Employment Prospects

Scientific and technical Sales Representatives work in such industries as biotechnology, medical devices, pharmaceuticals, chemical processing, computer and data processing services, electrical goods, electronics, and industrial machinery and equipment. They may be employed by a company or a manufacturer's agent firm. Many are self-employed manufacturer's agents.

According to the May 2006 OES survey (by the BLS), 390,280 Sales Representatives were employed by wholesalers and manufacturers that sold technical and scientific products.

The employment of these Sales Representatives in general is expected to increase by 12 percent through 2016. In addition, opportunities will become available as professionals retire, transfer to other occupations, or leave the workforce for various reasons. Applicants can expect intense competition. Job applicants can expect intense competition.

Job prospects in sales depend upon the health of the economy, consumer preferences, and other factors. The demand for scientific and technical Sales Representatives varies by industry. Currently, the medical manufacturing and pharmaceutical industries are strong and job opportunities for Sales Representatives should remain steady for a number of years.

Advancement Prospects

Sales Representatives pursue advancement in various ways. Those interested in administrative and management responsibilities can advance to such positions as sales trainer, sales supervisor, branch manager, district manager, or vice president of sales. Sales Representatives who have entrepreneurial ambitions can become independent manufacturer's agents.

Many Sales Representatives measure their success by earning higher incomes, meeting or exceeding sales targets, receiving sales accounts or territories of their choice, and becoming top sales representatives for their firms.

Some Sales Representatives use their experience to pursue opportunities in marketing, advertising, purchasing, or consulting.

Education and Training

Employers generally require that scientific and technical Sales Representatives have a bachelor's degree, preferably in a science or engineering field. Some companies prefer to hire candidates with a master's degree in business administration. These candidates may not need an undergraduate degree in science, as long as they show an aptitude in science or a willingness to master scientific or technical subject matter. Some employers hire candidates who have no college degrees if they have qualifying sales experience.

Employers usually provide formal training programs for entry-level Sales Representatives, which includes classroom instruction on such topics as sales techniques, marketing, and presentation skills. They also provide technical instruction on the products being sold. New Sales Representatives receive on-the-job training, and work under the supervision of senior representatives for several months before being allowed to work independently.

Experience, Skills, and Personality Traits

The ideal candidate for Sales Representatives of scientific and technical products is someone with several years of sales experience and related background knowledge in science, health, or engineering. Employers are also willing to hire scientists, engineers, and health professionals without sales experience as well as experienced sales people without any technical background if they show enthusiasm and a strong desire to succeed.

In order to generate new business and keep clients, Sales Representatives must have superior interpersonal and communication skills. Additionally, they need effective leadership, organizational, and problem-solving skills, as well as strong self-management skills, such as being able to work independently; manage multiple tasks; handle stressful situations; meet appointments; and manage time efficiently. Having adequate math and computer skills is also necessary.

Some personality traits that successful Sales Representatives share are being pleasant, enthusiastic, trustworthy, diplomatic, persuasive, persistent, self-motivated, creative, and flexible. Further, Sales Representatives are thick-skinned—as they must be able to handle rejections that come with the job.

Unions and Associations

Professional associations for scientific and technical Sales Representatives are available at the state, regional, and national levels. These societies offer professional services and resources such as education programs, professional, certification, and networking opportunities. A few examples of different national societies are the Agricultural and Industrial Manufacturers Representatives Association, the Electronics Representatives Association International, and the National Association of Medical Sales Representatives. In addition, scientific and technical Sales Representatives might join the National Association of Sales Professionals, which serves sales professionals in all industries. For contact information for these groups, see Appendix III.

Tips for Entry

1. As a high school student, see if working in the sales field might interest you. For example, you might get a part-time job as a sales clerk or volunteer in a fund-raising activity for your school.
2. Many Sales Representatives have found their jobs through word-of-mouth.
3. Job applicants should be prepared to go through several job interviews with a company, which may entail accompanying Sales Representatives on their rounds.
4. Take advantage of the Internet in your search for a Sales Representative position. You can find job listings as well as information about the companies where you would like to work. To learn if a company has a Web site, enter its name in a search engine.

ENTREPRENEURSHIP

ENTREPRENEUR
(SCIENCE AND TECHNOLOGY)

Duties: Start up and manage new business venture; perform duties as required

Alternate Title(s): Business Owner

Salary Range: $0 to $1,000,000+

Employment Prospects: Good

Advancement Prospects: Fair

Prerequisites:

Education or Training—Business training

Experience—Years of experience in the area and industry of the new business venture

Special Skills and Personality Traits—Leadership, management, problem-solving, communication, presentation, writing, interpersonal, and teamwork skills; bold enterprising, foresighted, creative, innovative, optimistic, persistent, confident, flexible, and self-motivated

Special Requirements—Professional licensure may be required; business licenses required

CAREER LADDER

Business Owner

Entrepreneur

Scientist, Engineer, or Other Science/Technology Professional

Position Description

Many scientists and others working in science and technology reach a point in their careers when they want to be their own boss. They decide to become an Entrepreneur. They have ideas for products or services that they strongly believe would fill a need in certain markets and be profitable. Thus, they are willing to take the risks involved in starting up a new manufacturing company, wholesale establishment, retail firm, or service (business that offers professional expertise and time to perform specific tasks).

To determine whether their proposed ventures are feasible, Entrepreneurs first conduct research. They perform market studies to get an idea of how their target audiences would accept their products or services. They learn about their competition—who they are, how the Entrepreneur's business would be similar and different from the competition, and so on. In addition, Entrepreneurs gather information to help them determine how to structure their business, what kind of facilities they would need, the types of employees they would need, and how much it would cost to start up their venture. Entrepreneurs also consult lawyers, accountants, business advisers, and successful business owners for help and advice.

Establishing new businesses requires much careful planning and decision making by Entrepreneurs. They address various legal issues. If they will be starting a business with other people, they draw up a business contract that formally defines the nature of their partnership. Entrepreneurs also decide on the best legal form—such as solo proprietorship, corporation, or limited liability company—for their business enterprise. Entrepreneurs may choose to form a board of directors to provide advice and guidance over their businesses. (Boards of directors are legally required to be formed for corporations.)

Entrepreneurs obtain all licenses and permits required by local, state, and federal governments for their type of business. Entrepreneurs who plan to sell products that they themselves have invented or created make sure that their exclusive rights to manufacture, use, and sell those products are protected. They obtain patents for inventions from the U.S. Patent and Trademark Office (USPTO). For creative works, such as books and software, Entrepreneurs formally register their copyrights with the U.S. Copyright Office.

Furthermore, Entrepreneurs are responsible for finding the means to finance their ventures. They might borrow money from themselves, friends, or family members. They might take out business loans from local banks or apply for business grants from government programs. They might also raise money through venture capitalists, who invest money in businesses in exchange for part ownership.

Entrepreneurs prepare business plans, or formal statements, about their proposed ventures. (These are important tools for securing funding for their enterprises.) In these business plans, Entrepreneurs describe the products or services they plan to sell, who their markets and competitors are, and why their products or services are unique or better than the competition. Entrepreneurs also outline how they plan to operate their business. In addition, they provide financial projections for the first few years as well as describe their marketing and sales strategies.

Once their business is up and running, Entrepreneurs now take on another role. As chief executive officers, they handle the overall direction and management of their businesses. Some of their responsibilities entail:

- planning and coordinating operational activities, including human resources, finance, accounting, facilities management, information technology, and marketing
- formulating policies and procedures that pertain to the general operations and various divisions
- hiring and training managers, professionals, technical staff, office staff, and other personnel
- making sure all bills and taxes are paid
- troubleshooting problems as they arise in any aspect of their business
- promoting their business by joining and networking with trade associations, local chambers of commerce, and other organizations

Most Entrepreneurs are involved in performing professional duties. For example, they might develop software products, conduct scientific research, or provide consulting services. As their businesses grow, many business owners find themselves focusing solely on management responsibilities.

Some experts say that it generally takes between three to 10 years for businesses to establish themselves in their markets and begin earning profits. Once their business has achieved their goals, Entrepreneurs often seek new challenges. Many Entrepreneurs become involved in acquiring other companies or investing their money in start-up ventures. Some Entrepreneurs sell their businesses and establish new ones to offer totally different products or services to the same markets or to venture into different markets.

Building a successful business takes hard work and dedication. Entrepreneurs typically work long hours each day, and often work six to seven days a week.

Salaries

Annual incomes vary yearly for Entrepreneurs. They can earn as little as nothing or as much as millions of dollars or more. It is also common for Entrepreneurs to lose money during their first years in operation.

Entrepreneurs may receive salaries as executive officers, top-level managers, or consultants from their companies.

Employment Prospects

Many businesses open and close each year. According to the U.S. Small Business Administration (SBA), there were approximately 671,800 new firms and about 544,800 business closures in the United States in 2005. (Note: Not all closures were due to failure.)

Entrepreneurial opportunities in science and technology are readily available for those individuals ready and willing to take advantage of them. Since the 1990s, new technology advancements and scientific discoveries have stimulated the establishment of many start-up companies in information technology (computers, software, semiconductors, communications equipment, and communications services), biotechnology, pharmaceuticals, medical technologies, and health care-related products.

Advancement Prospects

In general, Entrepreneurs measure their progress by achieving their business goals and objectives. For example, business owners might strive to earn a certain income or obtain contracts with specific clients or complete certain research and development projects by the end of a fiscal year. Entrepreneurs also gauge success through job satisfaction and recognition from their peers for their entrepreneurial talents and skills.

Education and Training

Entrepreneurs need basic business training, whether formal or informal, to succeed well in their ventures. Scientists can learn necessary skills through entrepreneurship courses offered by community colleges, university extension programs, and professional associations. In addition, many books, magazines, and Web sites about starting businesses are available. Also, many universities offer MBA (master's in business administration) programs specifically designed for scientists and engineers, in which they learn the basics of business tools such as balance sheets and market research.

Special Requirements

Entrepreneurs who offer services to the public may be required to hold appropriate professional licensure.

For example, geologists, hydrologists, and soil scientists may be required to be licensed or registered in the states where they practice.

As business operators, Entrepreneurs obtain appropriate local and state business licenses. For specific information about business licenses, contact the local (city or county) government administrative office in the city where you plan to operate your business.

Experience, Skills, and Personality Traits

Entrepreneurs typically start businesses in industries in which they have many years of experience. They are highly knowledgeable about the products and services that their new ventures offer.

Some skills that Entrepreneurs need to succeed are leadership, management, and problem-solving skills. They also need effective communication, presentation, and writing skills as well as excellent interpersonal and teamwork skills. Successful Entrepreneurs have several personality traits in common. Foremost, they are bold, enterprising, and foresighted. In addition, they are creative, innovative, optimistic, persistent, confident, flexible, and self-motivated.

Unions and Associations

Many business owners belong to trade and professional associations to take advantage of networking opportunities, training programs, and other valuable resources and services.

Professional associations for science and technical Entrepreneurs are available in some localities to serve the interests of those living in a particular region.

Tips for Entry

1. Many research universities and other organizations sponsor business incubation programs that help scientists start up and develop their businesses. These programs (sometimes called incubators) offer business and technical support services, assistance with finding finances, office space, shared office services, and so forth. You can learn more about incubators at the National Business Incubation Association Web site, http://www.nbia.org.

2. The U.S. Small Business Administration (SBA) offers various resources for entrepreneurs. To access its Web site, go to http://www.sba.gov. To learn about programs aimed at science and technical entrepreneurs, visit the SBA Office of Technology Web site at http://www.sba.gov/sbir.

3. Learn more about entrepreneurship on the Internet. One Web site you might visit is the "Small Business" section of *Wall Street Journal Online* at http://online.wsj.com/small-business. For more links, see Appendix IV.

MANAGEMENT CONSULTANT

Position Description

The ability to solve problems, create new ideas, and provide advice and suggestions are the services that Management Consultants offer their clients. They provide business advice to private corporations, from start-up companies to established multinational companies. Many Management Consultants also offer services to government agencies, nonprofit institutions, foreign governments, and other organizations.

Management Consultants may be independent contractors or salaried workers for a management consulting firm, accounting firm, or other business consulting company. Because they are not part of their clients' work-force, Management Consultants are able to remain objective and not be influenced by company politics.

Companies hire Management Consultants to handle a wide range of projects, such as:

- developing strategies for entering new marketplaces or remaining competitive within existing markets
- advising clients about merging, buying, and selling companies
- corporate restructuring
- improving some aspects of their operations such as production, marketing, human resources, and information systems

Some Management Consultants are generalists. They address any type of problem in any industry. Some consultants choose to specialize in specific industries such as health care, nonprofit organizations, biotechnology, or information technology. Others specialize in particular functions, such as organizational strategies, human resources, financial services, sales, or high-tech operations.

Management Consultants are assigned to projects in which they work closely with the clients' managers. With most projects, consultants follow a similar process. They begin by assessing their clients' situation and identifying the specific problems they must tackle. They then conduct research, which includes collecting appropriate client data, such as annual revenues or employment records. They interview executive officers, managers, and other employees within the organizations. Consultants also seek information from external sources such as government agencies and trade associations. Some consultants devise diagnostic surveys and market studies to gather data.

Consultants next analyze and interpret the data to develop solutions to their clients' problems. They use such tools as spreadsheets and mathematical models to gain insight into the problems. Consultants take into account such factors as the nature of an organization, its internal structure, its competition, and market trends as they prepare their recommendations.

Management Consultants submit reports of their findings and recommendations in written or oral form. Clients sometimes retain Management Consultants to help implement the suggestions they have made.

Management Consultants may work on two or more cases at a time. Depending on the projects, they might work independently or with other consultants.

Most Management Consultants are involved in business development. They continually seek out new clients. For example, they might make presentations to potential clients or promote their firms at professional conferences and trade shows. In addition, Management Consultants maintain relationships with existing clients for repeat business.

Management Consultants may be responsible for preparing proposals for prospective work, which describe how consulting firms plan to handle projects. (Companies usually solicit proposals from several firms for projects, and choose the proposal that best suits their needs.) Experienced consultants often perform supervisory, project management, and client relations duties.

Management Consultants typically work long hours, as much as 50 to 60 hours or more per week. Most consultants travel frequently, as they go and work at the clients' work sites, which may be in another city, state, or country. Consultants often spend several weeks or months away from home in order to complete their projects.

Salaries

Salaries for Management Consultants vary, depending on such factors as their education, experience, employer, and geographic location. Partners in top consulting firms can expect to earn six-figure annual incomes. Many firms also reward their employees with monetary bonuses for work performance.

Specific salary information for Management Consultants is unavailable. However, their earnings are similar to management analysts. According to the May 2006 *Occupational Employment Statistics* by the U.S. Bureau of Labor Statistics (BLS), the estimated annual salary for most management analysts ranged from $39,840 to $128,330. The estimated annual mean wage for those who worked in the management, scientific, and technical consulting industry was $91,150.

Employment Prospects

Management Consultants find employment with large and small management consulting firms. Some firms provide services to corporations in all industries, while others specialize in particular industries (such

as biotechnology) or specific functions (such as human resources). Some management consulting firms are affiliated with accounting firms, computer software companies, or technology firms. Government agencies also employ Management Consultants, known as management analysts. Furthermore, many Management Consultants are independent contractors.

The job outlook for Management Consultants should be steady over the long term, as organizations rely on outside help to improve their performance. However, the rate of job growth is dependent on the health of the economy. When the economy is on a downturn, there are fewer job openings and more layoffs in consulting firms.

According to the BLS, job growth is expected to grow in large consulting firms with international expertise and in smaller firms that specialize in biotechnology, health care, information technology, engineering, human resources, and other specific areas.

The competition is keen for entry-level as well as experienced positions. Because of the high salaries, prestige, and independent nature of this occupation, many college graduates and professionals are attracted to the job.

Advancement Prospects

Depending on their education and experience, Management Consultants begin their careers at the research associate or junior consultant level. They rise through the ranks as consultants, project managers, and partners. To advance in some firms, research associates may need to obtain further education.

Many Management Consultants use their positions as stepping stones to obtain top management positions in companies, investment banks, or venture capital firms. Those with entrepreneurial ambitions become independent consultants or start their own consulting firms.

Education and Training

Firms hire entry-level candidates with a bachelor's or advanced degree. Those with a bachelor's degree are typically hired for research associate positions, while candidates with a master's or doctoral degree are hired to junior consultant positions. For Management Consultant positions, many employers require that candidates hold a master's in business administration and/or a doctorate in a science, engineering, or social science discipline.

Employers typically provide Management Consultants with formal training programs and on-the-job training. Some firms put new hires who are Ph.D. graduates, scientists, engineers, and others with nonbusiness backgrounds through intense business training that last several weeks or months.

Experience, Skills, and Personality Traits

Consulting firms generally seek candidates who have business or industry experience. They hire college graduates, MBA's, and Ph.D.'s as well as professionals who have worked several years in their field. Many Management Consultants have switched to consulting from a career in finance, business, actuarial science, life science, chemistry, physics, or engineering.

Employers seek candidates who demonstrate excellent analytical, problem-solving, communication, and writing skills. In addition, they show strong presentation, interpersonal, and leadership skills. Furthermore, prospective consultants need effective computer and quantitative skills.

Being self-motivated, creative, tenacious, poised, curious, energetic, enthusiastic hardworking, and passionate are some personality traits that successful Management Consultants share.

Unions and Associations

Management Consultants might join local, state, or national societies to take advantage of professional services such as education programs and networking opportunities. Some national associations that consultants might belong to are the Institute of Management Consultants USA, Inc., the Professional and Technical Consultants Association, or the American Association of Healthcare Consultants. For contact information, see Appendix III.

Tips for Entry

1. Although a consulting job may be years away, you can begin preparing yourself now. You might enroll in, or audit, business courses. Read business books and publications, such as the *Wall Street Journal* and *Business Week*. Check out Web sites of consulting firms and talk with management consultants.

2. Contact the consulting firms where you would like to work to learn about their job openings. Also meet with your networking contacts to learn about current and possible upcoming vacancies. In addition, check with college career counseling centers for leads.

3. Consulting firms usually require their prospective job candidates to be interviewed several times by different staff members. One such interview is called the *case interview* in which candidates are given one or more mock business problems to solve. This allows firms to evaluate candidates' problem solving and communication skills as well as their understanding of basic business principles.

4. Use the Internet to learn more about Management Consultants. To get a list of relevant Web sites, enter the keywords *management consultant* or *management consulting* in a search engine. For some links, see Appendix IV.

TECHNOLOGY LICENSING ASSOCIATE

Special Skills and Personality Traits—Leadership, program management, research, marketing, writing, negotiation, communication, networking, interpersonal, and teamwork skills; self-motivated, discreet, diplomatic, ethical, creative, detail-oriented, and entrepreneurial

Position Description

In the academic world, scientists generally conduct research for the purpose of gaining further knowledge and understanding in their areas of interest. Many of the discoveries and technologies made in these academic laboratories have been further developed by companies to produce commercial products and services—such as pharmaceutical drugs, medical treatments, horticultural plants, food processing systems, educational software, Internet search engines, wireless services, energy-efficient appliances, construction materials, alternative fuels, crime lab equipment, and groundwater remediation technologies.

Academicians—faculty and students—are encouraged to license their innovations to private industry for the benefit of consumers as well as for their universities and the overall economy. The formal process of assigning the rights to their inventions to private companies is known as technology transfer. Professionals called Technology Licensing Associates are employed by American research universities to help faculty members and students protect their intellectual property rights and to find companies that are interested in licensing their technologies for commercial development.

Technology Licensing Associates work in an entrepreneurial spirit as they seek to develop successful partnerships between university researchers and private companies. Their job requires them to have a broad technical background and be knowledgeable in areas of business and law, including marketing, investments, contractual agreements, negotiations, patents, and intellectual property issues.

These technology transfer professionals generally cover scientific, engineering, mathematical, or medical areas in which they have expertise and backgrounds. They work closely with university scientists to recognize their research interests and accomplishments, as well as to identify new technologies emerging from research that may appeal to private industries. These specialists are also assigned a caseload of technologies to manage, in which they follow each invention through the phases from conception to commercialization.

For each assigned technology, these professionals are responsible for determining if it has the potential to be a consumable product or service. They decide if the innovation can be patented, and assist in the patent application process. A patent is a legal document that protects the property rights of invention owners to sell, use, or import their inventions exclusively. Parties who wish to utilize or sell patent holders' inventions must first obtain their permission. (The U.S. Office of Patents and Trademarks has the authority to grant patents in the United States.)

Another major responsibility of these technology transfer specialists is identifying companies that would be interested in licensing the various technologies within their portfolios. They actively market to potential corporate candidates, which involves providing them with concise and comprehensive written information about the innovations and meeting with them for further discussion.

In addition, Technology Licensing Associates assist in preparing confidentially, licensing, and other contractual agreements between researchers and interested companies. They also shepherd agreements through the negotiation and execution process. Some of them assist with the actual negotiation of royalties and other contractual terms and conditions. Furthermore, these technology transfer specialists are responsible for managing the license agreements and overseeing the business relationships among the researchers and universities and the private companies.

Technology Licensing Associates work in office settings under the guidance and instruction of technology transfer directors. Each workday is varied as they perform a variety of tasks, such as:

- developing and implementing commercialization strategies
- reviewing information about new innovations to determine the feasibility of commercializing them
- monitoring the progress of patent applications
- preparing marketing information about their assigned technologies
- developing plans for the transfer of technology to established firms or start-up companies
- advising researchers, university administrators, and corporate representatives about intellectual property policies and issues
- gathering information about patents, technologies, markets, or other matters through literature, computer databases, Internet sources, and interviews
- using computers to monitor the status of patent applications, contractual agreements, and other documents related to their assigned technologies
- making sure procedures and contracts are in compliance with university policies and rules as well as with appropriate laws and regulations
- preparing correspondence, reports, and contractual agreements

- maintaining up-to-date records, logs, and files
- attending meetings with scientists, attorneys, financial experts, university administrators, corporate representatives, technology transfer colleagues, or others
- supervising subordinates, student interns, or administrative staff
- assisting with the daily administrative operations of their offices

Technology Licensing Associates work a standard 40-hour schedule. When needed, they put in additional hours to complete their various duties, which may require working evenings and on weekends.

Salaries

Salaries for Technology Licensing Associates vary, depending on their education, experience, employer, and other factors. Salary information for this occupation is unavailable. An idea of their incomes may be gained by looking at the earnings of similar occupations. According to the May 2006 *Occupational Employment Statistics* survey by the U.S. Bureau of Labor Statistics, the estimated annual salary ranged between $30,620 and $95,890 for most professionals in the category of business and financial operations occupations.

Employment Prospects

In addition to working for research universities, technology licensing specialists are employed by federal laboratories, research institutes, and other nonprofit organizations. Mid- to large-sized private companies also hire these technology transfer professionals. In addition, these specialists find employment with firms that offer technology transfer services to private companies and nonprofit organizations.

Since the enactment of the 1980 Bayh-Dole Act, there has been a rapid growth in technology transfer, particularly among research universities. (This legislation, cosponsored by U.S. senators Birch Bayh and Robert Dole, enabled nonprofit research organizations to own and patent inventions that were developed under federal grants.) Almost all American research universities have established a technology transfer office, staffed with as few as three members or less and as many as 15 members or more.

The technology transfer field is a young field. In general, opportunities for technology licensing specialists become available as professionals transfer to other positions or occupations, or leave the workforce for various reasons. Employers will create additional jobs to meet growing needs as long as funding is available.

Advancement Prospects

As Technology Licensing Associates gain experience and higher skill levels, they are assigned more complex responsibilities. They also advance through job satisfaction and by earning higher salaries. Managerial and administrative opportunities are also available.

These university professionals may also choose to pursue technology transfer careers in private industry or in the federal government or other nonprofit organizations.

Education and Training

In general, employers seek candidates who possess master's or doctoral degrees in science, mathematics, or engineering disciplines. Some employers prefer to hire candidates who possess master's in business administration degrees or law degrees. Employers may choose candidates with bachelor's degrees if they have several years of qualifying experience. Candidates should have the proper scientific or technical training in the subject areas in which they would be working.

Many Technology Licensing Associates learn their skills on the job, while working under the supervision and guidance of experienced technology transfer professionals. Some universities offer internship or post-doctoral fellowship programs in technology transfer that provide participants with basic training.

Throughout their careers, Technology Licensing Associates enroll in continuing education and training programs to update their skills and keep up with advancements in their fields.

Experience, Special Skills, and Personality Traits

Employers hire candidates with different backgrounds, depending on their particular needs. For example, employers might prefer to hire attorneys, business professionals, marketing specialists, or scientists with experience in specific research areas. In general, employers seek candidates who have a strong science background and who are knowledgeable about such business and law areas as business development, marketing, contracts, and intellectual property. Having previous experience in technology transfer is desirable.

To perform well at this job, Technology Licensing Associates need strong leadership, program management, research, marketing, writing, and negotiation skills. They also need excellent communication, networking, interpersonal, and teamwork skills, as they must work well with many people from diverse backgrounds. Being self-motivated, discreet, diplomatic, ethical, creative, detail-oriented, and entrepreneurial are some personality traits that successful Technology Licensing Associates share.

Unions and Associations

Technology Licensing Associates can join professional associations to take advantage of networking opportunities, continuing education, and other professional services and resources. Some national societies that serve their interests are the Association of University Technology Managers, Licensing Executives Society International, and the Technology Transfer Society. For contact information, see Appendix III.

Tips for Entry

1. Visit the technology transfer office at your school and talk with staff members about your interest in learning about their work. Also find out if an internship or part-time position is available.

2. As a student, join a professional association that is involved in the technology transfer field. Attend conferences and meetings to network with professionals, and take advantage of seminars and workshops that the organization might sponsor.

3. Use the Internet to learn more about the technology transfer field. You might start by visiting the Web site of the Association of University Technology Managers. Its URL is http://www.autm.net. For more links, see Appendix IV.

EDUCATION AND COMMUNICATIONS

SCHOOLTEACHER

Position Description

Schoolteachers instruct students in grades kindergarten through 12 (K–12). Two of the core subjects for the K–12 curriculum are science and mathematics. Science teachers instruct basic concepts and skills in life science, physical science, and earth science. Math teachers instruct fundamental concepts and skills in arithmetic, geometry, and algebra.

Schoolteachers work in public, private, and independent institutions. Private establishments include boarding schools, day schools, military schools, and parochial schools (those that are affiliated with a religious denomination). Independent schools are also private, but they are not part of other organizations; they have their own board of trustees and develop their own source of funding.

In most school systems, the grades are divided into three levels: elementary school, middle school, and high school. Elementary schools may be configured as grades K to three, K to five, K to six, or K to eight. Elementary school teachers are usually responsible for teaching one class of children in all core subjects—math, science, language arts, and social science. Some teachers also provide instruction in computer skills, art, music, and physical education to their students. In many elementary schools, teaching specialists come in once or twice a week to teach those subjects.

The middle-level schools may be organized as either middle schools or junior schools. Most middle schools are made up of either grades five to eight or six to eight. Typically, teams of two to four middle school teachers are assigned to a class of students (for example, 80 students) at the same grade level. The team is responsible for the instruction of the four core subjects. Each teacher is responsible for teaching one or more subjects. For example, in a two-member team, one might teach math and science while the other teaches language arts and social studies. The exploratory classes—art, music, physical education, foreign language, health, and so on—are taught by specialists.

In some elementary schools and middle schools, science classes are taught by science teaching specialists. They may teach science to different grades in one school or travel to several schools during the week. In addition to teaching classes, science specialists act as resource teachers in the schools they serve. They help other teachers develop and plan science lessons for their classes.

Junior high schools are organized similar to high schools. They may consist of grades seven and eight or seven to nine, while high schools may be composed of grades nine to ten or ten to twelve. The school day is divided into several class periods and students rotate from class to class. Science and math teachers are specialists in their subject matter, and teach science or math to students in different grade levels.

Schoolteachers create daily lesson plans for their classes, following school curriculum guidelines. A lesson plan outlines what the teacher shall teach, including the concepts and skills to be taught, the purpose of the lesson, the learning objectives, the teaching methods, and the exercises and activities that shall reinforce learning.

Teachers prepare lessons by studying topics, gathering teaching materials, creating student materials, and setting up demonstrations or experiments. To help reinforce instruction, teachers use films, slides, videotapes, and other audiovisual equipment. Many teachers supplement instruction by having students work with computer programs and access the Internet during the class period. Science and math teachers also plan field trips to science museums, zoos, environmental centers, and similar venues.

Schoolteachers' days involve various activities. They take attendance, collect homework, review the previous day's lessons, present new lessons through lecture, demonstration, and modeling. Teachers check students' understanding of concepts and skills with written and oral exercises, quizzes, or tests and assign class work, homework, and projects. Schoolteachers also act as mentors to their students.

Schoolteachers are responsible for monitoring students' academic progress. They maintain a record book of students' test scores and grades for class assignments. At the end of each grading period, teachers evaluate their students' work and assign grades for their performance.

In many public schools, special education students— children with learning, emotional, and physical disabilities—are assigned to general education classrooms. Special education students each have an Individualized Education Program (IEP) that outlines the instructional goals and objectives that teachers are required to follow. When needed, they consult with special education teachers for assistance in implementing IEPs.

Schoolteachers have many other tasks, which vary with grade level. They might hold parent conferences, coach sports, advise school clubs, supervise schoolgrounds during recesses, or oversee school functions. Schoolteachers also participate in faculty meetings.

Schoolteachers work beyond the regular school day, and often complete their tasks (making lesson plans, calling parents, grading papers, etc.) during evenings and on weekends. Many schools are in session from September to June. Some schools have year-round sessions.

Salaries

Salaries for Schoolteachers vary and depend on such factors as their education, experience, employer, and geographic location. The U.S. Bureau of Labor Statistics (BLS) reports in its May 2006 *Occupational Employment Statistics* (OES) survey the following estimated salaries for most public and private schoolteachers: elementary school teachers, $30,370 to $72,720; middle school teachers, $31,450 to $73,350; secondary school teachers, $31,760 to $76,100.

In some schools, teachers can earn extra pay for coaching, being class advisers, sponsoring extracurricular activities, teaching summer school, or performing other jobs.

Employment Prospects

According to the BLS's May 2006 OES survey, approximately 3,192,660 elementary, middle, and secondary school teachers were employed by public and private schools in the United States. (This count excludes special education and vocational school teachers.) The BLS reports that the employment of Schoolteachers is expected to increase by 12 percent through 2016. In addition to job growth, teachers will be needed to fill vacancies as elementary, middle, and high school teachers, retire, transfer to other jobs, or leave the teaching field for other careers. Within the next several years, a large number of teachers throughout the nation are becoming eligible for retirement.

Teaching opportunities vary from region to region as well as from community to community. Jobs are more readily available in inner cities and rural areas. Opportunities are also favorable in the western states where the highest levels of student enrollment are expected to occur.

Many experts express alarm about a potential shortage of math and science teachers in the coming years. Some experts say there are an insufficient number of newly trained teachers to cover the number of retiring teachers. The greater concern, however, is a low supply of qualified teachers to replace those who decide to leave the field within their first few years in the classroom due to job dissatisfaction, low salaries, or other reasons.

Advancement Prospects

In most public school systems, teachers receive tenure after completing three to five years of continuous teaching service. With tenure, teachers cannot be fired from their jobs without just cause.

With further education and licensure, Schoolteachers can become counselors, librarians, curriculum specialists, school psychologists, or other school-related professionals.

Schoolteachers can also advance to positions in school administration. With additional education and licensure, public school teachers can become school principals and district administrators. In private and independent schools, teachers can work their way up to higher positions as school head, division head, or dean of students.

Education and Training

The minimum requirement to become Schoolteachers in most schools is a bachelor's degree. However many Schoolteachers hold a master's degree. Elementary and middle school teachers usually hold a degree in liberal studies. Middle school teachers may have a degree in other fields as long as they have completed the required course work to teach one or more core subjects. Junior high and high school teachers need at least a bachelor's degree in the primary subject that they are teaching.

All state-licensed teachers must complete an accredited teacher education program that includes a supervised field practicum.

In many schools, beginning teachers are assigned mentor teachers who advise them with curriculum development, and classroom management. Throughout their careers, Schoolteachers attend workshops, seminars, and courses to update their teaching skills as well as their knowledge about the subject matters that they teach.

Special Requirements

To teach in public schools, Schoolteachers must have valid teaching credentials. Elementary school teachers possess elementary education credentials. Middle school teachers hold elementary education, secondary education, or middle-grade credentials, depending on the requirements of their states. Junior high and high school teachers hold secondary education credentials with endorsements in the subjects that they teach.

Licensure requirements vary from state to state. (For specific information, contact the state board of education where you wish to teach.) Public school teachers may need to complete continuing education units and, eventually, a master's degree for licensure renewal.

Many private schools require teacher certification from the state board of education, a school accreditation group, or another recognized organization. Some schools, require internal certifications, which are obtained after completing their training programs.

Experience, Skills, and Personality Traits

Entry-level Schoolteachers usually have previous teaching experience as student teachers, substitute teachers, or teacher's aides. Many private and independent schools look for candidates who also have a strong background in sports, drama, community service, or other extracurricular activities.

To work with students, staff, and parents, Schoolteachers need excellent communication, teamwork, and interpersonal skills. Additionally, they need strong management and organization skills to complete their many different tasks each day. Successful Schoolteachers share several personality traits, such as being creative, enthusiastic, dependable, flexible, fair, patient, caring, and tolerant.

Unions and Associations

Various professional associations at the local, state, and national levels are available to Schoolteachers. They offer such professional services and resources as education programs, teacher resources, and networking opportunities. Some societies that serve the interests of science and math teachers are:

- National Council of Teachers of Mathematics
- National Science Teachers Association
- American Association of Physics Teachers
- National Association of Biology Teachers
- National Earth Science Teachers Association
- International Technology Education Association

Most public school teachers belong to either of these teacher unions: the American Federation of Teachers or the National Education Association. See Appendix III for contact information for the above organizations.

Tips for Entry

1. Gain experience working with children at the age level that you would like to teach. For example, you might tutor science or math students; work with children or youth groups; or volunteer at zoos, science museums, nature centers, or other institutions that offer children programs.

2. An alternative path for teacher licensure is available for those who prefer to obtain their credentials by teaching full time in classrooms under the supervision of certified educators. To learn more, contact your state board of education or school district office.

3. Submit an application even if jobs are not currently available. Call back from time to time to learn the status of your application.

4. To enhance their employability, some teachers voluntarily obtain certification from the National Board for Professional Teaching Standards. For more information, visit its Web site at http://www.nbpts.org.

5. Use the Internet to learn more about teaching science and mathematics. Two Web sites you might visit are the National Science Teachers Association, http://www.nsta.org; and the National Council of Teachers of Mathematics, http://www.nctm.org. For more links, see Appendix IV.

PROFESSOR

Duties: Provide instruction in science, mathematics, or engineering in colleges and universities; perform duties as required

Alternate Title(s): Lecturer, Instructor; a title that reflects a teaching specialty, such as Botany Professor or Professor of Mathematics

Salary Range: $32,000 to $146,000

Employment Prospects: Good

Advancement Prospects: Fair

Prerequisites:

Education or Training—Master's or doctoral degree in a math or science discipline

Experience—Teaching experience needed; research background may be required

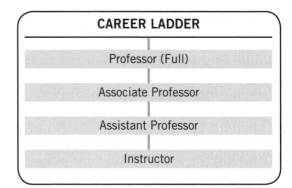

Special Skills and Personality Traits—Communication, presentation, interpersonal, teamwork, social, organization, and management skills; independent, adaptable, curious, flexible, and creative

Position Description

Many scientists and mathematicians are employed as Professors in two-year colleges, four-year colleges, universities, and medical schools. Their primary role is to teach and advise students as they complete their educational objectives in pursuit of their future careers as scientists, mathematicians, engineers, technologists, technicians, and educators. In addition, many Professors are involved in conducting basic and applied research that lead to important scientific discoveries and inventions that benefit society. Depending on the college setting, Professors may be responsible for just teaching or for a combination of teaching and conducting research.

Two-year colleges are also known as community colleges, junior colleges, or technical colleges. These colleges serve the educational needs of local communities and provide training for local professions, businesses, industry, and government agencies. Science and math professors teach courses that fulfill general education requirements that lead to associate degrees or occupational certificates. (General education courses in community colleges usually fulfill lower undergraduate requirements in four-year institutions.) Community college professors rarely are required to conduct research.

In four-year colleges and universities, Professors teach undergraduate as well as graduate students. Those in small liberal arts colleges focus primarily on teaching while professors at research universities divide their time among such responsibilities as teaching, conducting research, and producing scholarly works for publication.

Professors are part of a department or division that corresponds to their subject or field (such as physical geography, animal science, or bioinformatics). For each term, they are assigned to teach courses that are part of a prescribed curriculum. For example, a math professor at a community college might teach basic arithmetic, finite mathematics, geometry, and applied mathematics for the spring semester.

For each of their courses, Professors develop a course syllabus that outlines the topics to be taught as well as bibliographies for outside reading assignments. They are also responsible for preparing lectures and laboratory experiments. Depending on the course, Professors might lecture to hundreds of students in large halls, supervise students in laboratories, or lead small seminar discussions. Some Professors teach courses on cable or closed-circuit television as well as via the Internet.

Professors perform a wide range of duties, which vary daily. Some general tasks include preparing lectures, reading and critiquing student papers, creating examinations, grading tests, and performing administrative tasks. Professors are required to hold regular office hours to meet with students and advise them on academic and career matters. They also supervise students with their research projects. At large universities, teaching assistants are usually available to help Professors with administering exams, grading exams, and leading discussion sections.

Professors participate in faculty meetings where they make decisions on curriculum, equipment purchases, hiring, and other departmental matters. Professors also serve on academic and administrative advisory committees which deal with institutional policies. Additionally, they perform community service, such as providing consultation services to community agencies, nonprofit organizations, corporations, government agencies, and other institutions. Many Professors serve on committees, panels, or commissions established by government agencies.

Research professors conduct studies in areas that interest them. Some research projects are conducted in collaboration with colleagues within their discipline as well as from other disciplines. Professors are responsible for obtaining funds for their research projects, which pay for research equipment and supplies, travel to research sites, overhead costs, financial support for themselves and their research assistants, and so on. Furthermore, Professors are expected to have the results of their research published in scholarly journals, books, or electronic media.

Professors have flexible hours that may include teaching courses every day or every other day as well as teaching classes at night or on weekends. They typically put in 40 or more hours per week to teach courses, hold office hours, prepare for classes, grade papers and exams, conduct research, participate in meetings, and so on.

In recent years, colleges and universities have been hiring adjunct instructors to teach general education courses. Adjunct instructors teach one to three courses for an institution. They have limited administrative and student advising duties. Many are not given office space, so they spend little time on campus. Many part-time instructors teach at more than one institution in different parts of a city, county, or region. Some also teach courses for extension programs in community colleges, colleges, or universities.

Salaries

Salaries for Professors vary, and depend on such factors as their experience, education, academic institution, and geographic location. The U.S. Bureau of Labor Statistics (BLS) reports, in its May 2006 *Occupational Employment Statistics* survey, the following estimated salaries for most Professors in these disciplines:

- agricultural science—$41,440 to $118,180
- biological sciences—$37,620 to $145,600

- chemistry—$36,160 to $116,910
- computer science—$32,130 to $108,780
- environmental science—$32,890 to $119,260
- geography—$34,300 to $98,200
- geoscience (or earth sciences)—$37,330 to $121,500
- mathematics—$31,580 to $103,330
- physics—$39,580 to $120,210

Employment Prospects

Job prospects are expected to be strong in the next several years due to the increase in student enrollment and the large number of professors who are becoming eligible for retirement. According to the BLS, employment of Professors is expected to increase by 23 percent through 2016. In addition to job growth, opportunities will become available as Professors retire or transfer to other jobs.

Competition for tenure-track positions is high. Job prospects are more favorable for adjunct and full-time term positions. Opportunities with educational institutions that receive state government funding are limited by budgetary constraints.

Advancement Prospects

College Professors advance through the academic ranks as instructor, assistant professor, associate professor, and full professor. Tenure-track positions start at either the instructor or assistant professor level with tenure attained at the associate professor rank. With tenure, Professors have prestige, professional freedom, and job security for the rest of their academic career. Job satisfaction is extremely high, and few tenured Professors leave the profession.

Administrative and management positions are available to those interested in following this career path. Professors can pursue such positions as department chairs, academic deans, administrative directors, provosts, and presidents.

Education and Training

A master's degree is the minimum requirement needed to teach in two-year colleges, but many faculty members hold a doctoral degree. The minimum requirement at four-year colleges and universities is a doctoral degree.

Earning a doctorate takes several years of dedication. In general, students complete four years of undergraduate work, earning a bachelor's degree. This is followed by six to eight years of study for first a master's degree and then a doctoral degree. New Ph.D.s usually spend two or more years completing postdoctoral training before seeking permanent positions.

Experience, Skills, and Personality Traits

Depending on an educational institution's mission, candidates may need to demonstrate that they have a strong teaching or combined teaching and research background. For example, community colleges and smaller liberal arts colleges emphasize teaching over research, while research universities are interested in candidates with strong research experience.

Professors must have excellent communication and presentation skills as well as strong interpersonal and teamwork skills to establish rapport with students, colleagues, and administrators. They also need adequate social skills, as Professors attend various college functions. Furthermore, strong organization and management skills are needed to complete their various duties each day.

Successful Professors share several personality traits such as being independent, adaptable, curious, flexible, and creative. They have a strong desire to pursue knowledge in their field as well as to teach and share their knowledge with students.

Unions and Associations

Professors belong to different societies to take advantage of networking opportunities and other professional resources and services. They join local, state, and national professional associations. The Mathematical Association of America and the National Science Teachers Association are two organizations that serve the specific interests of science educators.

In addition, many Professors belong to professional associations that serve the general interests of college faculty, such as the National Association of Scholars or the American Association of University Professors. Community college instructors might also join the American Association for Adult and Continuing Education. Professors in public institutions are eligible to join the higher education divisions of the National Education Association or the American Federation of Teachers.

Many Professors also join scientific societies, such as the American Association for the Advancement of Science, the American Astronomical Society, the American Geological Institute, the American Institute of Physics, and the American Institute of Biological Sciences, that serve their particular interests. See Appendix III for contact information for all of the above organizations.

Tips for Entry

1. The Preparing Future Faculty (PFF) program offers graduate students an opportunity to experience teaching in colleges and universities at an apprentice level. For more information, check out the program's Web site at http://www.preparing-faculty.org.

2. To gain work experience, contact institutions about adjunct positions. Many colleges and universities maintain a list of qualified candidates whom they contact when new instructors are needed. It is common for institutions to hire instructors at the last minute to replace adjunct instructors who have suddenly left for full-time positions.

3. When applying for a position, read the job announcement carefully. Also learn something about the school and tailor your résumé and cover letter to fit the position. For example, if you know the school is more interested in teaching, then you would want to emphasize your teaching strengths and experiences.

4. The Internet can provide you with valuable sources for job banks as well as with developments and trends in higher education. Some Web sites you might want to visit include the American Association of University Professors, http://www.aaup.org; the American Association of Community Colleges, http://www.aacc.nche.edu; and the Chronicle of Higher Education, http://chronicle.com. For more links, see Appendix IV.

SCIENCE EDUCATOR
(NONSCHOOL SETTINGS)

Position Description

Science Educators are responsible for developing and implementing informal science education programs. Some Science Educators run programs in science museums, zoos, aquariums, botanical gardens, planetariums, environmental centers, and other institutions. Other educators manage programs that are sponsored by government agencies (such as NASA), universities and colleges, scientific organizations, and other groups.

Science Educators develop a wide variety of educational programs and activities around their institution's collections, exhibits, and natural resources. Their objective is to create programs that entertain audiences as well as teach them informally about science and technology. Educational programs include tours, demonstrations, classes, workshops, films, lectures, and field trips. Many programs use a hands-on or interactive format in which patrons manipulate objects, complete tasks, handle fossils, run lab experiments, or assist scientists with field studies.

Various programs are developed for different audiences—children, adults, families, and schools. For example, a science museum might offer after-school programs, summer camps, and junior docent programs for young people; family nights at its planetarium; field trips and lecture series aimed specifically for their adult patrons; special tours and workshops for student groups; and on-line learning programs at its website on the Internet.

Some Science Educators are involved in designing and delivering educational outreach programs. They travel to schools, youth centers, community centers, and other organizations and put on workshops and presentations. They use films, slideshows, and other multimedia tools to bring science to life in their lectures. They also utilize fossils, specimens, and other objects that their audiences can experience.

Some Science Educators develop programs that offer science curriculum and instruction support to teachers and other educators in formal settings. For example, environmental educators might conduct workshops for middle school teachers, demonstrating how to do enrichment activities for their lessons about the environment.

Depending on their experience, Science Educators may supervise one or more educational programs. Their duties include scheduling events, locating facilities to hold activities, obtaining supplies and equipment, managing the program budget, marketing the program, and preparing program evaluations. Science Educators are also responsible for developing and producing teaching materials and activities. In addition, they oversee programs on the days they happen, and supervise staff and volunteers that are involved in the program. Most Science Educators teach classes and workshops as well as give presentations and demonstrations.

Science Educators perform a variety of other tasks, which include:

- helping set up and maintain exhibits
- writing interpretive materials about exhibits, collections, or natural resources
- conducting tours of their facilities
- training and supervising junior staff, volunteers, and interns
- writing grant proposals for future or current programs
- producing marketing and public relations materials such as newsletters, informational brochures, and Web pages
- maintaining accurate records, preparing reports, writing correspondence, and completing required paperwork
- participating in meetings and conferences

Science Educators work part-time or full-time. They may be required to work evenings, weekends, and holidays. Those working for residential environmental education programs are usually required to live at the camps.

Salaries

Salaries for Science Educators vary, and depend on such factors as their education, experience, job responsibilities, and employer. Formal salary information about this occupation is unavailable. In general, they earn salaries similar to self-enrichment instructors, who teach nonacademic, nonvocational, and self-improvement courses in nonschool settings. The estimated annual salary for most self-enrichment teachers ranged between $17,740 and $66,600, according to the May 2006 *Occupational Employment Statistics* survey by the U.S. Bureau of Labor Statistics.

Employment Prospects

Most opportunities become available as Science Educators transfer to other positions. Many jobs are based on the funding of grant proposals, and so may last only for a specific period of time. The turnover rate for Science Educators in informal settings is high, but the competition for available positions is also strong.

Advancement Prospects

Science Educators can advance to supervisory and administrative positions, as program coordinators and directors. Those with higher ambitions can pursue a career path leading to directorships of museums, zoos, aquariums, and so forth.

Education and Training

Employers require that Science Educators have a bachelor's degree in a science discipline, education, or another related field. Some employers require that candidates have a master's degree, but may waive the requirement if candidates have qualifying work experience.

Science Educators are expected to continue their professional growth through self-study, enrollment in training and education programs, and networking with colleagues.

Experience, Skills, and Personality Traits

Employers generally prefer to hire candidates who have several years of teaching experience in informal science programs. They also have previous experience planning and implementing education or outreach programs in informal settings. In addition, they have a strong science background.

Science Educators need excellent interpersonal and teamwork skills, as well as strong communication and writing skills. They must be computer literate. They also need exceptional self-management skills, including the ability to handle multiple tasks, prioritize tasks, work independently, and handle stressful situations.

Some personality traits that successful Science Educators share are being creative, organized, flexible, enthusiastic, diplomatic, and self-motivated.

Unions and Associations

Science Educators join different professional societies (at local, state, and national levels) that serve their interests as museum professionals, educators, and scientists. These organizations offer training programs, networking opportunities, and other professional services and resources. Some professional associations at the national level that serve the interests of science educators include the National Science Teachers Association, the North American Association for Environmental Education, and the National Marine Educators Association.

Science Educators are eligible to join associations that serve different types of museums, such as the American Association of Museums, the Association of Science-Technology Centers and the Association of Zoos and Aquariums. Further, Science Educators can join scientific societies that serve their particular interests, such as the Society for Integrative and Comparative Biology, the American Geophysical Union, the Entomological Society of America, and the Paleontological Society.

See Appendix III for contact information for all of the above organizations.

Tips for Entry

1. You can start gaining experience in high school and college. For example, you might volunteer with education or outreach programs at a science museum, technology center, zoo, or another institution.
2. Many environmental and nature centers hire educators for temporary positions for their residential environmental education programs. These positions usually include room and board along with a weekly salary. Contact environmental organizations in your area for job listings.
3. Because Science Educator positions are limited, the job search may be a long one. Many Science Educators were museum volunteers or had worked in such positions as administrative assistants and gallery explainers while doing their job search.
4. Learn more about science education and outreach programs on the Internet. To get a list of relevant Web sites to visit, enter any of these keywords in a search engine: *science museum* (or *zoo* or *aquarium*) *education program.* For some links, see Appendix IV.

SCIENCE CURATOR

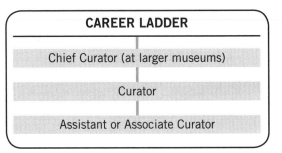

Position Description

Science Curators oversee the science and technology collections in museums and other institutions that exhibit these collections for viewing by the general public. Zoos, aquariums, nature centers, botanical gardens, arboretums, natural history museums, planetariums, and science centers are other types of such institutions. Science Curators also work in children's museums which offer interactive exhibits and education programs for young people.

In small institutions, curators are in charge of all collections. In larger institutions, several curators are employed to manage one or more collections. They are assigned to collections in their fields of expertise, such as paleontology, geology, botany, entomology, astronomy, or physics. Some institutions employ curators who only perform research or administrative duties.

Science Curators are responsible for the care and presentation of all the objects, materials, and specimens that are in science and technology collections. For example, a zoo curator oversees collections of live animals. Curators manage collections that belong to their institutions as well as those that are lent to them by donors or by other institutions.

While working with other staff members, such as archivists and conservators, curators develop and implement collections programs. Their duties include organizing and preserving collections, classifying items, conducting research, and storing collections safely and securely. Science Curators also publish magazine articles, monographs, and books about their collections. In addi-

tion, they make presentations at professional conferences as well as at meetings and functions of civic groups.

Science Curators are also in charge of developing exhibits that bring concepts of science and technology to life. They are responsible for choosing appropriate items for exhibits. They do research and write text (or labels) about the items to be displayed. They also determine the best way to design exhibits so that they communicate ideas clearly and in an entertaining manner.

Museums continually acquire new items by purchasing them or receiving them as gifts, or on loan, from other institutions. In the case of live animals and plants, many are acquired through reproduction or are collected in their natural habitats. Science Curators decide which acquisitions to make, as well as determine which objects to remove from collections to make way for new ones.

Curators perform various administrative tasks such as administering policies; managing budgets; maintaining collection records; training and supervising staff; writing grant proposals; and assisting in fund-raising. Many curators help with public relations and marketing tasks to promote programs, events, and activities. Some curators also participate in the development of science education and public outreach programs.

Some Science Curators are lecturers or adjunct instructors at colleges and universities, where they teach in undergraduate, graduate, or continuing education programs. They may teach courses in their field of science or in museum science. Some institutions are connected to research universities. In such cases, curator positions may be academic appointments. Like

SCIENCE WRITER

Position Description

Science Writers contribute to the general public's understanding of science and technology by describing and explaining scientific concepts and technical terminology in simple, yet accurate, language. They write news articles, magazine features, textbooks, instruction manuals, documentary scripts, grant proposals, marketing materials, content for Web pages, and so on.

The field of science writing is made up of several specialties. It is not uncommon for Science Writers to work in several specialized areas throughout their careers.

One specialty is science journalism. Science Writers in this area are commonly known as science reporters or science journalists. They report on current news about scientists, discoveries, inventions, events, issues, and other happenings in the science and technology world. They cover a wide range of topics—including medical studies, health, environmental issues, earthquakes, climate change, space programs, technology, archaeological findings, artificial intelligence, and science and technology policy, among others. The stories may take place at the local, state, national, or global level.

Science journalists work for newspapers, magazines, journals, television stations, radio stations, and Internet news services. Their audiences may be the general public or professionals (such as doctors, engineers, chemists, and astrophysicists). Some science journalists are also book authors, producing in-depth reportage about science and technical topics that interest them.

Some Science Writers specialize in the area of public relations and marketing. They are often known as public information officers or press writers, and are responsible for communicating the latest scientific research made by their employers to the public media and others. These information specialists work for universities, medical centers, pharmaceutical companies, biotechnology firms, high-technology corporations, government agencies, laboratories, research institutes, science museums, nonprofit health organizations, and so on.

Public information officers write press releases, and may write articles for in-house publications, speeches for executive officers, scripts for radio and television spots, and copy for their employers' Web sites. Many of them are also responsible for creating educational and promotional materials about the products their organizations manufacture and sell.

Still another specialty is medical writing. Medical writers work in various settings, such as biotechnology firms, medical schools, hospitals, pharmaceutical companies, government agencies, and nongovernmental organizations. They create a wide variety of written materials for their employers—for example, clinical study reports, position papers, regulatory documents, investigative drug brochures, and patient handbooks.

other professors, these curators are expected to teach, conduct research projects, produce scholarly work, and fulfill community service obligations.

Salaries

Salaries for Science Curators vary, depending on such factors as their education, experience, employer, and geographic location. Curators in large institutions typically earn higher salaries than curators in smaller institutions. The U.S. Bureau of Labor Statistics (BLS) reports in its May 2006 *Occupational Employment Statistics* survey that most curators earn an estimated annual salary that ranged from $26,320 to $80,030.

Employment Prospects

The turnover rate for curators is low; thus competition for any opening is keen, especially for positions with large museums. Most opportunities become available as curators retire or transfer to other positions.

Because most museums, zoos, aquariums, and similar institutions are nonprofit, positions are dependent on the availability of funding.

Advancement Prospects

Advancement opportunities are limited to obtaining curator positions with more complicated responsibilities. Thus, for example, curators in smaller museums might seek positions at larger ones. Curators with administrative and management ambitions can seek to become director of a museum, zoo, or planetarium.

Education and Training

Most employers hire Science Curators who hold a master's or doctoral degree in a relevant science discipline. For example, aquarium curators typically hold an advanced degree in such fields as oceanography or marine biology.

Many colleges and universities have graduate programs or certificate-based programs in museum studies with a focus in curatorship.

Experience, Skills, and Personality Traits

Employers choose candidates who have extensive experience working with collections that are similar to those in their type of institution.

To handle the different aspects of their jobs, Science Curators need excellent management and business skills as well as effective research, communication, computer writing, and self-management skills. They also must have strong interpersonal and teamwork skills, as they need to work well with many people of diverse backgrounds. Being creative, intuitive, curious, energetic, self-motivated, and flexible are some personality traits that successful Science Curators share.

Unions and Associations

Science Curators join professional associations to take advantage of education programs, networking opportunities, and other professional resources and services. Some national societies include the American Association of Museums, the Association of Zoos and Aquariums, the Society for the Preservation of Natural History Collections, and the Association of Science-Technology Centers. For contract information, see Appendix III.

Tips for Entry

1. To gain experience, volunteer at a museum, zoo, or other institution that interests you. Get involved in the different areas of operations.
2. Many museums have internship programs for college students. If an institution does not have one, contact it anyway and ask about interning there.
3. Get involved with professional organizations and conferences and network with your peers.
4. Learn more about museums on the Internet. Check out Web sites for the American Association of Museums, http://www.aam-us.org; and the Association of Science-Technology Centers, http://www.astc.org. For more links, see Appendix IV.

Many also write articles for newspapers, magazines, and Web sites.

Some Science Writers write science textbooks for school and college audiences. Some create educational materials for informal educational settings such as science museums, nature centers, and science programs. Other Science Writers specialize in writing grant proposals or developing and writing content for Web sites. Some Science Writers are involved with writing scripts for documentaries, educational films, and other multimedia. Many are technical writers who develop manuals and other documentation for technical devices, software programs, computer hardware, and various other consumer products.

A large part of Science Writers' work involves conducting research. Whether they are writing news articles, grant proposals, or technical manuals, Science Writers need to gather background information. They search through relevant scientific databases and read pertinent literature. They also interview scientists and other experts.

Unless they are writing personal commentary, Science Writers cannot put their own opinions or biases in their writings. In addition, they make sure that the information they are communicating is accurate and correct, and thus they check and often recheck their facts. They revise and edit their writing so that the language is clear and that their products adhere to standard writing formats and guidelines.

Some Science Writers are self-employed as freelance writers. They complete writing assignments or writing projects on a contractual basis for different clients. Freelance writers also perform tasks related to running a small business. For example, they do bookkeeping, pay bills and taxes, collect fees from clients, promote business, and maintain office supplies. Furthermore, they set aside time in their schedule just for seeking out future work.

Science Writers typically work more than 40 hours a week to complete their assignments. Their work can often be stressful, particularly when they juggle several assignments at a time and need to meet deadlines for each one.

Salaries

Salaries for Science Writers vary, depending on their education, experience, specialty, employer, and geographic location. The U.S. Bureau of Labor Statistics (BLS) reports (in its May 2006 *Occupational Employment Statistics* survey) the following estimated salaries for most of these professionals:

- reporters—$19,180 to $73,880
- public relations specialists—$28,080 to $89,220

- technical writers—$35,520 to $91,720
- writers and authors—$25,430 to $97,700

The Council for Advancement of Science Writers reports that earnings for experienced Science Writers and correspondents at major newspapers, national magazines, and network television stations may range from $60,000 to $100,000 or more.

Employment Prospects

Job competition is high for all writing occupations, particularly for entry-level positions. The BLS reports that employment of public relations specialists is expected to increase by 18 percent through 2016. Employment of technical writers should grow by 20 percent, while the employment of writers in general should increase by 13 percent.

Most opportunities for Science Writers become available as individuals retire, transfer to other jobs or careers, or advance to higher positions.

Advancement Prospects

Science Writers can advance to senior writer and editor positions, which usually involves performing supervisory and management duties.

Many Science Writers measure their success by gaining professional reputations and by earning higher incomes.

Education and Training

Educational requirements vary with the different employers. Minimally, Science Writers need a bachelor's degree in a scientific discipline, journalism, English, or another related field. Many Science Writers have a master's or doctoral degree in a science or engineering discipline.

Science Writers are involved in their own professional development. They keep up with science research as well as continue to improve their writing craft. Many Science Writers also learn new skills such as using graphics software or developing Web sites.

Experience, Skills, and Personality Traits

Employers prefer to hire Science Writers who have relevant writing experience—such as journalism, public relations, or technical writing—for the position to which they are applying. In addition, Science Writers have a general understanding of the subject matter in which they write.

Science Writers need excellent writing, organization, research, and communication skills. They must have strong interpersonal skills and the willingness to talk with strangers from different backgrounds. Science

Writers also need good self-management skills, such as the ability to meet deadlines, work independently, take initiative, and prioritize tasks accordingly. Freelance writers should have adequate business skills.

Some personality traits that successful Science Writers share are being creative, observant, flexible, disciplined, self-motivated, and persistent.

Unions and Associations

Science Writers join professional associations to take advantage of networking opportunities, job banks, and other professional services and resources. Different societies are available to serve the different interests of Science Writers. Some of these societies include:

- National Association of Science Writers
- Society for Technical Communication
- American Medical Writers Association
- ACE (Association for Communication Excellence in Agriculture, Natural Resources and Life and Human Sciences)
- Association of Health Care Journalists
- Society of Environmental Journalists
- Technology Section of the Public Relations Society of America

Many Science Writers also belong to writing societies such as the National Writers Union and the American Society of Journalists and Authors. Science Writers are also eligible to join scientific societies in their areas of interest, such as the American Geological Institute or the American Institute of Biological Sciences.

See Appendix III for contact information for all of the above organizations.

Tips for Entry

1. As a college student, join a professional writing association to take advantage of networking opportunities and other benefits.
2. Many scientific societies offer mass media fellowships for graduate students and Ph.D.'s.
3. Build a portfolio of your published work, as employers will want to see your writing samples.
4. Contact employers directly about permanent positions or freelance work.
5. Use the Internet to learn more about becoming a Science Writer. One Web site you might explore is from the National Association of Science Writers, http://nasw.org. For more links, see Appendix IV.

SCIENTIFIC ILLUSTRATOR

Position Description

Oftentimes scientific, medical, or technical information can be difficult to understand without the help of visual aids. Professionals known as Scientific Illustrators are responsible for creating artwork that visually explains complex concepts that people read in various media or hear during presentations. They produce exact and meticulous work such as anatomical drawings of plants, animals, and the human body, or diagrams of devices, equipment, and machinery. Scientific Illustrators also create artistic and stylized works in which they interpret scientific, medical, or technical ideas such as molecular bondings, geological events, ecological systems, and astronomical phenomena.

Scientific Illustrators use both traditional techniques (such as paints, colored pencils, and pen-and-ink) and computer programs to create drawings, diagrams, graphic designs, three-dimensional graphics, animations, and other visual aids for educators, professionals, companies, government agencies, museums, and others. Their work is used for instructional, informational, marketing, legal, and other purposes. For example, they may create artwork that appear in:

- science magazines, professional journals, e-zines, and other print or electronic publications
- science, engineering, or medical textbooks, reference books, and field guides
- educational pamphlets and brochures for hospitals, science programs, museums, or other organizations
- research project proposals, scientific papers, or scientific presentations
- employee training materials
- user manuals for software, computer hardware, scientific instruments, equipment, or machinery
- advertisements or promotional materials (such as posters, brochures, CD-ROMs, and online animations) of products and services
- business plans, catalogs, annual reports, and other institutional materials for organizations
- museum exhibits and displays
- demonstrative exhibits for attorneys to use to clarify scientific or technical issues or facts at court trials
- Web sites for academicians, physicians, hospitals, government agencies, private companies, and others

Some Scientific Illustrators hold staff positions in a wide range of settings, such as publishing houses, museums, universities, design studios, government agencies, and private companies in various industries. Others work as freelancers who offer their services to clients on a contractual basis.

Scientific Illustrators may have a background of fine art or science, or a combination of both. Many of these artists specialize in a particular area such as botany, paleontology, veterinary science, wildlife, astronomy, marine life, entomology, or ornithology. Some illustrators further specialize by focusing on a specific plant or animal species or a certain type of environment (such as wilderness or the underwater environment). Some artists work in the area of medical illustration, which is considered a separate field from scientific illustration. Medical illustrators may specialize in such areas as anatomical, surgical, or veterinary illustration.

Depending on the project, Scientific Illustrators may work alone or as part of a team that include graphic designers and other artists. Every project generally goes through the same phases. Scientific Illustrators normally begin each project by meeting with clients (who may be in-house) to discuss the parameters of the project. They determine such details as the purpose of the project, the audience, the information to be depicted, and the types of artwork needed.

A large part of their work involves doing research. These artists gather as much information as needed to learn about their subject matter. They examine reference materials (such as drawings, photographs, reports) that clients have given them as well as other literature they find in libraries, on electronic databases, and through the Internet. They also consult with scientists, physicians, technicians, and other experts with whom they may work closely throughout the project. When needed, they visit laboratories, hospital operating rooms, industrial plants, museums, archaeological digs, and other locations to gather information for their projects. They take their photographs and make sketches to use as reference when they craft their work.

When they have completed all of their research, they analyze the data and plan out the visuals. They create initial sketches, drafts, animations, or presentations for clients to review and approve before they make the final products. Accuracy is a crucial element to their work; consequently, they check the preciseness of the details. These commercial artists also make sure that their renderings fit into the context of the written materials that they illustrate. In addition, Scientific Illustrators are expected to create products that are easy to comprehend and are pleasing to the eye.

Scientific Illustrators work in clean, well-lighted offices or art studios. They spend many hours sitting or standing at drawing boards and worktables, or sitting before computers.

Full-time staff illustrators usually work a standard 40-hour week, while freelancers determine their own work schedules. Regardless of whether they are employees or freelancers, or work part time or full time, Scientific Illustrators put in long hours to complete projects on time.

Freelance artists are responsible for running their own business. They perform such tasks as negotiating contracts with clients, invoicing clients, paying bills and taxes, and maintaining artist and office supplies. Freelancers also set aside time to develop and implement marketing strategies to generate new business for themselves. Some freelancers continue to hold down staff positions as illustrators or work as teachers, artists, or research assistants.

Salaries
Earnings for Scientific Illustrators vary, depending on such factors as their education, experience, employer, and geographical location. Medical illustrators generally earn the highest wages. According to the May 2006 *Occupational Employment Statistics* survey by the U.S. Bureau of Labor Statistics (BLS), the estimated annual wages for most illustrators ranged between $18,350 and $79,390 and, for most multimedia artists, between $30,390 and $92,720.

The BLS reports that the annual mean wage for independent artists was $42,890. Freelance illustrators usually charge clients a flat rate, which varies according to the piece that they are creating. For some projects, freelancers bill clients by the hour.

Employment Prospects
Scientific Illustrators find staff positions or contractual work with book publishers, magazines, museums, government agencies, universities, medical schools, scientific research centers, law firms, and advertising agencies, among others. Manufacturers in the pharmaceutical, medical device, agricultural equipment, and various other industries also utilize the services of these artists to illustrate manuals, promotional materials, training materials, and so forth. In addition, Scientific Illustrators work for graphic arts firms that offer scientific or medical illustration services.

Job prospects are favorable for experienced Scientific Illustrators but the competition is keen. Some experts report that the demand for medical illustrators is currently greater than the number of available skilled artists. Opportunities for these professionals should continue to grow in the coming years due to the continual advancement of new technologies and treatments in the health care field.

Advancement Prospects
Scientific Illustrators generally measure advancement through job satisfaction, higher incomes, and recognition for the quality of their work. As employees, Scientific Illustrators can advance to supervisory and

managerial positions, but opportunities are limited. Entrepreneurial individuals can pursue careers as successful freelancers or owners of firms that offer scientific illustration services.

Education and Training

There are no standard educational requirements for an individual to become a Scientific Illustrator, although many employers prefer to hire candidates who possess college degrees. Most professionals hold a bachelor's or advanced degree in a scientific discipline or fine art. Some Scientific Illustrators have an educational background in both art and science. Many medical illustrators possess a master's degree in medical illustration.

Formal training in scientific illustration is limited. A few universities in the United States offer master's degree programs in medical illustration, which are accredited by the American Medical Association. Some colleges and universities offer certificate or degree programs in this field, while some botanical gardens and arboretums offer certificate programs in botanical illustrations. For information about some schools, see Appendix II.

Scientific Illustrators normally learn on the job. Throughout their careers, they update their skills in both traditional and digital media as well as learn more about scientific or medical subjects. They continue their education through self-study. They also enroll in courses, seminars, and workshops given by educational institutions, professional associations, and other organizations.

Experience, Special Skills, and Personality Traits

Both employers and clients prefer to hire candidates who have experience creating accurate scientific illustrations. Novice artists may have gained their experience through employment, volunteer work, or student projects. Employers also seek candidates who have a science background, or who demonstrate an interest and a basic understanding of the subject matter (aquatic biology, vulcanology, or space science) in which they would be working.

Along with having traditional drawing and painting abilities, Scientific Illustrators need strong computer skills, including the ability to utilize illustration, animation, desktop publishing, and other computer graphics software. They also must have effective analytical, research, communication, interpersonal, teamwork, and self-management skills. Being creative, precise, focused, detail-oriented, flexible, and self-motivated are some personality traits that successful Science Illustrators share. Furthermore, these artists must be able to handle criticism about their work.

Unions and Associations

Many Scientific Illustrators join professional organizations to take advantage of networking opportunities, professional certification, continuing education programs, and other professional resources and services. Some national societies that serve the different interests of Scientific Illustrators include the Guild of Natural Science Illustrators, the American Society of Botanical Artists, Inc., the BioCommunications Association, the International Association of Astronomical Artists, and the Health and Sciences Communications Association. The Association of Medical Illustrators specifically supports the interests of medical illustrators. Scientific Illustrators are also eligible to join the Graphic Artists Guild, a national union that advocates for fair wages and working conditions on behalf of its membership. For contact information for these organizations, see Appendix III.

Tips for Entry

1. Build a portfolio of your best work to show prospective employers or clients.
2. To gain experience, you might volunteer to do illustrations for nonprofit organizations, nature centers, or campus researchers.
3. If you plan to do freelance work, learn how to run and promote your business. Also be sure that you understand the principles of copyright laws as well as the basics of contractual agreements.
4. Networking is vital to succeeding as a Scientific Illustrator. Through your friends, colleagues, clients, former professors and employers, find out who may need an illustrator for current or future projects.
5. Use the Internet to learn more about Scientific Illustrators. You might start by visiting the Guild of Natural Science Illustrators Web site at http://www.gnsi.org. For more links, see Appendix IV.

APPENDIXES

APPENDIX I
EDUCATION AND TRAINING: HOW MUCH IS REQUIRED?

In this appendix, you will learn about the educational requirements that are needed for careers in the fields of science and mathematics.

HIGH SCHOOL

Many professionals recommend that students take as many science and math courses as possible to begin preparing for a science career. These include courses in biology, chemistry, physics, algebra, geometry, precalculus, and computing. In addition, students should also take courses in the humanities, social science, and business to gain a rounded background. High school students should also take courses in English and speech to build up strong reading, writing, and communication skills which are important for survival in college and the work world.

Four-year colleges and universities require college applicants to submit test scores from standardized college entrance exams, which may be the SAT or the ACT. For further information, talk with your high school counselor. On the Internet, go to http://www.collegeboard.com to learn about the SAT or to http://www.act.student.org to learn about the ACT.

BACHELOR'S PROGRAMS

Research opportunities as technologists, technicians, and research assistants are available to holders of bachelor's degrees. In the applied sciences, as well as in alternative science careers, the bachelor's degree is the minimum requirement for many positions. For example, many actuaries, environmental scientists, forensic scientists, technical writers, and science educators gained entry into their jobs with a bachelor's degree.

Science degree programs are four years long, but many students complete their studies in five or more years, especially if they hold part-time or full-time jobs. The first two years of any bachelor's program are spent fulfilling general requirements in science, social science, the humanities, and English. Students focus on completing coursework for their major during the last two years of their degree programs.

Undergraduate students gain a general background in their areas of interest (physics, geology, biology, mathematics, and so on). The ability to specialize in a particular subject is found at the graduate level.

To enhance future employability, many professionals suggest that students take a few basic courses in statistics, computers, and data management. In addition, students should continue to build and strengthen their reading, writing, and communication skills.

MASTER'S AND DOCTORAL PROGRAMS

Traditionally, the master's and doctoral degree programs are necessary steps toward becoming a research scientist. The master's program is usually one to two years long in a specialized area of study. Applicants for graduate school must submit their test scores from the Graduate Record Examinations (GRE), a standardized graduate entrance exam. For more information, check out the following Web site: GRE, http://www.gre.org.

Upon completion of their master's program, students enter a doctoral program which generally takes between five to eight years to complete. Doctoral students complete advanced classroom studies and lab research training. They are also required to write a dissertation that involves original research.

To find resources on the Internet related to the world of doctoral students in science, mathematics, and engineering, check out PhDs.org (by Geoff Davis) at http://www.phds.org.

POSTDOCTORAL TRAINING

Many Ph.D. graduates obtain postdoctoral positions for further research, training, and development of scientific skills in their field of interest. They may work in academic, government, industrial, nonprofit, or nongovernmental settings.

Postdoctoral posts are usually one to three years long, and recipients receive either a fellowship or a salary. Many Ph.D.s work in several successive postdoctoral positions before obtaining full-time employment.

To learn more about postdoctoral training positions, check out the following Web sites:

- *Science* Careers (from the journal *Science*), http://sciencecareers.science mag.org
- National Postdoctoral Association, http://www.national postdoc.org
- Fellowships at the National Academies (Advisers to the Nation on Science, Engineering, and Medicine), http://www.nationalacademies.org/grantprograms.html

SCIENCE MASTER'S PROGRAMS

The science master's program is a professional master's of science degree program in science or mathematics, which is offered by many colleges and universities in the United States. It is an alternative option to earning a doctoral degree for individuals who are interested in pursuing careers in industrial settings in such fields as insurance, research management, technology transfer, and consulting.

The professional science master's program is generally two years long and based in emerging or interdisciplinary fields such as bioinformatics, biotechnology, industrial mathematics, computational science, geographical information systems, industrial microbiology, and environmental sciences.

For further information about the professional science master's program, talk with your college adviser. You can also find information at the following Web site: Professional Science Master's http://sciencemasters.com.

TRAINING FOR CLINICAL RESEARCHERS

To conduct medical (or clinical) research, medical training is usually required. Physician-scientists, or medical scientists, obtain a medical degree or doctor of osteopathy degree. Many of them obtain a doctoral degree as well.

A bachelor's degree in premedicine or a scientific discipline is the minimum requirement needed to enter medical school. (Many medical schools also accept applicants with other majors if they have met other qualifying requirements.) You will need to take the Medical College Admission Test before you can apply for medical schools. On the Internet, you can learn more about this test at the Association of American Medical Colleges Web site. Go to http://www.aamc.org/students/mcat/start.htm.

Medical school is a four-year program. During the first two years, students study anatomy, physiology, pathology, pharmacology, and other sciences basic to medicine. They are also introduced to the fundamentals of health care and the examination of patients. Medical students gain practical experience working with patients in office, clinic, and hospital settings in the different medical disciplines during the last two years of medical school. After graduation from medical school, they then complete at least three years in graduate medical education programs (more commonly known as residency programs), where they obtain training in their chosen medical specialty, such as internal medicine or surgery. If they wish to specialize in a subspecialty, such as cardiovascular disease or medical oncology in internal medicine, they complete another one to three more years of training.

Educational training for medical students who also obtain a doctoral degree usually takes between seven to nine years to complete. These students are part of dual degree (M.D./Ph.D.) programs, which are offered at many medical schools. Students initially complete the first two years of medical school. During the next three to five (or more years), they do their graduate work in their chosen fields. After they have completed their dissertations, they then finish the last two years of medical school and complete training in their medical specialties.

For information about medical schools, visit the Association of American Medical Colleges Web site at http://www.aamc.org.

CONTINUING EDUCATION

Throughout their careers, most individuals continue their education to keep up with developments in their fields and to learn new skills. Informally, they read professional books and journals as well as network with colleagues and participate in professional meetings and conferences. They may also enroll in formal training and continuing education programs offered by professional societies, trade associations, colleges, and universities.

Some professionals may need to satisfy continuing education requirements in order to renew professional licensure or certification.

PAYING FOR YOUR EDUCATION

Scholarships, fellowships, grants, and loans are available to help students pay for their college education, from their undergraduate years up through their postdoctoral training. In addition, internship and work-study programs are available, which also give students the opportunity to gain practical work experience in actual work settings. These financial aid programs are sponsored by government agencies, professional societies, trade associations, research institutes, foundations, businesses, and other organizations.

For further information, high school students might consult their high school guidance counselor while college students might contact their financial aid offices and college career centers. School, college, and public libraries also carry current directories and guides to scholarships, grants, and loans. Furthermore, financial aid information can be found on the World Wide Web. For example, two Web sites that provide such information are FinAid!, http://www.finaid.org; and Student Aid on the Web (by the Federal Student Aid of the U.S. Department of Education), http://www.studentaid. ed.gov.

APPENDIX II
EDUCATION AND TRAINING RESOURCES

In this appendix, you will learn about Internet sources for education and training programs for some of the occupations that you learned about in this book. To learn about programs for other occupations not listed in this appendix, talk with school or career counselors as well as professionals in the field. You can also consult college directories produced by Peterson's or other publishers, which may be found in your school or public library.

Note: When a specific Web page is not given, click on either the education or careers link to find the listing of educational programs at an organization's Web site. You can also type *educational programs* into the Web site's search engine.

All Web site addresses were current at the time this book was being written. If a URL no longer works, enter the title of the Web page or the name of the organization or individual to find the new address.

GENERAL RESOURCES

The following Web sites provide links to various academic programs at the different colleges and universities in the United States:

- The Princeton Review, http://www.princetonreview.com
- Web U.S. Higher Education, a listing of two-year, four-year colleges, and universities (maintained by the University of Texas at Austin), http://www.utexas.edu/world/univ
- GradSchools.com, http://www.gradschools.com

ACTUARIAL SCIENCE

The Society of Actuaries provides a listing of colleges and universities that offer actuarial science programs at its Web site. The URL is http://www.soa.org.

ASTRONOMY

Dr. Tom Arny (Department of Astronomy, University of Massachusetts) provides a listing of astronomy programs on the following Web pages:

- undergraduate programs—http://www.astro.umass.edu/~arny/astro_ugprogs.html
- graduate programs—http://www.astro.umass.edu/~arny/astro_gradprogs.html

BIOCHEMISTRY

The American Society for Biochemistry and Molecular Biology provides a listing of academic departments in molecular biology, biochemistry, or chemistry with a biochemistry emphasis at its Web site. The URL is http://www.asbmb.org.

BIOINFORMATICS

The International Society for Computational Biology provides a listing of degree programs in bioinformatics at http://www.iscb.org.

BIOPHYSICS

The Biophysical Society provides a database of graduate programs in biophysics at http://www.biophysics.org/careers/databases.htm#education.

BIOTECHNOLOGY

The American Association of Pharmaceutical Scientists provides a listing of schools offering graduate programs in biotechnology at http://www.aapspharmaceutica.com/StudentCenter/prof_devel/pharmsci_programs/index.asp.

CHEMISTRY

The American Chemical Society provides a database of undergraduate and graduate programs in chemistry at its Web site. The URL is http://www.chemistry.org.

CLIMATOLOGY

The Climate Specialty Group of the Association of American Geographers provides a listing of graduate climatology programs at http://www.geography.du.edu/csg.

COMPUTER SCIENCE
(OR COMPUTING SCIENCE)

Here are two Web sites where you can learn about some academic programs in computing science:

- The Accreditation Board for Engineering & Technology (ABET) provides a listing for computing science programs accredited by ABET at http://www.abet.org/accredited_programs.shtml
- The Computing Research Association provides a database of departments granting doctorates in computing-related disciplines. Go to http://www.cra.org/reports/forsythe.html

EARTH SCIENCES (OR GEOSCIENCES)

Listings of various academic programs in the earth sciences can be found at the following Web sites:

- American Geophysical Union, http://agu.org/sci_soc/phd_urls.html
- Geoscience Departments WWW Directory–U.S. and Canada (maintained by Timothy Heaton, University of South Dakota), http://www.usd.edu/esci/geodepts.html

ENVIRONMENTAL SCIENCE

The following organizations provide listings of environmental science, environmental engineering, and related environmental programs at their Web sites:

- EnviroEducation.com: The Environmental School Directory, http://www.enviroeducation.com
- Air and Waste Management Association, http://www.awma.org

EPIDEMIOLOGY

A listing of epidemiology programs can be found at the following website: The World-Wide Virtual Library: Epidemiology (maintained by Department of Epidemiology and Biostatistics, University of California, San Francisco), http://www.epibiostat.ucsf.edu/epidem/epidem.html.

FOOD SCIENCE

The Institute of Food Technologists provides a listing of undergraduate and graduate programs in food science at http://www.ift.org.

FORENSIC SCIENCE

The American Academy of Forensic Sciences provides a listing of undergraduate and graduate programs in forensic science at http://www.aafs.org.

FOREST SCIENCE

The Society of American Foresters provides a listing of degree programs in forest science and forest technology at http://www.safnet.org.

GENETICS

A listing of graduate and postgraduate training programs in human genetics can be found at Gen Ed Net.org. The URL is http://www.genednet.org.

HEALTH PHYSICS

The Health Physics Society provides a listing of schools that offer bachelor's and advanced degrees in health physics at http://hps.org/students.

HORTICULTURE

The American Society for Horticultural Science provides a listing of two-year and four-years horticulture programs at http://www.ashs.org.

IMMUNOLOGY

The American Association of Immunologists provides a listing of graduate programs in immunology at http://www.aai.org/resources/graduate.htm.

MATERIALS SCIENCE

The Minerals, Metals and Materials Society (TMS) provides a listing of schools that have materials science programs at its TMS Career Resource Center Web site. Go to http://www.crc4mse.org/resources/colleges.html.

MATHEMATICS

The American Mathematical Society provides a directory of professional master's degree programs in the mathematical sciences at http://www.ams.org/tools/masters.html.

MEDICAL ILLUSTRATION

The Association of Medical Illustrators provides a list of accredited graduate programs at its Web site. The URL is http://www.medical-illustrators.org.

MEDICAL PHYSICS

The American Association of Physicists in Medicine provides a listing of graduate medical physics programs at http://www.aapm.org.

MEDICAL SCIENCE

The National Association of M.D./Ph.D. Programs provides a listing of joint medical/doctorate programs at its Web page, which is hosted by the Association of American Medical Colleges. Go to http://www.aamc.org/research/dbr/mdphd.

MEDICINE

For listings of medical programs, visit these Web sites:

- Association of American Medical Colleges, http://www.aamc.org
- The Princeton Review, http://www.princetonreview.com/medical

For listings of graduate medical education programs (or residency programs) and sponsoring institutions, go to the following Web page at the Accreditation Council for Graduate Medical Education Web site at http://www.acgme.org/adspublic.

METEOROLOGY
(OR ATMOSPHERIC SCIENCES)

The National Weather Association provides a listing of academic programs in meteorology or atmospheric science at http://www.nwas.org/links/universities.php.

MOLECULAR BIOLOGY

The American Society for Biochemistry and Molecular Biology provides a listing of academic departments in molecular biology at its Web site. The URL is http://www.asbmb.org.

OPERATIONS RESEARCH AND
MANAGEMENT SCIENCES

The Institute for Operations Research and the Management Sciences provides a listing of educational programs in operations research at http://www.informs.org.

PATHOLOGY

For listings of pathology programs, visit the following Web sites:

- Intersociety Council for Pathology Information, http://www.pathologytraining.org
- College of American Pathologists, http://www.cap.org

PHARMACOLOGY

American Society for Pharmacology and Experimental Therapeutics provides a listing of undergraduate and graduate programs in pharmacology at http://www.aspet.org/public/training_programs/training_programs.html.

PHYSICS

The American Institute of Physics provides a database of graduate programs in physics and related fields at its Web site called Gradschoolshopper.com. Go to http://www.gradschoolshopper.com.

RANGE MANAGEMENT

The Society for Range Management provides a list of professional programs in range management education at its Web site. The URL is http://www.rangelands.org.

REGULATORY AFFAIRS

The Regulatory Affairs Professionals Society provides a list of degree and certificate programs in regulatory affairs at its Web site. The URL is http://www.raps.org.

SCIENCE AND TECHNOLOGY POLICY

For a list of U.S. graduate programs, check out Guide to Graduate Education in Science, Engineering and Public Policy by the American Association for the Advancement of Science. To access this guide on the Internet, go to http://www.aaas.org/spp/sepp.

SCIENCE COMMUNICATION

A listing of science communication programs and courses can be found at:

- School of Journalism and Mass Communication, University of Wisconsin, Madison, http://journalism.wisc.edu/dsc
- The Society of Environmental Journalists, http://www.sej.org/careers/index.htm

SPACE PHYSICS

The American Geophysical Union's Space Physics and Aeronomy Section provides a listing of colleges and universities offering advanced degrees in space physics fields at http://spaweb.space.swri.edu/universities.html.

STATISTICS

The American Statistical Association provides a list of colleges and universities in the United States and

Canada that offer degree programs in statistics at http://www.amstat.org/education/SODS.

TEACHER EDUCATION

The National Council for Accreditation of Teacher Education provides a database of schools, colleges, and departments of education, which they have accredited, on its Web site. The URL is http://www.ncate.org.

TECHNICAL WRITING (OR TECHNICAL COMMUNICATION)

The Society for Technical Communication has a database of academic programs in technical communication at http://www.stc.org/edu.

TOXICOLOGY

The Society of Toxicology provides a listing of academic programs in toxicology at its Web site. The URL is http://www.toxicology.org.

VETERINARY TECHNOLOGY

The National Association of Veterinary Technicians of America provides a listing of veterinary technology programs at http://navta.net/education.

APPENDIX III
UNIONS AND PROFESSIONAL ASSOCIATIONS

In this appendix, you will find contact information and Web site addresses for the professional organizations that are mentioned in this book. Most of these organizations offer information about careers, job opportunities, training programs, educational resources, and professional certification programs.

Some organizations have a main office (or headquarters) with branch offices throughout the United States. Contact an organization's headquarters or contact person to find out if there is a branch in your area. Other local, state, regional, and international professional associations also represent many of the professions discussed in this book. To learn about other relevant professional societies and unions, contact local professionals.

Note: All contact information and Web site addresses were current when the book was being written. If you come across a URL that is no longer valid, you may be able to find an organization's new Web site by entering its name in a search engine.

BIOLOGICAL SCIENCES

American Arachnological Society
http://www.americanarachnology.org

American Association for Laboratory Animal Science
9190 Crestwyn Hills Drive
Memphis, TN 38125
Phone: (901) 754-8620
Fax: (901) 753-0046
http://www.aalas.org

American Association for the Advancement of Science
1200 New York Avenue NW
Washington, DC 20005
Phone: (202) 326-6400
http://www.aaas.org

American Association of Equine Veterinary Technicians
http://www.aaevt.org

American Chemical Society
1155 Sixteenth Street NW
Washington, DC 20036
Phone: (800) 227-5558 or (202) 872-4600
Fax: (202) 872-4615
http://www.chemistry.org

American Dairy Science Association
1111 North Dunlap Avenue
Savoy, IL 61874
Phone: (217) 356-5146
Fax: (217) 398-4119
http://www.adsa.org

American Fisheries Society
5410 Grosvenor Lane
Bethesda, MD 20814
Phone: (301) 897-8616
Fax: (301) 897-8096
http://www.fisheries.org

American Institute of Biological Sciences
1444 I Street NW
Suite 200
Washington, DC 20005
Phone: (202) 628-1500
Fax: (202) 628-1509
http://www.aibs.org

American Physiological Society
9650 Rockville Pike
Bethesda, MD 20814
Phone: (301) 634-7164
Fax: (301) 634-7241
http://www.the-aps.org

American Society for Biochemistry and Molecular Biology
9650 Rockville Pike
Bethesda, MD 20814
Phone: (301) 634-7145
Fax: (301) 634-7126
http://www.asbmb.org

American Society for Horticultural Science
113 South West Street
Suite 200
Alexandria, VA 22314
Phone: (703) 836-4606
Fax: (703) 836-2024
http://www.ashs.org

American Society for Microbiology
1752 N Street NW
Washington, DC 20036
Phone: (202) 737-3600
http://www.asm.org

American Society for Virology
http://www.asv.org

American Society of Agronomy
677 South Segoe Road
Madison, WI 53711

Phone: (608) 273-8080
Fax: (608) 273-2021
http://www.agronomy.org

American Society of Animal Science

1111 North Dunlap Avenue
Savoy, IL 61874
Phone: (217) 356-9050
Fax: (217) 398-4119
http://www.asas.org

American Society of Human Genetics

9650 Rockville Pike
Bethesda, MD 20814
Phone: (866) HUM-GENE or (301) 634-7300
http://www.ashg.org

American Society of Limnology and Oceanography

5400 Bosque Boulevard
Suite 680
Waco, TX 76710
Phone: (800) 929-2756 or (254) 399-9635
Fax: (254) 776-3767
http://www.aslo.org

American Society of Plant Biologists

15501 Monona Drive
Rockville, MD 20855
Phone: (301) 251-0560
Fax: (301) 279-2996
http://www.aspb.org

American Veterinary Dental Society

P.O. Box 803
Fayetteville, TN 37334
Phone: (800) 332-AVDS or (931) 438-0238
Fax: (931) 433-6289
http://www.avds-online.org

Animal Behavior Society

Indiana University
2611 East 10th Street
Bloomington, IN 47408
Phone: (812) 856-5541
Fax: (812) 856-5542
http://www.animalbehavior.org

Association for Computing Machinery

2 Penn Plaza, Suite 701
New York, NY 10121
Phone: (800) 342-6626 or (212) 626-0500
http://www.acm.org

Association of Applied IPM Ecologists

P.O. Box 12181
Fresno, CA 93776
Phone/Fax: (559) 907-4897
http://aaie.net

Association of Zoo Veterinary Technicians

http://www.azvt.org

Botanical Society of America

P.O. Box 299
St. Louis, MO 63166
Phone: (314) 577-9566
Fax: (314) 577-9515
http://www.botany.org

Coleopterists Society

http://www.coleopsoc.org

Ecological Society of America

1707 H Street NW
Suite 400
Washington, DC 20006
Phone: (202) 833-8773
Fax: (202) 833-8775
http://www.esa.org

Entomological Society of America

10001 Derekwood Lane
Suite 100
Lanham, MD 20706
Phone: (301) 731-4535
Fax: (301) 731-4538
http://www.entsoc.org

Genetics Society of America

9650 Rockville Pike
Bethesda, MD 20814
Phone: (866) 486-GENE or (301) 634-7300
http://www.genetics-gsa.org

Institute of Food Technologists

525 West Van Buren

Suite 1000
Chicago, IL 60607
Phone: (312) 782-8424
Fax: (312) 782-8348
http://www.ift.org

International Society for Computational Biology

Pharmaceutical Building
Room 3230
9500 Gilman Drive
MC 0743
La Jolla, CA 92093
Phone: (858) 822-0852
Fax: (760) 888-0313
http://www.iscb.org

National Association of Veterinary Technicians in America

P.O. Box 224
Battle Ground, IN 47920
Phone: (765) 742-2216
Fax: (765) 807-3360
http://www.navta.net

North American Benthological Society

http://www.benthos.org

Society for Conservation Biology

4245 North Fairfax Drive
Arlington, VA 22203
Phone: (703) 276-2384
Fax: (703) 995-4633
http://conbio.net

Society for Industrial Microbiology

3929 Old Lee Highway
Suite 92A
Fairfax, VA 22030
Phone: (703) 691-3357
Fax: (703) 691-7991
http://www.simhq.org

Society for Integrative and Comparative Biology

1313 Dolley Madison Boulevard
Suite 402
McLean, VA 22101
Phone: (800) 955-1236 or (703) 790-1745

Fax: (703) 790-2672
http://www.sicb.org

Society for Marine Mammalogy
http://www.marinemammalogy.org

Society of General Physiologists
P.O. Box 257
Woods Hole, MA 02543
Phone: (508) 540-6719
Fax: (508) 540-0155
http://www.sgpweb.org

Society of Veterinary Behavior Technicians
http://www.svbt.org

Society of Wetland Scientists
1313 Dolley Madison Boulevard
Suite 402
McLean, VA 22101
Phone: (703) 790-1745
Fax: (703) 790-2672
http://www.sws.org

CHEMISTRY

AACC International
3340 Pilot Knob Road
St. Paul, MN 55121
Phone: (651) 454-7250
Fax: (651) 454-0766
http://www.aaccnet.org

American Association for Clinical Chemistry
1850 K Street NW
Suite 625
Washington, DC 20006
Phone: (800) 892-1400 or (202) 857-0717
Fax: (202) 887-5093
http://www.aacc.org

American Association for the Advancement of Science
1200 New York Avenue NW
Washington, DC 20005
Phone: (202) 326-6400
http://www.aaas.org

American Association of University Professors
1012 Fourteenth Street NW

Suite 500
Washington, DC 20005
Phone: (202) 737-5900
Fax: (202) 737-5526
http://www.aaup.org

American Ceramic Society
735 Ceramic Place
Suite 100
Westerville, OH 43081
Phone: (866) 721-3322
Fax: (301) 206-9789
http://www.ceramics.org

American Chemical Society
1155 Sixteenth Street NW
Washington, DC 20036
Phone: (800) 227-5558 or (202) 872-4600
Fax: (202) 872-4615
http://www.chemistry.org

American College of Toxicology
9650 Rockville Pike
Bethesda, MD 20814
Phone: (301) 634-7840
Fax: (301) 634-7852
http://www.actox.org

American Institute of Biological Sciences
1444 I Street NW
Suite 200
Washington, DC 20005
Phone: (202) 628-1500
Fax: (202) 628-1509
http://www.aibs.org

American Institute of Chemists
315 Chestnut Street
Philadelphia, PA 19106
Phone: (215) 873-8224
Fax: (215) 629-5224
http://www.theaic.org

American Society for Biochemistry and Molecular Biology
9650 Rockville Pike
Bethesda, MD 20814
Phone: (301) 634-7145
Fax: (301) 634-7126

http://www.asbmb.org

ASM International
9639 Kinsman Road
Materials Park, OH 44073
Phone: (800) 336-5152 or (440) 338-5151
Fax: (440) 338-4634
http://asmcommunity.
asminternational.org

Association of Government Toxicologists
http://www.agovtox.org

Geochemical Society
Washington University
E&PS Building, Room 334
1 Brookings Drive, CB 1169
St. Louis, MO 63130
Phone: (314) 935-4131
Fax: (314) 935-4121
http://www.geochemsoc.org

Materials Research Society
506 Keystone Drive
Warrendale, PA 15086
Phone: (724) 779-3003
Fax: (724) 779-8313
http://www.mrs.org

Minerals, Metals and Materials Society
184 Thorn Hill Road
Warrendale, PA 15086
Phone: (800) 759-4867 or (724) 776-9000
Fax: (724) 776-3770
http://www.tms.org

National Association of Scholars
221 Witherspoon Street
Second Floor
Princeton, NJ 08542
Phone: (609) 683-7878
http://www.nas.org

Society for Biomaterials
15000 Commerce Parkway
Suite C
Mt. Laurel, NJ 08054
Phone: (856) 439-0826

Fax: (856) 439-0525
http://www.biomaterials.org

Society of Cosmetic Chemists
120 Wall Street
Suite 2400
New York, NY 10005
Phone: (212) 668-1500
Fax: (212) 668-1504
http://www.scconline.org

Society of Environmental Toxicology and Chemistry
1010 North 12th Avenue
Pensacola, FL 32501
Phone: (850) 469-1500
Fax: (850) 469-9778
http://www.setac.org

Society of Forensic Toxicologists
1 MacDonald Center
1 MacDonald Street
Suite 15
Mesa, AZ 85201
Phone/Fax: (888) 866-7638
http://www.soft-tox.org

Society of Toxicology
1821 Michael Faraday Drive
Suite 300
Reston, VA 20190
Phone: (703) 438-3115
Fax: (703) 438-3113
http://www.toxicology.org

PHYSICS AND ASTRONOMY

Acoustical Society of America
Suite 1NO1
2 Huntington Quadrangle
Melville, NY 11747
Phone: (516) 576-2360
Fax: (516) 576-2377
http://asa.aip.org

American Academy of Health Physics
1313 Dolley Madison Boulevard
Suite 402
McLean, VA 22101
Phone: (703) 790-1745, extension 25
Fax: (703) 790-2672
http://www.hps1.org/aahp

American Association for the Advancement of Science
1200 New York Avenue NW
Washington, DC 20005
Phone: (202) 326-6400
http://www.aaas.org

American Association of Physicists in Medicine
1 Physics Ellipse
College Park, MD 20740
Phone: (301) 209-3350
Fax: (301) 209-0862
http://www.aapm.org

American Association of University Professors
1012 Fourteenth Street NW
Suite 500
Washington, DC 20005
Phone: (202) 737-5900
Fax: (202) 737-5526
http://www.aaup.org

American Astronomical Society
2000 Florida Avenue NW
Suite 400
Washington, DC 20009
Phone: (202) 328-2010
Fax: (202) 234-2560
http://www.aas.org

American Geophysical Union
2000 Florida Avenue NW
Washington, DC 20009
Phone: (800) 966-2481 or (202) 462-6900
Fax: (202) 328-0566
http://www.agu.org

American Geophysical Union Space—Physics and Aeronomy Section
http://spaweb.space.swri.edu

American Institute of Physics
1 Physics Ellipse
College Park, MD 20740
Phone: (301) 209-3100
http://www.aip.org

American Nuclear Society
555 North Kensington Avenue

La Grange Park, IL 60526
Phone: (800) 323-3044 or (708) 352-6611
Fax: (708) 352-0499
http://www.ans.org

American Physical Society
1 Physics Ellipse
College Park, MD 20740
Phone: (301) 209-3200
Fax: (301) 209-0865
http://www.aps.org

American Physical Society— Division of Biological Physics
http://units.aps.org/dbp

American Physical Society— Division of Nuclear Physics
http://dnp.nscl.msu.edu

Biophysical Society
9650 Rockville Pike
Bethesda, MD 20814
Phone: (301) 634-7114
Fax: (301) 634-7133
http://www.biophysics.org

Health Physics Society
1313 Dolley Madison Boulevard
Suite 402
McLean, VA 22101
Phone: (703) 790-1745
Fax: (703) 790-2672
http://hps.org

International Association of Geomagnetism and Aeronomy
http://www.iugg.org/IAGA

International Union for Pure and Applied BioPhysics
http://www.iupab.org

National Association of Scholars
221 Witherspoon Street
Second Floor
Princeton, NJ 08542
Phone: (609) 683-7878
http://www.nas.org

EARTH SCIENCES

Air Weather Association
http://www.airweaassn.org

American Association of Petroleum Geologists
1444 South Boulder Avenue
Tulsa, OK 74114
Mailing Address:
P.O. Box 979
Tulsa, OK 74101
Phone: (800) 364-2274 or (918) 584-2555
Fax: (918) 560-2665
http://www.aapg.org

American Association of Stratigraphic Palynologists
http://www.palynology.org

American Association of University Professors
1012 Fourteenth Street NW
Suite 500
Washington, DC 20005
Phone: (202) 737-5900
Fax: (202) 737-5526
http://www.aaup.org

American Geographical Society
120 Wall Street
Suite 100
New York, NY 10005
Phone: (212) 422-5456
Fax: (212) 422-5480
http://www.amergeog.org

American Geological Institute
4220 King Street
Alexandria, VA 22302
Phone: (703) 379-2480
Fax: (703) 379-7563
http://www.agiweb.org

American Geophysical Union
2000 Florida Avenue NW
Washington, DC 20009
Phone: (800) 966-2481 or (202) 462-6900
Fax: (202) 328-0566
http://www.agu.org

American Institute of Hydrology
300 Village Green Circle
Suite 201
Smyrna, GA 30080
Phone: (770) 384-1634
Fax: (770) 438-6172
http://www.aihydro.org

American Institute of Professional Geologists
1400 West 122nd Avenue
Suite 250
Westminster, CO 80234
Phone: (303) 412-6205
Fax: (303) 253-9220
http://www.aipg.org

American Meteorological Society
45 Beacon Street
Boston, MA 02108
Phone: (617) 227-2425
Fax: (617) 742-8718
http://www.ametsoc.org

American Society of Civil Engineers
1801 Alexander Bell Drive
Reston, VA 20191
Phone: (800) 548-2723 or (703) 295-6300
Fax: (703) 295-6222
http://www.asce.org

American Society of Limnology and Oceanography
5400 Bosque Boulevard
Suite 680
Waco, TX 76710
Phone: (800) 929-2756 or (254) 399-9635
Fax: (254) 776-3767
http://aslo.org

American Water Resources Association
P.O. Box 1626
Middleburg, VA 20118
Phone: (540) 687-8390
Fax: (540) 687-8395
http://www.awra.org

Association for Women Geoscientists
P.O. Box 30645
Lincoln, NE 68503
http://www.awg.org

Association of American Geographers
1710 16th Street NW
Washington, DC 20009
Phone: (202) 234-1450
Fax: (202) 234-2744
http://www.aag.org

Association of American Geographers—Cartography Specialty Group
http://www.csun.edu/~hfgeg003/csg

Association of American Geographers—Climate Specialty Group
http://www.geog.du.edu/csg

Association of Environmental and Engineering Geologists
3773 Cherry Creek Drive N.
Suite 575
Denver, CO 80209
Mailing
P.O. Box 460518
Denver, CO 80246
Phone: (303) 757-2926
Fax: (303) 757-2969
http://www.aegweb.org

Cartography and Geographic Information Society
6 Montgomery Village Avenue
Suite 403
Gaithersburg, MD 20879
Phone: (240) 632-9716
Fax: (301) 632-1321
http://www.cartogis.org

Environmental and Engineering Geophysical Society
1720 South Bellaire
Suite 110
Denver, CO 80222-4303
Phone: (303) 531-7517
Fax: (303) 820-3844
http://www.eegs.org

Geographic and Land Information Society
6 Montgomery Village Avenue
Suite 403
Gaithersburg, MD 20879
Phone: (240) 632-9700
http://www.glismo.org

Geological Society of America
3300 Penrose Place
Boulder, CO 80301
Mailing Address:
P.O. Box 9140
Boulder, CO 80301
Phone: (303) 357-1000
Fax: (303) 357-1070
http://www.geosociety.org

International Association of Seismology and Physics of the Earth's Interior
http://www.iaspei.org

International Association of Volcanology and Chemistry of the Earth's Interior
http://www.iavcei.org

Marine Technology Society
5565 Sterrett Place
Suite 108
Columbia, MD 21044
Phone: (410) 884-5330
Fax: (410) 884-9060
http://www.mtsociety.org

National Association of Black Geologists and Geophysicists
723 Main Street
Suite 1006
Houston, TX 77002
Mailing Address:
4212 San Felipe
Suite 420
Houston, TX 77027
http://nabgg.com

National Council of Industrial Meteorologists
http://www.ncim.org

National Groundwater Association
601 Dempsey Road

Westerville, OH 43081
Phone: (800) 551-7379 or (614) 898-7791
Fax: (614) 898-7786
http://www.ngwa.org

National Weather Association
228 West Millbrook Road
Raleigh, NC 27609
Phone: (919) 845-1546
http://www.nwas.org

Oceanic Engineering Society
http://www.oceanicengineering.org

Oceanography Society
P.O. Box 1931
Rockville, MD 20849
Phone: (301) 251-7708
Fax: (301) 251-7709
http://www.tos.org

Paleontological Society
http://www.paleosoc.org

Seismological Society of America
201 Plaza Professional Building
El Cerrito, CA 94530
Phone: (510) 525-5474
Fax: (510) 525-7204
http://www.seismosoc.org

Society of Exploration Geophysicists
8801 South Yale
Tulsa, OK 74137
Mailing Address:
P.O. Box 702740
Tulsa, OK 74170
Phone: (918) 497-5500
Fax: (918) 497-5557
http://seg.org

Society of Vertebrate Paleontology
60 Revere Drive
Suite 500
Northbrook, IL 60062
Phone: (847) 480-9095
Fax: (847) 480-9282
http://www.vertpaleo.org

Urban and Regional Information Systems Association
1460 Renaissance Drive
Suite 305
Park Ridge, IL 60068
Phone: (847) 824-6300
Fax: (847) 824-6363
http://www.urisa.org

MATHEMATICS

American Academy of Actuaries
1100 Seventeenth Street NW
Seventh Floor
Washington, DC 20036
Phone: (202) 223-8196
Fax: (202) 872-1948
http://www.actuary.org

American Association of University Professors
1012 Fourteenth Street NW
Suite 500
Washington, DC 20005
Phone: (202) 737-5900
Fax (202) 737-5526
http://www.aaup.org

American Mathematical Society
201 Charles Street
Providence, RI 02904
Phone: (800) 321-4267 or (401) 455-4000
Fax: (401) 331-3842
http://www.ams.org

American Society of Pension Professionals and Actuaries
4245 North Fairfax Drive
Suite 750
Arlington, VA 22203
Phone: (703) 516-9300
Fax: (703) 516-9308
http://www.aspa.org

American Statistical Association
732 North Washington Street
Alexandria, VA 22314
Phone: (888) 231-3473 or (703) 684-1221

Fax: (703) 684-2037
http://www.amstat.org

Association for Computing Machinery

2 Penn Plaza
Suite 701
New York, NY 10121
Phone: (800) 342-6626 or (212) 626-0500
http://www.acm.org

Association for Women in Mathematics

11240 Waples Mill Road
Suite 200
Fairfax, VA 22030
Phone: (703) 934-0163
Fax: (703) 359-7562
http://www.awm-math.org

Casualty Actuarial Society

4350 North Fairfax Drive
Suite 250
Arlington, VA 22203
Phone: (703) 276-3100
Fax: (703) 276-3108
http://www.casact.org

Caucus for Women in Statistics

http://caucusforwomeninstatistics.com

Conference of Consulting Actuaries

3880 Salem Lake Drive
Suite H
Long Grove, IL 60047
Phone: (847) 719-6500
Fax: (847) 719-6506
http://www.ccactuaries.org

IEEE Computer Society's Technical Committee on Security and Privacy

http://www.ieee-security.org

Institute for Operations Research and the Management Sciences

7240 Parkway Drive
Suite 310
Hanover, MD 21076

Phone: (800) 446-3676 or (443) 757-3500
Fax: (443) 757-3515
http://www.informs.org

Institute of Mathematical Statistics

Business Office
P.O. Box 22718
Beachwood, OH 44122
Phone: (216) 295-2340
Fax: (216) 921-5661
http://www.imstat.org

International Association for Cryptologic Research

http://www.iacr.org

International Biometric Society

1444 I Street NW, Suite 700
Washington, DC 20005
Phone: (202) 712-9049
Fax: (202) 216-9646
http://www.tibs.org

Mathematical Association of America

1529 Eighteenth Street NW
Washington, DC 20036
Phone: (800) 741-9415 or (202) 387-5200
Fax: (202) 265-2384
http://www.maa.org

National Association of Scholars

221 Witherspoon Street
Second Floor
Princeton, NJ 08542
Phone: (609) 683-7878
http://www.nas.org

Society for Industrial and Applied Mathematics

3600 Market Street
6th Floor
Philadelphia, PA 19104
Phone: (215) 382-9800
Fax: (215) 386-7999
http://www.siam.org

Society of Actuaries

475 North Martingale Road
Suite 600

Schaumberg, IL 60173
Phone: (847) 706-3500
Fax: (847) 706-3599
http://www.soa.org

COMPUTER SCIENCE

ASIS International

1625 Prince Street
Alexandria, VA 22314
Phone: (703) 519-6200
Fax: (703) 519-6299
http://www.asisonline.org

ASME International

3 Park Avenue
New York, NY 10016
Phone: (800) 843-2763 or (973) 882-1167
http://www.asme.org

Association for the Advancement of Artificial Intelligence

445 Burgess Drive
Suite 100
Menlo Park, CA 94025
Phone: (650) 328-3123
Fax: (650) 321-4457
http://www.aaai.org

Association for Computing Machinery

2 Penn Plaza
Suite 701
New York, NY 10121
Phone: (800) 342-6626 or (212) 626-0500
http://www.acm.org

Association for Computing Machinery—Special-Interest Group for Artificial Intelligence

http://www.sigart.org

Association for Women in Computing

41 Sutter Street
Suite 1006
San Francisco, CA 94104
Phone: (415) 905-4663
Fax: (415) 358-4667
http://www.awc-hq.org

Association of Support Professionals
122 Barnard Avenue
Watertown, MA 02472
Phone: (617) 924-3944
Fax: (617) 924-7288
http://www.asponline.com

Computer Security Institute
600 Community Drive
Manhasset, NY 11030
Phone: (800) 250-2429 or (847) 763-9602
Fax: (847) 763-9606
http://www.gocsi.com

HDI
102 South Tejon, Suite 1200
Colorado Springs, CO 80903
Phone: (800) 248-5667 or (719) 268-0174
Fax: (719) 268-0184
http://www.thinkhdi.com

High Technology Crime Investigation Association
4021 Woodcreek Oaks Boulevard
Suite 156-#209
Roseville, CA 95747
Phone: (916) 408-1751
Fax: (916) 408-7543
http://www.htcia.org

IEEE Computer Society
1730 Massachusetts Avenue NW
Washington, DC 20036
Phone: (202) 371-0101
Fax: (202) 728-9614
http://www.computer.org

IEEE Robotics and Automation Society
http://www.ieee-ras.org

Information Systems Security Association
9220 SW Barbur Boulevard
#119-333
Portland, OR 97219
Phone: (866) 349-5818 or (206) 388-4584
Fax: (206) 299-3366
http://www.issa.org

ISACA
3701 Algonquin Road
Suite 1010
Rolling Meadows, IL 60008
Phone: (847) 253-1545
Fax: (847) 253-1443
http://www.isaca.org

AGRICULTURAL SCIENCE AND FOOD SCIENCE

American Chemical Society
1155 Sixteenth Street NW
Washington, DC 20036
Phone: (800) 227-5558 or (202) 872-4600
Fax: (202) 872-4615
http://www.chemistry.org

American Dairy Science Association
1111 North Dunlap Avenue
Savoy, IL 61874
Phone: (217) 356-5146
Fax: (217) 398-4119
http://www.adsa.org

American Meat Science Association
1111 North Dunlap Avenue
Savoy, IL 61874
Phone: (217) 356-5368
http://www.meatscience.org

American Society for Horticultural Science
113 South West Street
Suite 200
Alexandria, VA 22314
Phone: (703) 836-4606
Fax: (703) 836-2024
http://www.ashs.org

American Society of Agronomy
677 South Segoe Road
Madison, WI 53711
Phone: (608) 273-8080
Fax: (608) 273-2021
http://www.agronomy.org

American Society of Animal Science
1111 North Dunlap Avenue
Savoy, IL 61874

Phone: (217) 356-9050
Fax: (217) 398-4119
http://www.asas.org

Association of Women Soil Scientists
http://www.womeninsoils.org

Botanical Society of America
P.O. Box 299
St. Louis, MO 63166
Phone: (314) 577-9566
Fax: (314) 577-9515
http://www.botany.org

Crop Science Society of America
677 South Segoe Road
Madison, WI 53711
Phone: (608) 273-8080
Fax: (608) 273-2021
http://www.crops.org

Institute of Food Technologists
525 West Van Buren
Suite 1000
Chicago, IL 60607
Phone: (312) 782-8424
Fax: (312) 782-8348
http://www.ift.org

National Society of Consulting Soil Scientists, Inc.
P.O. Box 1724
Sandpoint, ID 83864
Phone: (800) 535-7148
Fax: (208) 263-7013
http://www.nscss.org

Poultry Science Association
1111 North Dunlap Avenue
Savoy, IL 61874
Phone: (217) 356-5285
Fax: (217) 398-4119
http://www.poultryscience.org

Society of Flavor Chemists
3301 Route 66
Suite 205, Building C
Neptune, NJ 07753
Phone: (732) 922-3393
Fax: (732) 922-3590
http://www.flavorchemist.org

Soil Science Society of America
677 South Segoe Road

Madison, WI 53711
Phone: (608) 273-8080
Fax: (608) 273-2021
http://www.soils.org

MEDICAL SCIENCE

American Academy of Pediatrics—Section on Epidemiology
141 Northwest Point Boulevard
Elk Grove Village, IL 60007
Phone: (847) 434-4000
http://www.aap.org/sections/
epidemiology

American Association for Clinical Chemistry
1850 K Street NW, Suite 625
Washington, DC 20006
Phone: (800) 892-1400 or
(202) 857-0717
Fax: (202) 887-5093
http://www.aacc.org

American Association for the Advancement of Science
1200 New York Avenue NW
Washington, DC 20005
Phone: (202) 326-6400
http://www.aaas.org

American Association of Bioanalysts
906 Olive Street
Suite 1200
St. Louis, MO 63101
Phone: (314) 241-1445
Fax: (314) 241-1449
http://www.aab.org

American Association of Immunologists
9650 Rockville Pike
Bethesda, MD 20814
Phone: (301) 634-7178
Fax: (301) 634-7887
http://www.aai.org

American Association of Pharmaceutical Scientists
2107 Wilson Boulevard
Suite 700
Arlington, VA 22201

Phone: (703) 243-2800
Fax: (703) 243-9650
http://www.aaps.org

American Association of Physicists in Medicine
1 Physics Ellipse
College Park, MD 20740
Phone: (301) 209-3350
Fax: (301) 209-0862
http://www.aapm.org

American Chemical Society
1155 Sixteenth Street NW
Washington, DC 20036
Phone: (800) 227-5558 or
(202) 872-4600
Fax: (202) 872-4615
http://www.chemistry.org

American College of Clinical Pharmacology
3 Ellinwood Court
New Hartsford, NY 13413
Phone: (315) 768-6117
Fax: (315) 768-6119
http://www.accp1.org

American College of Epidemiology
1500 Sunday Drive
Suite 102
Raleigh, NC 27607
Phone: (919) 861-5573
Fax: (919) 787-4916
http://www.acepidemiology.org

American College of Medical Physics
12100 Sunset Hills Road
Suite 130
Reston, VA 20190
Phone: (703) 481-5001
Fax: (703) 435-4390
http://www.acmp.org

American College of Preventative Medicine
1307 New York Avenue NW
Suite 200
Washington, DC 20005
Phone: (202) 466-2044
Fax: (202) 466-2662
http://www.acpm.org

American College of Radiology
1891 Preston White Drive
Reston, VA 20191
Phone: (703) 648-8900
http://www.acr.org

American Medical Association
515 North State Street
Chicago, IL 60610
Phone: (800) 621-8335
http://www.ama-assn.org

American Medical Technologists
10700 West Higgins Road
Suite 150
Rosemont, IL 60018
Phone: (800) 275-1268 or
(847) 823-5169
Fax: (847) 823-0458
http://www.amt1.com

American Physical Society
1 Physics Ellipse
College Park, MD 20740
Phone: (301) 209-3200
Fax: (301) 209-0865
http://www.aps.org

American Psychological Association—Division of Psychopharmacology and Substance Abuse
750 First Street NE
Washington, DC 20002
Phone: (800) 374-2721 or (202)
336-5500
http://www.apa.org/divisions/div28

American Public Health Association—Epidemiology Section
800 I Street NW
Washington, DC 20001
Phone: (202) 777-APHA
Fax: (202) 777-2533
http://www.apha.org/membergroups/
sections/aphasections/
epidemiology

American Society for Clinical Laboratory Science
6701 Democracy Boulevard
Suite 300

Bethesda, MD 20817
Phone: (301) 657-2768
Fax: (301) 657-2909
http://www.ascls.org

American Society for Clinical Pathology
33 West Monroe
Suite 1600
Chicago, IL 60603
Phone: (800) 267-2727 or (312) 541-4999
Fax: (312) 541-4998
http://www.ascp.org

American Society for Clinical Pharmacology and Therapeutics
528 North Washington Street
Alexandria, VA 22314
Phone: (703) 836-6981
Fax: (703) 836-5223
http://www.ascpt.org

American Society for Histocompatability and Immunogenetics
15000 Commerce Parkway
Suite C
Mt. Laurel, NJ 08054
Phone: (856) 638-0428
Fax: (856) 439-0525
http://www.ashi-hla.org

American Society for Investigative Pathology
9650 Rockville Pike
Bethesda, MD 20814
Phone: (301) 634-7130
Fax: (301) 634-7990
http://www.asip.org

American Society for Pharmacology and Experimental Therapeutics
9650 Rockville Pike, E 220
Bethesda, MD 20814
Phone: (301) 634-7060
Fax: (301) 634-7061
http://www.aspet.org

American Society for Reproductive Immunology
P.O. Box 284
Lake Bluff, IL 60044

Phone: (847) 578-8382
http://www.theasri.org

American Society of Phlebotomy Technicians
P.O. Box 1831
Hickory, NC 28603
Phone: (828) 294-0078
Fax: (828) 327-2969
http://www.aspt.org

Association for Molecular Pathology
9650 Rockville Pike
Bethesda, MD 20814
Phone: (301) 634-7939
Fax: (301) 634-7990
http://www.amp.org

Association for Pathology Informatics
9650 Rockville Pike
Bethesda MD 20814
Phone: (301) 634-7820
Fax: (301) 634-7990
http://www.pathologyinformatics.org

Association for Professionals in Infection Control and Epidemiology
1275 K Street NW
Suite 1000
Washington, DC 20005
Phone: (202) 789-1890
Fax: (202) 789-1899
http://www.apic.org

Association of Genetic Technologists
P.O. Box 15945-288
Lenexa, KS 66285
Phone: (913) 895-4605
Fax: (913) 895-4652
http://www.agt-info.org

Association of Medical Laboratory Immunologists
http://www.amli.org

Biophysical Society
9650 Rockville Pike
Bethesda, MD 20814
Phone: (301) 634-7114
Fax: (301) 634-7133

http://www.biophysics.org

Clinical Immunology Society
555 East Wells Street
Suite 1100
Milwaukee, WI 53202
Phone: (414) 224-8095
Fax: (414) 272-6070
http://www.clinimmsoc.org

College of American Pathologists
325 Waukegan Road
Northfield, IL 60093
Phone: (800) 323-4040 or (847) 832-7000
Fax: (847) 832-8000
http://www.cap.org

Health Physics Society
1313 Dolley Madison Boulevard
Suite 402
McLean, VA 22101
Phone: (703) 790-1745
Fax: (703) 790-2672
http://hps.org

National Society for Histotechnology
10320 Little Patuxent Parkway
Suite 804
Columbia, MD 21044
Phone: (443) 535-4060
Fax: (443) 535-4055
http://www.nsh.org

Society for Cardiovascular Pathology
http://scvp.net

Society for Epidemiologic Research
P.O. Box 990
Clearfield, UT 84098
Phone: (801) 525-0231
Fax: (801) 774-9211
http://www.epiresearch.org

Society for Mucosal Immunology
5272 River Road, Suite 630
Bethesda, MD 20816
Phone: (301) 718-6516
Fax: (301) 656-0989
http://www.socmucimm.org

Society for Pediatric Pathology
c/o United States and Canadian
Academy of Pathology (USCAP)
3643 Walton Way Extension
Augusta, GA 30909
Phone: (706) 364-3375
Fax: (706) 733-8033
http://www.spponline.org

United States and Canadian Academy of Pathology
3643 Walton Way Extension
Augusta, GA 30909
Phone: (706) 733-7550
Fax: (706) 733-8033
http://www.uscap.org

ENVIRONMENTAL PROTECTION AND CONSERVATION

Air and Waste Management Association
One Gateway Center, 3rd Floor
420 Fort Duquesne Boulevard
Pittsburgh, PA 15222
Phone: (800) 270-3444 or (412) 232-3444
Fax: (412) 232-3450
http://www.awma.org

American Association for the Advancement of Science
1200 New York Avenue NW
Washington, DC 20005
Phone: (202) 326-6400
http://www.aaas.org

American Chemical Society— Division of Environmental Chemistry
http://www.envirofacs.org

American Forage and Grassland Council
350 Poplar Avenue
Elmhurst, IL 60126
Phone: (800) 944-2342 or (630) 941-3240
Fax: (630) 359-4274
http://www.afgc.org

American Institute of Chemists
315 Chestnut Street
Philadelphia, PA 19106
Phone: (215) 873-8224
Fax: (215) 629-5224
http://www.theaic.org

American Planning Association
122 South Michigan Avenue
Suite 1600
Chicago, IL 60603
Phone: (312) 431-9100
Fax: (312) 431-9985
http://www.planning.org

American Society of Agronomy
677 South Segoe Road
Madison, WI 53711
Phone: (608) 273-8080
Fax: (608) 273-2021
http://www.agronomy.org

Association of Consulting Foresters of America
312 Montgomery Street
Suite 208
Alexandria, VA 22314
Phone: (703) 548-0990
Fax: (703) 548-6395
http://www.acf-foresters.com

Ecological Society of America
1707 H Street NW
Suite 400
Washington, DC 20006
Phone: (202) 833-8773
Fax: (202) 833-8775
http://www.esa.org

Forest Guild
P.O. Box 519
Santa Fe, NM 87504
Phone: (505) 983-8992
Fax: (505) 986-0798
http://www.foreststewardsguild.org

National Association of Environmental Professionals
389 Main Street
Suite 202
Maiden, MA 02148
Phone: (888) 251-9902 or (781) 347-8870

Fax: (781) 397-8887
http://www.naep.org

National Ground Water Association
601 Dempsey Road
Westerville, OH 43081
Phone: (800) 551-7379 or (614) 898-7791
Fax: (614) 898-7786
http://www.ngwa.org

Society for Range Management
10030 West 27th Avenue
Wheat Ridge, CO 80215
Phone: (303) 986-3309
Fax: (303) 986-3892
http://www.rangelands.org

Society of American Foresters
5400 Grosvenor Lane
Bethesda, MD 20814
Phone: (866) 897-8720 or (301) 897-8720
Fax: (301) 897-3690
http://www.safnet.org

Soil and Water Conservation Society
945 SW Ankeny Road
Ankeny, IA 50023
Phone: (515) 289-2331
Fax: (515) 289-1227
http://www.swcs.org

Water Environment Federation
601 Wythe Street
Alexandria, VA 22314
Phone: (800) 666-0206
Fax: (703) 684-2492
http://www.wef.org

OPPORTUNITIES IN GOVERNMENT

American Academy of Forensic Sciences
410 North 21st Street
Suite 203
Colorado Springs, CO 80904
Phone: (719) 636-1100
Fax: (719) 636-1993
http://www.aafs.org

American Association for the Advancement of Science
1200 New York Avenue NW
Washington, DC 20005
Phone: (202) 326-6400
http://www.aaas.org

American Chemical Society
1155 Sixteenth Street NW
Washington, DC 20036
Phone: (800) 227-5558 or
(202) 872-4600
Fax: (202) 872-4615
http://www.chemistry.org

American Geophysical Union
2000 Florida Avenue NW
Washington, DC 20009
Phone: (800) 966-2481 or
(202) 462-6900
Fax: (202) 328-0566
http://www.agu.org

American Institute of Physics
1 Physics Ellipse
College Park, MD 20740
Phone: (301) 209-3100
http://www.aip.org

American Mathematical Society
201 Charles Street
Providence, RI 02904
Phone: (800) 321-4267 or
(401) 455-4000
http://www.ams.org

American Society for Microbiology
1752 N Street NW
Washington, DC 20036
Phone: (202) 737-3600
http://www.asm.org

American Society of Questioned Document Examiners
P.O. Box 382684
Germantown, TN 38183
http://www.asqde.org

Association for Public Policy Analyses and Management
1029 Vermont Avenue NW
Suite 1150
Washington, DC 20005

Phone: (202) 496-0130
Fax: (202) 496-0134
http://www.appam.org

Association of Firearm and Toolmark Examiners
http://www.afte.org

Institute of Food Technologists
525 West Buren, Suite 1000
Chicago, IL 60607
Phone: (312) 782-8424
Fax: (312) 782-8348
http://www.ift.org

International Association of Bloodstain Pattern Analysts
http://www.iabpa.org

Society for Integrative and Comparative Biology
1313 Dolley Madison Boulevard
Suite 402
McLean, VA 22101
Phone: (800) 955-1236 or (703) 790-1745
Fax: (703) 790-2672
http://www.sicb.org

Society of American Foresters
5400 Grosvenor Lane
Bethesda, MD 20814
Phone: (866) 897-8720 or (301) 897-8720
Fax: (301) 897-3690
http://www.safnet.org

Society of Forensic Toxicologists
1 MacDonald Center
1 MacDonald Street
Suite 15
Mesa, AZ 85201
Phone/Fax: (888) 866-7638
http://www.soft-tox.org

OPPORTUNITIES IN INDUSTRY

Agricultural and Industrial Manufacturers Representatives Association
7500 Flying Cloud Drive

Suite 900
Eden Prairie, MN 55344
Phone: (952) 253-6230
Fax: (952) 835-4774
http://www.aimrareps.org

American Chemical Society
1155 Sixteenth Street NW
Washington, DC 20036
Phone: (800) 227-5558 or (202) 872-4600
Fax: (202) 872-4615
http://www.chemistry.org

American Marketing Association
311 South Wacker Drive
Suite 5800
Chicago, IL 60606
Phone: (800) AMA-1150
http://www.marketingpower.com

American Society for Quality
600 North Plankinton Avenue
Milwaukee, WI 53203
Mailing Address:
P.O. Box 3005
Milwaukee, WI 53201
Phone: (800) 248-1946 or (414) 272-8575
Fax: (414) 272-1734
http://www.asq.org

Electronics Representatives Association International
300 West Adams Street
Suite 617
Chicago, IL 60606
Phone: (312) 527-3050
Fax: (312) 527-3783
http://www.era.org

IEEE Professional Communication Society
http://www.ieeepcs.org

Institute of Food Technologists
525 West Van Buren
Suite 1000
Chicago, IL 60607
Phone: (312) 782-8424
Fax: (312) 782-8348
http://www.ift.org

Marketing Research Association
110 National Drive
2nd Floor
Glastonbury, CT 06033
Phone: (860) 682-1000
Fax: (860) 682-10110
http://www.mra-net.org

**National Association of Medical
Sales Representatives**
2776 South Arlington Mill Drive
Suite 504
Arlington, VA 22206
Phone: (800) 580-6960
http://www.medicalsalescareer.com

**National Association of Patent
Practitioners**
4680-18i Monticello Avenue
PMB 101
Williamsburg, VA 23188
Phone: (800) 216-9588
Fax: (757) 220-2231
http://www.napp.org

**National Association of Sales
Professionals**
8300 North Hayden Road
Suite 207
Scottsdale, AZ 85258
Phone: (480) 951-4311
http://www.nasp.com

National Writers Union
113 University Place, 6th Floor
New York, NY 10003
Phone: (212) 254-0279
Fax: (212) 254-0673
http://www.nwu.org

Project Management Institute
4 Campus Boulevard
Newtown Square, PA 19073
Phone: (610) 356-4600
Fax: (610) 356-4647
http://www.pmi.org

**Qualitative Research
Consultants Association**
1000 Westgate Drive
Suite 252
St. Paul, MN 55114
Phone: (888) 674-7722 or
(651) 290-7491

Fax: (651) 290-2266
http://www.qrca.org

**Regulatory Affairs
Professionals Society**
5635 Fishers Lane
Suite 550
Rockville, MD 20852
Phone: (301) 770-2920
Fax: (301) 770-2924
http://www.raps.org

**Society for Technical
Communication**
901 North Stuart Street
Suite 904
Arlington, VA 22203
Phone: (703) 522-4114
Fax: (703) 522-2075
http://www.stc.org

ENTREPRENEURSHIP

**American Association of
Healthcare Consultants**
5938 North Drake Avenue
Chicago, IL 60059
Phone: (888) 350-2242
http://www.aahc.net

**Association of University
Technology Managers**
60 Revere Drive
Suite 500
Northbrook, IL 60062
Phone: (847) 559-0846
Fax: (847) 480-9282
http://www.autm.net

**Institute of Management
Consultants USA, Inc.**
2025 M Street NW
Suite 800
Washington, DC 20036
Phone: (800) 221-2557 or
(202) 367-1134
Fax: (202) 367-2134
http://www.imcusa.org

**Professional and Technical
Consultants Association**
P.O. Box 2261
Santa Clara, CA 95055
Phone: (800) 747-2822 or
(408) 971-5902

Fax: (866) 746-1053
http://www.patca.org

Technology Transfer Society
2005 Arthur Lane
Austin, TX 78704
http://www.t2society.org

EDUCATION AND COMMUNICATIONS

ACE
Building 116, Mowry Road
P.O. Box 110811
Gainesville, FL 32611
Phone: (352) 392-9588
Fax: (352) 392-8583
http://www.aceweb.org

**American Association for
Adult and Continuing
Education**
10111 Martin Luther King, Jr.
Highway
Suite 200C
Bowie, MD 20720
Phone: (301) 459-6261
Fax: (301) 459-6241
http://www.aaace.org

**American Association for the
Advancement of Science**
1200 New York Avenue NW
Washington, DC 20005
Phone: (202) 326-6400
http://www.aaas.org

**American Association of
Museums**
1575 I Street NW
Suite 400
Washington, DC 20005
Phone: (202) 289-1818
Fax: (202) 289-6578
http://www.aam-us.org

**American Association of
Physics Teachers**
1 Physics Ellipse
College Park, MD 20740
Phone: (301) 209-3311
http://www.aapt.org

American Association of University Professors
1012 Fourteenth Street NW
Suite 500
Washington, DC 20005
Phone: (202) 737-5900
Fax: (202) 737-5526
http://www.aaup.org

American Astronomical Society
2000 Florida Avenue NW
Suite 400
Washington, DC 20009
Phone: (202) 328-2010
Fax: (202) 234-2560
http://www.aas.org

American Federation of Teachers
555 New Jersey Avenue NW
Washington, DC 20001
Phone: (202) 879-4440
http://www.aft.org

American Geological Institute
4220 King Street
Alexandria, VA 22302
Phone: (703) 379-2480
Fax: (703) 379-7563
http://www.agiweb.org

American Geophysical Union
2000 Florida Avenue NW
Washington, DC 20009
Phone: (800) 966-2481 or (202) 462-6900
Fax: (202) 328-0566
http://www.agu.org

American Institute of Biological Sciences
1444 I Street NW
Suite 200
Washington, DC 20005
Phone: (202) 628-1500
Fax: (202) 628-1509
http://www.aibs.org

American Institute of Physics
1 Physics Ellipse
College Park, MD 20740
Phone: (301) 209-3100
http://www.aip.org

American Medical Writers Association
40 West Gude Drive
Suite 101
Rockville, MD 20850
Phone: (301) 294-5303
http://www.amwa.org

American Society of Botanical Artists, Inc.
47 Fifth Avenue
New York, NY 10003
Phone: (866) 691-9080 or (212) 691-9080
Fax: (212) 691-9130
http://www.amsocbotartists.org

American Society of Journalists and Authors
1501 Broadway
Suite 302
New York, NY 10036
Phone: (212) 997-0947
Fax: (212) 768-7414
http://www.asja.org

Association of Health Care Journalists
Missouri School of Journalism
10 Neff Hall
Columbia, MO 65211
Phone: (573) 884-5606
Fax: (573) 884-5609
http://www.healthjournalism.org

Association of Medical Illustrators
P.O. Box 1897
Lawrence, KS 66044
Phone: (866) 393-4264
Fax: (785) 843-1274
http://www.ami.org

Association of Science-Technology Centers
1025 Vermont Avenue NW
Suite 500
Washington, DC 20005
Phone: (202) 783-7200
Fax: (202) 783-7207
http://www.astc.org

Association of Zoos and Aquariums
8403 Colesville Road
Suite 710
Silver Spring, MD 20910
Phone: (301) 562-0777
Fax: (301) 562-0888
http://www.aza.org

BioCommunications Association
http://www.bca.org

Entomological Society of America
10001 Derekwood Lane
Suite 100
Lanham, MD 20706
Phone: (301) 731-4535
Fax: (301) 731-4538
http://www.entsoc.org

Graphic Artists Guild
32 Broadway, Suite 1114
New York, NY 10004
Phone: (212) 791-3400
http://www.gag.org

Guild of Natural Science Illustrators
P.O. Box 652
Ben Franklin Station
Washington, DC 20044
Phone: (301) 309-1514
http://www.gnsi.org

Health and Sciences Communications Association
39 Wedgewood Drive
Suite A
Jewett City, CT 06351
Phone: (860) 376-5915
http://www.hesca.org

International Association of Astronomical Artists
http://www.iaaa.org

International Technology Education Association
1914 Association Drive
Suite 201
Reston, VA 20191

Phone: (703) 860-2100
Fax: (703) 860-0353
http://www.iteaconnect.org

Mathematical Association of America

1529 Eighteenth Street NW
Washington, DC 20036
Phone: (800) 741-9415 or (202) 387-5200
Fax: (202) 265-2384
http://www.maa.org

National Association of Biology Teachers

12030 Sunrise Valley Drive
Suite 110
Reston, VA 20191
Phone: (800) 406-0775 or (703) 264-9696
Fax: (703) 264-7778
http://www.nabt.org

National Association of Scholars

221 Witherspoon Street
2nd Floor
Princeton, NJ 08542
Phone: (609) 683-7878
http://www.nas.org

National Association of Science Writers

P.O. Box 890
Hedgesville, WV 25427
Phone: (304) 754-5077
http://nasw.org

National Council of Teachers of Mathematics

1906 Association Drive
Reston, VA 20191
Phone: (703) 620-9840

Fax: (703) 476-2970
http://www.nctm.org

National Earth Science Teachers Association

http://www.nestanet.org

National Education Association

1201 16th Street NW
Washington, DC 20036
Phone: (202) 833-4000
Fax: (202) 822-7974
http://www.nea.org

National Marine Educators Association

http://www.marine-ed.org

National Science Teachers Association

1840 Wilson Boulevard
Arlington, VA 22201
Phone: (703) 243-7100
Fax: (703) 243-7177
http://www.nsta.org

National Writers Union

113 University Place
6th Floor
New York, NY 10003
Phone: (212) 254-0279
Fax: (212) 254-0673
http://www.nwu.org

North American Association for Environmental Education

2000 P Street NW, Suite 540
Washington, DC 20036
Phone: (202) 419-0412
Fax: (202) 419-0415
http://naaee.org

Paleontological Society

http://www.paleosoc.org

Public Relations Society of America—Technology Section

33 Maiden Lane
11th Floor
New York, NY 10038
http://www.prsa.org/networking/sections/technology

Society for Integrative and Comparative Biology

1313 Dolley Madison Boulevard
Suite 402
McLean, VA 22101
Phone: (800) 955-1236 or (703) 790-1745
Fax: (703) 790-2672
http://www.sicb.org

Society for Technical Communication

901 North Stuart Street
Suite 904
Arlington, VA 22203
Phone: (703) 522-4114
Fax: (703) 522-2075
http://www.stc.org

Society for the Preservation of Natural History Collections

http://www.spnhc.org

Society of Environmental Journalists

P.O. Box 2492
Jenkintown, PA 19046
Phone: (215) 884-8174
Fax: (215) 884-8175
http://www.sej.org

APPENDIX IV
RESOURCES ON
THE WORLD WIDE WEB

Listed in this appendix are Web sites and Web pages that can help you learn more about many of the professions that are discussed in this book. You will also find some resources that offer career and job search information.

Note: All Web site addresses were current when this book was being written. For a Web site address that no longer works, you may be able to find its new one—try entering the name of the organization or Web page in a search engine.

CAREER AND JOB INFORMATION

AAAS Career Center
http://www.aaas.org/careercenter

America's Career InfoNet
http://www.careerinfonet.org

CareerOneStop
http://www.careeronestop.org

Career Prospects in Virginia
http://www.ccps.virginia.edu/
    career_prospects

Career Voyages
http://www.careervoyages.gov

CollegeGrad.com
http://www.collegegrad.com

ISEEK
http://www.iseek.org

Monster
http://www.monster.com

Occupational Employment Statistics
U.S. Bureau of Labor Statistics
http://www.bls.gov/oes

Occupational Outlook Handbook
U.S. Bureau of Labor Statistics
http://www.bls.gov/oco

O*NET OnLine
http://online.onetcenter.org

PhDs.org: Science, Math, and Engineering Career Resources
http://www.phds.org

Science Careers
(from the journal *Science*)
http://sciencecareers.sciencemag.
    org

Sloan Career Cornerstone Center
http://www.careercornerstone.org

USA Jobs—The Federal Government's Official Job Site
http://www.usajobs.opm.gov

SCIENCE—GENERAL INFORMATION

Alfred P. Sloan Foundation
http://www.sloan.org

Eric Weisstein's World of Science
A Wolfram Web Resource
http://scienceworld.wolfram.com

MadSci Network
http://www.madsci.org

National Academy of Sciences
http://www.nasonline.org

National Academies Press
http://www.nap.edu

National Science Foundation
http://www.nsf.gov

PBS—Scientific American Frontiers
http://www.pbs.org/saf

Public Library of Science
http://www.publiclibraryofscience.
    org

ACTUARY

Actuarial Grads Network
http://www.actuarialgrads.com

Actuarial Outpost
http://www.actuarialoutpost.com

Actuary.com
http://www.actuary.com

AGRICULTURAL TECHNICIAN

Agriculture Network Information Center
http://www.agnic.org

American Farm Bureau
http://www.fb.org

Sustainable Agriculture Research and Education
http://www.sare.org

USDA Animal and Plant Health Inspection Service
http://www.aphis.usda.gov

ANIMAL SCIENTIST

American Registry of Professional Animal Scientists
http://www.arpas.org

Animal Agriculture Links
AgricultureLaw.com
http://www.agriculturelaw.com/
links/animalag.htm

Animals and Animal Products
U.S. Cooperative State Research, Education, and Extension Service
http://www.csrees.usda.gov/nea/
animals/animals.cfm

Aquaculture Network Information Center
http://aquanic.org

AQUATIC BIOLOGIST

Bridge
Sea Grant Ocean Sciences Education Center
http://www.vims.edu/bridge

National Marine Fisheries Service
http://www.nmfs.noaa.gov

ARTIFICIAL INTELLIGENCE SCIENTIST

AI Topics
Association for the Advancement of Artificial Intelligence
http://www.aaai.org/aitopics

AI Depot
http://ai-depot.com

ASTRONOMER

American Association of Amateur Astronomers
http://www.astromax.com

American Association of Variable Star Observers
http://www.aavso.org

Astronomical Observatory Links
The NGC/IC Project
http://www.ngcic.org/obs.htm

Astronomical Society of the Pacific
http://www.astrosociety.org

National Aeronautics and Space Administration (NASA)
http://www.nasa.gov

BIOCHEMIST

Biochemistry Links
by Dr. Jeffrey Cohlberg, California State University, Long Beach
http://www.csulb.edu/~cohlberg/
biochemlinks.html

Biochemical Society
http://www.biochemistry.org

The Biology Project: Biochemistry
http://www.biology.arizona.edu/
biochemistry/biochemistry.html

BIOINFORMATICS SCIENTIST

Bioinformatics.org
http://bioinformatics.org

National Center for Biotechnology Information
http://www.ncbi.nlm.nih.gov

BIOLOGICAL TECHNICIAN

ActionBioscience.org
http://www.actionbioscience.org

American Institute of Biological Sciences
http://www.aibs.org

BIOLOGIST

Biology Browser
http://www.biologybrowser.org

Federation of American Societies for Experimental Biology
http://www.faseb.org

Organization of Biological Field Stations
http://www.obfs.org

Tree of Life Web Project
http://www.tolweb.org

BIOPHYSICIST

Resources in Biophysics
Biophysical Society
http://www.biophysics.org/
education/resources.htm

Structural Biophysics Web Resources
Stephen White Laboratory at UC Irvine
http://blanco.biomol.uci.edu/
WWWResources.html

BIOTECHNOLOGIST

Bio.com Career Center
http://www.bio.com/jobs

BioTech
University of Texas Institute for
    Cellular and Molecular Biology
http://biotech.icmb.utexas.edu

biotechbasics.com
http://www.biotechbasics.com

**Biotechnology and Genomics
Overview**
U.S. Cooperative State Research,
    Education, and Extension
    Service
http://www.csrees.usda.gov/nea/
    biotech/biotech.cfm

Biotechnology Institute
http://www.biotechinstitute.org

BiotechnologyJobs.com
http://www.biotechnologyjobs.com

BOTANIST

**American Society of Plant
Biologists**
http://www.aspb.org

**American Society of Plant
Taxonomists**
http://www.aspt.net

Botany.Com
http://www.botany.com

Internet Directory for Botany
http://www.botany.net/IDB

CARTOGRAPHER

**American Congress on
Surveying and Mapping**
http://www.acsm.net

**Geography and Map Reading
Room**
Library of Congress
http://www.loc.gov/rr/geogmap

**Maps: Links@
nationalgeographic.com**
http://www.nationalgeographic.
    com/maps/map_links.html

CHEMICAL TECHNICIAN

Chemicals Technology
http://www.chemicals-technology.
    com

ChemTechLinks
American Chemical Society
http://www.chemtechlinks.org

CHEMIST

**American Board of Clinical
Chemistry**
http://apps.aacc.org/abcc

**National Registry of Certified
Chemists**
http://www.nrcc6.org

**WWW Virtual Library: Links
for Chemists**
http://www.liv.ac.uk/Chemistry/
    Links/links.html

**World Wide Web Resources in
Chemistry**
Hiram College Library
http://library.hiram.edu/sub_chem.
    htm

CLIMATOLOGIST

Climate Organizations
Virginia State Climatology Office
http://climate.virginia.edu/orgs.htm

Earth Science Office
http://www.ghcc.msfc.nasa.gov

**WWW Virtual Library:
Paleoclimatology and
Paleooceanography**
http://www.datasync.com/~farrar/
    www_vl_paleoclim.html

COMPUTER SCIENTIST

**Computer Professionals for
Social Responsibility**
http://cpsr.org

Computing Careers
by Association for Computing
    Machinery
http://computingcareers.acm.org

**MIT Computer Science and
Artificial Intelligence
Laboratory**
http://www.csail.mit.edu

CRIMINALIST

**American Board of
Criminalistics**
http://www.criminalistics.com

**American Society of Crime
Laboratory Directors**
http://www.ascld.org

**Carpenter's Forensic Science
Resources**
http://www.tncrimlaw.com/forensic

Dr. Henry Lee
http://www.drhenrylee.com

**International Association for
Identification**
http://www.theiai.org

**Young Forensic Scientists
Forum**
http://www.aafs.org/yfsf

CROP SCIENTIST

**American Seed Trade
Association**
http://www.amseed.com

**Food and Organization of the
United Nations**
http://www.fao.org

NewCROP
Center for New Crops and Plant
    Products
Purdue University
http://www.hort.purdue.edu/
    newcrop/default.html

U.S. Department of Agriculture
http://www.usda.gov

**Weed Science Society of
America**
http://www.wssa.net

CRYPTOGRAPHER

American Cryptogram Association
http://www.cryptogram.org

An Overview of Cryptography
by Gary C. Kessler
http://www.garykessler.net/library/crypto.html

International Financial Cryptography Association
http://ifca.ai

National Cryptologic Museum
http://www.nsa.gov/museum

ECOLOGIST

American Society of Naturalists
http://www.amnat.org

Ecology.com
http://www.ecology.com

ECO World: Global Environmental Community
http://www.ecoworld.com

Society for Ecological Restoration
http://www.ser.org

ENTOMOLOGIST

American Board of Forensic Entomology
http://research.missouri.edu/entomology

Bug Bios: Insects on the Web
http://www.insects.org

Bugwood Network
Department of Entomology, University of Georgia
http://www.bugwood.org

ENTREPRENEUR

Entrepreneurial Connection
http://www.entrepreneurialconnection.com

Ewing Marion Kauffman Foundation
http://wwww.kauffman.org

National Association for the Self-Employed
http://www.nase.org

National Business Incubation Association
http://www.nbia.org

ENVIRONMENTAL CHEMIST

EnvironmentalChemistry.com
http://environmentalchemistry.com

Links
Division of Environmental Chemistry, American Chemical Society
http://www.envirofacs.org/links.html

National Registry of Certified Chemists
http://www.nrcc6.org

ENVIRONMENTAL PLANNER

Environmental Planning Online
UC Berkeley Library
http://www.lib.berkeley.edu/ENVI/environ.html

Planners Network
http://www.plannersnetwork.org

ENVIRONMENTAL SCIENTIST

Envirolink: The Online Environmental Community
http://www.envirolink.org

Environmental Careers Organization
http://www.eco.org

Institute of Professional Environmental Practice
http://www.ipep.org

National Registry of Environmental Professionals
http://www.nrep.org

ENVIRONMENTAL TECHNICIAN

National Association of Local Government Environmental Professionals
http://www.nalgep.org

Ubiquity
by Nicholas D'Amato
http://www.geocities.com/RainForest/8974/homepage.htm

EPIDEMIOLOGIST

U.S. Centers for Disease Control and Prevention
http://www.cdc.gov

The World-Wide Web Virtual Library: Epidemiology
http://www.epibiostat.ucsf.edu/epidem/epidem.html

FEDERAL SCIENTIST

Federal R&D Project Summaries
http://www.osti.gov/fedrnd

Partnership for Public Service
http://www.ourpublicservice.org

FOOD SCIENCE TECHNICIAN

CareersinFood.com
http://www.careersinfood.com

Food and Agriculture Organization of the United Nations
http://www.fao.org

FOOD SCIENTIST

U.S. Food and Nutrition Information Center
http://fnic.nal.usda.gov

U.S. Food Safety and Inspection Service
http://www.fsis.usda.gov

The World of Food Science
http://www.worldfoodscience.org

FORESTER

American Forests
http://www.americanforests.org

Davies and Company
Karl Davies
http://www.daviesand.com

National Association of State Foresters
http://www.stateforesters.org

GENETICIST

American Board of Genetic Counseling
http://www.abgc.net

American Board of Medical Genetics
http://www.abmg.org

Association of Genetic Technologists
http://www.agt-info.org

genomics.energy.gov
U.S. Department of Energy Office of Science
http://genomics.energy.gov

GEOGRAPHER

Center for International Earth Science Information Network
http://www.ciesin.org

Geography
U.S. Geological Survey
http://geography.usgs.gov

National Geographic Society
http://www.nationalgeographic.com

U.S. National Park Service
http://www.nps.gov

GEOGRAPHIC INFORMATION SYSTEMS (GIS) SPECIALIST

Global Spatial Data Infrastructure Association
http://www.gsdi.org

National Center for Geographic Information and Analysis
UC Santa Barbara
http://www.ncgia.ucsb.edu

WebGIS
http://www.webgis.com

GEOLOGIST

Earth Science Resources: Geology Oceanography, Astronomy and Ecology
by R. Hays Cummins, Miami University
http://jrscience.wcp.muohio.edu/html/earthsci.html

Guide to Human Resources in the Geosciences
http://guide.agiweb.org

National Association of State Boards of Geology
http://www.asbog.org

GEOPHYSICIST

Earth Science World—Gateway to the Geosciences
http://www.earthscienceworld.org

National Geophysical Data Center
http://www.ngdc.noaa.gov

U.S. Department of the Interior
http://www.doi.gov

HEALTH PHYSICIST

Health Physics Internet Resources
Oak Ridge Associated Universities
http://www.orau.org/busops/ivhp/health-physics/hp-links.htm

The Radiation Information Network
http://www.physics.isu.edu/radinf

RadWaste.org
http://www.radwaste.org

HORTICULTURAL SCIENTIST

American Horticultural Society
http://www.ahs.org

enPlant: Home of Awesome Plant Science Careers
Ohio State University
http://enplant.osu.edu

The Horticultural Web
http://www.horticulture.com

International Society for Horticultural Science
http://www.ishs.org

Jobs in Horticulture
http://www.hortjobs.com

HYDROLOGIST

Global Hydrology Resource Center
http://ghrc.msfc.nasa.gov

Hydrologic Information Center
National Weather Service
http://www.weather.gov/oh/hic

Hydrology Section
American Geophysical Union
http://hydrology.agu.org

Spatial Hydrology.com
http://www.spatialhydrology.com

IMMUNOLOGIST

Immune Central
http://www.immunecentral.com

The Immunology Link Home Page
http://www.immunologylink.com

National Institute of Allergy and Infectious Diseases
http://www3.niaid.nih.gov

INFORMATION SECURITY SPECIALIST

Computer Security Resource Center
National Institute of Standards and Technology
http://csrc.nist.gov

Cybercrime and Internet Issues
http://www.vaonline.org/internet.html

Scheier.com
http://www.schneier.com

MANAGEMENT CONSULTANT

Association of Management Consulting Firms
http://www.amcf.org

Guerrilla Consulting Blog
by Mike McLaughlin
http://guerrillaconsulting.typepad.com

MARKET RESEARCH ANALYST

American Marketing Association
http:www.marketingpower.com

Council of American Survey Research Organizations
http://www.casro.org

MATERIALS SCIENTIST

Materials Science and Engineering Career Resource Center
http://www.crc4mse.org

Materials Science Resources on the Web
by Lorraine J. Pellack
http://www.istl.org/02-spring/internet.html

Scientific.Net: Materials Science
http://www.scientific.net

MATHEMATICIAN

The Math Forum
Drexel University
http://www.mathforum.com

Mathematical Sciences Career Information
http://www.ams.org/careers

MEDICAL PHYSICIST

American Board of Medical Physics
http://www.abmpexam.com

American Board of Radiology
http://www.theabr.org

International Organization for Medical Physics
http://www.iomp.org

MEDICAL SCIENTIST

American Academy of Osteopathy
http://www.academyofosteopathy.org

American Board of Medical Specialties
http://www.abms.org

American Osteopathic Association
http://www.osteopathic.org

Association of American Medical Colleges
http://www.aamc.org

The Student Doctor Network
http://www.studentdoctor.net

U.S. National Institutes of Health
http://www.nih.gov

MEDICAL TECHNOLOGIST/ MEDICAL TECHNICIAN

American Association for Laboratory Animal Science
http://www.aalas.org

Clinical and Laboratory Standards Institute
http://www.nccls.org

Laboratory of Clinical Science
Division of Intramural Research Program, National Institute of Mental Health
http://intramural.nimh.nih.gov/lcs/home.html

Science Information Resources
Science refdesk.com
http://www.refdesk.com/factsci.html

METEOROLOGIST

University Corporation for Atmospheric Research
http://www.ucar.edu

U.S. National Oceanic and Atmospheric Administration
http://www.noaa.gov

WW2010: The Weather World 2010 Project
http://ww2010.atmos.uiuc.edu

MICROBIOLOGIST

American Society for Cell Biology
http://www.ascb.org

Microbe Library
http://www.microbelibrary.org

MOLECULAR BIOLOGIST

Biology Links
Department of Molecular and Cellular Biology, Harvard University
http://mcb.harvard.edu/biolinks.html

NATURAL RESOURCES TECHNICIAN

American Fisheries Society
http://www.fisheries.org

LakeNet
http://www.worldlakes.org

The Nature Conservancy
http://nature.org

U.S. Fish and Wildlife Service
http://www.fws.gov

NUCLEAR PHYSICIST

The ABCs of Nuclear Science
Nuclear Science Division, Lawrence Berkeley National Laboratory
http://www.lbl.gov/abc

Institute for Nuclear Theory
http://int.phys.washington.edu

Nuclear Energy Institute
http://www.nei.org

OCEANOGRAPHER

Center for Coastal
  Environmental Health and
  Bimolecular Research
U.S. National Oceanic and
  Atmospheric Administration
http://www.chbr.noaa.gov

Hopkins Marine Station Career
  Information
http://hopkins.stanford.edu/careers.
  htm

Preparing for a Career in
  Oceanography
Scripps Institution of Oceanography
http://www.siommg.ucsd.edu/
  slices/index.html

Scripps Institution of
  Oceanography
http://sio.ucsd.edu

OPERATIONS RESEARCH ANALYST

INFORMS OR/MS Resource
  Collection
http://www2.informs.org/Resources

Operations Research: The
  Science of Better
http://www.scienceofbetter.org

PALEONTOLOGIST

Paleontology at the U.S.
  Geological Survey
http://geology.er.usgs.gov/paleo

The Paleontology Portal
http://www.paleoportal.org

PATENT AGENT

From Patent to Profit
http://www.frompatenttoprofit.com

Patent Law Links.com
http://www.patentlawlinks.com

World Intellectual Property
  Organization
http://www.wipo.int

PATHOLOGIST

American Board of Pathology
http://www.abpath.org

American College of Veterinary
  Pathologists
http://www.acvp.org

Pathology and Laboratory
  Medicine Internet Resource
  Page
University of Rochester Medical
  Center
http://www.urmc.rochester.edu/
  path/Internet/Index.htm

PHARMACEUTICAL CHEMIST

Drug Information Association
http://diahome.org

Medzilla.com
http://www.medzilla.com

U.S. Food and Drug
  Administration
http://www.fda.gov

U.S. Pharmacopeia
http://www.usp.org

PHARMACOLOGIST

American Board of Clinical
  Pharmacology
http://abcp.net

Pharmaceutical Education and
  Research Institute
http://www.peri.org

Pharmaceutical Research and
  Manufacturers of America
http://www.phrma.org

PHYSICIST

Argonne National Laboratory
http://www.anl.gov

Fear of Physics
http://www.fearofphysics.com

The Net Advance of Physics
http://web.mit.edu/redingtn/www/
  netadv

Physics Central
http://www.physicscentral.com

PhysLink.com
http://www.physlink.com

U.S. Department of Energy
http://www.energy.gov

PHYSIOLOGIST

Careers and Mentoring
The American Physiological Society
http://www.the-aps.org/careers

WWWVirtual Library:
  Physiology and Biophysics
http://neocortex.med.cornell.edu/
  VL-Physio

PROFESSOR

Higher Education Resources
National Science Digital Library
http://nsdl.org/resources_for/
  university_faculty

Teaching Resources on the Web
Faculty and TA Development, Ohio
  State University
http://ftad.osu.edu/sites.html

U.S. Cooperative State Research,
  Education, and Extension
  Service
http://www.csrees.usda.gov

PROGRAMMER

Institute for Certification of
  Computing Professionals
http://www.iccp.org

National Association of Programmers
http://www.napusa.org

PROJECT MANAGER

ALLPM.COM: The Project Manager's Homepage
http://www.allpm.com

gantthead.com: The Online Community for IT Project Managers
http://www.gantthead.com

Project Management.com
http://www.projectmanagement.com

QUALITY PROFESSIONAL

International Organization for Standardization
http://www.iso.org

Quality Resources Online
hosted by Bill Casti, CQA
http://www.quality.org

U.S. Consumer Product Safety Commission
http://www.cpsc.gov

RANGE SCIENTIST

U.S. Bureau of Land Management
http://www.blm.gov

U.S. Natural Resources Conservation Service
http://www.nrcs.usda.gov

REGULATORY AFFAIRS SPECIALIST

Center for Bio/Pharmaceutical and Biodevice Development
San Diego State University
http://www.interwork.sdsu.edu/cbbd

U.S. Food and Drug Administration
http://www.fda.gov

ROBOTICS RESEARCHER

NASA Internet Robotics Resources Index
http://ranier.hq.nasa.gov/telerobotics_page/internetrobots.html

Robotics Online
http://www.roboticsonline.com

Web Resources on Robotics
ORNL Research Libraries
http://www.ornl.gov/Library/robotics.htm

SALES REPRESENTATIVE

Manufacturers' Agents National Association
http://www.manaonline.org

Manufacturers' Representatives Educational Research Foundation
http://www.mrerf.org

Sales Vault
http://www.salesvault.com

SCHOOLTEACHER

Educational REALMS
http://www.ericse.org

Education Week
http://www.edweek.org

goENC.com
http://www.goenc.com

K-12Jobs.com
http://k12jobs.com

The Math Forum
Drexel University
http://www.mathforum.com

National Association of Independent Schools
http//www.nais.org

National Board for Professional Teaching Standards
http://www.nbpts.org

TeachersCount
http://www.teacherscount.org

Teachersplanet.com
http://teachersplanet.com

U.S. Department of Education
http://www.ed.gov

SCIENCE AND TECHNOLOGY POLICY ANALYST

AAAS Center Science, Technology, and Congress
http://www.aaas.org/spp/cstc

AAAS Science and Policy Programs
http://www.aaas.org/spp

Council for Agricultural Science and Technology
http://www.cast-science.org

Institute of Medicine
http://www.iom.edu

National Council for Science and the Environment
http://ncseonline.org

RAND Corporation
http://www.rand.org

SCIENCE CURATOR

Animals—Sea World/Busch Gardens
http://www.seaworld.org

MuseumLink's Museum of Museums
http://www.museumlink.com

Natural History Museums and Collections
http://www.lib.washington.edu/sla/natmus.html

SCIENCE EDUCATOR

Federal Resources for Educational Excellence
http://free.ed.gov

National Science Digital Library
http://nsdl.org

Office of Workforce Development for Teachers and Scientists
Office of Science, U.S. Department of Energy
http://www.scied.science.doe.gov/scied/sci_ed.htm

The Science Page
http://sciencepage.org

SCIENTIFIC ILLUSTRATOR

Biomedical-Illustration.com
http://biomedical-illustration.com

Hunt Institute for Botanical Documentation
http://huntbot.andrew.cmu.edu

Illustrators' Partnership of America
http://www.illustratorspartnership.org

Science-Art.com
http://www.science-art.com

SCIENCE TECHNICIAN

Science Information Resources
http://www.refdesk.com/factsci.html

SCIENCE WRITER

Council for the Advancement of Science Writing
http://www.casw.org

Science Writing and Net Resources Links
by Larry Krumenaker
http://nasw.org/users/larryk/swlinks.htm

WritersNet
http://www.writers.net

WritersResources.com
http://www.writersresources.com

SEISMOLOGIST

Center for Earthquake Research and Information
The University of Memphis
http://www.ceri.memphis.edu

Incorporated Research Institutions for Seismology
http://www.iris.edu

SOIL SCIENTIST

Agricultural Systems
U.S. Cooperative State Research, Education, and Extension Service
http://www.csrees.usda.gov/nea/ag_systems/ag_systems.cfm

NRCS Soils Web site
U.S. Department of Agriculture
http://soils.usda.gov

U.S. Agricultural Research Service
http://www.ars.usda.gov

U.S. National Agricultural Library
http://www.nal.usda.gov

SPACE PHYSICIST

Center for Science Education
UC Berkeley Space Sciences Laboratory
http://cse.ssl.berkeley.edu/scientists.html

Jet Propulsion Laboratory
http://www.jpl.nasa.gov

NASA Polar, Wind, and Geotail Projects
http://www-istp.gsfc.nasa.gov

National Space Science Data Center
http://nssdc.gsfc.nasa.gov

Space Physics Textbook
Space Physics Group of Oulu
http://www.oulu.fi/~~spaceweb/textbook

Universities Space Research Association
http://www.usra.edu

STATISTICIAN

FedStats
http://www.fedstats.gov

WWW Virtual Library: Statistics
http://www.stat.ufl.edu/vlib/statistics.html

TECHNICAL SUPPORT SPECIALIST

bleepingcomputer.com
http://www.bleepingcomputer.com

CompInfo—The Computer Information Center
http://www.compinfo-center.com

Tech Support Alert
http://www.techsupportalert.com

TECHNICAL WRITER

Newbie TechWriter
by Paul Dunham
http://www.cloudnet.com/~pdunham/newbietechwriterhome.html

Techwr-L
by RayComm, Inc. Resource
http://www.techwr-l.com

TECHNOLOGY LICENSING ASSOCIATE

Association of University Technology Managers— Links
http://www.autm.net/aboutTT/aboutTT_links.cfm

Licensing Executives Society International
http://www.lesi.org

Office of Technology
U.S. Small Business Administration
http://www.sba.gov/sbir

Technology Transfer and Licensing
by Franzen Hopper Enterprises
http://users.erols.com/cohenjosh/
120600tran.html

U.S. Copyright Office
http://www.copyright.gov

U.S. Patent and Trademark Office
http://www.uspto.gov

TOXICOLOGIST

American Board of Forensic Toxicology
http://www.abft.org

American Board of Toxicology
http://www.abtox.org

American Board of Veterinary Toxicology
http://www.abvt.org

EXTOXNET—The Extension Toxicology Network
http://extoxnet.orst.edu

VETERINARY TECHNICIAN

American Society for the Prevention of Cruelty to Animals
http://www.aspca.org

Center for Veterinary Medicine
U.S. Food and Drug Administration
http://www.fda.gov/cvm

NetVet Veterinary Resources and the Electronic Zoo
http://netvet.wustl.edu

VOLCANOLOGIST

Alaska Science Forum: Volcanoes Index
http://www.gi.alaska.edu/
ScienceForum/volcanoes.html

Cascades Volcano Observatory
http://vulcan.wr.usgs.gov

Center for the Study of Active Volcanoes
http://www.uhh.hawaii.edu/~csav

ZOOLOGIST

Ark Animals.com
http://www.arkanimals.com

Online Zoologists
by Wesley R. Elsberry and Diane J. Blackwood
http://www.rtis.com/nat/user/
elsberry

GLOSSARY

AAAS American Association for the Advancement of Science.

actuarial science The application of mathematics to identify financial risks, uncertainties, and probabilities that could occur in the future.

adjunct instructor An individual who teaches part-time at a college or university.

administrative Relating to the daily management of an office, program, or organization.

advanced degree A college degree earned beyond a bachelor's degree.

agronomy The study of plants and soils in their surrounding environments.

algorithm The set of logical steps used for solving a mathematical problem.

analysis A detailed examination of something in order to better understand it.

anatomy The study of the internal structure of living organisms.

animal science The study of animals that are used for food, fiber, work, recreation, and companionship.

application The act of using the knowledge and skills of one's discipline for a practical purpose.

applied research Scientific studies that are conducted for practical purposes, such as developing new products, methodologies, or technologies.

applied sciences Science fields in which scientific principles are used for practical purposes; for example, medical science, biotechnology, horticulture, and forensic science.

artificial intelligence (AI) The study of computational models that describe human thinking processes.

associate degree The degree earned upon fulfilling the requirements of a two-year college program.

astronomy The study of the solar system and the universe; this discipline is also known as astrophysics.

astrophysics Another name for astronomy.

atmospheric science Another name for meteorology, the study of the Earth's atmosphere.

bachelor's degree The degree earned upon fulfilling the requirements of a four-year college program.

basic research Scientific studies that are conducted to gain new knowledge and understanding about a subject.

biochemistry The study of how chemicals combine and react within the cells.

bioinformatics The scientific management of all biological information that is stored in computer databases.

biological sciences Life sciences; the various disciplines and subdisciplines of biology.

biology The study of humans, animals, plants, and one-celled organisms.

biomedical research Scientific studies which involve finding ways to prevent, treat, and cure human diseases and conditions.

biophysics The application of physics to the study of life systems.

bioscientist A scientist who studies biology or one of its disciplines or subdisciplines.

biotechnology The study and practice of using living cells and materials to create pharmaceutical, diagnostic, agricultural, and other products.

botany The study of plants.

BLS Bureau of Labor Statistics; the agency in the U.S. Department of Labor that collects, processes, analyzes, and distributes statistical data about labor economics.

candidate A job applicant whom an employer is interested in hiring.

career The occupation a person chooses as his or her line of work.

career center The college office that helps students and alumni plan their careers as well as find employment.

cartography The study and practice of making maps.

chemistry The study of chemicals, or substances, which make up all living and nonliving matter.

climatology The study of the climate, the pattern of weather that occurs over a long period of time in a geographical area.

clinical research Studies which involve testing experimental drugs and treatments on human subjects; the final stages of development of new drugs.

communication skills The speaking and listening abilities a worker needs to successfully perform his or her job.

compliance The meeting of requirements set forth by a specific law or regulation.

computational model   A mathematical model.

computer hardware   All physical parts of a computer; also all computer-related equipment such as a printer or modem.

computer model   A computer program used to create a mathematical, or computational, model.

computer science   The study of computational foundations upon which the operation and design of computers and computer systems are based.

conservation   The protection of air, water, soil, and other natural resources.

criminalistics   The application of science to the analysis, identification, and evaluation of physical evidence that is collected at a crime scene.

crop science   The study and application of growing and managing field crops such as wheat, rice, potatoes, legumes, and cotton.

cryptography   The study of codes and the methods of analyzing and breaking codes.

database   An organized collection of facts and figures that is stored in a computer and that can be accessed and manipulated.

detail-oriented   Able to pay close attention to the various aspects of a task, project, or job.

DNA   Deoxyribonucleic acid; the genetic code of a living organism.

data   Information, including facts and figures.

discipline   A field of study, such as biology, geology, or soil science.

doctorate (or doctoral degree)   An advanced degree; the degree earned upon fulfilling the requirements of a postgraduate program.

duty   A task or responsibility that a worker has been hired to do.

earth sciences   The scientific disciplines that study the Earth, its oceans, and its atmosphere; may also include the disciplines that study space and the solar system.

ecology   The study of how ecosystems are organized and how plants and animals interact with each other in their surroundings.

ecosystem   A geographical area and all living and nonliving things that reside within that area.

entomology   The study of insects and related arthropods such as spiders, ticks, and centipedes.

entrepreneurial   Being willing to risk starting a new business.

entry-level position   A job that a person can obtain with little or no work experience.

environmental science   The study of how human activities affect the environment as well as the practice of preventing, treating, and controlling environmental problems such as air pollution.

EPA   Environmental Protection Agency; the U.S. agency that enforces federal environmental laws.

epidemiology   The study of human health and disease.

estimated wages   An amount that is close to the actual pay a worker earns.

ethical   Behaving justly and honestly.

experience   Paid and volunteer work that an individual has done that is related to the position for which he or she applies.

FDA   Food and Drug Administration; the agency in the U.S. Department of Health and Human Services that enforces federal food and drug laws.

fellowship   An award given to professionals or doctoral-degreed scientists to further their study and training in their field.

flexible   Able to handle changes.

food science   The application of science to the development and production of safe, healthy, and tasty food products that meet customers' satisfaction.

forensic science   The application of sciences to the study of legal and regulatory matters.

forest science   The study and practice of forest conservation and management.

GIS   Geographic information system; the technology used for collecting, storing, and manipulating geographic information on computers.

GPS   Global Positioning System; the technology that uses satellites to automatically pinpoint locations anywhere on Earth.

General Schedule (GS)   The pay schedule used for most federal employees.

genetics   The study of heredity, or how traits, are passed between generations.

geography   The study of the physical processes and human activities that occur on the Earth's surface.

geology   The study of the structure, composition, processes, and history of the Earth.

geophysics   The application of physics to study the Earth's interior.

geosciences   Another name for the earth sciences.

graduate medical education   Medical residency; the years of medical training that medical graduates perform to gain practical experience.

health physics   The study of radiation and the risks and problems it causes.

horticulture   The study of growing fruits, vegetables, and ornamental plants.

hydrology   The study of the water (or hydrologic) cycle.

IEEE Institute of Electrical and Electronic Engineers.

immunology The study of the body's immune system.

independent contractor A self-employed, or free-lance, professional.

independent research Scientific studies in which scientists can choose the topics they wish to research.

industry A group of individuals and organizations that are engaged in the same kind of business enterprise.

internship The period of employment as a trainee or a low-level assistant in order to gain experience.

interpersonal skills The abilities a worker needs to communicate and work well with others on the job.

life process Circulatory, respiratory, or other life system that performs a specific function to keep an organism alive.

life science The study of living things—humans, animals, plants, and microscopic organisms.

life system The cells, tissues, and organs that work together to perform a specific function in a living organism; for example, the circulatory, respiratory, or skeletal system.

market A specific group of people or organizations that have been targeted as likely buyers for a particular product or service.

master's degree An advanced degree that is earned upon fulfilling the requirements of a one- or two-year graduate program.

materials science The study of the properties and applications of metals, ceramics, and various other materials.

mathematical model A mathematical equation that describes the components of a problem and their relationship to each other; also called a computational model.

mathematics The study of measurement, properties, and relationships of quantities and sets.

medical physics The application of radiation, heat, lasers, and other physical tools to the study of diagnosing and treating human diseases and health problems.

medical sciences The scientific disciplines that are involved in the study of medicine.

meteorology The study of the Earth's atmosphere.

methodology A particular set of procedures used to conduct research.

microbe A microorganism such as a virus, mold, alga, or bacterium.

microbiology The study of bacteria, viruses, fungi, and other microbes (or microorganisms).

modeling The use of mathematical equations to predict what may happen.

molecular biology The study of the structure and function of DNA, RNA, and the proteins that reside in the cell nucleus.

morphology The form and structure of a living thing.

nanotechnology A technology that designs and produces very tiny materials, devices, and circuits made from single atoms and molecules.

NASA National Aeronautics and Space Administration; the federal agency that oversees the U.S. space program.

natural resources Air, water, food, shelter, and all other things that are produced in nature and that living organisms need in order to survive.

natural sciences The science disciplines that study natural phenomena.

networking Making contacts with colleagues and other people who may be able to provide information about job openings.

nongovernmental organization A nonprofit organization that is not part of a government agency or business.

nuclear physics The study of the nucleus of the atom.

oceanography The study of the Earth's oceans and coastal environments.

operations research The application of mathematics and other sciences to solve complex problems related to running organizations; this discipline is also known as management science or decision technology.

organism A living thing—human, animal, plant, or microbe.

Ph.D. Doctor of Philosophy.

paleontology The study of fossils of microbes, plants, and animals that lived on Earth over thousands or millions of years ago.

patent The legal right that allows a person to sell his or her invention exclusively.

pathology The study of how cells and tissues are altered by disease; also a medical practice.

pharmacology The study of drugs and how they can best treat or prevent disease and illness.

physical anthropology The study of how the human body has adapted, changed, and evolved over time; this discipline is both a biological science and a social science.

physical sciences The sciences, such as physics and astronomy, that study the nonliving world.

physics The study of matter and energy.

physiology The study of the life processes (such as the respiratory system) that keep organisms alive.

plant A building or group of buildings where manufacturing processes take place; also a building (or buildings) where electric energy is made.

postdoctoral Relating to academic work or research done by a person after earning a doctoral degree.

principle A basic truth, rule, or law.

problem-solving skills The abilities a worker needs to analyze, interpret, and solve problems on the job.

process A series of related steps, activities, or events that must occur in sequence in order for a task to be successfully completed.

product development The phases that a company goes through to turn an idea into a product that can be sold on the market.

production The process of manufacturing products.

project management The oversight and coordination of the activities for a work project.

protocol A standard operating procedure.

psychiatry The medical practice that diagnoses and treats patients with mental problems.

quality Having all the required characteristics; being free of any defects or deficiencies.

quality assurance program All the activities involved in ensuring the quality standards of raw materials, production processes, and final products.

quality control program All the activities involved in checking quality of raw materials, packaging, and products during the production processes.

RNA Ribonucleic acid; the molecules that transmit the DNA code to other parts of the cell.

range science The study and practice of the conservation and management of rangelands such as grasslands, wetlands, and savannas.

regulatory Having to do with government regulations.

research A scientific investigation.

research and development The process of developing new or improved processes, products, or services.

research assistant An individual who provides technical support to research scientists.

research associate An individual who performs complicated research tasks under the supervision of scientists.

research grant Money given by a government agency, corporation, or other organization to researchers so that they may complete their research projects.

research scientist A scientist who conducts research in his or her area of interest.

robotics The scientific study and practical application of robots.

sample A small amount of soil, blood, or body tissue that is taken from the source for scientific or medical examination.

seismology The study of earthquakes.

self-management skills The abilities a worker needs to perform his or her duties without constant supervision.

social sciences The scientific disciplines (such as psychology, sociology, economics, and geography) that study people and their interactions and activities.

software Programs that instruct computers how to operate automatically; also programs that allow computer users to perform specific tasks such as word processing.

soil science The study of soils within their environments.

space physics The study of the physical processes that occur in space.

specialist An individual who has expertise in a particular occupation; for example, a regulatory affairs specialist.

specimen Sample; a small amount of soil, blood, or body tissue that is taken from the source for scientific or medical examination.

start-up venture A new business or company.

statistics The study of the collection, organization, analysis, and interpretation of large masses of numerical data.

subdiscipline A field of study that is part of a major area of study; for example, physical oceanography, marine chemistry, and marine biology are subdisciplines of oceanography.

task A duty or job that an employee must perform.

taxonomy Classification.

teamwork skills The abilities a worker needs to work as part of a group on a job or on a work project.

technician An individual who has the practical technical knowledge and skills of a particular occupation; for example, a chemical technician.

technique A technical method used in conducting scientific research.

technologist A scientist who is involved in the practical application of a science; for example, a food technologist.

technology The application of science for practical purposes.

technology transfer The formal process of assigning the rights of an invention owned by a nonprofit research scientist to a private company for development into commercial products.

toxic   Poisonous.

toxicology   The study of poisonous, or toxic, substances.

translational research   Applied research.

URL   Universe Resource Locator: the address of a Web site on the Internet.

USDA   United States Department of Agriculture.

USPTO   United States Patent and Trademark Office.

volcanology   The study of volcanoes.

zoology   The study of the animal kingdom.

BIBLIOGRAPHY

A. PERIODICALS

Various periodicals are available for the different scientists, technicians, managers, educators, and other professionals that are described in this book. These include magazines, journals, newspapers, newsletters, webzines, and electronic news services.

Many of the print magazines allow limited free access to their articles on the Web. Some of the Web-based publications are free, whereas others require a subscription to access certain issues and other resources. Some publications offer free subscriptions to students or professionals.

Listed below are just a few of the scientific and technical magazines that are available in libraries, on magazine stands, and on the Web. To learn about other print and online publications, talk with librarians, educators, and professionals for recommendations. Also check out professional and trade associations. Many of them publish journals, newsletters, magazines, and other publications.

The following are a few publishers who produce scientific and technical journals for different professionals. Visit their Web sites to view a listing of what they offer.

- Academic Press (imprint of Elsevier Science), http://www.academicpress.com/journals
- Oxford University Press, http://www.oxfordjournals.org
- Wiley InterScience, http://www.interscience.wiley.com
- Nature Publishing Group, http://www.nature.com

Note: Web site addresses were current when this book was written. If a Web site address no longer works, you may be able to find its new address by entering the name of the publication into a search engine.

Adjunct Advocate
http://www.adjunctnation.com

Advance for Medical Laboratory Professionals
Phone: (800) 355-1088
http://laboratorian.advanceweb.com

Air and Space Magazine
Phone: (800) 766-2149
http://www.airandspacemag.com

American Scientist
Phone: (800) 282-0444 or (919) 549-0097
Fax: (919) 549-0090
http://www.americanscientist.org

Career Cornerstone News
Sloan Career Cornerstone Center
http://www.careercornerstone.org/scccnews/scccnews.htm

The Chronicle of Higher Education
Phone: (800) 728-2803 or (815) 734-1216
http://chronicle.com

Computer World
Phone: (888) 559-7327
http://www.computerworld.com

Discover Magazine
Phone: (800) 829-9132
http://www.discovermagzine.com

Edutopia Magazine
http://www.edutopia.org

Electronic Journal of Science Education
http://ejse.southwestern.edu

Forensic Magazine
http://www.forensicmag.com

Industry Week
http://www.industryweek.com

Invention and Technology
Phone: (800) 777-1222 or
(515) 247-7631
http://inventionandtechnology.com

Journal of Extension
http://www.joe.org

Learners Online
http://www.learnersonline.com

National Geographic
Phone: (800) 647-5463
http://www.nationalgeographic.com

Nature
Phone: (866) 839-0194
http://www.nature.com

New Scientist
Phone: (888) 822-3242
http://www.newscientist.com

Nuts and Volts
Phone: (877) 525-2539 or (818) 487-4545
Fax: (818) 487-4550
http://www.nutsvolts.com

Operations Research
http://www.informs.org/site/OperationsResearch

Popular Science
Phone: (800) 289-9399
http://www.popsci.com

Science Magazine
Phone: (202) 326-6417

Fax: (202) 842-1065
http://www.sciencemag.org

Science News Online
http://www.sciencenews.org

Scientific American
Phone: (800) 333-1199
Fax: (712) 755-7118
http://www.sciam.com

Sky & Telescope
Phone: (800) 253-0245
Fax: (617) 864-6117
http://www.skypub.com

Technology Review
Phone: (800) 877-5230
http://www.techreview.com

Universe Today
http://www.universetoday.com

ZDNet
http://www.zdnet.com

B. BOOKS

Listed below are some book titles that can help you learn more about science and science careers. To find other books, ask a librarian for help. You might also ask professionals to recommend titles for you to read.

GENERAL INFORMATION

Committee on Science, Engineering, and Public Policy. *Enhancing the Postdoctoral Experience for Scientists and Engineers.* Washington, D.C.: National Academies Press, 2004. Available on the Web. http://www.nap.edu.

Derry, Gregory Neil. *What Science Is and How It Works.* Princeton, N.J.: Princeton University Press, 1999.

DK editors. *Ultimate Visual Dictionary.* New York: DK Publishing, Inc., 2006

Daintith, John, and Elizabeth Martin, editors. *A Dictionary of Science,* 5th ed. Oxford: Oxford University Press, 2005

Eberhart, Mark. *Why Things Break: Understanding the World by the Way It Comes Apart.* New York: Harmony Books, 2003.

Reader's Digest Association. *Reader's Digest: How in the World?* Pleasantville, N.Y.: Reader's Digest Associaztion, 1990.

Yount, Lisa. *Contemporary Women Scientists.* New York: Facts On File, Inc., 1994.

CAREER INFORMATION

Committee on Science, Engineering, and Public Policy. *Careers in Science and Engineering.* Washington, D.C.: National Academies Press, 1996. Available on the Web. http://www.nap.edu.

Easton, Thomas *A. Careers in Science.* Chicago: VGM Career Books, 2004.

Feibelman, Peter J. *A Ph.D. Is Not Enough! A Guide to Survival in Science.* Reading, Mass: Addison-Wesley Publishing Co., 1993.

Fiske, Peter S., Ph.D. *Put Your Science to Work: The Take-Charge Career Guide for Scientists.* Washington, D.C.: American Geophysical Union, 2001.

Flowers, Lawrence O., ed. *Science Career: Personal Accounts from the Experts.* Lanham, Md.: Scarecrow Press, 2003.

Goldreich, Gloria, and Esther Goldreich. *What Can She Be? A Scientist.* New York: Holt, Rinehart and Winston, 1981.

Kelsey, Jane. *Science.* Lincolnwood, Ill.: VGM Career Horizons, 1997.

Kreeger, Karen Young. *Guide to Nontraditional Careers in Science.* Philadelphia, Penn.: Taylor & Francis, 1999.

Louise, Chandra B. *Jump Start Your Career in BioScience.* Durham, N.C.: Peer Productions, 1998.

Reeves, Diane Lindsey. *Career Ideas for Kids Who Like Science.* New York: Checkmark Books, 2007.

Robbins-Roth, Cynthia, editor. *Alternative Careers in Science: Leaving the Ivory Tower.* Boston: Elsevier Academic Press, 2006.

Rothwell, Nancy. *Who Wants to Be a Scientist? Choosing Science as a Career.* New York: Cambridge University Press, 2002.

Shenk, Ellen. *Outdoor Careers: Exploring Occupations in Outdoor Fields.* Mechanicsburg, Penn.: Stackpole Books, 2000.

Sullivan, Megan. *All in a Day's Work: Careers in Science.* Arlington, Va.: NSTA Press, 2006.

U.S. Bureau of Labor. *Career Guide to Industries, 2008–2009 Edition.* Washington, D.C.: Bureau of Labor Statistics, 2008. Available on the Web. http://www.bls.gov/oco/cg.

U.S. Department of Labor. *Occupational Outlook Handbook 2008–2009 Edition.* Washington, D.C.: Bureau of Labor Statistics, 2008. Available on the Web. http://www.bls.gov/oco.

Xie, Yu and Kimberlee A. Shauman. *Women in Science: Career Processes and Outcomes.* Cambridge, Mass.: Harvard University Press, 2003.

BIOLOGICAL SCIENCES

Camenson, Blythe. *Careers for Plant Lovers and Other Green Thumbs.* 2nd ed. Chicago: VGM Career Books 2004.

Cassedy, Patrice. *Biotechnology.* Farmington Hills, Mich.: Lucent Books, 2003.

Higginson, Mel. *Scientists Who Study Wild Animals.* Vero Beach, Fla.: The Rourke Corporation, Inc., 1994.

Imes, Rick. *The Practical Entomologist.* New York: Simon and Schuster/Fireside, 1992.

Janovy, John, Jr. *On Becoming a Biologist.* New York: Harper & Row, Publishers, 1985.

Maynard, Thane. *Working with Wildlife: A Guide to Careers in the Animal World.* New York: Franklin Watts, Grolier Publishing, 1999.

Miller, Louise. *Careers for Animal Lovers and Other Zoological Types.* Chicago, Ill.: VGM Career Books, 2001.

Raven, Peter H., et.al. *Biology,* 7th ed. Boston: McGraw-Hill, Higher Education, 2004.

Reeves, Diane Lindsey, and Nancy Heubeck. *Career Ideas for Kids Who Like Animals and Nature.* New York: Checkmark Books, 2000.

Tagliaferro, Linda. *Genetic Engineering Progress in Peril.* New York: Lerner Publications Company, 1997.

Walker, Maryalice. *Entomology And Palynology: Evidence from the Natural World.* Philadelphia: Mason Crest Publishers, 2005.

Walker, Sharon. *Biotechnology Demystified.* New York: McGraw-Hill Professional, 2006.

Winter, Charles A. *Opportunities in Biological Science Careers.* Chicago: VGM Career Books, 2004.

CHEMISTRY AND MATERIALS SCIENCE

Breslow, Ronald. *Chemistry Today and Tomorrow: The Central, Useful, and Creative Science.* Washington, D.C.: American Chemical Society, 1997.

Friary, Richard J. *Jobs in the Drug Industry: A Career Guide for Chemists.* San Diego, Calif.: Academic Press, 2000.

Woodburn, John H. *Opportunities in Chemistry Careers.* Chicago: VGM Career Books, 2002.

PHYSICS AND ASTRONOMY

Hawking, Stephen W. *A Brief History of Time: From the Big Bang to Black Holes.* New York: Bantam Books, 1998.

Orange, Daniel, Ph.D., and Gregg Stebben; Denis Boyles, Series Editor. *Everything You Need to Know about Physics.* New York: Pocket Books, 1999.

Stott, Carole, and Amie Gallagher. *The New Astronomer.* New York: DK Publishing, 1999.

Tribble, Alan C. *Tribble's Guide to Space.* Princeton, N.J.: Princeton University Press, 2000.

EARTH SCIENCES (OR GEOSCIENCES)

Bolt, Bruce A. *Earthquakes,* 5th ed. New York: W. H. Freeman and Co., 2006.

Camenson, Blythe. *Great Jobs for Geology Majors,* 2nd edition. New York: McGraw-Hill, 2007.

Decker, Robert, and Barbara Decker. *Volcanoes,* 4th ed. New York: W. H. Freeman and Co., 2006.

Krueger, Gretchen Dewailly. *Opportunities in Petroleum Careers.* Lincolnwood, Ill.: VGM Career Horizons, 1999.

Lambert, David. *The Field Guide to Geology.* New York: Checkmark Books, Facts On File, 1998.

Novacek, Michael. *Time Traveler: In Search of Dinosaurs and Ancient Mammals from Montana to Mongolia.* New York: Farrar, Straus, and Giroux, 2002.

Sommer, Shelly, and Tasha Wade. *A to Z GIS: An Illustrated Dictionary of Geographic Information Systems.* Redlands, Calif.: Esri Press, 2006.

Thurman, Harold V., and Alan P. Trujillo. *Essentials of Oceanography,* 7th ed. New York: Prentice Hall, 2001.

Whybrow, Peter J., editor. *Travels with the Fossil Hunters.* New York: Cambridge University Press, 2000.

Wyckoff, Jerome. *Reading the Earth: Landforms in the Making.* Mahwah, N.J.: Adastra West, Inc., 1999.

MATHEMATICS

Ferguson, Niels and Bruce Schneier. *Practical Cryptography.* New York: Wiley, 2003.

Reeves, Diane Lindsey. *Career Ideas for Kids Who Like Math.* New York: Checkmark Books, 2000.

Sterrett, Andrew, editor. *101 Careers in Mathematics.* Washington, D.C.: The Mathematical Association of America, 1996.

COMPUTER SCIENCE

Bone, Jan. *Opportunities in Robotics Careers.* Lincolnwood, Ill.: VGM Career Horizon, 1993.

Darling, David. *Beyond 2000: Computers of the Future.* Parsippany, N.J.: Dillon Press, 1996.

Hawkins, Lori, and Betsy Dowling. *100 Jobs in Technology.* New York: Macmillan, Inc., 1996.

Henderson, Harry. *Career Opportunities in Computers and Cyberspace.* New York: Checkmark Books, 2004.

Jefferis, David. *Artificial Intelligence: Robotics and Machine Evolution.* New York: Crabtree Publishing Co., 1999.

Maupin, Melissa. *Computer Engineer.* Mankato, Minn.: Capstone Books, 2001.

Reeves, Diane Lindsey, and Peter Kent. *Career Ideas for Kids Who Like Computers.* New York: Ferguson, 2007.

Stair, Lila B., and Leslie Stair. *Careers in Computers.* Chicago: VGM Career Books, 2002.

Vacca, John R. *Computer Forensics: Computer Crime Scene Investigation.* Hingham, Mass.: Charles River Media, 2002.

Wickelgreen, Ingrid. *Ramblin' Robots: Building a New Breed of Mechanical Beasts.* New York: Franklin Watts, 1996.

AGRICULTURAL SCIENCE AND FOOD SCIENCE

Garner, Jerry. *Careers in Horticulture and Biology,* 2nd ed. New York: McGraw-Hill, 2006.

Goldberg, Jan. *Opportunities in Horticultural Careers.* Lincolnwood, Ill.: VGM Career Horizons, 1995.

MEDICAL SCIENCE

Friedlander, Mark P., Jr. *Outbreak: Disease Detectives at Work.* Minneapolis, Minn.: Lerner Publications, 2003.

Loue, Sana. *Case Studies in Forensic Epidemiology.* New York: Kluwer Academic/Plenum Publishers, 2002.

Mahon, Connie R., Linda A. Smith, and Cheryl Burns. *An Introduction to Clinical Laboratory Science.* Philadelphia: Saunders, 1998.

Snook, I. Donald, Jr., and Leo D'Orazio. *Opportunities in Health and Medical Careers.* New York: VGM Career Books, 2004.

Stonier, Peter D., editor. *Careers with the Pharmaceutical Industry.* Chicester, N.J.: Wiley 2003.

Zannos, Susan. *Careers in Science and Medicine.* Bear, Del.: Mitchell Lane Publishers, 2001.

ENVIRONMENTAL PROTECTION AND CONSERVATION

Basta, Nicholas. *The Environmental Career Guide: Job Opportunities with the Earth in Mind.* New York: John Wiley and Sons, Inc., 1991.

Environmental Careers Organization. *The Complete Guide to Environmental Careers in the 21st Century.* Washington, D.C.: Island Press, 1997.

Environmental Careers Organization and Kevin Doyle. *The ECO Guide to Careers That Make a Difference: Environmental Work for a Sustainable Future.* Washington, D.C.: Island Press, 2004.

Fanning, Odom. *Opportunities in Environmental Careers,* 7th ed. Chicago: VGM Career Books, 2002.

Nelson, Corinna. *Working in the Environment.* Minneapolis, Minn.: Lerner Publications, 1999.

Quintana, Debra. *100 Jobs in the Environment.* New York: Macmillan Publishing Company, Inc., 1996.

OPPORTUNITIES IN GOVERNMENT

Camenson, Blythe. *Opportunities in Forensic Science Careers.* Chicago, Ill.: VGM Career Books, 2001.

Echaore-McDavid, Susan, and Richard A. McDavid. *Career Opportunities in Forensic Science.* New York: Ferguson, 2008.

Fletcher, Connie. *Every Contact Leaves a Trace: Crime Scene Experts Talk About Their Work from Discovery Through Verdict.* New York: St. Martin's Press, 2006.

Lyle, D. P. *Forensics for Dummies.* Indianapolis, Ind.: Wiley Publishing, Inc., 2004.

Saferstein, Richard. *Criminalistics: An Introduction to Forensic Science,* 8th edition. Upper Saddle River, N.J.: Prentice Hall, 2004.

OPPORTUNITIES IN INDUSTRY

Baker, Sunny, Kim Baker, and Michael Campbell. *The Complete Idiot's Guide to Project Management.* 3rd ed. Indianapolis: Alpha Books, 2003.

Brown, Sheldon S. *Opportunities in Biotechnology Careers.* New York: McGraw-Hill, 2007.

Chirico, JoAnn. *Opportunities in Science Technician Careers.* Lincolnwood, Ill.: VGM Career Horizons, 1996.

Echaore-McDavid, Susan. *Career Opportunities in Aviation and the Aerospace Industry.* New York: Ferguson, 2005.

Goldberg, Jan. *Opportunities in Research and Development Careers.* Lincolnwood, Ill.: VGM Career Horizons, 1997.

Lindsell-Roberts, Sheryl. *Technical Writing for Dummies.* New York: John Wiley and Sons, 2001.

McDavid, Richard A., and Susan Echaore-McDavid. *Career Opportunities in Engineering.* New York, N.Y.: Ferguson, 2007.

Pringle, Alan S., Sarah S. O'Keefe, and Bill Burns. *Technical Writing 101: A Real-World Guide to Planning and Writing Technical Documentation.* Research Triangle Park, N.C.: Scriptorium Press, 2000.

Steinberg, Margery. *Opportunities in Marketing Careers.* New York: McGraw-Hill, 2006.

Wells, Donna. *Biotechnology.* Tarrytown, N.Y.: Benchmark Books, 1996.

ENTREPRENEURSHIP

Mariotti, Steve, with Debra DeSalvo and Tony Towle. *The Young Entrepreneur's Guide to Starting and Running a Business.* New York: Times Books, 2000.

Poltorak, Alexander, and Paul J. Lerner. *Essentials of Licensing Intellectual Property.* Hoboken, N.J.: Wiley, 2003.

Sindermann, Carl J., and Thomas K. Sawyer. *The Scientist as Consultant: Building New Career Opportunities.* New York: Plenum Press, 1997.

Speser, Phyllis. *The Art and Science of Technology Transfer.* Hoboken, N.J.: Wiley, 2006.

EDUCATION AND COMMUNICATIONS

Barker, Kathy. *At the Bench: A Laboratory Navigator.* Cold Spring Harbor, N.Y.: Cold Spring Harbor Laboratory Press, 2005.

Blum, Deborah, Mary Knudson, and Robin Marantz Henig, editors. *A Field Guide for Science Writers.* New York: Oxford University Press, 2006.

Echaore-McDavid, Susan. *Career Opportunities in Education* and Related Services. New York: Ferguson, 2006.

Lee, Jennifer B., and Miriam Mandelbaum. *Seeing is Believing: 700 Years of Scientific and Medical Illustration.* New York: New York Public Library, 1999.

Reis, Richard M. *Tomorrow's Professor: Preparing for Academic Careers in Science and Engineering.* New York: IEEE Press, 1997.

Wood, Phyllis. *Scientific Illustration: A Guide to Biological, Zoological, and Medical Rendering Techniques, Design, Printing, and Display.* New York: Van Nostrand Reinhold, 1994.

INDEX

horticulture technician 154
horticulturist 11, 142
housing specialist 100
hydrogeologist 79
hydrologist 72, **79–81**, 194, 207, 216
hydrometeorologist 79

I

immunologist **176–179**
industrial chemist 197
industrial forester 205, 206
industrial microbiologist 6
information developer 250
information security administrator 134
information security analyst 135
information security architect 134
information security manager 135
information security specialist 133,
   134–136
information system auditor 135
information systems security
   specialist 134
instructor 270
instrumentation specialist 82
intellectual property attorney 246
interpretive specialist 100
invertebrate paleontologist 87
invertebrate zoologist 15

J

Java programmer 131

L

laboratory assistant 233
laboratory technician 32, 51, 77, 154,
   160, 233
landscape architect 195
landscape designer 12, 143
landscape gardener 206
land surveyor 74
lawyer 42, 74, 109, 146
lecturer 270
legislative analyst 224
lepidopterist 20
librarian 74, 267
life scientist 2
limnologist 15, 18, 79
livestock producer 152
lobbyist 14, 195, 206, 209
location specialist 100

M

management analyst 114, 115, 259
management consultant **259–261**

manager 152
manufacturer's agent 252, 253
marine biologist 11, 18, 76
marine chemist 76
marine educator 273
marine geochemist 76
marine geologist 76
marine geophysicist 90
marine scientist 76
market analyst 247
market forecaster 152
marketing researcher 111
market research analyst **247–249**
market research specialist 247
materials scientist **48–50**
mathematical statistician 111
mathematician **108–110**
math professor 270
math teacher 266, 267
meat inspector 152
mechanics engineer 129
medical doctor 3, 16, 46, 152, 164,
   167, 171. *See also* physician
medical entomologist 20
medical geneticist 24, 25
medical health physicist 63
medical illustrator 281, 282
medical laboratory scientist 186
medical laboratory technician 190
medical laboratory technologist 3,
   190
medical microbiologist 5, 6
medical oncologist 164
medical physicist 63, **183–185**
medical physiologist 22
medical radiation physicist 183
medical scientist 2, **164–166**, 170,
   217
medical technician 186, **190–192**
medical technologist **186–189**, 190,
   191
medical toxicologist 46
medical writer 278
medicinal chemist 41, 173
metallurgist 48
meteorologist **82–84**
microbiologist 2, **5–7**, 8, 164, 216, 228
middle school teacher 266
mining geophysicist 90
molecular biologist **27–28**, 164
mucosal immunologist 176
museum curator 3, 14, 16, 42, 88
mycologist 11

N

naturalist 12, 14, 16
natural resources specialist 209

natural resources technician **211–212**
network administrator 133, 139
nontraditional occupations for
   scientists. *See* alternative careers for
   scientists
nuclear physicist 56, **61–62**
nursery manager 143

O

observational astronomer 66
observing assistant 67
ocean engineer 76
oceanographer **76–78**, 194, 217
operational meteorologist 82, 83
operations analyst 115
operations research analyst 108, 109,
   114–116
optical engineer 67
optics physicist 56
organic chemist 40
ornithologist 15

P

paleoclimatologist 85
paleontologist **87–89**
palynologist 87
parasitologist 5
park ranger 3, 74, 149, 195, 206, 209
park technician 211, 212
patent agent 42, **245–246**
patent analyst 245
patent examiner 3
pathologist **167–169**
pediatrician 164
pediatric pathologist 167
pest control specialist 21
petroleum geologist 73
petroleum geophysicist 91
pharmaceutical chemist **173–175**
pharmaceutical sales representative
   252
pharmacist 42, 170, 173
pharmacological chemist 173
pharmacologist 164, **170–172**, 173
phlebotomy technician 190
physical geographer 99
physical meteorologist 82
physical oceanographer 76
physical therapist 3
physician 42, 109, 165, 176, 188. *See
   also* medical doctor
physician assistant 188
physician-scientist 164
physicist **56–58**, 59, 61, 108, 217
physiologist **22–23**, 164
planner 14